Library of
Davidson College

Nuclear Madness

Nuclear Madness

Religion and the Psychology
of the Nuclear Age

Ira Chernus

State University of New York Press

The following publishers have generously granted permission to reprint copyrighted material:

Basic Books, for *The Broken Connection* by Robert Jay Lifton, copyright ©1979 by Basic Books, Inc.
Harper & Row, for *Re-Visioning Psychology* by James Hillman, copyright ©1975 by Harper & Row Publishers, Inc.
Penguin Books, for *The Politics of Experience and the Bird of Paradise* by R. D. Laing, copyright ©1967 by Penguin Books, Ltd.
Tavistock Publications for *The Divided Self* by R. D. Laing, 2d ed., copyright ©1965 by Tavistock Publications
University of Notre Dame Press for *The Forbidden Forest* by Mircea Eliade, copyright ©1978 by University of Notre Dame Press

Published by
State University of New York Press, Albany

© 1991 State University of New York

All rights reserved

Printed in the United States of America

No part of this book may be used or reproduced in any manner whatsoever without written permission except in the case of brief quotations embodied in critical articles and reviews.

For information, address State University of New York Press, State University Plaza, Albany, N.Y., 12246

Production by M. R. Mulholland
Marketing by Fran Keneston

Library of Congress Cataloging in Publication Data

Chernus, Ira, 1946-
    Nuclear madness : religion and the psychology of the nuclear age / Ira Chernus.
       p.   cm.
    Includes bibliographical references.
    ISBN 0-7914-0503-6 (alk. paper). — ISBN 0-7914-0504-4 (pbk. : alk paper)
    1. Nuclear warfare—Religious aspects.   2. Nuclear warfare--Psychological aspects.   I. Title.
BL65.A85N82   1991
327.1'74'019—dc20
                                                                   90-32195
                                                                       CIP

10 9 8 7 6 5 4 3 2 1

For Miguel, and his generation:
the infinite possibility of the future

Contents

Acknowledgments		ix
Introduction		1
Part I.	Psychic Numbing and Nuclear Imagery	7
1.	Numbing, Imagery, and the Schizoid Strategy	9
2.	Numbing and Imagery as Social Fantasy	29
3.	The Neurosis of Modernity	47
4.	Disarmament and the Modern Ego	71
5.	The Theory of Psychic Numbing Reconsidered	95
Part II.	Nuclear Madness	121
6.	Nuclear Madness: A Model	123
7.	Nuclear Madness: The Cold War Era	145
8.	Nuclear Madness: Deterrence, Détente, and Disarmament	163
Part III.	Madness and Transformation	191
9.	The Meaning of the End of the World	193
10.	The Myth of Nuclear Origins	219
11.	The Hell and Renaissance of Madness	253
12.	Madness and Peace	273
Notes		291
Bibliography		317
Index		327

Acknowledgments

I want to thank my colleagues in the Religious Studies Department of the University of Colorado at Boulder, who have consistently supported my rather unorthodox academic pursuits, and especially Lynn Ross-Bryant and David Carrasco, who read chapters of the manuscript in progress and offered valuable suggestions. Thanks also to Daniel Noel, who read and commented on parts of the manuscript, and to Carola Sautter and Megeen Mulholland at SUNY Press, who enabled me to turn the manuscript into a book. Special thanks to Ed Linenthal, who encouraged me to persist in this project at an early stage when I might have abandoned it. As always, my deepest thanks to Ann, who inspired me to care enough to take up this work and cooperated generously when I needed the time to do it, and now to Miguel, our ray of hope, who has taught me much more than I could ever teach him, or anyone.

Introduction

As the last decade of the millennium begins, it is hard to know whether to speak of the nuclear threat, the arms race, and the Cold War in the past or present tense. The nuclear threat no longer occupies the headlines, nor does it occupy the consciousness of very many Americans. There is a broad consensus supporting the government's arms control efforts, the momentum of the Strategic Defense Initiative is significantly slowed, and there is a new era of amity between the superpowers. A nation that contemplated "winning a nuclear war" less than a decade ago now speaks enthusiastically of "the end of the Cold War."

For many disarmament activists this dramatic turnabout vindicates the twin pillars of their decade-long efforts: education and moral suasion. The nuclear disarmament movement has traditionally approached the nuclear dilemma in this twofold manner. On the one hand it sees the issue as an intellectual one: if we were sufficiently educated, learned the facts, and thought about them clearly, we would choose disarmament. On the other hand, it also proclaims a moral challenge: if we would only have sufficient love for our planet, or humanity, or life, or our children, we would choose disarmament. No doubt these appeals to mind and heart have made an impact. The American public is now better educated on nuclear issues and increasingly troubled by the moral dilemmas of nuclear security.

Yet the disarmament movement's ultimate goal of nuclear abolition remains far distant—perhaps as distant as ever. Nuclear weapons still exist by the thousands, and many of them, at least, are under the control of men who are perfectly prepared to use them in certain circumstances. The actual reductions in nuclear weaponry remain very minimal. Most Americans expect the arms race and the nuclear threat to continue, in some form, for the foreseeable future. So the disarmament movement's successes should heighten our perplexity over its traditional question: Why nuclear weapons? Why do the people of this democracy permit their lives to remain imperiled?

The dilemma can no longer be attributed to a paucity of public knowledge and debate. Nor can it simply be charged to widespread immorality. Most Americans proclaim their love for their land, their children, and themselves unashamedly. For some this love leads to antinuclear sentiments, for others it leads to a pronuclear stance. But there is little reason to doubt that the love is just as genuine in either case. Perhaps that is why moral appeals are no more successful than intellectual appeals in removing the nuclear threat. It is hard for us to see what other approach might be available, though, because the two tracks of antinuclear activism are the two tracks laid down for all moral problem solving in the foundations of Western culture. The first rests on the premise of classical Greek thought (and its Enlightenment revival) that evil stems from ignorance, that those who know the right will inevitably do the right. The second rests on the biblical premise that evil stems from a misguided or perverted will. In the present case, however, it seems that those who are committed to nuclear abolition do need a new diagnosis of the problem.

Some disarmament advocates already entertain a third approach. They focus not on problems of thinking or willing but of feeling, or in more general terms on psychological problems. Probably the best known psychological diagnosis is summed up in Robert Jay Lifton's term *psychic numbing.* According to this view the essential problem lies not in the way we think or choose but in our failure to think and choose at all, and this is essentially a failure of imagination—a lack of images of the threat. Psychic numbing is a very real phenomenon, and a psychological perspective offers fruitful new approaches to the nuclear dilemma. But it seems to me that the crucial problem is not an absence of images but rather the kind of images we use to think about the nuclear issue. Somehow these images must promote psychic numbing. If so, then it matters little whether we think about the Bomb or not. In either case, we will remain numb and unable to make meaningful changes in the status quo.

This book therefore takes Lifton's theoretical model as its starting point and builds upon it, developing a broader model that can account for both the proliferation of nuclear imagery and the persistence of psychic numbing. Lifton suggests that psychic numbing must be understood as in some sense a religious problem. My own previous research suggests that most of our nuclear images have striking analogues in traditional religious images.[1] So it seems especially fruitful to probe the problem from the perspective of the psychology of religion. My approach to the problem begins with two theorists of psychology and religion who have influenced Lifton's own thought—R.D. Laing and Paul Tillich. The first three chapters apply their thought to the psychodynamics of the Cold War and the superpowers' arms race. Since the Cold War remains with us as our very recent past, as the subtext of our present nuclear discourse, and as an ever-present possibility for the future, I speak of it in the present tense.

Nevertheless the feeling that the nuclear threat is safely behind us is now very much a part of the psychology of the nuclear age. So a book about the nuclear age must speak in the present tense about both the persistence and the relative amelioration of the nuclear dilemma. Chapter 4 addresses the psychodynamics of the growing feeling of confidence and the images that support it. My conclusion is that the same factors underlying the psychic numbing and nuclear imagery of the Cold War are still at work, though creating somewhat different symptoms, as we enter the 1990s. Therefore I find a unity in the psychological and religious underpinnings of the nuclear age. And I argue that the disease underlying all our nuclear symptoms has been incubating in the body politic since long before 1945.

Chapters 5 and 6 develop a theoretical model of this disease, which popular intuition long ago diagnosed in the phrase *nuclear madness*. I do not suggest that this diagnosis be accepted naively and literally, as if the nation were no different from a psychotic individual. Nor, though, do I think the phrase is merely a rhetorical slogan. I explore it here as a particularly apt metaphor whose rich psychological and religious meaning can be spelled out with a good deal of precision. Chapters 7 and 8 use this metaphor to trace the history of nuclear imagery, showing that the shift from "winning a nuclear war" to "the end of the Cold War" is a movement from one symptom of nuclear madness to another. And I argue that the disarmament movement of the eighties, by generally endorsing this shift, revealed its complicity in the madness.

One can not simply walk away from a pervasive public madness. So the final chapters search the metaphor of madness for a positive route that might lead to a new, more constructive understanding of war and peace in the nuclear age. My guides here are Mircea Eliade and James Hillman, who suggest that madness may be understood as a call for total transformation of world and self. I have chosen these guides, recognizing that others might be equally valuable, because I am familiar with their work and find it especially valuable for casting new light on the nuclear age.[2]

This book is not a call to action. It is a call to deeper and more imaginative thought about both the Bomb and our culture. The disarmament movement has paid relatively little attention to theory and needs a stronger theoretical component. Theorists of modernity (and postmodernity)[3] have paid insufficient attention to the Bomb. Even if weapons of self-annihilation were all to disappear tomorrow, any sound interpretation of the modern West would still have to account for all the years in which those weapons were developed, deployed, and condoned. Any sound interpretation would also have to account for the many nonnuclear paths to self-destruction that we continue to pursue. What artifact of our culture is more telling and emblematic of our culture's self-destructiveness than the Bomb?

The "we" of this book is confined to "we, the people of the United States." I write about the United States because it is the only nation I can claim to understand even minimally. It is also the country I want to address directly as a concerned citizen. If in some ways a focus on the American people seems too narrow, in other ways it may seem too broad. Many people find comfort in believing that a small elite controls all policymaking in America and bears all the blame for the nuclear dilemma. Others focus on problems of conflicting social pressures and political interests. Surely there are elites and vested interests that are crucial in shaping nuclear policy. Academics have given intensive study to these particular forces (in part because social scientific methods are best suited to such study).

But it is all too easy to cast the blame on others and absolve ourselves of responsibility. Many Americans know that elite interests promote nuclear armament for their own financial and political gain. Yet this awareness has created relatively small changes in public policy. In fact, the nation as a whole has consistently supported some form of nuclear armament ever since 1945. A study conducted at the height of antinuclear sentiment in 1983 found only about one out of five Americans clearly supporting the views of the nuclear disarmament movement.[4] The problem can not be solved by addressing only the ways in which elites and special interests thwart the will of the people, for it is a problem that implicates every member of society. A fruitful theory of the nuclear age must be broad enough to encompass both the machinations of the few and the acquiescence of the many. So the focus of this book is on the nuclear dilemma as experienced by the average person (although I hope that it will also shed light on the experience of elites and special interests).

It is certainly a risky enterprise to make sweeping generalizations about an entire nation, its average person, and its cultural milieu. Perhaps the only thing riskier is to refrain from such generalizations. The kinds of broad-brush interpretations I present here cannot be verified or falsified by empirical data. They are hypothetical constructs and metaphorical models. Societies have always understood themselves most meaningfully through such constructs and models, not through empirically verifiable research. Exploring the metaphor of madness reminds us that only metaphors can express the full truth of the human condition. It also reminds us that metaphors are the most critical agents in changing our historical conditions. So I offer not scientific fact, but rather a personal exploration, in which I hope readers can find a mirror of their own experience. If my interpretation gives the appearance of all-embracing certainty, I am the first to acknowledge that this is merely an appearance. The more I study nuclear weapons and public attitudes toward them, the more I am baffled by the irreducible mystery at the core of the thing.

I present my interpretations not to replace or dispute others, but rather to stimulate others. No one model can claim to hold the sole truth, since no one model can disprove any other. Many can be fruitful if they offer plausible self-understandings and if their metaphors point to new directions for public policy and public awareness. Some models are especially fruitful because they create an intersection for different avenues of interpretation. Others are fruitful because they pursue one avenue as far as it can go. I have chosen the latter approach, following a particular avenue of psychology and religion to a rather extreme terminus. This does not imply that the nuclear dilemma should be, or could be, reduced to a purely religious and psychological problem. I have chosen this course simply because it yields a new perspective that is as yet largely unexplored. If it is illuminating, it will obviously have to join with other perspectives to give a full understanding of the issue.

Now more than ever we need many radical, and radically different, diagnoses that root us in a totally new position to see the problem from a totally new perspective. For this purpose, nothing is more practical than a new theory, because nothing else can so thoroughly explode our accustomed viewpoints—except, perhaps, the one final explosion that may forever destroy all viewpoints. Though my discussion may seem to stray far from practical concerns, it is always directed toward the most practical of all concerns: human survival.

Part I
Psychic Numbing and Nuclear Imagery

1

Numbing, Imagery, and the Schizoid Strategy

When Robert Jay Lifton first visited Hiroshima in 1962, he was surprised to learn that no one had yet done any serious psychological study of the *hibakusha*—the survivors of the August 6, 1945, atomic bombing. Lifton stayed in Hiroshima for half a year, holding in-depth interviews with scores of *hibakusha* and interpreting his findings in the light of his psychiatric training. In a broader sense, though, Lifton never left Hiroshima, for he came to believe that the atomic Bomb had inflicted its psychological scars not just on the *hibakusha* but on all of us. To describe and diagnose those scars, he developed a new vocabulary and a new paradigm for both psychological disease and psychological health. That paradigm is spun from the thread he first found in Hiroshima: his belief that nuclear weapons have generated a worldwide psychological health crisis of massive proportions, an epidemic of psychic numbing.

The Theory of Psychic Numbing

The central premise of Lifton's psychological paradigm is that "human existence itself can be understood as a quest for vitalizing images and image-constellations."[1] The fundamental motivation for all human thought and behavior is the need to feel alive, and this need is met only when one has mental images of oneself as truly alive. The self must be grounded in images of itself as a biological and historical unity, an ongoing integrated vital organism. This grounding depends, in turn, on a basic trust in life itself as a dependable structure in which the self is permanently embedded, which will continue beyond every individual's death. The individual cannot have secure images of vitality unless there is some assurance that life itself is secure.

Typically, this basic trust is expressed in a symbolic sense of immortality, an image-constellation that can take one of four modes: biological continuity through descendants, spiritual continuity through some kind of resurrection or immortal soul, cultural continuity through one's enduring works, or continuity as part of the eternal course of nature. Each of these modes symbolizes both the death of the individual and the survival of the individual's meaning.

What happens when there is no grounding in modes of symbolic immortality? Lifton's answer is summed up in the phrases for which he is best known: *psychic numbing* and *death in life*. These concepts were born from his encounter with the *hibakusha* of Hiroshima:

> In Hiroshima, people I interviewed told me how, when the bomb fell, they were aware of people dying around them in horrible ways but that, within minutes or even seconds, they simply ceased to feel. They said such things as "I simply became insensitive to human death," or referred to a "paralysis of the mind." I came to call this general process psychic numbing . . . . It would continue over weeks, months, or even years, and became associated with apathy, withdrawal, depression, despair, or a kind of survivor half-life with highly diminished capacity for pleasure, joy, or intense feelings in general.[2]

Whenever people survive an encounter with massive death, Lifton contends, the psychodynamics of the *hibakusha* are likely to be repeated. According to his theory, a massive death encounter calls into question every form of symbolic immortality; it raises the possibility that the stream of life as a whole may come to an end. Therefore it undercuts the grounding of the self and undermines every image of personal vitality. For the ungrounded self, every new stimulus that calls for new inner imagery evokes the threat of death. This threat can lead the self to refuse to seek new imagery at all. When the formative process thus shuts itself down, the result is psychic numbing. The self imposes upon itself a "form of symbolic death in order to avoid a permanent physical or psychic death."[3]

On the basis of this theory, Lifton puts forth his well-known idea that psychic numbing is the central fact of the nuclear age. The twentieth century, with its world wars, its unprecedented holocausts, and especially its threat of nuclear annihilation, has forced us all to encounter death on a massive scale. So Lifton concludes that we are all psychically numbed survivors. We fail to respond to the nuclear threat, he claims, because we have no adequate images of the Bomb and its effects. We have no images because we are numbed survivors of our encounter with the massive death embodied in the Bomb. Precisely because the potential consequences of nuclear weapons undermine all four forms of symbolic immortality, we have choked off our formative process and rendered ourselves unable to head off those consequences.

Lifton acknowledges his debt to other thinkers in developing his concept of psychic numbing. He describes numbing using Paul Tillich's definition of neurosis: "the way of avoiding nonbeing by avoiding being."[4] He also cites R.D. Laing's early work as an important influence on his own; he sees Laing's concept of 'the false self' as substantially identical to his own idea of numbing: "What Laing calls 'the false self' I prefer to call the dead self, or deadened self. That view is in keeping with Laing who, at another point, speaks of 'the murder of the self.' "[5] But Lifton is the only psychologist who has elaborated this concept specifically in response to the nuclear threat. There is no doubt that this is an achievement of signal importance in our understanding of the nuclear age. Its value has been widely appreciated, and it remains the most influential psychological interpretation of the nuclear dilemma. Within the nuclear disarmament movement, psychic numbing has become almost a cliche.

Yet Lifton's theory has received surprisingly little careful scrutiny. Nor have its implications been sufficiently recognized. The core of his argument is that when people feel threatened by imminent death they may paradoxically choose death as an escape route from the threat. This can happen not only to individuals but to whole societies. His most radical claim is that modern American society (and perhaps modern Western society as a whole) has chosen this route in the nuclear age. Although we are terrified of impending mass annihilation—and precisely because we are terrified of impending mass annihilation—we simultaneously desire a collective "murder of the self." *Death in life* describes not only our psychological plight but our deepest desire: just as much as we want life, we also want the national and global death that we fear. Part I of this book will examine Lifton's theory and its radical implications, with special reference to the ideas of Laing and Tillich that have informed the theory.

Psychic Numbing: Some Problems in the Theory

While Lifton's analysis surely deserves the acclaim it has received, it is open to question because it rests on the premise that we have no adequate images to embody the nuclear threat. Yet the nuclear age has triggered an explosion of films, novels, short stories, poems, television dramas, and even comic books that have made nuclear imagery a familiar part of the landscape of contemporary imagination. It may be argued that the power of these images is blunted by the common perception that they are merely for entertainment. But one need only turn to the newspapers, news magazines, and television and radio news reports to find the same images at work: the missile streaking from its silo, the vanished city, the desolation of nuclear winter, the nuclear family huddled in its bomb shelter, the heroic survivors rebuilding their society, the calculated gambles of nuclear diplomacy, the shrewd gamesmanship of the arms control table. All these, and many more, are the vividly familiar images that shape our responses to the Bomb. As Lifton says, all our utterances and even our perceptions must be based on inner imagery. Every word in our endless stream of discourse about nuclear weapons is evidence of our rich nuclear imagery.

So it is misleading to suggest that in 1945 there was a sudden break in the nation's image-making process triggered by the bombings of Hiroshima and Nagasaki. On the contrary, those bombings set off an immediate efflorescence of images. While some of these were unfocussed fragments, some were creative attempts to discover coherent new images commensurate with the new reality. Most notably, there was a widespread perception of the Bomb as a radically new kind of weapon whose global destruction could harm its possessors as much as its targets. There were also early images of the Bomb as a technological savior, an instrument of total domination, an unprecedented moral dilemma, and a turning point in human history—a harbinger of apocalypse or utopia. All these images have persisted, with innumerable transformations, to the present day. Lifton himself has shown that some of these images represent not a loss but a revival of a traditional mode of symbolic immortality. He groups such images under the rubric of *nuclearism*, the belief that the Bomb can provide salvation and immortality. In nuclearism a very old religious form, death as the path to resurrection, is applied to nuclear holocaust.

If nuclear images show that our psychic processes continued to function after 1945, it is equally important to recall that our society was beset by radical doubts about the modes of symbolic immortality long before 1945. Those radical doubts are apparent in many of this century's greatest intellectual and cultural creations. Long before 1945, the idea of death as sheer meaningless nothingness had sunk deep roots in Western life. The advent of nuclear weapons may have intensified this process and the psychic numbing it generated, but nuclear weapons certainly did not begin the process.

Lifton accepts some degree of continuity between pre- and post-1945 images of war and destruction. He accounts for this through his concept of 'totalism.' During periods of rapid social change, he contends, when prevailing cultural patterns are called into question, there is a symbolic dislocation that undermines the validity of all images and especially images of symbolic immortality. This "creates a special kind of uneasy duality . . . a general sense of numbing . . . and a form of image release, an explosion of symbolizing forays in the struggle to overcome collective deadness . . . a protean historical situation in which, in terms of imagery and sometimes behavior, everything becomes possible."[6] Inevitably, some of these possibilities—often the most extreme—are seized by the society as a potential vehicle for revitalization. These are totalized; they are held with absolute fanatic certainty. All of the society's institutions and public processes are brought under their sway. The death threat they are meant to stave off is projected onto some other group, which is then victimized, often with extreme violence. In projecting death onto the scapegoated other, everything becomes possible, even mass executions, extermination camps, and, in nuclearism, nuclear holocaust.

This concept of totalism is a crucial element in Lifton's work because it offers one solution to a difficult theoretical problem: How can psychic numbing, a concept developed in terms of individual psychodynamics, be ascribed to societal processes and institutions? But the concept raises other problems that it does not solve. Although it accounts for some continuity with prenuclear images of destroying the enemy, it fails to account for the central uniqueness of the nuclear age: images of destroying the enemy inevitably evoke images not only of revitalizing but of destroying one's own society too. Nor does totalism adequately account for the process of psychological self-destruction in psychic numbing. Lifton does point out that totalism involves a hope of stopping the process of history, which requires further numbing. But he puts little emphasis on this self-perpetuating dynamic of numbing. Nor does he explain how it can coexist with the simultaneous "explosion of symbolizing forays," the apparent urge to revitalization that is the dominant focus of his discussion. The theoretical problem is to make sense of an explosion of images that reinforces numbing rather than counteracting it.

But this is not merely a theoretical problem. It also raises the very pressing practical problem of whether numbing can be counteracted at all. Lifton raises grave doubts on this point. Although he urges his readers to redirect the movement toward revitalization and aim it at more life-enhancing images, his paradigm cannot explain why this has not already occurred, and it offers little theoretical explanation of how it might occur in the future. Perhaps this is why Lifton says relatively little about specific remedies.[7] His prescriptive writings consist largely of alerting readers to the dangers of psychic numbing and urging them somehow to muster the will to break through their numbing. But the "somehow" remains rather vague. Lifton's paradigm implies that breakthroughs against numbing will be exceedingly difficult and rare. The record of history, with sporadic outbursts of nuclear concern followed by long years of relative passivity, seems to validate that prediction.

These theoretical, empirical, and pragmatic problems do not vitiate the importance of Lifton's analyses. Psychic numbing is a very real phenomenon, and psychology must understand numbing if it is to respond adequately to the nuclear dilemma. But these problems do indicate the criteria for an appropriate psychological paradigm in the nuclear age. The paradigm must account for the persistence of psychic numbing, explaining why numbing compounds itself. But it must also account for the multitude of nuclear images and show why these images allow numbing to grow, rather than diminishing it. It must make sense of the physical and psychological self-destruction imaged in the Bomb. It must account for both continuities and differences between the prenuclear and postnuclear situations. And it must be able to generate possibilities for political response that break through the numbing. These are criteria that Lifton himself lays down.

The task, then, is not to dismantle Lifton's theoretical structure but to build upon it in ways that come closer to fulfilling the goals he has so persuasively articulated. One way to begin this task is to follow Lifton's own lead and turn to the thinkers who guided him in developing his theory. Perhaps there are elements in their thought undeveloped in Lifton's work that can offer a more comprehensive concept of psychic numbing. Two of these thinkers who have especially important implications for the psychology of religion are the two mentioned above: R.D. Laing and Paul Tillich. It will be most useful to consider Laing's work first and then, in a later chapter, to examine the contribution that Tillich's work can make.

The Schizoid Strategy

It is understandable that Lifton stresses the influence of Laing's early work, by which he means especially Laing's first book, *The Divided Self*. Lifton thereby distances himself from Laing's later, more radical writings, which remain on the intellectual fringe today. For a few years Laing enjoyed (or endured) considerable notoriety; this may be the main source of his subsequently diminished influence. Once he became a prime symbol of "the sixties" it was difficult to read his work objectively. Opinion was inevitably shaped by the reader's feelings about the radical social change he symbolized. When most intellectuals decided that "the sixties" was a passing phase now safely behind us, Laing's work was generally shelved with the same judgment. On the left, his rejection of political orthodoxies brought him a similar fate. Laing's choice of an increasingly elliptical and confessional style also contributed to his declining influence.

But now enough time has passed to reread and reevaluate without all the passion. The result is to discover that Laing's writings of the 1960s still provide valuable insights on psychology and society. Perhaps it is unfortunate that Laing abandoned the clear expository style of his first book, for there is a systematic thread unifying all these writings (though he often chose to obscure it). This thread is explicitly stated in *The Divided Self*: the problem of a sense of personal unreality, which Laing calls "ontological insecurity." In exploring this theme, Laing acknowledges his debt to a long line of existentialist thinkers from Kierkegaard to Sartre and Tillich. But his own descriptions of the phenomenon have a unique richness. With unparalleled subtlety he traces the intricate knots that bind both psyche and society when people feel that their own reality is radically insecure. Those knots turn out to be strikingly similar to the knots binding nuclear superpowers locked in a Cold War.

"A man may have a sense of his presence in the world as a real, alive, whole, and, in a temporal sense, a continuous person," the young Laing writes. "Such a basically ontologically secure person will [have] . . . a sense of his integral selfhood and personal identity, of the permanency of things, of the reliability of natural processes."[8] But a man or woman need not have such a sense. There are some people who feel "more unreal than real; in a literal sense, more dead than alive."[9] While they may fear physical death, that fear reflects a more fundamental conviction of a psychic death that is already happening to them. For such people, both self and world come to seem unreliable, discontinuous, and disintegrating. Every moment seems to threaten a total loss of reality that would turn the self into nothing-at-all. Everything and everyone is a potential thief, ready to rob one's last shred of personal reality.

How do these people imagine that such a dreadful loss of reality might occur? As Laing explored the inner fantasies of his psychiatric patients, he found three recurring themes that ring eerily true in the shadow of the Bomb.[10] The one that he calls "engulfment" includes fears of being swallowed up, smothered, stifled, drowned, or buried. "The image of fire recurs repeatedly. . . . Some psychotics say in the acute phase that they are on fire, that their bodies are being burned up." The second theme, "implosion," is a fear of "the world as liable at any moment to crash in and obliterate all identity as a gas will rush in and obliterate a vacuum." "Petrification," the third theme, denotes dread of "the possibility of turning, or being turned, from a live person into a dead thing, into a stone, into a robot, an automaton," as well as the emotional and physical effects of this dread: inner feelings of "emptiness, deadness, coldness, dryness, impotence, desolation."[11] These vivid images form the world of the ontologically insecure self, a world that is itself insecure, oppressive, and imprisoning.

These images also form the world of the nuclear superpowers, for all have their counterparts in familiar nuclear images: the obliterating crash of a nuclear blast, engulfment in the mushroom cloud, the implosion of rushing winds and firestorms, the frozen world of nuclear winter, the empty desolation of Hiroshima in 1945, the trancelike numbing of stupefied survivors, the cold aridity of a dead planet. So they suggest that nuclear imagery and nuclear policy may be understood as responses to ontological insecurity. The analogy between the insecure self and the superpower may therefore hold an important key to understanding the psychodynamics of Cold War rivalry and the nuclear arms race.

In working with patients whose anxiety reached such acute levels, Laing found many trapped in the dilemma typified by one who "knew of no half-way stage between radical isolation in self-absorption or complete absorption in all there was. He was afraid of being absorbed into Nature, engulfed by her, with irrevocable loss of self."[12] Yet they still had to live with others in the world, so they needed a strategy for survival. The strategy that some discovered was to live a schizoid life. Schizoids build a defensive wall by fantasizing an inner 'true self' that lives in radical isolation, detached from both body and behaviors. Since only the body and its behaviors, which they imagine as a 'false self,' come into contact with the world and other people, only the false self can be harmed, they believe. Yet the false self cannot really be harmed because it is experienced as already unreal and dead. To confirm this strategy, schizoids also fantasize all other bodies and behaviors—the sum total of the external world—as equally unreal and dead. When an unreal self meets an unreal world, nothing can really happen.

In acknowledging his debt to Laing, Lifton identifies his own notion of 'the dead self'—the death in life of psychic numbing—with Laing's concept of the false self and 'the murder of the self.' But this identification overlooks an important distinction. When Laing speaks of the murder of the self, he is discussing schizophrenia. When he speaks of the false self he is describing the schizoid strategy, which can be a prelude to schizophrenia but is not itself a psychotic state. In fact, the schizoid strategy creates a deadened false self in order to keep the true self alive. The false self seems to offer freedom from ontological threat—freedom to invent external reality as one would like it to be and to revel undisturbed in the invention. The goal is an inner world where one is in control of everything and subject to nothing—isolated, invulnerable, and omnipotent. The schizoid chooses invulnerable omnipotence—the radical self-absorption of the true self—as the only viable alternative to the total annihilation of complete absorption in or engulfment by the world.

Annihilation and Omnipotence

Nuclear superpowers seem to feel trapped between the same two alternatives that define the schizoid strategy, and they respond with the same images of invulnerable omnipotence. The Bomb was viewed from the outset as "the big one," "the winning weapon," the "hammer" that would give America unprecedented control over world affairs.[13] Announcing the bombing of Hiroshima, President Truman declared America "the most powerful nation in the world—the most powerful nation perhaps in all history."[14] The nation, like a schizoid, believed more than ever in its self-image as a superpower. Identifying with the nation and its Bomb, average citizens could now see themselves fulfilling a grandiose vision of imperial conquest. The culmination of this vision was the hope for a *pax Americana*, a world order held stable by America's irresistible force. Policymakers at the highest levels have acted upon this vision throughout the nuclear age, brandishing the nuclear sword to make it a reality.[15]

Were they prepared to carry out their threats? In the first decade of the nuclear age, at least, they probably were: "The highest American policy committee, the National Security Council, secretly decided that if the United States went to war it should feel free to use nuclear weapons 'as other munitions,' and set forth grandiose war aims: international Communism would be dismantled and the Soviet Union would be divided into powerless segments."[16] Three decades later, Colin Gray, an influential Reagan administration advisor, spoke for many who hoped to revive this Cold War image when he urged that the U.S. develop plans to actually use its nuclear weapons for "the destruction of Soviet political authority and the emergence of a postwar world order compatible with Western values."[17] While many Americans have questioned the wisdom of such planning, fewer object to the vision of American hegemony—the "We're Number One" syndrome—that drives it. The bombs, bombers, missiles, and missile launchers that are so often pictured in the press, even when the accompanying text addresses arms control and peace efforts, offer vivid pictorial symbols of our enduring omnipotence fantasy. And the Single Integrated Operating Plan (SIOP) for nuclear conflict is still intended to let the president fulfill Truman's fantasy: total control of an infinitely powerful arsenal.[18]

The omnipotence fantasy is also reflected in the various strategies of nuclear deterrence. With the amount of violence at our disposal apparently infinite, it seems possible to compel the whole world to live within our chosen deterrence fantasy forever. But deterrence images speak more loudly of the complementary fantasy: just as freedom behind the false self means omnipotence, so security means isolation and invulnerability. Ontological insecurity makes every relationship a potential pitfall. Relationships can only be arenas for self-preservation at best, never for true self-enhancement. Thus the best relationship is one in which the other is unable to touch the self. Of course once the self is cut off from the other it can have no real knowledge of the other; it can only relate to its fantasy images of the other.

The world of mutual deterrence is a perfect image of a society of schizoids. Deterrence strategies are based not on what "the other side" is actually doing, but on our perceptions (and fears) of what the other might do—or merely be able to do—at any time in the future in a worst case scenario. Psychologists have long noted that deterrence strategies make it increasingly dificult for us to have any real knowledge of "the other side"; instead they persuade us to believe ever more firmly in our own frightening fantasies.[19] Inevitably those fantasies convince us that we must be absolutely invulnerable. It is hardly surprising that each side also strives to develop whatever defensive system it can technologically and economically afford. The American Strategic Defense Initiative (SDI or "Star Wars") plan, as originally proposed by Ronald Reagan in 1983, is perhaps the ultimate analogue to the false self—a fantasy of a shield providing perfect protection against whatever attack the other might mount.

As long as there is reality and life in the world, however, the world remains independent, unpredictable, and threatening. The schizoid can feel completely secure only by imagining the world as a vast empire of inert objects ruled by the self's unfettered will. The appeal of nuclear deterrence rests in part on such a fantasy. Each side renders the other too petrified to make a move. Each side maps out its global strategy as if every other nation were merely a piece in the strategists' puzzle—an object that can be manipulated at will. The ultimate result is the Pentagon officer (and no doubt his Moscow counterpart) choosing nuclear targets at random, never stopping to think that each new pin in the map may represent several million dead human beings.[20]

Images of annihilation and images of invulnerable omnipotence nearly exhaust the repertoire of Cold War imagery. Thinking about the Bomb is defined largely by these two mutually exclusive alternatives. Absolute control of the Bomb's dangers is proclaimed as the only possible alternative to the absolute unleashing of those dangers. But controlling the Bomb is generally equated with controlling the enemy's threat. So Cold War thinking about political relationships also assumes a schizoid quality. As in the schizoid's fantasy world, one must be either absolutely independent or absolutely dependent. There is no middle ground, no place for thinking about mediating possibilities. All thinking, and acting, is defined by the stark simple contrast of good and evil.

The Spiral of Insecurity

But the schizoid's life is hardly simple. Laing's analyses in *The Divided Self* demonstrate that the competing schizoid fantasies of isolated omnipotence and annihilating absorption actually foster and intensify each other. The schizoid's life is an endless oscillation between these two sets of mutually reinforcing images, with no third possibility in sight. Again, the life of the superpowers displays the same pattern. The fear of annihilation quite understandably generates fantasies of nuclear omnipotence. The reverse process is less easily understandable, but it is readily apparent: alongside the enduring sense of America as "Number One" are persistent images of impending nuclear holocaust. And there is an equally persistent call to "catch up in the arms race," betokening an enduring fear that we are constantly losing the race for omnipotence. No doubt the military services and defense contractors promote this fear for self-serving reasons. But the significant point is how readily and regularly the public has believed it.

In Laing's view, this fear reflects the price that schizoids inevitably pay for omnipotence images that restrict their reality to a fantasy realm. Deprived of an independent and changing world, the true self is deprived of any chance for growth. Without actual contact between self and others, the self grows increasingly empty and sterile. The more it confines itself to omnipotence fantasies, the more impotent it senses itself becoming in reality. The feeling of inner unreality increases, and with it the fear of every external reality. Simultaneously, the false self system that the individual has constructed as an avenue to freedom becomes increasingly rigid and lifeless. As part of the inert imprisoning outer world, it becomes a prison itself, bringing the oppressive threat of petrification to the true self's doorstep.

The schizoid's insecurity is further magnified by another basic principle of ontological insecurity: in a world where everything seems threatening, the self must suspect that its own intentions are always reciprocated. When freedom is defined as omnipotence, the very existence of the other serves as evidence of this reciprocity. As long as the other exists as an independent reality, there is always a chance that it might be able to act independently; thus the self is not omnipotently free. So the other inevitably appears intent on depriving the self of its freedom. "If one experiences the other as a free agent, one is open to the possibility of experiencing oneself as an *object* of his experience and thereby of feeling one's own subjectivity drained away. . . . Any other is then a threat to his 'self' (his capacity to act autonomously) not by reason of anything he or she may do or not do specifically, but by reason of his or her very existence."[21]

Moreover, since the schizoid self can only interpret this reciprocal intent as the other's quest for omnipotence, the other's freedom is inevitably equated with the terrifying possibility of the other's omnipotence. By definition, the self and the other cannot both be omnipotent simultaneously; either one or the other must perish. The self feels compelled to annihilate the other, then, not for anything it has done or might do but simply because it exists. Yet as the self attempts to render the other a lifeless object, it must see the other as trying to do the same to itself. So the self can never free itself of its fear that its reality might be taken away. Every move against the other further convinces the self that its fear is justified, so it becomes a move against its own sense of security.

Many psychologists have described the role of projection in political affairs: we accuse the enemy of wanting to do precisely those things that we want to do to them. The situation is actually more complex though. We project onto the enemy not simply our unconscious desires but our unconscious fearful recognition that our desires are robbing us of our own reality. The same dynamic may generate popular images of the nuclear "mad scientist," who becomes our enemy by threatening to annihilate us with his Frankenstein's monster. Ultimately, though, we accept the scientist and his monster because we fear the loss of our national security. The fear is all too genuine, though we attribute it to a fantasied source. Each time we respond to the fear with renewed efforts at invulnerable omnipotence—each time we try to do unto others what we think they want to do unto us—we only end up feeling more insecure and more eager to lay all the blame on the enemy.

In relations between superpowers, not all fears are ungrounded. It is plausible to suspect that most intentions are empirically reciprocated. Moreover, as each side acts on its fantasies of imperial omnipotence its behavior becomes increasingly manipulative (which seems perfectly justified since other nations are imagined to be merely inert things); naturally the objects of this manipulation oppose it and act to defend themselves. But it is pointless to argue about whether and when our political fears are justified. Superpowers, like schizoids, assume that direct contact with outside reality is dangerous; they avoid the danger by avoiding genuine relationships with others and relating only to their fantasy images of others. The content of those fantasies matters less than the mere fact of substituting fantasy for reality.

Our nuclear fantasies, like our nuclear arsenals, are intended to create a wall of deterrence that wards off all reality and condemns us to pure fantasy, leaving no way to test the actuality behind our fears. Every fear, whether totally or only partially rooted in fantasy, increases our sense of unreality. Every fear reinforces the schizoid defenses that shut out reality and increase our insecurity. This ever-deepening vicious spiral is the basic pattern of schizoid life, a life in which every effort toward increased security makes one less secure. If the nuclear superpowers are living the same kind of life in their Cold War rivalry, Laing's analysis would go far toward resolving an enduring contradiction between nuclear means and ends: the more we depend on nuclear arsenals to protect national security, the less secure we actually feel, because (as most Americans readily admit) the weapons that we depend on to save us can only be used to destroy us. As Laing's analysis proceeds to further dimensions of the schizoid strategy, it leads deeper into this web of contradiction.

The Path to Self-Destruction

Omnipotence and annihilation fantasies helped shape international relations long before the nuclear age. Images of engulfment, implosion, petrification, fire, cold, desolation, and the like have always been part of these fantasies. But the Bomb has made these images seem all too believable on a global scale, and it has forced every such image directed against the other to rebound back at oneself. This should make the futility of the schizoid strategy clear. When faced with futility, though, the schizoid self resorts to other attempts at escape that only imprison it more firmly in its dilemma. A similar escalation occurs among the nuclear superpowers, who embrace a further set of fantasies that seem uniquely suited to the nuclear age.

One logical response to deepening fear is to declare external reality so dangerous that it must be physically destroyed. Here the self fantasizes its own omnipotence carried to the ultimate step: a final act of universal annihilation that leaves only a dead desolate world, either frozen and petrified or engulfed in flames, insuring that no one and nothing can henceforth do it any harm. The self does unto others, in fantasy, just what it fears the others will do unto it. This is, of course, the source of the oldest and perhaps the most seductive of all nuclear images—the image of "winning" a world-destroying nuclear cataclysm, with "our side" somehow surviving in splendid and perfectly secure isolation.

This fantasy of destruction is more than just a desperate defensive maneuver. It also expresses the self's anger toward the world. Recognizing that all the reality it longs for is outside its wall of deterrence, the self longs to be nourished by that reality and accuses the external world of depriving it of its ontological needs. The world as a whole, including the loved ones in it, becomes the hated enemy. This hatred is compounded by the self's jealousy, "its envy of the rich, vivid, abundant life which is always elsewhere; always there, never here."[22] Of course this belief in the abundant life elsewhere is largely fantasy too. But the inner self is trapped within the world of its own fantasies. So it sees world-annihilation as a deserved punishment, a justified expression of anger.

Nor does the self give up hope of attaining the reality that it sees always elsewhere. Its deepest motive for destruction may be a fantasy of safely absorbing the reality it destroys: "The self tries to destroy the world by reducing it to dust and ashes, without assimilating it. . . . It becomes a question of 'getting' life and realness in some way that will not result in the annihilation of the self."[23] This question is easily answered in the fantasy of surviving a global holocaust and taking for oneself all the reality that has been destroyed. Of course the superpower, like the self, can only end up feeling more insecure, since it must simultaneously fantasize its desires as reciprocated by the world at large.

The trap is tightened when the self, or the nation, realizes that it cannot fool itself completely, no matter how ardently it holds its contradictory fantasies. While feeling itself enriched by the reality it has so violently seized in destruction fantasies, the inner self also realizes that it has in fact annihilated the very reality for which it longed. It realizes, on some level, that it is in fact alone in an empty world and therefore even more ontologically impoverished. The image of surviving the final destruction is very cold comfort. The insecurity and fear that generated the vicious spiral are only intensified, and some new solution must be found. So the self turns from world-destruction to self-destruction.

This fateful turning is illuminated by Laing's prototypical patient who "knew of no half-way stage between radical isolation in self-absorption or complete absorption in all there was." After describing him as "afraid of being absorbed into Nature, engulfed by her, with irrevocable loss of self," Laing completes the description with this surprising and crucial twist: "yet what he most dreaded, that also he most longed for."[24] Nor is this patient's case an isolated exception: "It seems to be a general law that at some point those very dangers most dreaded can themselves be encompassed to forestall their actual occurrence."[25] The schizoid's motto becomes, "Do unto yourself before others do unto you." If this general law of the schizoid strategy is also a general law in the nuclear age, it would go far toward explaining the self-destructive patterns of life in the shadow of the Bomb.

To illustrate this general law, Laing points to an example particularly relevant to the nuclear dilemma: "Thus, to forego one's autonomy becomes the means of secretly safeguarding it. To play possum, to feign death, becomes a means of preserving one's aliveness. To turn oneself into a stone becomes a way of not being turned into stone by someone else."[26] Petrification seems to render the self immune to change, forestalling implosion from the outside world. But it also provides an enhanced image of the self as a fixed point, a center around which the world can and must revolve. Immobilization becomes immovability; the feared fate is embraced; the problem becomes the solution.

The analogous process in nuclear imagery is readily apparent. Each superpower aims to render the other too petrified to make a move. "Firmness" naturally becomes a key weapon in their war of words. Calls for "firm resolve" and a "firm stance" against the enemy remain unquestioned. Nuclear policy has become increasingly focussed on "sending a message to the other side," and that message inevitably speaks of our unshakable firmness.[27] Just as the superpowers are petrified of each other's deterrent forces, so within each nation the fear of nuclear destruction petrifies potential dissenters and freezes the society in its commitment to the status quo. Genuine alternatives cannot even be imagined, much less debated. The body politic turns itself to stone and enters the death in life of psychic numbing. Perhaps this is why the image of the frozen world of a "nuclear winter"—the scientific predictions that even a limited use of nuclear weapons might freeze and destroy the global ecosphere—made hardly a scratch in the body politic.

The Lure of Nothingness

The ultimate test of firmness among superpowers is the willingness to take the risk of nuclear winter and use one's nuclear weapons. Of course the certainty of nuclear retaliation makes this a formidable risk. Yet most deterrence theories conclude that nuclear arsenals are useless unless the superpowers are resolutely prepared to use them. In terms of schizoid imagery, the superpowers must be willing to imagine engulfing themselves in nuclear fire. But Laing's general law of schizoid life suggests that the superpowers may harbor this image quite willingly. Just as schizoids may petrify themselves in their fantasies, he contends, so they may also fantasize engulfing themselves. Indeed, the Bomb and the demand for nuclear "resolve" offer a unique opportunity to maintain petrification and engulfment fantasies simultaneously. By both routes, the superpowers imagine themselves losing their reality completely and becoming nothing.

Such fantasies of self-annihilation reflect more than just the strategy of doing unto yourself before others do unto you. They also reflect the schizoid's desire for freedom. The inner self is bent on remaining absolutely free and unfettered. But every free choice in life commits the self to being "something," fixing it in the concreteness of the choice. To the inner self every act thus appears to be a constriction of freedom; if every act makes us "something," true freedom lies only in being "nothing." "The deed is always (or at least he believes it to be) a pretended, a supposed performance, and he may actively cultivate as far as he can that 'inner' negation of all that he does in an effort to declare everything that he does 'null and void,' so that in the world, in reality, in 'the objective element,' nothing of 'him' shall exist."[28] The petrification of psychic numbing is one way to negate the self.

Another way to become nothing at all is to be invisible. Schizoids often fear the gaze of the other as a sort of radar or even "death ray"[29] that can penetrate the defensive wall of the false self, petrifying and enslaving the true self. As this fear grows, the inner self becomes obsessively concerned to keep itself secret and hidden; it fears not only implosion and petrification, but also that the other will discover the self's deepest secret—its inner emptiness. One need hardly say that such an obsession with secrecy, based on fear of the penetrating radar gaze and death ray of the enemy, is a basic staple of nuclear age imagery. In the early years of the nuclear age, secrecy was generally seen as the key to implementing omnipotence fantasies.[30]

But the paradoxical corollary does need to be stated clearly: as much as the schizoid self fears being seen it also desperately wants to be seen. The enemy's spying eye holds a reality that can turn the self into nothing at all. And beneath the self's desire for annihilation lies a longing to be filled with revitalizing reality. Since all reality resides elsewhere, the self longs for the very contact with the enemy that it fears. So the self must somehow let itself be seen, while still pretending that it cannot be seen, in an endless succession of security lapses. The very existence of a constantly spying enemy can be a tenuous but precious lifeline to external reality.

Once the enemy is called upon to petrify, spy on, and penetrate the self, ontological insecurity grows, of course. The inner self must respond to its growing awareness that it is impoverishing its own reality through this maze of fantasy. This makes the enemy even more valuable, since the reality the self needs is always "out there" in the enemy's domain. With no inner resources left to respond to its mounting sense of danger, the self may turn back to plans for stealing or otherwise seizing reality from the enemy. But this means a renewal of omnipotence fantasies, which can only lead deeper into the dilemma. The self is still not bereft of resources, though. As a final attempt at saving itself, it may go beyond hopes of being seen and petrified to a fantasy of being filled with the simultaneously annihilating and revitalizing reality it craves. One way to do this is to live on the brink of annihilation: "A further attempt to experience real alive feelings may be made by subjecting oneself to intense pain or terror. . . . The cold schizoid person may 'go for kicks,' court extreme thrills, push himself into extreme risks in order to 'scare some life into himself!'"[31]

Life in the nuclear age, lived every moment on the brink of annihilation, is the penultimate "kick." Ultimately, however, the facsimile of reality it provides may not be enough. If the enemy possesses all life and reality, the self has only one place to turn: it must embrace its fantasies of being engulfed or invaded by the enemy. And it uses its omnipotence fantasies to plan manipulative behaviors that provoke attack by the other. This kind of provocation may, in fact, be the secret purpose of the manipulative fantasies of schizoids and of superpowers. Every fantasy of omnipotence incurs the risk that fantasies of engulfment and invasion will be acted out. This may be the deepest lure of omnipotence fantasies: the chance to imagine breaking down the deterrent wall of the false self and opening the true self to the enemy's reality. Provoking the other to engulf the self is simultaneously a strategy for self-engulfment (embracing one's fate in order to forestall it), a way to insure that one will be forever nothing at all, and a means of permanently filling oneself with the other's reality.

The schizoid self, longing to be an invulnerable superpower, points to the ultimate meaning of superpower policies and politics. At the end of its fantasy road lies the fantasy of death in life—of a self-induced death that will guarantee a life of freedom and security, precisely the two values we claim to preserve with our nuclear arsenal. The most terrifying nuclear images, the images that convince us we cannot destroy the enemy without destroying ourselves, may therefore be the most alluring. As they perversely tantalize us with their possibilities of universal implosion and global engulfment, they touch our deepest fantasies of perfect security and limitless freedom. So we speak of "blowing up the world" and "blowing ourselves up" with an ease, even a readiness, that seems strangely at odds with our anxiety. And we flirt with the brink of worldwide catastrophe, as if lured to that brink by some implacable power. What might that power be, if not the promise of salvation embodied in the image of universal destruction? In this ultimate schizoid fantasy, the ultimate problem—total loss of reality—is embraced as the ultimate solution.

Laing's analysis of the schizoid pattern, and its analogies in the nuclear age, are easiest to follow if laid out in somewhat linear fashion, as they have been here. But in lived reality the situation is much more complex. By the time the schizoid appears in the doctor's office, all of the fantasies of the inner self are already in full bloom, generating and reinforcing each other in an apparently endless maze. By the time we come to diagnose the superpower in the nuclear age, it is wandering in a strikingly similar maze. Images of invulnerable omnipotent isolation, annihilating absorption, petrification, implosion, engulfment, world-destruction, self-destruction, and all the rest join together to form a closed system—a nuclear cage—from which no escape seems possible. As in a hall of mirrors, each image we embrace forces us to confront other images. Those others may be more menacing, but they are also more seductively appealing, for each appears to be the solution to the threat inherent in the others. The nuclear cage is so tightly closed precisely because each image carries ambivalent meanings of both threat and salvation from threat. So we find ourselves embracing all these conflicting images simultaneously.

2

Numbing and Imagery as Social Fantasy

The parallels between schizoid and superpower are striking enough to suggest the hypothesis that somehow our whole society, in pursuing the Cold War rivalry, behaves as if it were a schizoid individual: the strategy we pursue to stave off the threat of destruction merely increases our sense of impending destruction. But how can the psychodynamics of a disturbed individual be replicated in an entire nation? Is it even legitimate to apply a theory developed solely in individual psychotherapy to a global political phenomenon? Laing himself never claimed that it is legitimate. Although his writings in the 1960s became increasingly concerned with social and political affairs, he never linked those later analyses directly to *The Divided Self*. He never explicitly claimed that ontological insecurity was at the root of the nuclear disturbance or any other societal disturbance.

Yet Laing did claim that his notion of the false self was directly applicable to society at large, and he explained in some detail how that application could legitimately be made. Therefore, since *The Divided Self* insists that ontological insecurity is the source of the false self system, his corpus of writings as a whole implicitly claims that ontological insecurity is now a social, and hence political, phenomenon. If his later writings are examined in political terms, with continuing reference to the guiding theme of ontological insecurity, they can show how and why a whole nation comes to act as if it were a schizoid. The "as if" is crucial here; it is clearly unwise to treat society through literal application of individual psychodynamics. But when Laing's early thought is linked to his later thought in ways he himself did not spell out, it suggests that it is more than merely a rhetorical flourish to view a social group as a "divided self." It is a metaphor with a compelling logic behind it, and it offers a new understanding of how nuclear imagery is rooted in and reinforces psychic numbing.

Social Fantasy and the False Self System

In all his writings Laing insisted that a person is never merely an object, separable from its environment. A person is fundamentally a locus of interactions with the environment and especially with other people. The schizoid strategy must therefore be understood as a function of the individual's relationships in society. In other words, there is an essential continuity between the supposedly normal self and the inauthentic false self. The false self strategy is only possible because it is offered—and perhaps demanded—by "normal" others. So it is not only the schizoid individual, but society as a whole, that is implicated in the dynamics of schizoid fantasy and psychic numbing. Laing's writings provide one view of how such fantasy and numbing can pervade a whole society.

The process begins, he suggests, at birth. No sooner has the baby entered the world than the relatives gather around, debating the crucial questions: "What kind of baby is she? Who does she take after?" Once consensus is reached, the issue is settled. Perhaps it is decided that little Susie takes after Aunt Martha, who was especially attached to her mother. In Laing's terminology, Aunt Martha's relationship with her mother (Susie's grandmother) is 'mapped' onto Susie's relationship with her mother. In the next generation, Susie's relationship with her mother may be mapped onto Susie's daughter's relationship with her mother (Susie). These kinds of mappings can go on within families for an astonishing number of generations. No one ever tells us what to do. They simply tell us, explicitly and implicitly, who we are like and what we are like and how we do in fact relate: "One's first social identity is conferred on one. We learn to be whom we are told we are."[1]

Identity formation means learning accepted definitions of reality as well as self. When basic values are at stake, the world simply says, "This is how things are. This is how you are." As we go on from backyard to schoolyard to homes and jobs of our own, the same process is repeated. Laing's notion of mapping adds an original twist to the familiar sociological idea of attributed and learned social roles, for he contends that mapping always involves falsification of reality. The basic formula of mapping is "this is like that": baby is like mother (or father or aunt or uncle), teacher is like parent, learning is like racing, dating is like buying, prospering is like conquering, dying is like failing, and so on. Ultimately, the whole cosmos can be mapped in this way. So identity, as a product of mapping, is a false self system: a composite of all the fantasies we are taught to act out. Since identity is assigned, attributed, and taught by others, the individual false self system must reflect "normal" social reality. Individual false selves are drawn from, and reinforce, the common pool of fantasy available at the time. Because this common fantasy denies its metaphoric quality, it falsifies our experience and compels us to deny what we know to be true—to affirm that each thing is something that it is not.

The false self system falsifies our experience even more radically by limiting our possibilities and then systematically hiding itself behind a facade of "normalcy." In imagination, one can be and do anything, as every young child knows. But even imagination is molded by the social fantasy, usually at a very young age, so that the child learns to imagine that it is nothing but an ordinary little child. Growing up is essentially a process of abandoning the infinite possibility of the true or inner self—"our personal idiom of experiencing . . . imagination, dreams, fantasy, and beyond that to even further reaches of experience"[2]—and replacing it with the finite structures and strictures of the regnant false self system. As "normal" people, "we are aware of the *content* of experience, but are unaware that it is illusion. We see the shadows, but take them for the substance."[3] Every sacrifice of our own truthful experience makes us feel more unreal, intensifies our ontological insecurity, and therefore roots us more deeply in the soil from which the schizoid strategy grows.

The False Self System and the Nuclear Age

This interpretation of social identity throws new light on the relationship between psychic numbing and nuclear imagery. Nuclear images, like all images, are not just private intrapsychic events. They grow out of an immense network of interpersonal and social communications that create and reinforce the mappings of fantasy. We cannot begin to think about the nuclear issue without stepping into this social fantasy; once we do, it is difficult to escape. But this fantasy functions as part of a publicly shared false self system. It is detached from living reality and can not respond authentically to changes in reality; it is a prescription for death in life. Every new nuclear image only deadens us more and removes us further from reality.

A catalog of the mappings involved in the nuclear fantasy could well be endless. Different interpreters would focus on different aspects of experience to explain the mappings projected onto the Bomb. For sociologists, the Bomb may embody the in-group's self-image as it desires to annihilate the out-group. For political scientists, it may be a fantasy of the nation's "manifest destiny." Economists may see it representing a lust for unlimited resources. Psychologists may identify nuclear weapons with interpersonal hostility, dominance needs, repressed rage, or magical defenses against insecurity. Freudians will find a mapping of infantile omnipotence desires. Jungians will find archetypal patterns of all sorts. Theologians will consider the Bomb a mapped replication of our traditional image of God. But all will attest the existence of a social fantasy.

Fantasy is at work in the images surrounding the Bomb as well. We understand the arms race because we know what a race is: a head-to-head competition with a winner and a loser. We contemplate building bomb shelters because we have all fallen asleep in mother's arms and awakened safely the next morning. We consent to new weapons development because proverbial wisdom and common sense tell us to plan today for unexpected contingencies tomorrow. We rise to the various challenges of the nuclear age because we already know the thrill of overcoming obstacles and receiving praise. All our experiences, as children and parents, as workers and players, as lovers and haters, find their way into the psychological labyrinth of nuclear imagery. For that labyrinth is just one corner of the much larger maze of social fantasy in which we live every moment of every day.

Why do we embrace a social fantasy world suffused with nuclear terror? The issue—as our politicians and generals regularly remind us—is security. But in Laing's view it is not, as these leaders would have us believe, a question of military or political or economic security. It is a question of ontological security. No matter how dangerous its component parts, the social fantasy system weaves an irresistible ontological web, a nexus of fantasy that beckons with the illusory promise of secure reality. The strongest strand in that web is personal identity. "We would rather be anywhere, as long as we are somewhere. We would rather be anyone, as long as we are someone. We can *cling* to being a Christian, a married man, a housewife, a dutiful daughter, to attributions, even unpleasant ones."[4]

We cling to these attributions, sometimes desperately, because the alternative is to be no one at all, to be unreal. This alternative is precisely the danger that the schizoid's false self system aims to ward off (although it ends up courting the very danger it fears). As the social fantasy system defines us, it also defines other people; it makes them someone rather than no one, and it makes us feel even more secure. "The quality of reality experienced inside the nexus of phantasy may be enchanting. Outside it is cold, empty, meaningless, unreal. It is not desirable and, thank God, it is not possible to leave."[5]

While Laing argues that a limited identity saves us from a sense of unreality, he does not articulate the converse: it also saves us from an equally threatening sense of unlimited reality. In a culture riddled with the fear of unreality, there is no way to cope with the anxiety inherent in the infinite possibility of the not-yet-real. The prospect of being anything you want to be is just as appalling as the prospect of being no one at all. So we rely on the false self system that safely defines us to safely confine us too. As we learn who and what we are, we build an individual false self embedded in an apparently universal system. Thus we acquire a numbed outer shell that allows us to employ the schizoid strategy for staving off threats to our reality while living perfectly "normal" lives. We can play out the intricate scripts of the social fantasy—play at being "just ourselves"—without ever running the risk that our true inner selves will be hurt, for they cannot be touched by anything, or anyone, in external reality.

Of course immersion in the nexus of fantasy is immersion in the very unreality we most fear. If the root cause of our dedication to that fantasy is our abiding sense of unreality, then we are taking refuge in the problem itself as if it were the solution and exacerbating the danger. This is the schizoid pattern that we act out so clearly in the nuclear arms race. But since the social fantasy defines and constitutes our sense of reality, no one is aware of the growing danger of unreality. Indeed everything feels more real inside the nexus, and we may live our entire lives enmeshed quite comfortably in this communal web:

"The *normal* state of affairs is to be so immersed in one's immersion in social phantasy systems that one takes them to be real. . . . We are dead, but think we are alive. We are asleep, but think we are awake."[6]

Terror and the Family of Nations

In lived experience, the nexus of fantasy is indistinguishable from the nexus of people who embody and induct us into the social fantasy. That means, first and foremost, the family. From earliest childhood, the family "comes to serve as a defense or bulwark against total collapse, disintegration, emptiness, despair, guilt, and other terrors."[7] Growing older, we enlarge the nexus, but the principle remains the same. Each member of the nexus depends on the others and serves the others while serving the self. All are bound together primarily by their common need to preserve common fantasies. Indeed Laing claims that the true social cement is not the particular content of communal fantasies but rather the individuals' reciprocal commitment to uphold the common fantasies of the moment, whatever they might be. If a new fantasy comes along—if, for example, World War II is mapped onto the Cold War—it is no easy matter to question it. Every question threatens the unquestioning reciprocal loyalty that is the group's only common bond. As fantasies come and go, each member of the nexus is held hostage to all the others, unable to question "reality" because ontological security itself is at stake. Loyalty is the highest ethic of society: "It is the ethic of the Gadarene swine, to remain true, one for all and all for one, as we plunge in brotherhood to our destruction."[8]

A modern nation-state is such a nexus, according to Laing. As a social and experiential reality, it exists only as long as its members feel bound to one another and recognize each other as participants in this common, but essentially empty, bond. In truth it is a most precarious reality, since it has no real existence in itself. Yet security and identity are entrusted to the nation, so it must somehow be made to appear the least precarious of realities. "The condition of permanence of such a nexus, whose sole existence is each person's experience of it, is the successful reinvention of whatever gives such experience its *raison d'être*. If there is no external danger, then danger and terror have to be invented and maintained. . . . The invention of Them creates Us, and We may need to invent Them to reinvent ourselves."[9]

We may invent "the Russians," for example, as an experiential reality, just as "the Russians" invent "the Americans," to give Us a continuous sense of being who We are; We know We are Us because We are not Them. Having invented Them, We may find it convenient to use Them as a recurrent scapegoat. If all our problems are caused by "the Russians," we have no problems of our own worth worrying about. So the problems generated and amplified within the nexus are projected from the inner to the outer realm. Our principal problem, as always, is our fear of unreality. And our maneuvers to preserve and strengthen our reality are sure to embed us in the self-defeating complexities of the schizoid strategy and increase the unreality we fear. Yet it is a simple matter to project the unreality produced by projection back onto the projection: insofar as everything threatening our reality is evil, evil is unreality, and "the Russians" are evil, so they must be the embodiment of unreality. Yet we know that "the Russians" are very real, because we experience Them really threatening us with unreality. So we have no choice but to destroy Them: "*They* exist to be destroyed and are destroyed to be reinvented. We need not worry that the kill ratio between Them and Us will get too high. There are always more where *they* came from. From *inside Us.*"[10]

It matters very little precisely who They are. Whether "the Russians," "the Commies," "the terrorists," "invaders from outer space," or whatever, they are never anything more than the inverse image of Us. They are just as insubstantial as Us, for both are simply reifications of patterns of perception and interaction, first projected, then introjected, then accepted as inevitable reality. Yet we sacrifice our inner freedom to the fantasied security of national loyalty and its concomitant fantasy of fighting against Them. "The peculiar thing about Them is that They are created only by each one of us repudiating our own identity. When we have installed Them in our hearts, we are only a plurality of solitudes in which what each person has in common is his allocation to the other of the necessity for his own actions. . . . Although I can make no difference, I cannot act differently"[11]—because if I even think about acting differently, "What about the Russians?"

The Russians presumably ask with equal sincerity, "What about the Americans?" The same dynamic is probably at work with the same compelling effect on the other side of the Iron Curtain. Just as they are Them to us, so we are Them to them. Just as we gladly offer our authentic being to our nation in return for protection from Them, so they offer theirs equally gladly to their nation in return for protection from us, whom they call Them. As we both drain ourselves of authentic reality, we both hide more insistently behind the false self and the schizoid life that it demands.

We both hide more insistently, too, behind the wall of nuclear deterrence that grows ever higher. How else can We be sure of being stronger than Them? On both sides, nuclear images have been locked into an all-encompassing gridwork of national political fantasy, a gridwork forged by our schizoid political life. On both sides, the fantasies of nuclear strategy become the distorted reflection of a publicly shared schizoid strategy, which sees no middle ground between annihilation and invulnerable omnipotence. Our Bomb becomes a symbol of national greatness, a rallying point for fervent reaffirmations of group loyalty, and an embodiment of the nation's very reality, while Their Bomb is seen as the ultimate proof of just how dangerous They really are and just how badly we need Our Bomb. Ontological insecurity, now crystallized around the Bomb, requires us to draw the Iron Curtain between Us and Them ever more firmly.[12]

The Bomb thus demands loyalty to the nexus, and loyalty to the nexus demands loyalty to the Bomb. If one piece of the fantasy is pulled out, might not the whole structure come crashing down around us? Both superpowers use the Bomb to tighten the knot of the national nexus. On both sides of the Iron curtain, the argument is just as compelling: since They are preparing to destroy Us, We must prepare to destroy Them. "So long as they *are*, we are in danger. So we must destroy them. If we must destroy them, they must destroy us to prevent us destroying them, and we must destroy them before they destroy us before we destroy them before they destroy us. . . . [This] is where we are at the moment."[13] This is probably where we have always been, as long as there has been an Us and a Them.

At the moment, though, we are also in a new place, a place where no one can destroy Them without simultaneously destroying Us too. Both sides play the same game in pursuit of a common goal, security, for both face a common threat of "total collapse, disintegration, emptiness"—which comes, above all, from the Bomb itself. This new essential fact should be enough to show us that the fiercely competing superpowers are actually a nexus bound together in a common enterprise. It should be easy enough to see that their violence stems from holding each other hostage to the mutual goal of keeping the superpower game alive. Laing's observation on a family that drove one member mad is surely just as true of the nuclear arms race: "The game's the thing: not perhaps fundamentally even a matter of winning it, but of perpetuating it."[14] As mirror images of each other, "both sides come more and more to resemble each other. The uroboros eats its own tail. The wheel turns full circle. Shall we realize that We and They are shadows of each other?"[15]

Probably not, Laing's theory suggests, for we are all caught in a knot that we don't know how to untie. "It seems a comparatively simple knot, but it is tied *very, very* tight—around the throat, as it were, of the whole human species,"[16] for it is a global knot binding East and West together in a single global nexus. The louder the U.S. and the U.S.S.R. denounce each other as enemies, the tighter they embrace each other as partners in upholding a mutual schizoid fantasy. Since each side is other to the other, each depends on the other for its own existence. National security, in its true ontological meaning, rests on the willingness of the enemy to continue being an enemy. In the family of nations, as in any family, one's enemy is one's most valued ally—and vice versa.

The "family of nations" is more than a figure of speech. The force of Laing's analysis here rests on the observation that the link between the family and international relations is not just analogical or metaphorical. From nuclear family to nuclear arms race, the world is a single seamless web of interlocking fantasies; the family, the school, the company, the city, the nation, and the global community all share and sustain the same nexus of illusory reality. Yet that reality is nothing but a shadow whose best kept secret is that it is nothing but a shadow. The nexus must therefore be built on suspicion, terror, and violence. Our nearest and dearest must become our enemies.

Violence and the Family of Nations

The paradoxical interplay of love and violence in every nexus begins at home. Young children are not content with or even aware of the shadows of socially sanctioned illusions. They naturally incline toward substance and toward independent exploration of their own possibilities. So they must be inducted into the social fantasy system by force. Children must be taught to prize loyalty to the nexus above all else; their own unique authentic experience and their freedom to explore its infinite possibilities must be destroyed. The job of the family is to carry out this teaching-by-destruction quickly and ruthlessly, recreating the child to fit the rules of the game. The family builds the new, loyal child on twin pillars:

> (i) a fantasy of the external world as extraordinarily dangerous; (ii) the generation of terror inside the nexus at this external danger. The "work" of the nexus is the generation of this terror. This work is *violence*. The stability of the nexus is the product of terror generated in its members by this work (violence) done by the members of the group on each other. Such family "homeostasis" is the product of reciprocities mediated under the statutes of violence and terror.[17]

The violence generated by the nexus is directed less toward the enemy than toward the fellow members, who pose a greater, albeit unspoken, threat to each other than does the enemy. For if the enemy is merely the shadow of ourselves, it is always possible (at least in theory) that one of Us might recognize that They are no different from Us and question the fundamental bond that holds Us together. Since that bond is actually only our mutual agreement not to question the bond, each of us holds all the others hostage in a conspiracy of mutual terror. Each must constantly compel the others in the nexus to continue playing the game—to refuse to see and say the truth—for if one person refuses to play the game, the game may collapse, taking with it our last tenuous shreds of security and reality.

We depend mightily upon our loved ones (parents and siblings, in the first instance) to uphold the false self system that defines and confines our reality. We depend upon them to offer us a reality outside ourselves, to keep on feeding us our very being. Yet we fear that they may snap our fragile hold on reality, so in our loving we give only a false self, and we receive only a false self in return. This love only makes us feel emptier, more detached, and more frustrated than ever. The more we are fed on such an illusory reality the less real and secure we feel. It must be the fault of the others, we assume. An inevitable spiral of mutual anger and recrimination sets in: the more we mistrust and suspect them, the more we feel compelled to compel them to provide us with our reality, threatening to destroy them if they refuse. Of course they feel just as compelled to compel us, so we feel their violence, justify our suspicions, and become even more violent toward them.

Through it all we feel that the other is not genuinely there, not really feeling or being moved by either our anger or our love. Ultimately love becomes a desperate need suffused with hatred, and "in phantasy, one destroys what one hates, and hates what one cannot have since one has destroyed it. The unresponsive or impervious other induces a sense of emptiness and impotence in self. . . . The more self destroys other, the more empty self becomes. The more empty the more envious, the more envious the more destructive."[18] This is the sorry state of love, as Laing sees it, in a world of impoverished selves.

When we leave the supposed comforts of the family nest and go out into the world, we naturally find more of the same. From the local ballfield to the international diplomatic and military battlefield, all social structures replicate the same patterns of envy, hostility, and struggle. All pledge their allegiance to the motto of every nexus: "Do unto others before they do unto you." The path to security is always via threat of destruction, both received and given, and willingness to carry out that threat. The violence encased in the Bomb and in all our nuclear images is only an immense magnification of the violence inherent in every family. Though the scale is changed, the principles remain the same. And at every turn those principles dictate that security and reality itself must be founded on violence. In such a world, exhortations to love our fellow man or woman, or even our own children, are hardly likely to reverse the course toward nuclear destruction.

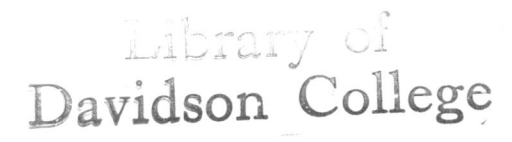

The cycle seems unbreakable. Every act of destruction and every threat commits us more firmly to the false self system it is intended to protect. The more firmly we are committed, the more enmeshed we are in the web of suspicion and violence. As the size of the nexus grows, so does the scale of violence. But we embrace and encourage this growth because it means more and more people sharing our schizoid fantasies, confirming our false selves, and making our illusory reality seem more indubitably secure. Nuclear images, as the centerpiece of the international fantasy nexus, work the same paradoxical effect as all shared fantasies. They offer a heightened feeling of reassuring reality while simultaneously draining the world of genuine reality and fostering the spread of deadening illusion. This is what the partners in the nuclear nexus, as in any nexus, desire.

A nexus is always dedicated to the schizoid strategy of freezing reality in its status quo; the spiral of insecurity makes every change appear threatening. As the members fight desperately to freeze their own identities, their inert false selves, each insists with equal fervor that all the others remain just as rigidly frozen. Authentic individual experience, with its unlimited possibility, must succumb to the rigid uniformity of the social fantasy. Attributed identities, mapped fantasies, enforced loyalty, and mutual terror and violence are all potent weapons in this battle. But the Bomb and its images may be our most potent weapons today. Since their web of fantasy encompasses the whole family of nations, denying the possibility of any alternative, they make our shared fantasy seem absolutely unquestionable and uniquely real. So we cling to our images of nuclear violence, direct them against the enemy, and reap a twofold gain: committing ourselves more firmly to the social fantasy and its schizoid strategy while managing to forget the fundamental violence we are wreaking upon each other and upon ourselves. Because our violence seems so normal, we barely notice it. In this atmosphere, the threat of military violence can be taken for granted, while the possibility of violence against ourselves simply means more of the same.

Mystification, Invalidation, Collusion

"It is not enough to destroy one's own and other people's experience. One must overlay this devastation by a false consciousness inured, as Marcuse puts it, to its own falsity."[19] The nexus has three more weapons in its arsenal to achieve this final triumph. Laing calls them "mystification," "invalidation," and "collusion." Mystification, in its broadest sense, means masking a reality by denying its existence or calling it something else. All fantasy is mystification of a sort. But it becomes especially virulent when one experience is mapped onto another that is its very opposite. In the nuclear age, obvious examples are easy to find. Planning for war is called planning for peace. Arms increases are called paths to arms reduction. Increasing the nuclear danger is called protecting national security.

Every description of reality is also an injunction to experience reality and respond to it in a certain way. When others describe reality falsely, they lead us to feel and act falsely—often directly contrary to our own best interests. Through injunctions, a nexus can go one step further and mystify individuals to the point where they cannot feel or act at all. The simplest way to achieve this is to give an individual two or more conflicting injunctions and demand that all be accepted simultaneously. "Various internal and external systems playing off against each other neutralize the command system so that one can't move; one is immobilized, actually brought to a standstill by the contradiction."[20]

Like a classic double bind, the constant barrage of conflicting nuclear images evokes such a no-win situation while blocking all the exit routes. Things must change to build a better future so that we can continue standing fixedly for firm traditional values. Something must be done to improve our security, yet every step to make us more secure simultaneously makes us less secure. For example, if we want to make the world safer, we should build smaller, more accurate bombs that provide a more compelling second-strike deterrent. But smaller bombs can also be used for a decapitating first strike, so they destabilize the world and increase the risk of war. So to make the world safer we should build bigger bombs. But if you get rid of two big bombs for every new small bomb, you are reducing nuclear arsenals; so reducing arms means increasing the risk of war. To do the right thing, you must do the wrong thing. To do good, you must do evil.

It is little wonder that the average person, assaulted by this welter of contradiction, ends up immobilized. When language and reality are so thoroughly bent out of any meaningful shape, we cannot begin to look for truth even if we want to. The rare individual who suspects that things are not what they are said to be usually succumbs to bewildering confusion, emotional exhaustion, and the fear of madness. It is just too difficult, and too frightening, to know the truth when "everyone knows" that one's truth is "really" a lie. One can quickly come to feel like Alice, but the world is hardly a wonderland. The surprising fact is not that so few speak up and raise questions but that anyone speaks up at all.

Occasionally, though, someone does step forward to challenge the social fantasy. The nexus, knowing that mystification may not be foolproof, is ready with its second weapon, invalidation. When a challenge arises, it is not enough simply to prevent its expression or even to suppress inner feelings of doubt. The deviant doubter must return to the fold by forgetting the doubt completely, believing that it never existed, and restoring the false consciousness inured to its own falsity. This is the goal of invalidation. Its first phase is apparent in common media images of antinuclear protesters as well-intentioned people who are, unfortunately, misguided enough to seek simplistic solutions for complex problems. In other words, they do not understand the "true" definition and nature of reality. Protesters are urged to feel guilty for misunderstanding reality, troubling their fellow citizens unnecessarily, and unwittingly endangering national security. By and large, though, their actions are written off as minor irritations, temporary aberrations, and regrettable (though correctable) lapses of common sense. Indeed society often seems to enjoy having protesters play out their traditional role in the nuclear fantasy, just as the rebellious child plays a time-honored role in the family nexus. The drama is entertaining, it provides a convenient scapegoat for the nexus' troubles, and the very familiarity of protest helps to reassure the average citizen that no serious problem exists, since nothing new has occurred.

The longer and more vigorous the protests, however, the more likely that invalidation will move on to its second phase. The deviant experience must be labeled as evil: the work of Communists, or outside agitators, or a rebellious streak, or just plain badness.[21] But now the average citizen may begin to suspect that a real problem exists, since evil must always be taken seriously. So if protest cannot be silenced quickly by vilification, the typical pattern of pathological families may be played out in the public arena: one who refuses to play the game will become no longer bad but mad. When society slaps the "madness" label on a protester, it sincerely believes it is right: "Attempts to wake before our time are often punished, especially by those who love us most. Because they, bless them, are asleep. They think anyone who wakes up, or who, still asleep, realizes that what is taken to be real is a 'dream' is going crazy."[22] Perfectly sincere psychiatrists have been doing this to individual patients for years. Many people have reported their fears of nuclear war being transformed by their therapists into neurotic or even psychotic symptoms of all kinds. When disarmament protests grow more intensive, they are likely to evoke media images depicting the protesters as "crazies"—a view that many Americans seem predisposed to accept. Once convinced that the protesters are just a lunatic fringe, the national nexus can rest more assured than ever that it has no problem. Who listens to crazy people? We do, however, try to cure them of their aberrant delusions.

Invalidation is a powerful tool. "In order for such transpersonal invalidation to work, however, it is advisable to overlay it with a thick patina of mystification. For instance, by denying that this is what one is doing, and further invalidating any perception that it is being done by ascriptions such as 'How can you think such a thing?' 'You must be paranoid.' And so on."[23] This mystification helps in the effort to drive the deviants mad and convince them to want to be cured. But it also helps in the effort to immobilize the public. Mystification calls nonviolent protesters disturbers of the peace, while violent weapons are called "Peacekeepers." It labels protesters a threat to national security, while weapons of omnicide are relied on for security. Popular images of protest thus add to the paradox and intensify the paralysis.

Mystification and invalidation are most successful when they are group efforts. When everyone else agrees on the accepted injunctions, assertions, and attributions, the individual is virtually helpless. With deviant inner experience expunged, "normal" behavior is sure to follow: "Induce people all to want the same thing, hate the same thing, feel the same threat, then their behavior is already captive."[24] They stop making trouble and once again "behave themselves," but the selves now behaving are once again false selves. To insure its triumph, therefore, the nexus employs the ultimate weapon in its arsenal: collusion—the tacit agreement to deny the falsifications, deny what is going on, and then deny the denial.

In every nexus, "the game *is* the game of mutual self-deception. . . . An essential feature of this game is not admitting that it is a game."[25] Collusion is the ultimate mystification of experience. Not only is there a rule against admitting what is going on, and a rule against admitting the collusion that forbids admitting what is going on, but for extra protection there is usually a rule against admitting the rule against collusion. "A clean-cut operation of repression achieves a *cut-off*, so that (a) we forget X, (b) we are unaware that there is an X we have forgotten, (c) we are unaware that we have *forgotten* X, (d) and unaware that we are unaware that we have forgotten we have forgotten X."[26] A person in such a "doubly false position feels 'real'; without *'feeling'* numb, he is numbed by this very feeling of reality."[27]

Collusion draws the knots of mystification and invalidation tightly around antinuclear dissenters, but it draws them even more tightly around those who refuse to ask questions. It responds to growing doubts and insecurity by heightening that insecurity, thereby heightening the need for a compulsive embrace of familiar numbing fantasies. So there cannot even be a rule against wondering whether self and world might somehow be false; to have such a rule would admit the possibility of doubt. In fact the rule against having a rule against asking questions is the most sacred rule of all: "It's a free country." All sides of the issue can be openly discussed, debated, and investigated. Indeed, there must be a rule against doubting whether we are free, and then a rule against recognizing that rule as a rule. After all, why would we need the Bomb to protect our freedom if we were not really free?

But looking at the issue from every side often means simply rearranging the mappings of a fantasy world. Nuclear imagery, like all social fantasies, does offer choices, but all available alternatives lie within the confines of the fantasy, so every choice leads deeper into the fantasy. Choices that might lead out of the fantasy would lead right out of the reality that "everyone" inhabits, so genuine alternatives, and hence the possibility of genuine change, must be denied. The fundamental rules of the game must remain unchallenged because there is a rule against having a rule against breaking these rules—so in fact there are no rules and there is no game. It all vanishes, just like the problems that cannot exist because we all agree to deny ever having denied the possibility that they might exist.

The result is the sense of helplessness epitomized by the nuclear dilemma. No one, it seems, can act decisively to change things; no one is really responsible; no one is in charge. Everyone is simply carrying out orders. And no one even knows quite where the orders come from, since the crucial orders are the subtle injunctions that tell us how to experience reality just like everyone else. "This human scene is a scene of mirages, demonic pseudo-realities, because everyone believes everyone else believes them."[28] Thus the individual is compelled to make a decision when no authentically independent or constructive decision is allowed. The easiest way to escape the pain of such a trap is to detach oneself psychologically by experiencing both false self and world as unreal. In the typical pattern of interpersonal knots, the problem is seized as a solution and numbing is intensified. In the end, no one cares that authentic decision making has vanished. Since all action is futile, why bother to weigh and choose between alternatives? A numbed acceptance of the status quo seems more reasonable—and more satisfying.

Answers and Questions

R.D. Laing's analyses trace the logical links connecting the nuclear family, the nation as family, and the family of nations in the nuclear age. At the core of all these analyses is the insight that every level of society is pervaded by a fear of personal unreality. This ontological insecurity impels us to accept a communal false self system that only makes us feel more insecure and deepens our numbing. The schizoid strategy described in *The Divided Self* is replicated on an ever larger scale, but its essential features remain the same. This is not to say that a nation can be understood as if it were literally the same as a schizoid individual. But it does suggest that Laing's concept of the schizoid strategy is a powerful metaphor and a valuable heuristic tool for understanding the nuclear dilemma.

The false self system that we all share is a fabric woven from the intricately tangled thread of schizoid fantasy, with its myriad images of annihilation and invulnerable omnipotence. Our nuclear images, and the political images surrounding them, thus all stem from the same ontological insecurity that is at the root of our psychic numbing; some are actually images of that petrified numbing installed in the nuclear fantasy. If we felt compelled to choose between psychic numbing and nuclear imagery, we would feel the conflict of a double bind. Having nuclear weapons, though, we need not choose between images and numbing. Nor need we choose between images of omnipotence and annihilation, petrification and engulfment, or world-destruction and self-destruction. The schizoid strategy of the nuclear age offers us all these quite comfortably side by side, reinforcing each other in an apparently seamless whole. We avoid the schizoid's fate of endlessly bouncing from one fantasy to another by living within the sum total of all of them, the nuclear fantasy embodied in the Bomb.

Laing's thought, applied to the nuclear age in ways he himself did not articulate, finds a hidden logic in the apparently illogical and self-defeating policies of the Cold War, the nuclear arms race, and the pursuit of national security through nuclear weapons. It also provides answers to some of the questions raised, but unanswered, by Robert Jay Lifton's theory of psychic numbing: Why, in the midst of numbing, do nuclear images proliferate, and how do they enhance rather than diminish numbing? Why are images of physical self-destruction embraced? How do they reinforce tendencies to psychological self-destruction? But the exposition of Laing's views offered here has not yet answered other questions that Lifton raises: Why did the psychodynamics underlying both nuclear imagery and numbing set in long before 1945? What is distinctive about the post-1945 situation? Most importantly, what can be done to break through psychic numbing?

The answers to these questions depend on answering a more basic question: If the schizoid strategy and the social false self system are motivated by ontological insecurity, what is the source of this insecurity? Why should our society be so riddled with a fear of losing its reality that it goes to such extreme lengths in trying to preserve its reality? Is not our reality the one fact that is self-evident, needing no special measures to preserve it? Some might suggest that the Bomb itself is responsible for our ontological insecurity. No doubt the nuclear threat has exacerbated our insecurity and trapped us more firmly in the schizoid strategy. But if the schizoid strategy explains how we came to be under the nuclear threat, then the insecurity that generated the strategy that generated the threat must have existed before nuclear weapons existed. So we are still in need of a theory to explain our society's pervasive ontological insecurity. One resource for solving this problem is a resource upon which both Laing and Lifton have already drawn: the thought of Paul Tillich.

3

The Neurosis of Modernity

R.D. Laing and Robert Jay Lifton show little direct concern for theological issues in their writings. Yet both have found much value in the work of the theologian Paul Tillich. In theological circles Tillich, who began as a critic of tradition, is now virtually a pillar of tradition. His ideas are common currency, having been commented on and criticized at great length. Certainly his interpreters and critics have moved far beyond his own thought in numerous valuable directions. Yet if Tillich is ranked among the old masters of theology, he has earned that rank by the richness of his thought. Like all old masters he can still offer new insights when approached from new perspectives.

Laing, Lifton, and other psychologists have opened up a new perspective by setting aside Tillich's own principal concerns, religious faith and philosophical truth, to approach him as an interpreter of the human psyche. They demonstrate that one need not share Tillich's faith commitments and theological affirmations in order to turn his insights to good psychological advantage. In an earlier era, some socialist thinkers who did not share Tillich's theological concerns found much value in his social and cultural criticism. Going a step further, Tillich's psychology can be combined with his social and cultural thought to explain why ontological insecurity became the precarious foundation of Western modernity. That explanation, and its relevance to the nuclear dilemma, is the subject of this chapter.[1]

Infinitude and Existential Anxiety

There are obviously problems in appropriating a religious thinker to address secular concerns. Tillich's thought is grounded from first to last in the issues and language of theological ontology. He defines faith as "ultimate concern": caring infinitely about that which is truly infinite. Since all beings are inherently finite, only Being is infinite and therefore worthy of ultimate concern. So his theology is an inquiry into the nature of Being and the human being's relation to Being. Psychologists cannot use such language very readily. But they may quite legitimately sidestep the philosophical and theological difficulties of the concept of Being by translating it into their own terms and developing an ontological psychology. Many psychologists who would not talk about Being are still quite willing to speak, as Laing does, of an individual's "sense of personal reality" in more or less quantitative terms. There are some people, they would say, who simply do not feel fully real.

The psychology implicit in Tillich's concept of ultimate concern goes one step further. It contends that everyone must feel some measure of personal unreality. His analysis here follows familiar lines of modern European existentialist thought. We meet the limits of our reality, he reminds us, when we feel the gap that inevitably separates us from other people and from the world. Eventually, we know, our separation will be total, in death. As separated, precarious, contingent beings, we do not feel fully real. We try to overcome our separation by participating in the world. Unlike other animal species, though, we have no specific relations to people or things forced upon us. We must constantly choose the nature of our connections with the world. The essential defining quality of human reality is thus open-ended possibility: that which might be but is not now real. Since the largest part of our being is, at any given moment, pure potentiality, we can never feel entirely actual or perfectly real. The more free we feel—the more we strive to transcend ourselves by creating tomorrow's new reality out of today's unreality—the more we sense just how open-ended, indeterminate, and unreal we are.

Whatever interaction with the world we choose, Tillich points out, it must be expressed in symbolic forms of word, action, or relationship. Symbolic forms, freely chosen, concretize the values and concerns that make life worth living. Ideally we could bridge the gap between ourselves and our world perfectly if we could embody our values perfectly in daily life. We could feel completely real if our lives felt completely meaningful. But we inevitably fall short of this ideal. There is always an empty spot where some part of life seems to be without meaning; there is always a sense of guilt for failing to live up to our own highest values. The gap between ideals and reality is just part of the larger gap between self and world. Symbolic forms are our only means to actualize our possibilities and fill the gap. Yet in creating these forms we project an inner possibility into the world as a fixed, static, discrete reality that is now separated from ourselves. Every attempt to overcome separation thus leads to further separation, heightening our sense of unreality. And it inevitably leads to demands for new choices, entangling us further in the complexities of finite freedom and its unrealities.

In sum, our sense of personal reality is limited along each of the six axes that constitute the basic structures of Being: separation from the world and participation in the world, dynamic change and static form, freedom to become what we want to be and destiny to become what we must be. These are the dimensions of finitude that many modern thinkers affirm in one way or another. Although Tillich clearly derives much of this analysis from other philosophers with whom he shares the label "existentialist," he goes beyond existentialist humanism by pointing to a central thread running through this whole analysis: in every case, we feel some degree of imperfection only because we can imagine a state of perfection. We feel partially real only because we can imagine a state of total reality. In fact, the very concepts of 'partial reality' and 'imperfection' entail a prior awareness of their opposites. So as soon as we acknowledge our limitedness, we necessarily invoke the logical alternative: that we might have been unlimited. We acknowledge the gap between actuality and possibility, between the finitude of what we are and the infinitude of what we might imaginably be. This capacity to imagine and desire perfection is the mainspring of life:

> Man is able to understand in an immediate personal and central act the meaning of the ultimate, the unconditional, the absolute, the infinite. . . . Man is driven toward faith by his awareness of the infinite to which he belongs, but which he does not own like a possession. This is in abstract terms what concretely appears as the "restlessness of the heart" within the flux of life. . . . Man experiences a belonging to the infinite which, however, is neither a part of himself nor something in his power. It must grasp him,

and if it does, it is a matter of infinite concern. Man is finite, man's reason lives in preliminary concerns; but man is also aware of his potential infinity, and this awareness appears as his ultimate concern.[2]

Every concern that motivates us in life is a token of our ultimate concern, the particular value that holds out the promise of perfect fulfillment. Whenever we actualize some possibility, we dream of actualizing all possibilities; whenever we enact a partial reality we are striving toward complete reality. Of course infinitude is unattainable. In every act we sense the gap between our imperfection and the perfection we seek. So every act makes us feel less than fully real. But precisely because the goal is unattainable, we can go on striving toward it forever. Like a mathematical asymptote, it is a limit-concept that draws us ever closer.

The lure of this limit reflects a uniquely human gift: the ability to think and live in absolutes, to extrapolate from the finite reality of the given world to the infinite reality of the possible. We can imagine infinite reality because our relationship to the world is so open-ended, because our essential reality is so laden with pure possibility. But we pay a heavy price for this gift. We can imagine infinite reality only as the sum total of all our possibilities, all that is not yet real. To imagine infinite reality is thus, simultaneously and necessarily, to imagine infinite possibility, which means infinite unreality.

The infinitude of possibility that stretches before us is, in Tillich's view, both a limitless promise that grounds our reality and a limitless abyss that threatens to swallow up every limited reality, including our own. This infinitude is "at the same time the No and the Yes over things . . . the absolute Nothing and the absolute Something."[3] As soon as we are aware of our finitude we see ourselves stretched between the poles of total reality and total unreality, and we must face the possibility of falling wholly to the latter side and vanishing into nonexistence. As soon as we make choices and call up our feelings of relative unreality, we must also confront our fears of absolute unreality. The risk of self-transcendence becomes an infinite risk. The awareness of this risk of ontological extinction is anxiety. Since everyone desires perfect reality, everyone experiences their own reality as finite and therefore feels anxiety.

Tillich's analysis aims to elucidate the irreducible paradoxes of finite existence. We can feel real only when we affirm ourselves by freely transcending ourselves and participating in symbolic meanings. But every such act must make us feel somewhat unreal. The hidden core of every act of self-transcendence is the desire for perfect reality. The more we affirm this core the more we affirm ourselves and the more real we feel. But the more we desire perfect reality, the more we must open ourselves to the realm of infinite possibility, feel our own finitude, and therefore feel the threat of total unreality. To feel more real we must increase our anxiety and risk feeling more unreal. To feel fully real and alive we must risk feeling fully unreal.

Religion is the realm in which we encounter this ultimate promise and ultimate risk. "The religious aspect points to that which is ultimate, infinite, unconditional in man's spiritual life. Religion, in the largest and most basic sense of the word, is ultimate concern."[4] Religion affirms that, paradoxically, finite human beings can experience themselves as surpassing or being freed from the limits of ordinary everyday life. But it offers infinite fulfillment only at the price of infinite risk of the self. Infinitude must always be represented for finite human beings by some finite "piece" of reality, which becomes a symbol pointing toward infinitude and demanding infinite surrender of the self, while itself remaining finite. This means that infinitude must always be tempered by finitude; perfect infinitude remains impossible. As we acknowledge the dimension of infinitude and feel ourselves drawn toward it, therefore, we also come face to face with the inherent anxiety of our finitude and recognize that we must experience our anxiety fully in order to transcend it. Religion does not remove anxiety, Tillich insists. Rather, as it brings us to the infinite ground that is also an abyss, it offers a grounding that enables us to risk the threat of the abyss. It gives us "the courage to be."

Neurotic Anxiety

What happens to those who refuse to take this infinite risk and try to evade the inevitability of anxiety? Tillich answers with his theory of neurosis. Neurotics, he contends, are more sensitive than other people to the possibility of infinite unreality (perhaps because they are more sensitive to the possibility of infinite reality). So they refuse to take the risk of anxiety. They deny their desire for unlimited reality in order to avoid the possibility of losing their limited reality. They restrict their lives to the purely finite realm. Or, in Robert Jay Lifton's terms, they become physically numb; Lifton has defined psychic numbing using Tillich's definition of neurosis as "the way of avoiding nonbeing by avoiding being."[5]

For Tillich, then, normal anxiety is the threat of unreality we feel when we are open to limitless possibility, responding to changing realities with the freedom of self-transcendence. Neurotic anxiety is the threat of unreality we refuse to feel when we deny our aspiration to infinitude, refusing to exercise the freedom of self-transcendence. A neurotic tries to avoid the anxiety of self-transcendence by avoiding the situation that breeds it—the encounter of a separate being with a changing and uncontrollable world:

> The self which is affirmed is a reduced one. Some or many of its potentialities are not admitted to actualization, because actualization of being implies the acceptance of nonbeing and its anxiety. . . . He affirms something which is less than his essential or potential being. He surrenders a part of his potentialities in order to save what is left. . . . This is, so to speak, the castle to which he has retired and which he defends with all means of psychological resistance against attack.[6]

Neurotics mask their growing feeling of unreality with the apparent security of a rigid life in a rigid, radically finite world. They construct an imagined world that corresponds directly to their own limited needs and desires, a world robbed of all otherness. They learn to forget how to respond to the real demands of the real world. No new choices are made and no new meanings considered. Life becomes a monologue with an inert world that is only one's own static reflection. Neurosis is therefore inevitably self-defeating: attempting to save life's reality, it ends up draining life of its reality.

Although neurosis tries to avoid unreality by refusing to face the fearful side of reality, it actually generates more fears, hoping to pin its anxiety to real concrete objects. Yet its fears are often highly unrealistic. Neurotics fear much that is not actually threatening. On the other hand, because they see only what they want to see (and can afford to see), neurotics often fail to fear things that really are threatening. Their impregnable, because largely imaginary, "castle" is ultimately a mask for the fond illusion of immortality, in Tillich's opinion. It excludes every threat to life by treating it as unreal; the more threatening and imminent the danger, the more likely it is to be ignored.

The hope of saving life by sacrificing life is inevitably in vain, however, for the threat of unreality grows on every side. Neurotics end up caught between two intolerable threats, "two types of nightmare. . . . The one type is the anxiety of annihilating narrowness, of the impossibility of escape and the horror of being trapped. The other is the anxiety of annihilating openness, of infinite, formless space into which one falls without a place to fall upon."[7] The world of neurosis is therefore a vicious ever-tightening circle. Life becomes increasingly more rigid and more rigidly defended against an ever-increasing sense of threat. Whether that threat is imagined as a trap or a formless void, it is a symbolic image of the nightmare of infinite unreality. Every attempt to use neurotic defenses to escape from this nightmare only leads further into it. Thus the core of every neurosis is a mounting spiral of ontological insecurity.

Radical Finitude and the Neurosis of Modernity

In most times and places, neurotic anxiety plagues only a few unfortunate individuals amidst a generally health populace, Tillich claims. However, "there is a moment in which the self-affirmation of the average man becomes neurotic." Such a moment is evident in "the mass neuroses which usually appear at the end of an era," he asserts, and then he asks: "To what degree are present-day Existentialist descriptions of man's predicament caused by neurotic anxiety?"[8] Tillich breaks off the discussion at this point without answering his own question, but the context indicates that his answer would be: "To a very high degree." He attributes this mass neurosis to rapid social change that undermines the average person's confidence and courage (comparing our own time to the late Roman Empire and waning of the Middle Ages). But a more radical view is implicit in the total corpus of Tillich's work. This view contends that modernity is unique and that only the full spectrum of its unique features can account for the scope, meaning, and ubiquity of its neurosis. On this view the self-destructiveness of nuclear imagery and psychic numbing is rooted in the self-destructiveness of modernity's neurosis.

At the center of Tillich's view of modernity is his notion of 'radical finitude.' Life in the twentieth century West, Tillich contends, is still shaped by the three great forces that created the industrial society of the eighteenth and nineteenth centuries: science, technology, and capitalism. Each of these forces has the same overriding characteristic—total adherence to finite reality:

> We come out of a time in which existence was directed toward itself, in which the forms of life were self-sufficient and closed against invasions of the eternal. Not a single phase of that life out of which we have come, not even the explicitly religious phase, was exempt from this attitude. Even the forces which assailed it became its victims. We come out of a time which no longer possessed any symbols by which it could point beyond itself. Capitalist society rested undisturbed in its finite forms.[9]

Tillich's past tense here indicates that he was optimistic that his own protest would join with others to produce a fundamental change. Yet his later writings and an honest look at present-day society both indicate that in fact the forces attempting to assail modernity still become its victims. Although the present century has seen some protest against self-sufficient finitude, the protest has failed to alter the basic structure of modern Western life, as Tillich's writings describe it.

There is a great irony in this, Tillich points out, for modern science, technology, and capitalism each grew out of aspirations for genuine self-transcendence beyond the finite level. Science began in the search for the ultimate meaning of nature, for the Creator's eternal laws shining through the material world. Technology began as a quest for ultimate self-transformation through the transformation of nature. Capitalism began as a drive for emancipation from an oppressive hierarchical society; the ideal was for everyone to transcend themselves as far as their individual talents and initiative could carry them. In each case, a concrete vision of perfection was driving human life beyond itself. In each case, however, the spirit of finite self-sufficiency eclipsed the spirit of self-transcendence, and the dimension of infinitude was excluded from the common stock of cultural realities.

These finitized visions came together in the utopian ideal of unlimited progress and perfection through material abundance. All of nature became a mechanical object to be taken apart and controlled—a means to an end—underscoring the scientific estrangement of human consciousness from its natural environment. Ultimately nature became an enemy, for its untamed reaches represented chaos and death, the impassable limit to the imposition of control. Technology, on the other hand, represented the perfect ordering of life and thus the dream of eternal life. When the victory of life over death was believed inevitable, perfect reality was imagined as a goal realizable in mundane reality, not a transcendent limit. The gap between real and ideal was closed, rendering life one-dimensional. But the goal was to be attained by sequential realization of an endless stream of finite possibilities. So every purpose became a means to some future goal, a goal that was always receding into a more distant future. The vision of a simultaneous realization of all possibilities was ruled out in principle.

With material prosperity raised to the level of ultimate concern, society made itself a replica of science's objective world, a huge machine of finite parts interacting only in cause and effect relations. As all things became inert commodities to be possessed and controlled, so people became commodities too. Education became primarily socialization into the production/consumption machine. Government became preoccupied with keeping the machine well oiled and pursuing peace—which now meant the optimal situation for global capitalist expansion. As the machine required more complex bureaucratic organizations to keep it going, everyone from the most powerful capitalist to the lowliest worker had to adapt to the demands of the whole.

> Man is supposed to be the master of his world and himself. But actually he has become a part of the reality he has created, an object among objects, a thing among things, a cog within a universal machine to which he must adapt himself in order not to be smashed by it. But this adaptation makes him a means for ends which are means themselves, and in which an ultimate end is lacking. Out of

this predicament of man in the industrial society the experiences of emptiness and meaninglessness, of dehumanization and estrangement have resulted. Man has ceased to encounter reality as meaningful.[10]

Wherever we look, then, we see modern Western culture making immense, and immensely successful, efforts to exclude the dimension of infinitude—not only as a living reality but, more importantly, as a possibility. All our social institutions and processes conspire to make us forget that experiences of infinitude are within the range of human potential. The religious symbols that once embodied the dream of perfect reality have been stripped of their power, and the very nature of modernity insures that no new symbols can arise to take their place. It is not enough, then, to say that this is an age of anxiety. The crucial point is that this age of anxiety has no antidote, no path to point beyond our feelings of limited, partial reality. Thus it has become an age of universal neurosis.

Neurosis and the Nuclear Age

Tillich's understanding of neurosis, coupled with his critique of modernity, shows how the psychodynamics of nuclear images and nuclear numbing in the Cold War world are rooted in the neurotic fears characteristic of modernity. Neurosis tries to avoid unreality by refusing to face the fearful side of reality. The tremendous achievements of science and technology make us virtually fearless in the face of nature. The evil spirits that once populated waterways and wilderness and darkness are banished. So we learn to fear other people: the ethnic and racial minorities, the Communists, or whatever others are most convenient at the time. We cling to these fears so persistently just because our potential range of fears has become so narrow. Fixation on a small number of intensely held fears is a prime characteristic of neurosis.

Neurotic fears assume a special quality of unreality in two senses: they express the threat of unreality in especially vivid symbolic terms, and they are often unrealistic. The pervasive fears of our own day display both these qualities. Among all the others, we especially fear the shadowy, impalpable, unknowable other: the terrorist, the thief in the night, the infiltrating spy, the stranger on the other side of the street—or the tracks, or the world—whom we will never meet. All these people are unreal to us, yet we guard ourselves against them with special caution, spending huge portions of our wealth to buy security, because we never know what They will do next. Our publicly shared fears do little to concretize our anxiety. For the most part, they simply reinforce our sense of helplessness in the face of intangible dangers. So we feel compelled to limit our anxiety by neurotically limiting our world and our own possibilities. Many of these fears may be unfounded and others exaggerated, but we simply have no way to find out the facts.

Neurotics cherish their unrealistic fears as a buffer against reality. They strip genuine dangers of their reality for the same reason. Whenever possible, they ignore real dangers and refuse to feel fear at all. If fear cannot be avoided, the second-best line of defense is to talk about the danger (sometimes incessantly) without internalizing it or intending to respond to it. In our societal neurosis, this verbal defense is quite common. We cannot totally ignore our fears about environmental destruction, urban decay, or the threat of nuclear annihilation. "It's a terrible problem," we say. "Someone really ought to do something." With that we confirm our own impotence. We diminish our reality in the face of the problem so that we can diminish the reality of the fear and danger. In a life of radical finitude this maneuver is especially easy. Subject and object, person and world, life and death are permanently separated in any event. Thus the danger, even if it represents death itself, becomes just one more object "out there," too far away to touch—or to touch our lives. So we deaden ourselves to very real dangers and sink back into psychic numbing. The more dangers there are, the easier it is to feel totally detached and numb.

Yet as we take refuge in our pure subjectivity, we also take refuge in our sense that we are just objects, cogs in the machine, inert and incapable of response. Ignoring our capacity to act, we settle into a convenient fatalism. "It's all too overwhelming," we say. And in fact we are quite easily overwhelmed. In the narrow shelter of our finitized world, we systematically train ourselves to be incapable of contemplating threats to the whole. Embedded in temporality, we can only deal with concerns of the short run. Our minds boggle in trying to think of global centuries-long consequences. And a nuclear threat that conjures up eternity with its image of "the end of all life" is impossible to take in—which is just the way neurotics want it.

In the framework of Tillich's thought, this limited perspective must be linked directly to what he calls the dominant form of anxiety today: the anxiety of meaninglessness. Tillich traces the meaninglessness of Western modernity back to the demise of universally shared values, meanings, and symbols. Rapid social change, he says, undermines all specific beliefs and concerns in a whirlpool of relativism. But here again his own thought points beyond this focus on change to a broader view of modernity, for he sees the loss of particular meanings as a symptom of a much larger problem: the loss of ultimate concern, concern for the infinite meaning and purpose of the whole. Partial meanings can be fulfilling only when they point to and participate in a symbolic vision of perfect meaning and perfect reality. If that vision disappears, partial meanings merely confirm us in the anxiety of partial reality and soon lose their value.

This is just what has happened, Tillich indicates, in modernity. Under the guise of scientific objectivity, a wall has been erected between public institutions and private feelings. The public realm of the production/consumption machine is now proclaimed morally neutral. The state, as manager of the machine, exempts itself in principle from questions of value and religion; all its policies, including its nuclear policies, are (at least theoretically) based solely on rational calculations and "reasons of state." All questions of meaning are relegated to the subjective dimension of personal feelings and private opinions. But even this private realm consists only of partial realities. Reality can no longer be experienced by the whole person, and the person can no longer experience the whole of reality. So one can ask about the meanings of parts of one's life, but the question of the meaning of the whole is in principle meaningless. Every value becomes simply a means to some other value, which is in its turn just a means. Each can only be a link in a chain whose sole purpose is to perpetuate itself to no end. The more passionately we search for our own unique meanings in the privacy of our own unique lives, the more our lives are radically finitized and emptied of meaning.

Occasionally threats to the whole may arise that force us to consider the nature of our concern for the totality of life. The nuclear threat is the most obvious case in point. But we avoid confronting this issue, as we avoid confronting our realistic fears, by claiming that it is just too big to comprehend. Again, there is truth in this claim. In a rare private moment we may wonder about the ultimate meaning of our individual lives, though we are denied an answer. But the Bomb is squarely in the middle of the public realm, where questions of ultimate meaning are impossible. We cannot connect our finite lives with ultimate meaning, nor can we connect our private lives with public meaning, so we cannot hope to connect our finite private lives with the ultimate public question of meaning implicit in the Bomb. We simply cannot ask that question. The language of public political discourse has no place for it.

Those who try to inject ultimate value terms into the nuclear weapons debate inevitably face this problem of language boundaries. First they are asked to reduce their terms to a concrete policy option within the parameters of the current political debate. If they comply, their value concerns may be appended to the political discussion as useful embellishment. Even when these value terms are genuinely the source of political opinions, they are only received into mainstream discourse when presented as appendages to currently debated political options. If questions of ultimate meaning can not be reduced to the "realistic" terms of finite public policy questions, they will probably be written off by the mainstream as "idealistic" and therefore irrelevant. Through these various maneuvers we insure that we can not ask such questions in the public realm. Nor do we want to. By and large, we feel saved from the threat of anxiety by our meaninglessness.

Finitude and Freedom

Once again there is a tragic irony underlying this development. Modern industrial society was founded on the ideal of autonomy. The freely choosing individual was to become the infinite value, the ultimate meaning. This ideal seemed to be the great liberation from the cramped confines of medieval society. To insure autonomy, culture followed science in relegating all questions of meaning to the realm of inner feelings. But once the individual was dichotomized into public and private person, an ultimate meaning encompassing all of life became *a priori* impossible. Freedom came to be defined as unfettered choice among finite alternatives. Thus every decision could only be a partial commitment, limited and often opposed by some other part of the self. The vacillating self-conflicted self became its own impediment to the centered acts that are the essence of true freedom.

Unable to make meaningful personal choices, the individual was even less able to resist the production/consumption machine. That machine, left to pursue its own course unimpeded by questions of meaning, gained the power to define and delimit all permissible paths for self-affirmation. Whether fulfillment was sought in meaningful work, family life, service to the nation, or even organized religion, all demanded integration into the society built on the machine. Freedom dwindled to consumerism—the freedom to choose among indistinguishable commodities and meaningless means. With genuine freedom inevitably slipping away, society might naturally feel driven to political extremes "in defense of freedom." But those extremes only tighten the grip of radical finitude and restrict the range of personal possibilities. And this may be just what a neurotic society wants. Despite our rhetorical insistence that nothing is more important to us than the defense of freedom (the rhetoric which justifies our nuclear arsenal), the truth may be quite otherwise.

When meaning is eroded and doubt abounds, the ground is ripe for conformity, Tillich contends. Doubt is a reminder that the certainty of every truth is limited because human knowledge is limited. But this awareness of finitude is precisely what neurosis must avoid. So it refuses to entertain doubts even when they are realistically called for. The neurotic "flees from his freedom of asking and answering for himself to a situation in which no further questions can be asked and the answers to previous questions are imposed on him authoritatively. . . . Meaning is saved, but the self is sacrificed."[11]

In traditional societies, the threat of meaninglessness may have demanded conformity to an indubitable ultimate meaning shared by all. But today conformity requires us to deny ultimate meaning altogether. Since no concern of the group can have ultimate meaning, the group and its neurosis are raised to ultimacy. In the modern era, the group is typically the nation-state, and conformity is praised as virtuous loyalty to "our way of life." In place of true freedom, we get the conformity of patriotism. Anyone within the nation who raises doubts about "our way of life" must be suspected of dangerous disloyalty and dealt with accordingly. Calls for specific changes and reforms cannot be evaluated on their individual merits; they can only be seen as so many threats to the status quo. So every proposal for meaningful change must be either incorporated into the status quo (i.e., framed within the current policy alternatives) or vigorously suppressed (for example, by imprisoning the civilly disobedient). When political protest mounts, the majority must affirm the nation's existing reality ever more vociferously as the best of all possible worlds. Any alteration in one strand of the fabric of society seems to threaten the entire structure, even if that strand is a Bomb that can destroy the whole structure in a single day.

Beneath our nuclear "defense of freedom," then, Tillich's analysis uncovers the same foundation that undergirds every aspect of our lives: the desire for, and satisfaction of, neurotic security. The fundamental structures of industrial society are all built on the project of avoiding the threat of limitless unreality by compulsively ignoring and denying the possibility of limitless reality. Every facet of our society contributes to this project; every actuality and every ideal feed its pervasive power. Tillich's claim that modern Western culture lacks an ultimate concern is, thereore, not quite accurate. His own thinking reveals, behind every individual goal and meaning, behind even the preservation and expansion of the production/consumption machine, an ultimate meaning: escape from ultimate concern and meaning, denial of the dimension of infinitude, maintenance of the societal neurosis.

This could be called the perfect neurosis. Not only does it deny the threat of unreality but also, by denying the very possibility of absolute reality, it denies that there is any threat to be denied. With the desire for perfection banished from consciousness, the gap between finite reality and the ideal of infinite reality is totally repressed. Since anxiety, as awareness of finitude, depends on awareness of this gap, anxiety is also repressed. The neurosis is invisible because nothing can stand outside it to attest and challenge its restricted vision. Since everyone lives within it, it appears to be just the perfectly ordinary life of ordinary healthy people. Like every neurosis, however, it is self-defeating. Our collective attempt to avoid the threat of infinite unreality by restricting our reality only leaves us feeling further bereft of personal reality. Having committed ourselves to radical finitude, we have no way to escape from ontological insecurity. It is now the precarious foundation of our common life.

The Bomb as a Symbol of Radical Finitude

Tillich's thought opens up a view of psychic numbing as a public religious phenomenon—a societal neurosis rooted in the loss of ultimate concern. If it is to offer an adequate interpretation of the nuclear age, though, it must also account for the abundance of nuclear images and show that they actually reinforce numbing. In Tillich's terms, it must show that the Bomb is not only a symptom but a symbol of our mass neurosis; i.e., that it participates directly in the neurotic qualities to which it points. Demonstrations of this claim are not hard to find.

Nuclear imagery is obviously saturated with elements of modern science and technology. In popular imagination, nuclear weapons readily conjure up images of a totally scientific and technological world. The physicists who "unlocked the secrets of the atom" with their analytical wizardry and arcane technical language are emblematic of the triumphs and terrors of modern science. Military planners are also pictured as technological wizards. In their subterranean war room, with its computers generating numbers and diagrams and flashing maps, they calculate megatonnage yields and kill ratios in purely quantitative terms. Under their command, computer-like young soldiers are riveted to their data display screens, doing their duty dispassionately in total detachment from the actual world far above their heads. In remote missile launch rooms, equally computer-like soldiers automatically throw the proper switches in the mechanical sequence they have rehearsed so often that they are now nothing but parts of the machine. (This image also recalls the scientific psychologist who has tested these young men and certified them sufficiently devoid of feeling to fit the requirements of the job.)

Indeed the entire nuclear weapons system, with all its personnel, is popularly understood as one huge machine in which all parts are interconnected; we reflect this perception when we refer to all the nuclear warheads in the world in the singular: the Bomb. But the nuclear machine is only part of the larger production/consumption machine which is the essence of the nation itself. For the average person, our nuclear arsenal and our wealth of commodities combine to entitle us to the status of superpower. There is a long-standing (though now increasingly questioned)[12] conception that expanding weapons industries create an expanding economy. The link between the Bomb and the corporate capitalist economy is most obvious in the overriding image of the nuclear age, the Cold War between capitalism and communism. In this image the world is permanently divided into two finite entities that are implacably opposed to each other. When the Cold War is pictured as unending, the nuclear arsenal becomes the eternal savior—the part of our machine that must protect the entire machine forever.

A desire to control and dominate is inherent in the science, technology, and capitalism of modern culture, as it is in every neurosis. The public perception of nuclear weapons reflects this desire. The Bomb and the label "superpower" are inextricably linked to images of national strength which are ubiquitous in the media, and these in turn evoke images of domination, even if the latter are not consciously admitted. At times the Pentagon has spoken openly about "fighting a protracted nuclear war" and "defeating the Soviet Union at any level of conflict" (goals that may still be actual U.S. policy).[13] And media discussion of nuclear weapons issues is consistently couched in traditional war-fighting terms: challenge and response, attack and defense, superior and inferior forces, victory and defeat. Most Americans readily accept this vocabulary in media treatments of the issue, though they simultaneously claim to believe that there can be no winner in a nuclear war.[14]

Of course everyone agrees that there could be a loser in a nuclear war, in the sense that one's nation might be destroyed. So images of national strength are legitimated by concerns for defense and the fear of being dominated. But these concerns are marked by the vagueness characteristic of neurotic anxiety. Most Americans have very little notion of the Soviet Union as a concrete actuality. Nor is there much precise definition of just what "the Soviet threat" really is. The common image of "the Soviet threat" resembles the shadowy impalpable other that we fear and shun in so many areas of our lives.

"The Soviet threat" has loomed so large in public perception mainly because it has been conflated with the threat of nuclear technology and nuclear war (a conflation legitimized by the traditional assumption that only the Soviets would initiate nuclear war). Popular images of nuclear technology are informed by only the barest minimum of scientific knowledge, and the empirical reality of a large-scale use of nuclear weapons eludes scientific understanding. So our fear of being dominated by the Soviets merges into a larger sense of a vague threat that cannot be objectively grasped or concretized. Our normal processes of reality testing are rendered inadequate. We are all reduced to the status of neurotics dealing with unrealistic sources of anxiety while refusing to examine genuine threats realistically.

Like an individual neurotic, therefore, society retreats to an imagined "castle" of safety. Tillich contends that every neurotic "castle" is built on an illusion of immortality aimed at fending off the threat of unreality. Fantasies of immortality have certainly haunted, and at times dominated, the nuclear age. The apocalyptic vision of a purifying nuclear cataclysm is often written off as a lunatic fringe fantasy. But the belief in apocalyptic redemption is so deeply rooted in Western culture that none of us are totally free of its impact. The more we deny its appeal for us the more seductively it works on our unconscious hopes and desires. Similarly, the distinctively American faith in eternal renewal—the pioneer spirit that can always start over again—can never be totally disengaged from our fantasy images of nuclear catastrophe. These cultural traditions are concretized in the survivalist and shelter-building fads that emerge in every generation (though with varying impacts). Even those who reject them as totally unrealistic are often irresistibly fascinated by them.[15] And if illusions of apocalyptic rebirth are abandoned, illusions of an eternally dependable nuclear deterrent shield arise to take their place, promising the same freedom from the threat of unreality.

As nuclear images entwine themselves with neurotic fears, they touch directly upon the anxiety of meaninglessness. Scientific and military experts are often pictured as human cogs in the nuclear machine, detached from all questions of personal meaning and value. Nuclear diplomacy follows nuclear technology into the public realm, where objective considerations of national security are believed to oust all subjective concerns. Yet there is a persistent suspicion that the Bomb charged with making us more secure has simultaneously made us less secure. Across the political spectrum there is an (often unspoken) awareness that nuclear weapons entangle us in a web of paradox and contradiction that typifies the absurdities of our age. Nuclear imagery is often tainted with a hint of absurdity, and there is more than a hint in such fictional images as Dr. Strangelove and such nonfictional images as Postal Service plans for mail delivery after the holocaust.[16]

The Trap and the Void

The intimate link between neurosis and nuclear imagery is especially evident in the two nightmare images that Tillich finds characteristic of neurosis: the annihilating trap of narrowness and the empty dark void of formlessness. "Both faces of the same reality arouse the latent anxiety of every individual who looks at them. Today most of us do look at them," he writes (again implying a societal neurosis).[17] Most obviously, we look at them in our images of the Bomb. It is easy to recognize images of nuclear war that resemble an empty dark void. The idea of a "nuclear winter" only underscores the popular image of a postholocaust world plunged into darkness, devoid of meaningful forms and perhaps of life itself. There is a less obvious dimension of openness in our most emblematic image of nuclear explosion, the mushroom cloud, which seems to spread expansively, scattering debris and fallout over an endless area. Every explosion carries this connotation of opening up and spreading out; when we want to depict an explosion visually we fling our arms out wide. Nuclear explosions carry this image to its utmost degree.

Images of narrowness and entrapment are less pervasive but still evident in the nuclear age. For much of this age, the overriding image of nuclear war has been one of survivors huddled in their tiny subterranean bomb shelter. While the popularity of that image waxes and wanes, there is a continuing sense that the Bomb itself has us trapped. We feel hemmed in on every side as we look for escape from the nuclear dilemma and seem unable to find it. It is widely believed that nuclear weapons are now a permanent feature of the human landscape, a burden that we must carry forever. Naturally this feeling that we are hemmed in intensifies our sense that we must defend ourselves. Here, too, the burden that hems us in is actually our societal neurosis.

But these nuclear images have another side, for each can easily be seen as the antidote to the traumatic anxiety evoked by the other. Each set of images is as appealing as it is terrifying. The appeal of entrapment is easy to understand: neurosis is essentially a quest for inviolable rigidity to forestall the threat of falling apart. This quest underlies government demands for "firmness" and a "rigid defense posture" to be implemented in the various deterrence strategies, which are so central in the rhetoric of the arms race. Behind all the apparently logical arguments on behalf of deterrence lie beguiling images like "the nuclear shield," "the nuclear umbrella," and "the wall of deterrence." All these strategies and images reflect a psychological need to feel absolutely invulnerable, to live in a world where each side stalemates the other so perfectly that neither can make a move. In typical neurotic fashion, we believe that if no movement is possible, then no harm can come to us. So we are willing, even eager, to be trapped and held as nuclear hostages as long as we can trap our rivals and hold them hostage too. The fatalism so often associated with the nuclear issue is surely tied to this desire to be trapped.

We readily imagine the Bomb itself protecting us from the infinite unreality of endless openness. But the narrow trap that looks like protection turns out to be another neurotic path to ontological insecurity.[18] So we just as readily imagine the Bomb freeing us from imprisoning narrowness; the image of a world exploded into innumerable pieces becomes appealing as well as threatening. This image caricatures the ideal of freedom that the Bomb is held to defend: the more finite pieces there are for the consumer's free choice, the more free the consumer feels. Behind this conception of freedom lies an embrace of finitude itself as an escape from the intolerable threat of infinitude; we may feel that the very existence of division and separation protects us. The Iron Curtain offers the ultimate image of a world permanently divided. Nuclear weapons offer the ultimate image of a world permanently shattered into pieces that can never be united. Once the cage is blown apart and everything is radically atomized, there will be no possibility of transcending our finitude—which may be just the security we want.

The neurotic meaning of nuclear images indicates that the Bomb is not just a symptom and symbol of our societal neurosis. It is also the guarantor of our neurosis, assuring that radical finitude, with its nightmare visions of entrapment and void, will continue to define our world. Since nothing else can symbolize and protect our finitude as powerfully as the Bomb, we may well perceive it as indispensable for our national security, which is really our neurotic security. We may well rely on it alone to secure the freedom of "the free world," which is really a neurotic self-constriction of our sense of reality that deepens our ontological insecurity. In these circumstances, we can not even try to apprehend annihilation as an empirical threat. We can only use it as the ultimate defensive weapon, standing guard over the radical finitude we defend at the risk of our lives.

The Bomb as a Symbol of Neurotic Ambivalence

We cling to images of the trap and the void because each holds out the promise of protecting us against the other. Yet these nuclear images hold a more complex meaning and a more ambiguous appeal. Each can claim to protect us from the others because all are images of the same threat: the infinite unreality inherent in both annihilating openness and annihilating narrowness. As they exert their irresistible fascination on us, luring us toward the fate we fear, they force us to realize that we are clinging to that fate even as we flee it. Our most powerful symbol of finitude is equally the ultimate expression of our frustrated desire to transcend finitude.

Virtually all the images of the nuclear age can be seen as attempts to point toward infinitude, and virtually all have analogues in traditional religious myth and symbolism.[19] On the level of specific images there are abundant examples: the magical weapon, the invulnerable shield, the underground tomb or cave, the apocalyptic battle, the heroic warrior, the evil monster, the cosmic dice game, the fires and ice of hell, the endless night, the living or grateful dead, the purified reborn world. There are also more general themes such as omnipotence, eternity, perfect order, death and resurrection, fate, chance, and sacrifice. All of these are as fundamental to our thinking and feeling about nuclear weapons as they are to the history of religions. And all point to the domain of infinitude. When the balanced stasis we seek is built on visions of endless conflict and the endless existence of nuclear weapons, it bespeaks a vision of infinite stasis—of eternity. When the destruction we prepare is unlimited, it reflects a desire for an infinitely constricting trap and an endless void.

When the craving for control is manifest in weapons of limitless destructive power, it reveals a craving for infinite power. A neurotic society, like a neurotic individual, is deeply ambivalent about infinite power. While it makes itself a replica of a totally finitizing machine, it longs to imbue that machine with infinite power and thus render itself omnipotent. We cannot have omnipotence, though, because other nations also have nuclear arsenals. So we are driven into an endless spiral of increasing our power only to find that the other side has increased its power, which seems to compel us to increase our power, and so on. The endlessness of this spiral is its essential feature, for what we actually desire is endless power. Yet neurotics fear omnipotence as much as they desire it. So it may be no accident that we have locked ourselves into a quest for omnipotence that is doomed to fail. As Tillich points out, power is the primary metaphor for Being itself. So the quest for omnipotence is actually a quest for infinite reality. Yet since the desire for infinite reality entails a risk of infinite unreality, it leads back to radical finitude and its twin nightmare images of infinite unreality: the trap and the void.

A similarly vicious spiral is manifest in other aspects of nuclear imagery. We look to the Bomb for unlimited security and stability, only to find ourselves increasingly insecure and unstable. We look to the Bomb to give us an apocalyptic transcendence of history yet find ourselves ever more burdened with the terrors of history. We look to the Bomb for the freedom of unfettered autonomy but it only immobilizes us with its fear. We look to the Bomb for unlimited new life but it brings only the threat of unlimited death. In every case we are caught in the same neurotic self-contradiction that shaped modernity: desiring infinitude yet guarding ourselves successfully against infinitude. Now, however, we use the Bomb to symbolize both the desire and frustration of the desire.

The endless paradoxes of nuclear imagery show the Bomb to be the prime symbol of our desire for the perfect coincidence of opposites promised by every religious image. But since our radical finitude systematically blocks every movement toward the coincidence of opposites, we must also nullify the potentially integrating power of this image. So we choose as our integrating symbol the ultimate symbol of universal shattering and finitizing.[20] We stake our quest for perfect reality on an image that insures that the opposites it brings together must contradict and frustrate each other. Our desire to transcend finitude remains unconscious because it is repressed by our need for absolute finitude. The desire for infinitude is expressed with inescapable public clarity in our nuclear images and our nuclear arsenal, however, so it demands more strenuous efforts of repression that only strengthen it.

The Bomb itself is the principal symbol and instrument of this repression; we look to the problem as if it were the solution. With the range of the possible reduced to the given, the only possible response is a more rigid and constricting affirmation of the given—another step deeper into neurosis. As a result, every step we take toward the fulfillment of perfect reality leaves us feeling more estranged from and emptied of reality. Every effort to enhance our security only makes us feel closer to the trap and the void.

Every nuclear image embodies this self-defeating pattern, so every nuclear image locks us more firmly into our numbing and into the ontological insecurity at its heart. As long as this societal neurosis prevails, and as long as the Bomb is its first line of defense, it matters little whether we think about the nuclear threat or not: the same forces will shape both our thinking and our not thinking. Nuclear imagery and psychic numbing will reinforce each other. Together they will reinforce our commitment to our neurotic sense of freedom and national security and to our nuclear arsenal, which is the cornerstone of that neurotic freedom and security.

A Tillichian analysis of the nuclear age answers many of the questions raised by Robert Jay Lifton's theory of psychic numbing. Like R.D. Laing's thought, Tillich's accounts for the prevalence of psychic numbing and for the nuclear imagery that reinforces numbing. His analyses also show, like Laing's, why images of physical self-destruction and processes of psychological self-destruction are self-perpetuating. But Tillich's approach goes beyond Laing's because it can explain why ontological insecurity is so pervasive in our society. His theory accounts for both the continuities and discontinuities between the pre- and post-1945 situation; it shows why we so readily embraced a new image of infinite power within the familiar confines of radical finitude.

Tillich's perspective is a complement, not an alternative, to Laing's. The neurotic described by Tillich has much in common with the schizoid described by Laing (not surprisingly, since Laing drew much from Tillich's psychological thought). Both have unrealistic fears and unrealistic relationships to the world; both seek ontological security in ways that only make them more insecure. An adequate theory of psychic numbing and nuclear imagery can be built upon these two theories. At the same time, of course, it must also incorporate the valuable insights offered by Lifton. And, most importantly, it must point to new political possibilities that will lead beyond the nuclear trap and void. One way to approach this task is to turn back to Lifton's psychological paradigm and reinterpret it in light of Tillich's and Laing's focus on ontological insecurity. Before that issue is addressed, however, an important objection to this whole line of thinking should be considered.

4

Disarmament and the Modern Ego

At this point readers who have followed the nuclear issue in the American media during the 1980s might want to raise a critical objection while breathing a sigh of relief. "No doubt all this talk of annihilation fears and omnipotence fantasies was once quite relevant," they might insist. "The Cold War era was a scary time; perhaps even a bit pathological. But soon that will all be just a memory. We are well on our way to a new era of common sense and cooperation. The will to end the nuclear threat is there on both sides of the Iron Curtain—which is itself rapidly coming down—and it is just a matter of time until the disarmament negotiators work out the details." Hence the sigh of relief. Most Americans might argue that even if the previous chapters offer persuasive interpretations of the Cold War era, their relevance to the late eighties and the nineties is questionable.

The 1980s did bring major changes in nuclear rhetoric and nuclear attitudes. The Reagan-Bush regime, which came into office with nuclear sabres rattling, ended the decade listing disarmament and a Cold War thaw among its greatest accomplishments and highest priorities for the future. This was surely a response to a major shift in public opinion—a shift fueled by fears that have largely been calmed. But is a new interpretation really needed to account for the present situation? This chapter aims to show that in fact the approach developed in the previous chapters is still very relevant, because it can account for the present as well as the past of the nuclear age. The key to this argument lies in a facet of R. D. Laing's thought not yet discussed: modernity's total commitment to the rational ego and its scientific "objective look." This commitment, which is central to images of nuclear omnipotence, is equally central to images of disarmament, nuclear balance, and superpower détente.

Science, Technology, and the Ego

For Laing, as for Tillich, the scientific worldview and its technological achievements lie at the heart of modernity. In the domain of scientific objectivity, the rational Cartesian ego is king. But from Laing's viewpoint the king looks suspiciously like a schizoid, for the Cartesian revolution is a fundamental pillar of modernity's false self system. As modernity heightens our ontological insecurity, it drains us of our own authentic selves and leaves us with nothing but its own distinctive, and distinctly schizoid, version of the false self:

> Having been tricked and having tricked ourselves out of our minds, that is to say out of our own personal worlds of experience, out of that unique meaning with which we potentially may endow the external world, simultaneously we have been conned into the illusion that we are separate "skin-ecapsulated egos." Having at one and the same time lost our *selves* and developed the illusion that we are autonomous *egos*, we are expected to comply by inner consent with external constraints, to an almost unbelievable extent.[1]

But there is nothing so unbelievable about the extent of the demand, nor about our willing compliance. We see the "objective look," with its assumption of a radical separation of mind from matter, as essential to our security. The compulsive defense of this wall of separation clearly resembles a compulsive schizoid defense. Schizoids see every contact with people and things in external reality as threats to their own tenuous reality. Since external reality refuses to disappear, schizoids become mere observers, aware but uninvolved, with neither desire nor ability to relate and respond. All their actions are relegated to the inert false self.

Similarly, Laing stresses that scientific objectivity shrinks the knower to a pinpoint of pure rational ego-consciousness, protected from contact with the objects of knowledge by a supposedly unbreachable wall between the two. Each of us is bidden to build the wall a little higher while always remaining on the proper side. For extra protection, the known—including the human body, personality, and relationships—is reduced to mere matter, which is declared false, numb, and dead. When a pinpoint ego meets a dead world, no relationship is possible, nor is any desired. Thus it is easy to take science's final step—the eclipse of human experience altogether. As the human observer is replaced by more precise technological instruments, "the human world itself is, in a sense, eliminated. We have come back to our senses but they themselves are now instruments."[2]

Laing finds the principal source of the nuclear threat in this scientific dehumanization: "*We* have been abolished and can only wait to be demolished. . . . The world has already been destroyed in theory. Is it worth bothering to destroy in practice? We and the world we live in faded out of scientific theory years ago."[3] Yet his own theory suggests that both the Bomb and the "objective look" that made it possible are symptoms of the deeper problem of ontological insecurity and the schizoid strategy. The ego postulated by the modern West's social fantasy system has just those qualities that the schizoid strategy requires. Not only is it permanently detached from the world, it is itself virtually nothing, a mere point of pure consciousness. Yet working through the false self system it can encompass all of reality in a single overarching rational system. Unconstrained by materiality, it can hope to manipulate, conquer, and control reality at will, thereby gaining omnipotence in deed as well as thought.

These hopes are vividly embodied in all the scientific and technological imagery surrounding nuclear weapons, as the ego glories in its greatest technical conquest, "the harnessing of the atom." The same hopes are embodied in the language of those nuclear strategists who speak of "surgical strikes" that would give decision makers "finely calibrated options" to control the "level of escalation" in a nuclear "exchange." During the 1980s increasing numbers of Americans came to reject this kind of language and its implicit fantasy of perfect control through technical precision. Many rejected it because it seems to have an air of unreality about it, as if unreal people are dealing with an unreal world. Some even suggested that it is pathological—as indeed it is in Laing's terms. So there was widespread relief when this warfighting rhetoric gave way, in the media and the highest levels of government, to the rhetoric of disarmament.

The Ego and Disarmament

Few Americans noticed, however, that the same underlying assumptions are equally evident in the language of disarmament and arms control, where all efforts toward peace are entrusted to technologically trained experts who can negotiate the bewildering maze of technical problems that block the way to agreements. In science, government, and the military alike, the watchword remains "objectivity," no matter what nuclear policy options are being pursued. This suggests that as disarmament policies come to the fore Laing's notion of the false self is still relevant, for the nuclear issue is even more deeply immersed in the inertness that is the false self's chief characteristic.

There is a nearly universal assumption that disarmament through the arms control negotiation process is the only viable way out of the nuclear trap. But this faith in arms control is faith in a process of mutual constriction. It looks forward to a day when the rational ego's expertise will devise a set of agreements so perfectly balanced that each side will be eternally immobilized and prevented from moving against the other.[4] The test of every prospective arms control treaty is its capacity to eliminate all risk. The disarmament movement's most successful initiative of the eighties—the nuclear freeze—reflects the same desire to freeze reality as a way of defending ourselves. Images of political stasis, permanence, and rigidity also abound in eras of détente. If the situation can be eternally frozen, we hope, we and the whole world can be eternally safe. So the new-found friendship between the superpowers resembles the friendships developed by schizoids. They are mutually negotiated arrangements for interacting without the prerequisite of all genuine human interaction: the risk of mutual vulnerability. No new political or military initiative can gain popular support unless it is first proven to be virtually risk-free.

All the emerging proposals for perfectly secure arms control treaties and negotiated settlements seem reasonable enough. In truth, though, all aim to defend us principally against the schizoid's real enemy—the inevitable flux of reality itself, whose code name in our political discourse is "instability." A society suffering acute ontological insecurity must see every change as a threat to its tenuous reality and therefore fear "instability" above all. No doubt the threat may be labeled differently at different times. In some eras it is "the Russians" or "the Communists"; in others it is the Bomb itself or the "terrorists" who could, with a bit of purloined plutonium and a suitcase, incinerate a city. But despite these changes our goal remains the same: "stability," which is a political code word for the extreme of psychic numbing—a world too petrified even to contemplate change.

Therefore, we increasingly pin our hopes for national security on the numbing power of the false self system and its apparently reasonable technological program. Just as we used to prize the "firmness" of a "rigid defense posture" above all, so we now prize "firmness" at the negotiating table as the only way to achieve the parity we must have at all costs. Since our goal is a stable balance that we believe will benefit the whole world, it seems perfectly reasonable, even benign, to cast ourselves as the immovable center from which the newly balanced world order proceeds, and as the rigidly vigilant center from which that balance is maintained—by threat of renewed force if necessary. Yet the "stability" we seek is actually the permanent petrification that the schizoid fears yet embraces, hoping to avoid death by becoming dead in life.

If the world and the nations in it are already dead, it matters little whether a given nation be treated as enemy or friend. In either case, all danger is denied. So an enemy nation can become a friend (or vice versa) very easily, and sometimes surprisingly rapidly. Communist China was transformed from enemy to ally almost overnight by the Nixon administration. The Soviet Union was changed, more gradually but no less strikingly, from "evil empire" to dialogue partner during the Reagan administration. Such eras of détente, even more than eras of overt enmity, validate Laing's perception of the family of nations as a nexus, in which both sides cooperate in keeping the international false self system alive. As Laing notes: "The game's the thing: not perhaps fundamentally even a matter of winning it, but of perpetuating it."[5] Détente means that the partners in the nexus openly admit their mutual desire to play the same game. In Laing's analysis of the nexus, the partners continue to play the game largely because each hopes to get reality from the other. As the false self assumes more and more control, schizoids feel increasingly drained of reality, so they turn to others to try to get reality without incurring any risk. One way to do this is to let the other spy on oneself, as the superpowers do with their growing willingness for mutual inspection of military facilities and nuclear weapons tests. Indeed all the recent moves toward superpower cooperation may be seen as attempts to open oneself up to the other's reality without risking one's own.

As in any nexus, though, the game still depends on mutual coercion masquerading as mutual concern. The transformation from enemy to ally is so easy because within the nexus one's closest ally always remains one's enemy. Therefore the pursuit of détente and disarmament need not mean a halt to weapons production. Most Americans believe that we must still keep up our guard, that new weapons can compel the enemy to negotiate arms reduction, that deterrence is necessary until the disarmament process is complete, and that some nuclear deterrence capability will thus be necessary for a very long time—perhaps forever. But deterrence and disarmament seem very compatible in the public mind because both reflect the same basic principle: that humanity can be saved by a technologically constructed and constricting static balance, using the Bomb itself to save us from its horrors.

The "Safe Bomb" Fantasy

Underlying all these beliefs is the drive toward human control and domination. All bespeak the same desire to achieve perfect control of the greatest power known to us—the infinite power that creates all life. One could hardly imagine a more grandiose omnipotence fantasy. As in the schizoid strategy, omnipotence is linked to a fantasy of perfect safety: when the Cold War ends, when perfect parity is achieved, when nuclear weapons production and deployment is totally codified by perfectly equitable and verifiable treaties, then the Bomb's threat will be perfectly contained. We can keep our nuclear arsenals yet be invulnerable to their destructive capacity—or so we seem to imagine. Not only can we make the Bomb safe, in this fantasy image, but by increased attention to environmental health and safety in the production process we can learn to make the Bomb safely too. The Bomb is treated as an inert object incapable of acting back upon us.

Since this "safe Bomb" fantasy depends on absolute faith in the rational ego, which confines itself to the purely finite realm, it is a major triumph for modernity's ultimate concern: its absolute commitment to radical finitude. So it is easily absorbed into the societal neurosis that Tillich describes. Focusing on disarmament and détente, public rhetoric persuades us that our rationality now has both of the historic sources of "instability"—the Soviet Union and the Bomb—securely in hand. The fantasy of perfect "stability" and a "safe Bomb" assures us that we need no longer fear losing our reality. We no longer fear the nuclear void because we have placed ourselves inside the perfectly rational, and therefore invulnerable, trap that the ego's technical expertise has built.

The illusion of invulnerable omnipotence has always been the goal of the superpower game. Never before, perhaps, has the game been played so skillfully. By the end of the 1980s there was a broad consensus, encompassing nearly the whole American political spectrum and gaining power around the world, validating the optimistic vision of the "safe Bomb" fantasy. From the perspective of Laing's social theory, though, this consensus might best be seen as a mystification designed to insure acquiescence in the social fantasy system. One of the most powerful techniques of mystification is to repeat apparently unquestioned and therefore unquestionable assumptions that "everyone knows."

So, for example, "everyone knows" that we all want peace; the disagreements are only over how best to attain it. "Everyone knows" that we all want to reduce nuclear weapons in the long run, but it can't be done overnight. "Everyone knows" that negotiated verifiable arms control agreements are the way to eliminate nuclear weapons. "Everyone knows" that a stable balance of power is the path to peace and security. "Everyone knows" that the Cold War is gradually ending and a new era of peaceful cooperation beginning, that the folly of the nuclear arms race is increasingly recognized, and that disarmament will therefore proceed at a judicious but steady pace. "Everyone knows" all these things and more.

Each of these assumptions may mask a truth that is just the opposite of its claim. Yet in the public media—and increasingly in private discussion—there is simply no room for the possibility that these assumptions might be false. Just as in past decades, the process of mystification is compounded by purveying logically contradictory beliefs that generate a double bind situation. We must embrace a new flexibility while remaining as firm as ever. We must make a breakthrough to détente while keeping up our vigilance against the enemy. We must end the arms race while insuring that we not fall behind in the arms race; indeed we may have to build new weapons just to make sure that we get rid of these weapons. We must encourage "the other side" to take more steps toward disarmament by refusing to match their previous steps.

As we pursue these mystifications, we assure their success through the collusion of mutual self-deception. Both superpowers share an equally strong commitment to obscuring the true nature of the game they are playing together. Around the world, then, we all agree to deny that there is any mystification going on at all. We proclaim that all our words and deeds are the most obviously logical—in fact the only logical—steps toward peace and national security. We insist that debate on the nuclear issue is now more free and open than ever—as it no doubt is, as long as it remains safely within the bounds of the socially sanctioned false self system. Within those bounds, the experts spin an amazingly complex world of competing arms control proposals, strategic options, force modernization plans, technological initiatives, and the like. These images, which define the parameters of "realistic" debate, are all cast in terms of the ego's fantasy of pure objectivity. So the individual self, reduced to a "skin-encapsulated ego," finds a striking symmetry between its private imaginings and the public fantasy. This symmetry gives life a reassuring sense of realness and helps to deny feelings of ontological insecurity, especially when the content of the public fantasy insists that the world is growing safer every day. But it may also help to detach us further from the reality of our world. The collective nuclear fantasies that the experts create and the media duly report to us may coincide with empirical actualities in only random, and often tangential, ways.

Disarmament Fantasies and Actualities

Many media images suggest that the nuclear danger is a thing of the past—even an object of nostalgia, according to influential journalist William Broad.[6] Yet for every step toward disarmament, superpower cooperation, and increased safety in the weapons production process, one can cite a countervailing step toward a continuing arms race, Cold War rivalry, and nuclear danger. As Americans optimistically proclaim "the end of the Cold War" and a new era of safety, they may be detaching themselves ever further from reality.

Strobe Talbott noted at the beginning of 1990 that the Bush administration was still commited to "an array of new strategic nuclear weapons—the MX and Midgetman intercontinental missiles, the B-1 and B-2 (Stealth) bombers, and the Trident II submarine launched missile."[7] Though there is growing support for cutting defense spending, few if any of the cuts will affect nuclear weapons systems. As Admiral Gene La Rocque (Ret.) summarized the situation: "*The old Cold Warriors are still in charge.* . . . Just about every new weapon the Pentagon wants gets funded by the Congress. Nuclear weapons for war-fighting such as the MX and Trident II missiles continue to have a high priority. Congress and the Bush Administration show little interest in really reducing military spending."[8] And liberals still consider it a major victory if they can hold SDI funding to "only" two or three billion dollars per year.

In late 1989 the *New York Times* editorialized that the Bush administration "seems to be deliberately going nowhere in strategic arms talks."[9] The only actual reduction in nuclear weapons as yet is the elimination of intermediate nuclear forces in Europe. And there are reports that American short-range missiles will soon be retrofitted to have virtually the same capacities as the missiles banned by the INF treaty.[10] Critics of the arms control process have long contended that most agreements actually ratify the acquisition of new arms in relatively balanced numbers rather than reducing arms. They note that even arms reduction treaties may simply spur research on new weapons to replace the eliminated weapons and slip through loopholes in the treaties.[11] Surveying America's nuclear force reductions at the beginning of the decade, the *Bulletin of the Atomic Scientists* concluded: "For the next few years decreases are likely to continue in the number, but not the capability, of U.S. strategic weapons."[12] Although the American government professes concern about the dangers of nuclear proliferation, there is little sense of urgency about this issue on the part of the government or the public.

The government's professed concerns for environmental safety at nuclear production plants are also mixed signals. For example, Secretary of Energy James Watkins proclaimed in 1989 that the Department of Energy (DOE) would now place safety concerns above production quotas. But he also insisted that western states must receive radioactive waste from nuclear plants, despite those states' objections, because if they refused the "precursor to building a strategic triad would be impaired."[13] When the states persisted in their refusal, the DOE reminded them that it had the legal right to compel them to take the waste, for reasons of "national security."[14] The DOE announced elaborate plans to improve health and safety, but the head of a House subcommittee on hazardous wastes asserted that "these so-called house cleanings are an illusion, because the same personnel continue to run the plants, and contaminate the environment."[15] Some critics even suggest that the DOE may be confessing the dangers of its aging facilities primarily to build support for funding a whole new generation of such facilities.

Some popular media images suggest that the Cold War attitudes traditionally used to justify weapons production may also continue. *U.S. News and World Report*, for example, cited the fears of "some analysts" that if America had only 18 Trident submarines (each carrying nearly 200 highly accurate warheads), its national security would be jeopardized.[15a] *Newsweek* made the case in more sweeping terms:

> Just because communism is crumbling in the Soviet Union does not mean Washington can ignore the military threat to Europe. A noncommunist Russia would still have 60 divisions west of the Urals, and a nationalist right-wing regime might be tempted to use them. . . . What if Washington withdrew its nuclear umbrella from its allies? Without the glue of common defense, the world might slip into hostile trading blocs, Europe vs. North America vs. Asia. Worse, Tokyo might ally with Moscow. These are powerful arguments for maintaining U.S. primacy in defense of the West.[16]

This traditional attitude is still reflected in government policy, not only in weapons research and production, but in plans to use the weapons. The Single Integrated Operating Plan is reportedly being revised to stress "decapitating" the Soviet leadership and destroying Soviet mobile and defensive missiles as priorities in a nuclear "exchange."[17] Of course the details of actual policy remain, as always, largely hidden from view. But it appears that proponents of some version of the nuclear warfighting strategy still have significant influence in military planning.[18]

In all the government's apparently dovish rhetoric, there is an overwhelming insistence that the Bomb's dangers can and will be abolished without abolishing the Bomb itself. There is never any doubt that technical expertise can make the Bomb safe. A cynical critic might even suspect that the government is fostering the illusion of safety in order to insure that production and deployment remain unimpeded despite growing public fears. Regardless of the government's conscious aims, the unconscious effect of the "safe Bomb" fantasy is clearly to move the nation deeper into unreality and psychic numbing. The *Bulletin of the Atomic Scientists* editorially summarized the situation: "Weapons of mass destruction may be out of mind, but they certainly aren't out of the U.S. military budget, which has only been chipped down a bit from the record level it hit under Ronald Reagan. In the meantime, many members of the more active 'attentive' public have turned their financial support and attention strictly to other matters, absentmindedly choosing to ignore the connections among issues and the continuing risk posed by nuclear weapons."[19]

Although the *Bulletin* described the situation accurately, the public may be doing more than just "absentmindedly ignoring" the nuclear risk and its connections to other issues. We may be shoring up our collective commitment to the radical finitude of the schizoid strategy. On the one hand, the images we publicly profess are increasingly shaped by the "objective look" of the rational ego, which is so central in our collective schizoid strategy. On the other hand, the images embodied in nuclear actualities are still largely the traditional fantasies of annihilation and military omnipotence. So the "safe Bomb" fantasy may now be playing the same role as the schizoid's false self: masking buried fantasies of annihilation and omnipotence. Our seeming rationality thus separates us from the reality in which we live both politically and psychologically. By committing ourselves to the common fantasy of the nuclear debate, we actually drain ourselves of reality by denying our own authentic experience of dread in the face of the nuclear threat—which is just what the schizoid strategy requires.

As inner reality dwindles, more and more of life is handed over to the apparent pure objectivity of the false self system. Perhaps we admire all the wonders of science and technology primarily because they insure that our numbed dehumanized world will continue to be the comforting daily reality. Perhaps we embrace the "safe Bomb" fantasy of détente and arms control for much the same reason; propagating an image of an immutably frozen future, we can more easily treat the present world as if it were dead and unreal and thus confirm our own death in life. But the more we immerse ourselves in the technical fantasies of the rational ego, the more we exacerbate the underlying problem of ontological insecurity, embracing the problem as if it were the only possible solution.

Embracing the problem means embracing the Bomb; throughout all the changes in nuclear imagery and the superpower game, the one constant is that the weapons continue to be produced and deployed. If the most recent phase of the nuclear age is a recoiling from fantasies of engulfment and implosion only to take refuge in petrification fantasies, then we should expect that the future will bring a predictable reaction: the fear of losing our reality in the narrow trap will lead us back to fantasies of the void, with their attendant Cold War and "warfighting" policies. This is not to deny that Americans genuinely want to enhance peace and security by ending the nuclear threat. The problem is rather that we are trapped by an ambivalence we do not understand; as "divided selves" we both want and do not want an end to the threat. We do not know how to disengage from it because we do not understand its psychological roots.

Laing's theoretical perspective, supplemented by Tillich's, can open up an adequate understanding of those roots, and it can account equally well for all phases of the nuclear age's numbing and imagery. It can reveal in some detail how current nuclear imagery numbs us just as effectively as its predecessors. (This conclusion remains valid as this book is completed in the spring of 1990. It is possible, though perhaps unlikely, that changes in nuclear imagery in the next few years will create a significantly different situation that calls for a different analysis. In any event, the present analysis does account for an important part of our nuclear imagery in the past; see the discussion in chapter 8 below.)

Yet neither Laing nor Tillich seem to offer a viable concrete alternative. Tillich's early vision of Christian socialism has found little response in the United States. His ontological language of faith, which is increasingly criticized on the theological left and was never popular on the right, is hardly likely to gain a broader public hearing. Laing's antidote is clear enough in its general outlines: we must be open to our own authentic experience, replacing social fantasy with individual imagination. But he has little to say about how to achieve this or about the specific nature of imagination. Perhaps the closest he comes is the conclusion of the last substantive essay in *The Politics of Experience*. Here, at the culmination of his most influential and radical writing, he says cryptically: "True sanity entails in one way or another the dissolution of the normal ego . . . the emergence of the 'inner' archetypal mediators of divine power . . . and through this death and rebirth, the eventual reestablishment of a new kind of ego-functioning, the ego now being the servant of the divine, no longer its betrayer."[20]

Laing names C. G. Jung as the one psychologist who has shown the way to a rediscovery of religious experience through conscious evocation of inner archetypal images, noting that few have followed Jung on this path. Laing himself hardly chooses to articulate this path at all. Yet there are some psychologists who have gone far beyond Laing, and even beyond Jung, in pursuing this vision of archetypes as divine powers and the ego as their servant. Among them, perhaps the most influential today (at least in the United States) is James Hillman. Hillman's work extends Laing's analysis of the contemporary ego in a number of directions that can be linked directly to the nuclear dilemma in both its past and present forms.

The Heroic Ego

James Hillman's archetypal psychology is founded on the fundamental belief of C. G. Jung that "the psyche consists essentially of images."[21] Every experience, according to archetypal psychology, is essentially shaped by some set of fantasies. The question to be asked about nuclear weapons, then, as about every other phenomenon, is: What fantasy images are embedded in our attitudes and behaviors? Hillman's answer is that the Bomb, like every facet of modernity, reflects the fantasies of "monotheistic consciousness." These fantasies translate the Western religious heritage into a secular form; though we may no longer be devoted to the one deity of traditional religion, we remain devoted to oneness itself as a deity, an ultimate value.

This ideal of pure unity keeps alive the fantasy of what Hillman calls the "heroic ego." The human being is still cast as a unified independent will, enjoined to champion good over evil and bring unity out of diversity. And the aim of modern secularity is to give human beings the glory once reserved for God: rational control over the chaos of nature. This is the heroic ego's mission—a mission that Laing sees as a collective commitment to the schizoid strategy. As the schizoid's ego shrinks toward nothingness, it must strive to unify everything, for it hopes to control everything. And it must prepare to fight heroically, for it sees itself beset by uncontrollable enemies on all sides. Just as the church felt compelled to eliminate heretics, the modern state feels compelled to war against all who oppose its single-minded vision of the good. Although the particulars of that vision may change from time to time, they always remain centered on monotheistic ego values: independence, individualism, free choice, free enterprise, and unlimited development of unique personal identity.

Sometimes the mission of protecting and advancing the good is acted out in images of the Cold War and the arms race. Like so many visions of singleness, this scenario is played out on a radically dualistic stage, with the Iron Curtain as the line of demarcation. The Bomb is seen as the great unifier, "the big one" that can bring the "Red menace" to its knees. Hillman suggests that monotheistic consciousness often embraces the dualism that appears to be its opposite. It seeks out simple abstract demarcations of right and wrong or good and evil because these are the most convenient base for its unifying maneuvers. Its motto is "divide and conquer."

At other times the cause of the good is advanced through images of détente, deterrence, and disarmament. But these are even more clearly based on visions of global unity. When the Iron Curtain seems to be coming down, Americans interpret it as a triumph for monotheistic American values that seem to be sweeping the world. Regardless of which images dominate at a particular time, the entire nation is always expected to stand united in defense of its values. "Firmness" and unbending "resolve"—the most cherished virtues of the heroic ego—remain the watchwords of national policy, whether acted out in the bomb shelter or at the negotiating table.

The Bomb was developed primarily as an instrument of political domination, to preserve the unity that we call "stability." But it was also developed because it was "technically sweet" (in Robert Oppenheimer's famous phrase).[23] It seemed to be the culmination of the heroic ego's struggle to dominate nature, symbolizing limitless control in every realm. The heroic ego welcomes the challenge of grappling with a problem, going into action, and overcoming every obstacle. Challenge has always been a central theme in nuclear imagery too. The most common justification for nuclear armament, of course, is the challenge of staying ahead of, or keeping up with, or catching up to the enemy. Nuclear armament has always been imaged as a race, and calls for national "resolve" always sound a strong note of challenge. The threat of nuclear cataclysm has also been transformed into a challenge—a test of the nation's courage in confronting danger. Even the actuality of cataclysm has sometimes been cast in these terms, with a postholocaust world viewed as the ultimate test not only of courage but also of technological ingenuity. When *Life* magazine advocated fallout shelters in 1961, for example, it suggested that the heroic ego is a distinctively American virtue: "[Shelters] will give all Americans the hope that they, like their forebears, can some day abandon the stockades to cross whatever new mountains of adversity or trial may lie ahead."[23]

For the modern ego technological achievement is a moral, political, and spiritual value—even a path to salvation.[24] Technical perfection is its ultimate goal, for it sees every flaw as a threat to perfect order. So the media, the ego-voice of the nation, depict both nuclear experts and the general public moving toward a perfect solution of the nuclear dilemma. The possibility of failure is rarely mentioned, and there is hardly a whispered hint that the task might be impossible. The focus of the quest may become disarmament rather than winning the war, but the heroic ego and its values still have center stage. The fantasy behind disarmament negotiations is a fantasy of a world perfectly unified by a perfectly verifiable treaty. The challenge now is to bargain toughly, to show a united will lest the enemy mistake our resolve, and to support new weapons systems as "bargaining chips." But media images allow little doubt that the experts and their technical rationality can some day tie up all the loose ends in an enduring perfect order. And this vision of salvation is reported by objective journalists in a matter-of-fact style as literal truth.

Literalism

Hillman's most valuable contribution to understanding the nuclear dilemma is the link he makes between the content and the form of the heroic ego's images. Not only do the ego's images all speak of oneness, but they are all experienced in the mode of oneness; i.e., literally. The essence of literalism is singleness of vision. It demands a single meaning for every word, event, or idea. It insists that nothing is "really real" except empirically verifiable facts. Literalism objectifies, quantifies, and simplifies because it must reject all confusion, ambiguity, and mystery. Its ultimate goal is to keep reality itself unified, orderly, precise, and single. In pursuit of this goal, it divides all experience into dualities and insists that opposites must be kept apart. Literalism is the natural milieu for the schizoid ego striving to control an uncontrollable world.

But the world's chaos is mediated to the mind through the chaos of the mind's own polyvalent imagery. A fantasy image never has a single clear meaning. It is more like a hall of mirrors, opening up an infinite web of interconnected, ambiguous, and entangling meanings. Fantasy compels us to see reality from many angles simultaneously; it is inherently polytheistic. So the ego must also strive to suppress all internal imagery. It must become an imperial power, colonizing the dark continents of imagination and rendering them unconscious in the name of its own enlightening consciousness. The ego cannot dispense with images altogether, of course. But it can hope to win its battle against imagination by choosing images that enshrine its own unique values and then literalizing those images. Literalism and the heroic ego are inseparable partners.

The triumph of monotheistic ego consciousness in modernity has insured the triumph of literalism, making it, in Hillman's opinion, "the besetting sin today."[25] We may admit that dreams, fictions, utopias, secret fears, superstitions, hallucinations, and the like are in some sense real, because they are forms of human experience. But we generally insist that these imagined realities are not "really real" because they are not concrete, publicly observable, objective data. (Those who argue that spiritual or psychic phenomena are "really real" usually feel compelled to present them in literal terms as objective realities, which merely underscores the point.)

Since monotheistic consciousness is at the center of the culture that produced nuclear weapons, it has determined not only our nuclear images but also the way we hold those images. The images of the Bomb that actually determine our attitudes and actions are the ones we hold literally. This literalism lends itself as readily to Cold War strategy as to schizoid strategy. Literalism divides the world into true and false, and then good and evil, with no middle ground allowed. It pits two monisms against each other in order to enshrine one and destroy the other. It is therefore the characteristic mode of a culture bent on an apocalyptic crusade to wipe out all evil. But its true goal is to enshrine singleness itself. Every enemy is a projection not only of a particular fantasy, but of the polyvalent power of fantasy itself. When Cold War strategy gives way to disarmament strategy, the crusade may be redirected at wiping out the nuclear threat. But the true enemy is still the uncontrollable complexities of reality, and our principal weapon is still objective literal thought.

Hillman traces the history of literalism back to the ancient world. Both Hellenistic philosophy and Israelite religion were grounded in the search for a single truth, he contends. Both therefore distrusted the polyvalent images of myth and fantasy. These two streams merged in the extreme single-mindedness of Christianity, which taught that the one God sent his only son to reveal a single truth through a single church. Although modern science is often pitted against Christianity, Hillman sees a direct link between the two in their common commitment to monotheistic literalism. The Cartesian revolution reduced the open-ended multifaceted mind to the singleness of the objective ego. Sensual feelings were reduced to sense data. Emotional feelings were reduced to abstract conceptualizing processes. Yet, like Christianity, modern science remains embedded in a rich matrix of fantasies. Chief among those fantasies, in both cases, is the fantasy of wiping out all fantasies.

For Hillman the crucial link between Christian tradition and modern science is late medieval nominalism, the theory that words are arbitrary names with no inherent meaning or power of their own. As nominalism triumphed in Western thought, rich complex universals were abandoned in favor of simple, particular, single-meaning terms. "The plain man of common sense with his fists full of facts is a nominalist and his view of reality has obtained."[26] It has certainly obtained in the media's treatment of nuclear issues. Every mention of overwhelming military, diplomatic, or technical complexities implies a "fist full of facts" as the only viable route to solutions. This nominalism is now called "realism" (a word that originally denoted the very opposite of nominalism); the most damning charge the media can bring against any opinion on the nuclear issue is to label it "unrealistic." As Cold War fantasies have given way to disarmament hopes, the reign of fact-laden "realism" has become more powerful than ever. No opinion can gain a hearing unless it is couched in the technical language of weaponry, strategy, and *realpolitik.* The litmus test of every new proposal is its immediate practicality and empirical verifiability.

Of course literalism cannot abandon abstract concepts altogether. But it can, and does, nullify the distinction between concrete facts and abstract ideas. As nominalism drains abstractions of their imaginal content and power, it leaves behind only an empty conceptual shell. Conceptualization tames the unruly image and imposes order on it by destroying its open-ended ambiguity. Defined and confined, the concept becomes a dead object placed on the same sorting shelf as scientific facts, a mere counter to be used in games of thought and speech.

Both concrete and abstract words are further enfeebled by modern linguistic theory, which sees words and concepts as empty containers, devoid of any essential connection to the world and its objects. Thus it fosters nominalism's heritage; words gain increasing prominence while they become increasingly arbitrary, powerless, and untrustworthy. Orwell's "newspeak" is an inevitable result. Preparation for war is preparation for peace; the threat of extinction promises security; evil is the breeding ground of good. Such contradictions are easily tolerated because the concepts they incorporate have no inherent meanings and evoke no response. They are flat, one-dimensional, interchangeable units, amenable to any manipulation. Immense concepts like "apocalypse," "extinction," "global security," and "world peace" are equally empty. They might once have triggered deep responses in the depths of the soul, but now they fail to move us. They merely fill up space on the page. All words have equal value and impact—or lack of value and impact. All are simply more grist for the ego's mill.

Literalism and Psychic Numbing

The crusading literalism that Hillman describes impacts modernity, and numbs modernity, most powerfully through scientific objectivity. It remolds all experience in terms of its own paradigmatic image: inert matter. Its vision is restricted to the opaque material world—a superficial world taken at face value, a world that is only what it appears to be and cannot be seen through. Ideas, words, and feelings take on the same qualities as physical objects. So do other people and ultimately our own selves. All appear wholly impersonal, quantifiable, amenable to manipulation and control. Every reality becomes an inert object with no multivalent interactions, no complex ramifications, and no creative tensions that might lead to unpredictable changes.

Literalism's analytical focus, seeing only the most limited realities, also denies the possibility of experiencing reality in its totality. The absence of connections and the denial of wholeness combine to restrict the mind to the realm of instrumental technical reasoning. Experience is confined to the conscious rational level on which A can never simultaneously be not-A. There can be no higher all-encompassing perspective to give meaning to limited realities. In such a world, filled with statistics, computer projections, and abstract theoretical models, everything becomes just a radically finite means to some other means. The endless complexities of human reality, and an ultimate meaning for all those complexities, disappear. The ego's world and self are reduced to collections of discrete, mechanistically connected, predictable, and therefore apparently safe objects.

Denying the uncontrollable complexities of imagination, literalism also cuts the mind off from its innate sense of possibility. It creates a static world, in which the possible is confined to the given of present perception, as if it were complete and unalterable. Literalizing others along with itself, the ego binds the others too; it forgets that all are acting out shared fantasies. All become stuck, as if in the mud, in their superficial materialism, unable to figure out what is really the matter. Without distance from the immediacy of experience, the mind cannot imagine historical depth or future alternatives. With its reality frozen in literalized images, it cannot help becoming numb. Certainly there is change in our world. But if there can be no experience of the whole there can be no change in the whole. All change must be confined to the realm that literalism defines as real: the smallest possible units of incremental change. And since the possible is equated with the given, all change must take place within that given; i.e., within the limits of the consensually validated fantasy that we call "progress." Indeed, everything can be allowed to change because the structure within which these changes occur appears to be safely immutable.

The numbing effects of literalism are most vividly evident in the popular images of the disarmament process and the "safe Bomb." A nearly universal consensus insists that only the gradual step-by-step process of arms control and environmental reform can reduce the weapons' threat. There is an endless stream of new projects and proposals to make progress in averting the nuclear threat; hyperactivity is one good way to avoid facing our inner psychological depths. But all these innovations only act out new variations on the same old tragic dramas. All reduce the nuclear dilemma to a discrete series of technical problems, requiring that other nations be reduced to a discrete series of technical problems as well. The Bomb and all those who might wield it become as inert as the matter from which the weapons are made. Only this literalizing approach fits the dominant canons of "realism," so it alone can be accepted as really real. Yet if Hillman is right, this is a narrow perspective whose ultimate result is to validate the very worldview that created the nuclear threat in the first place. As long as our nuclear images are all held purely literally, we are bound to perpetuate our numbing, and therefore perpetuate the threat, no matter what particular images or policies hold sway. We will be unable to imagine genuinely new possibilities because we are unable to imagine very much at all.

Literalism's crusade against imagination is endless, because the fantasies generated by the open psyche are our fundamental reality and will not go away. The more we deny the reality of fantasy, the more we starve ourselves of our personal reality and lock ourselves in to the self-defeating spiral of the schizoid strategy. Literalism thus exacerbates our ontological insecurity and drives us to replace our own waning reality with the apparent reality of the communal fantasy. We feel compelled to insist that this fantasy world, and only this world, is "really real," and that our worldview is a literally accurate representation of all reality. In a world that defines truth solely as literal truth, every new reality—including the Bomb and our efforts to control it—must be apprehended literally and thus intensify psychic numbing. This separation from our own reality and the world's reality is the psychological essence of the process that we call "being realistic."

The Ego and Its Repressions

Literalism and the objective look came to dominate the Western worldview with the Enlightment vision of universal progress. All embodied what Hillman sees as the ego's age-old dream: clarity, rationality, and light forever eclipsing life's 'shadow side' of evil, death, and nothingness. The modern ego's first step in pursuing this dream is to deny the reality of dream and fantasy and reduce its own shadow side fantasies to nothing but fear of literal physical death. In the manner of all mythic heroes, it affirms that physical death can be overcome, either technologically through medicine or spiritually through resurrection and immortality. In the early years of the nuclear age both these hopes combined in the belief in civil defense and bomb shelters as technological assurances that global death would be followed by national resurrection.

As that belief has lost its tacit public support, the heroic ego looks increasingly to arms control, nuclear deterrence, and environmental reform to escape the nuclear threat. This may appear to be a step toward realism. In fact, though, it takes the ego a significant step closer to denying the shadow side altogether. The early civil defense plans assumed the possibility (and often the inevitability) of widespread death and suffering. The dream of a "safe Bomb" is the dream of a world totally free from the shadow of the Bomb while still embodying its prized ego values in the Bomb. Contemporary public consciousness seems convinced that death and suffering need never be faced, if only the technical rationality of the experts is allowed full sway and the nation's resolve is firm.

In its war against the inner realm of fantasy, the modern ego finds another useful weapon in the literalism of political ideology. Building on its nominalistic heritage, it reduces complex ideas to simplistic conceptual images and acts them out literally in simplistic social roles. So we arm ourselves in the name of "peace" or "the free world" (or "the working class" or "the revolution"), hiding our fearful fantasies behind a shining mask of self-righteous morality. The ego takes its ideologies and moral slogans so seriously, Hillman contends, because it takes them so literally. It cannot see that its own viewpoint is merely one among many that inevitably coexist in every mind. Locked into an immobilized reality of its own making, the ego must compel others to accept its own ideology as uniquely true or even inevitable.

Yet the ego, single-mindedly fighting for moral virtue, ultimately undermines its own aim because it believes in its morality so literally. Once reality is reduced to mere matter, what moral restrictions should or could be binding upon us? Our selves, our relationships, and our civilization, like our things, seem to us nothing but inert objects. They "are just dead," Hillman says (echoing Laing), "so why not destroy them, they are dead anyway."[27] Although the ideologies surrounding the "safe Bomb" fantasy appear to be more moral than their Cold War predecessors, they retain the same literalizing moralizing style. So they may lull us into a false sense of security while actually reinforcing our feeling that anything is permitted, since the world is "just dead anyway."

Perhaps the greatest danger of the "safe Bomb" fantasy is that precisely because it represses our former fantasies of annihilation and omnipotence it insures their continued hold upon us. Hillman agrees with most depth psychologists that repressed thoughts, emotions, and images will inevitably return. But he stresses that, when repressed through literalism, they will return literally, in "ungainly, obsessive, literalistic ways, affecting consciousness with precisely the qualities it strives to exclude."[28] This principle plays a central role in shaping our nuclear images. When we deny the call of irrational death for a place in our imaginal life, we find ourselves bedazzled by compelling obsessions with irrational death—and killing—as physical realities. Always bent on domination, living in a world of constant challenge, and taking every conflict on the level of literal physical concreteness, we are inevitably fascinated by images of physical power, aggression, and destruction.

Even when we pursue policies to control destructive technologies, we are held by nuclear images and technologies in an apparently mysterious grip. Even when political realities as well as rhetoric seem to dictate dissolving our nuclear arsenals, real progress toward that goal is agonizingly slow. Even when declaratory policy finds no reasonable use for the weapons, actual policy may plan to use them as traditional instruments of war. Hillman's theorizing helps to clear up the mystery: the shadow side, he contends, returns in its most ungainly literal form as the indispensable tool for virtuously repressing the shadow side. No matter how well intentioned our "safe Bomb" ideologies may be, these attempts to repress the shadow side are inevitably self-defeating because they actually preserve the shadow they hope to dispel. In light of declaratory policy, nuclear holocaust may occur only as an apparent accident, countering all the world's best intentions to avert it. Or, in light of the actual policy pursued in some military quarters, it may appear to be the most moral act of all, in a perverse conclusion to the heroic ego's perversely self-righteous morality. Regardless of declaratory or actual policies, however, holocaust remains a very real possibility because we have psychologically negated the Bomb's living actuality.

James Hillman's archetypal psychology offers a useful complement to R. D. Laing's picture of the schizoid strategy. It shows why the schizoid must play the role of a heroic ego—why fantasies of omnipotence become fantasies of splitting reality in two, overcoming the challenge of the enemy, and imposing perfect unity. It shows why these fantasies, and indeed the whole world, must be taken literally. And it shows how the repression of annihilation fantasies, along with all other fantasies, undermines the schizoid's sense of personal reality and potentiates ontological insecurity. The repressed fear returns, but it is experienced—and combatted—as a literal reality; literalized visions of omnipotence generate literalized visions of annihilation, and vice versa. Literalism potentiates the spiral of insecurity that Laing describes and makes it that much more inescapable.

Hillman's analysis also underscores the conclusion drawn from Laing and Tillich: just as a single theoretical model can account for both psychic numbing and nuclear imagery, so a single model of numbing and imagery can account for both the arms race and disarmament, for both the Cold War and its thaw. All these disparate phenomena can best be understood as different manifestations of a single malady, which Robert Jay Lifton first identified as psychic numbing. It seems clear that Lifton's theory must be amplified to provide a fuller picture of the nuclear age. But this does not mean that Lifton's theory can be ignored. Rather it must be reinterpreted so that its valuable insights may be preserved and enhanced. It may turn out that Lifton's work holds the key to the deepest roots of the nuclear dilemma.

5

The Theory of Psychic Numbing Reconsidered

Robert Jay Lifton's theory of psychic numbing first took shape in his encounter with the abnormal in Hiroshima and then proceeded to a vision of normalcy in his new psychological paradigm. But it is easier to discuss the results of his work by reversing the order, for his paradigm of well-being is the key to understanding his concept of psychic numbing. In order to reinterpret the concept of psychic numbing, it will first be necessary to examine and reinterpret Lifton's understanding of psychological health.

The Formative Process and the Life of the Self

The best place to begin in outlining Lifton's paradigm is at the beginning—the birth of the human being. The neonate emerges into a radically new world filled with a chaotic jumble of strange stimuli. If the neonate took in all these stimuli, or took in some portion of them at random, it would die. To survive, it must select just those elements in the environment that are meaningful for its own life processes. The astonishing fact to be explained is that nearly all infants carry out this complex selection process successfully from the moment of birth. In Lifton's view, we must assume that infants are normally born with an innate ability to filter out irrelevant stimuli. He calls this most essential human trait "the inchoate image."[1]

It is an image, for it is something like an inner pattern that mirrors and fits the environment to which the baby must relate. But it is inchoate, for it is not truly an inner picture. It is merely a tendency for the baby to perceive the world in certain predetermined ways. When the baby is first offered the breast, for example, it does not in any way think or internally image "a breast." Yet somehow it knows that this is a highly significant stimulus. More importantly, the stimulus releases energies in a specifically patterned way; the baby responds appropriately with a desire to suck. The inchoate image is thus "an interpretive anticipation of interaction with the environment,"[2] which coordinates the constant exchange of psychosomatic energy between the baby and the world. As a result of this constant exchange, the baby not only stays alive but feels alive.

Much of the foundation for this paradigm rests on the work of ethologists who have studied animal behavior. Animals, like humans, live by innate images. But there is a crucial difference:

> In nonhuman species the overall pattern tends to be relatively fixed and limited in variation, and in that sense can be called instinctual. Human newborns *seem* to start out that way too, but from the beginning their inchoate imagery contains the potential for the more elaborate and varied environmental encounters they are to have. And over the course of the human life cycle every "act" or "response" becomes infused with symbolized function. If the term "reaction chain" can be used at all, it is open, attuned to a self-generating human imagination with its endless flow of prospective inner forms. The human brain requires that we do no less. As in the case of other animals there are biological limits to the process. These are most clear during early infancy, but the extraordinary human symbolic repertoire makes sharp definition of any such limits extremely difficult.[3]

Lifton puts special emphasis on the "self-generating" quality of human images. Inchoate images, as "prospective inner forms," exist and affect the psyche before any corresponding stimuli are encountered. External stimuli, once encountered, cannot evoke any response unless they are mediated by a psychic image. And the image can evoke responses independent of any external stimulus. (This is readily obvious in dream images, which can evoke not only emotional responses but also physical responses such as laughter, tears, sweat, and orgasm.) Moreover, inner imagery can go through innumerable expansions and transformations in the absence of any external changes. The inner image wants, or perhaps even needs, to grow and flourish of its own accord, regardless of its concern for survival. So the image functions as an independent stimulus which, by itself, calls forth a response, and the possibilities for inner stimulus-response interactions are virtually limitless.

As the infant grows, it learns to filter out irrelevant perceptions and sensations more efficiently. At the same time, the inner image acquires a constantly expanding series of symbolic meanings: memories, thoughts, feelings, fears, hopes, and other associations. Some of these arise from interactions with the environment and others are internally generated by interactions among images. As the infant grows into childhood and then adulthood, its fund of psychic images grows richer, more active, and more complex. Therefore learning, and ultimately survival, require an increasingly adept filtering of both external and internal stimuli.

This learning process is possible only because every human being is born into a particular culture. Some images grow out of the unique experience of the individual, but many (perhaps most) are drawn from the pool of meanings offered, and often imposed, by the culture. Society has a vital stake in insuring that each of its members meets particular stimuli with particular socially approved responses. From the earliest moments of the infant's life, the group is trying to shape the inner flow of images in what it considers the proper direction. Culture's fundamental task, it may be said, is to fill out the rudimentary schemas for interaction with symbolic meanings that are taken so much for granted as to appear innate.

Over time, images of related features of the world cluster together in ever larger mental structures, bringing with them their associated symbolic meanings. For example, the breast joins with the mother's face and hands and arms, and then with other parts of the mother's body, to create the visual and symbolic image of 'mother.' That image later joins with similarly generated images of 'father' and 'brothers' and 'sisters' to create the wider image of 'family.' When a series of such related images becomes stabilized in its constellation, it produces what Lifton calls a "form," "a relatively ordered recreation of all that I have experienced in that realm, bodily and psychically. Each represents my way of feeling and knowing that aspect of my existence."[4] A form is only relatively ordered, because it retains the same tendency to growth and openness to future possibility found in the inchoate image. The formative process is thus in principle self-accelerating and constantly expanding. The sum of all forms, in Lifton's view, the largest configuration, is the form of 'the self' by which we symbolize our sense of being a single coherent and continuing organism in interaction with a coherent world—and perhaps with humanity as a whole (or what Lifton has called the "species self").[5]

Lifton's paradigm of the normal psyche culminates in his insight that both life and the sense of being alive depend on the free flow of the formative process. As forms grow into larger configurations, they bring wider varieties of stimulus energy into the mind, trigger a broader flow of inner image development, release more energy in new patterns of response, and increase the self's feeling of vitality. As long as images and forms can go on developing, the self feels motivated to interact with the world in new ways and realize new possibilities. All these aspects of the formative process are mutually reinforcing. Vitality—the subjective feeling of aliveness—is necessary for a wider range of interactions, but those interactions are the fuel that feeds the flame of vitality. Lifton often stresses that vitality is the prerequisite for meaningfulness, but he also asserts that meaningful forms are prerequisite for vitality. All these qualities are so many parts of a single formative process that is essential for biological life itself. But mere survival is never the goal of the formative process. Rather, "an overall sense of organismic vitality [is] the central motivating principle for psychic action. . . . Indeed human existence itself can be understood as a quest for vitalizing images and image-constellations."[6]

Symbolic Immortality and Psychic Numbing

But is there in fact one single principle at the root of all psychic action? Following Lifton's own analysis it would seem not, since the quest for vitalizing images is the product of two prior desires: the desire for survival and the desire for inner image development. It is important to keep these desires conceptually distinct because they represent two distinct sides of the psyche.

The desire for survival demands images that can limit the interchange between psyche and world and prevent the psyche from drowning in a flood of overwhelming stimuli (both external and internal). The world and the psyche are always changing, of course, and demanding that images change too. But every change means a temporary breakdown in protective structure and a risk of stimulus overload. So the psyche, insofar as it seeks survival, must see changes as threats. It responds to these threats by filtering out new kinds of stimuli that have no meaningful place in its previously familiar patterns. When this is not possible or fruitful, it learns to take in these new stimuli by filtering and shaping them to fit its familiar patterns. But the overall goal of filtering remains the same: preventing the chaos of stimulus overload by limiting change to the minimum necessary to maintain homeostatic balance with the environment.

The innate desire for image growth presents a very different picture. It demands images that actualize the widest range of potentialities and realize the largest scope of possibilities. To this end, it desires a constantly expanding interchange of energies among the self's images and between self and world. Its great fear is not stimulus overload but rather just the opposite—a rigidity that threatens to stifle or even end the process of growth. So it sees no need to limit stimuli. Indeed it may even seek stimulus overload, for an uncontrolled flood of stimuli can trigger hyperactivity of inner imagery.

The psyche's quest for vitality is thus compounded of two very different needs that pull it in two opposite directions. Both fixed structures that limit interactions and ever-changing structures that open up new interactions seem to be prerequisites for a vitalizing flow of psychosomatic energy. Yet each threatens to undercut the other and thereby erode vitality. Whether the psyche is overwhelmed by stimuli or whether it withers from lack of stimuli, the result is an absence of forms and images—an absence of structured interactions—which spells death for the psyche. This intrapsychic conflict and its attendant threat are reproduced in every mental image and every mental act.

In Lifton's view, the self is permanently caught (with greater or lesser intensity) on the horns of this dilemma. The ideal solution is a perfect compromise between the two basic needs—a constantly changing but relatively stable balance between stasis and growth, yielding a relatively stable rate of change within relatively fixed forms. The closer the self approaches this ideal compromise, the more dependable its energy flow, and the more alive it feels. So the self's quest for vitalizing images is actually a quest for the perfect middle ground between its two fundamental desires. No self ever attains this golden mean permanently. But as long as the self can stay relatively balanced between structure and openness it will feel alive.

The prerequisite for relative balance is what Lifton calls "grounding." The self must be grounded in a sense of itself as a biological and historical unity, an ongoing integrated vital organism. This grounding depends, in turn, on a basic trust in life itself as a dependable balance of structure and change in which the self is permanently embedded, and which will continue beyond every individual's death. The prerequisite for basic trust is an image-constellation or form that can symbolize both the death of the individual and the survival of the individual's meaning through biological, spiritual, cultural, or natural continuity. This is what Lifton calls "symbolic immortality."

When there is no adequate form of symbolic immortality, the result is psychic numbing. Though Lifton's many discussions of psychic numbing view it from varying perspectives, they all point toward a basic (though often implicit) theory of the phenomenon rooted in his larger paradigm. According to this theory, a massive death encounter calls into question every form of symbolic immortality; it raises the possibility that the stream of life as a whole may come to an end. Therefore it undercuts the grounding of the self. For the ungrounded self, every experience of psychological change evokes the threat of death for two reasons. Without assurance of life continuity, the self fears that the decentering caused by changing forms and images may be permanent. Since the decentered self has no stable patterns for filtering stimuli, permanent decentering means a threat of being annihilated by overwhelming stimuli. At the same time the decentered self also fears that it may search for new imagery corresponding to the new stimuli but fail to find any, leaving it bereft of all stimuli and all interactions with the world. When symbolic immortality is undermined, therefore, the self feels the threat of annihilation from every new stimulus that calls for new inner imagery.

This fear of annihilation, both from too few and too many stimuli, can lead the self to refuse to seek new images at all. When the formative process thus shuts itself down, the result is psychic numbing or death in life. This is what has happened to all of us, Lifton contends, under the threat of nuclear annihilation. We are simply too petrified to accept, or even seek, adequate images of the Bomb and its effects. Precisely because the potential consequences of nuclear weapons undermine all four forms of symbolic immortality, we have choked off our formative process and rendered ourselves unable to head off those consequences. In fact we may even hasten those consequences by following the path of totalism. This path begins when the prevailing forms of symbolic immortality are undermined; it ends when images of the enemy as totally evil generate the project of exterminating the enemy, even at the risk of exterminating oneself.

Psychic numbing is not irreversible, in Lifton's view. In fact it generates its own counteracting and healing energies in a search for new forms of symbolic immortality. The efforts toward revitalization through totalism are an example, however distorted, of this self-healing tendency. Another, healthier, example is evident in a fifth mode of symbolic immortality, qualitatively different from the other four, which Lifton calls "experiential transcendence." He suggests that this mode is the experiential root of the other four because its hallmark is escape from awareness of time, and all modes of symbolic immortality must reflect the self's ability to rise above the mortal effects of time. Conversely, experiential transcendence must be embodied in one of the other four modes if it is to have enduring value. The essence of this fifth mode as Lifton describes it lies in

> the state of near-perfect centering. With inner forms in harmony, psychic action is intense and focused. . . . [It is] an inner experience of "uncentering" or breaking down of existing psychic forms followed immediately by a vivid sense of reintegration and recentering. . . . The self feels uniquely alive—connected, in movement, integrated—which is why we can say that this state provides at least a temporary sense of eliminating time and death. What it eliminates is the destructive side of the death symbol—proximate imagery of separation, stasis, and disintegration.[7]

Experiential transcendence is the point at which this paradigm comes closest to traditional religious concepts and contemporary views of religious experience. It seems to imply something like a death and resurrection.

Lifton stresses the religious dimension as necessary, and perhaps even central, to an adequate psychology—especially to a psychology that can point the way out of the darkness of nuclear threat: "To consider the significance of imagery of extinction we need a model that not only includes immediate everyday experience, as addressed in most psychological work, but also questions of larger human connectedness—of what Paul Tillich called 'ultimate concern.' This dimension has generally been left to philosophers and theologians, but I believe that it must be part of a scientific psychology as well."[8] When Lifton calls for psychology to return to the "domain of 'ultimate concern' . . . the ecology of infinity,"[9] he seems to recognize that for Tillich the word *ultimate* is virtually synonymous with *infinite*.

Lifton's Paradigm: A Theoretical Critique

Apparently Lifton believes that his own paradigm successfully incorporates the infinitude of ultimate concern into scientific and clinical psychology. But the way he develops this theme raises some doubt. He asserts that, with the concept of ultimate concern, Tillich "was attempting to equate all modes of symbolic immortality with theological transcendence";[10] i.e., with infinitude. In Lifton's own writings, symbolic immortality and ultimacy or infinitude are used virtually interchangeably. But this equation of the two concepts is misleading. For Tillich, if a symbolic image of immortality is to transcend finitude it must be understood as a symbolic representation of eternity, not merely endless continuity in time.[11] Yet Lifton's view of immortality seems confined to endless temporality. The four modes of symbolic immortality all center on some thing or things that continue on in life after the individual's physical death. They make death acceptable only because it is transcended by continuing finite life.

In Tillich's terms, these four modes may be symbols of ultimate concern, but they need not be. They may be merely finite cognitive beliefs, and they may express merely a hope for endless continuity in time. Even if they do serve as symbols of ultimate concern, they should not be simply identified with the element of ultimacy or infinitude itself; the finite symbol should not be confused with that to which it points. (Lifton's confusion of the two concepts is surprising, since he reports having discussed the concept of immortality with Tillich.)[12]

Lifton's notion of experiential transcendence might seem closer to what Tillich means by ultimate concern, but it too fails to meet Tillich's criteria. For Tillich, an ultimate concern must grasp the whole person, and it must embrace all the polarities of existence in their fullness. Yet in experiential transcendence, Lifton claims, the self embraces only its desires for connection, movement, and integration, while it eliminates the opposing elements of separation, stasis, and disintegration. If so, then the self excludes half of its own reality, for these opposing elements, and the desire for them, are ineluctable elements in the psyche: the psychic filtering process places a premium on stasis while the countervailing growth process constantly moves toward disintegrating static structures, and both processes demand a considerable degree of separation between self and world. Of course both processes demand various forms of connection, movement, and integration as well. All six elements must work together in pursuit of the psyche's twin goals.

In religion, as Tillich understands it, all these opposites are paradoxically harmonized. Moreover, each one bespeaks both the promise of life and the threat of death. It is not a matter of the threatening abyss—what Lifton calls "uncentering"—appearing and then disappearing in a subsequent phase of recentering, as Lifton's description of transcendence has it. Rather the two possibilities are manifest simultaneously, each necessarily implying the other. From Tillich's perspective, Lifton describes the self in its highest moment as a finite self, cut off from half of its own possibilities and therefore from half of its own reality. The message is that even when human life comes closest to infinitude it is inevitably limited to partial reality. Such a finitized experience of transcendence may point toward infinitude, but it need not. Like the other modes of symbolic immortality, it can just as easily (perhaps even more easily) become an apparently satisfactory substitute that blunts desire for anything more.

Lifton sees the need for the psyche to step beyond its own finitude, but he is unable to take that theoretical step himself. He is held back because he must stand on the foundation of his paradigm, a foundation which demands that the psyche and its images remain finite. All images reveal their finitude both in their nature as limiting structures and in their inevitable destiny to be transformed and ultimately to disappear. If all images are finite, then forms, a composite of finite images, must be finite, and the self, the highest form, must be finite too. This self can feel alive only when its images are changing finite structures. All its interactions, effected by limited images and forms, must be limited, so it can never feel limitlessly alive. In the context of Lifton's paradigm, experiential transcendence and symbolic immortality must remain within the orbit of finitude because they are means to ground the self in its own life and the stream of life, which are limited realities.

But the quest for vitality that Lifton puts at the center of his paradigm is more than just inherently self-limiting. It is inherently self-defeating, for it is a compromise between two antithetical aims: the security of enduring forms and the growth of constantly changing forms. Each psychic process is constantly fending off perceived threats from the other by maximizing its own energy. As each process limits the other it increases the perceived threats to the other, and the other responds in kind. This cycle has no end. The self will inevitably feel its vitality threatened from both sides and seek more vitality, thereby deepening its dilemma. The ideal of a perfect middle ground is no escape from finitude, for the best of compromises is only an inherently unstable compound of partial realities that limit and undermine each other. Even moments of experiential transcendence can only offer a sort of psychic refueling stop to keep forms relatively stable yet open to change. The essence of the experience lies in the profit that the finite self derives from its own integration, its intensified attachment to life, and its detachment from death; i.e., from a reinforcement of its finitude.

In this paradigm, the self must always feel its vitality threatened, even if it is grounded in a sense of its own life and the continuing stream of life. Understandably, the self will make its own quest for vitality its ultimate concern, the primary motivation for all psychic action. As Lifton himself puts it in another context: "The simple point is that extreme self-absorption is a way of struggling with what are perceived as extreme threats to the self."[13] When the self must constantly perceive itself as a threat to itself, it cannot help being extremely self-absorbed. By raising its fragmented self and its vain quest for the perfect compromise to the level of ultimate concern, the self can only confirm itself in its limited reality and limited vitality. Every step it takes in its quest for vitality only fixes it more firmly in its orbit of finitude. Lifton's speculations about a species self do not point a way out of this dilemma. The species self, which is only the individual self multiplied several billion times, is still a finite self.

Clearly Lifton hopes for something more. The core of his analysis of the nuclear age lies in his insight that nuclear weapons, with their capacity to end all human life, undercut the plausibility of all four modes of symbolic immortality. Experiential transcendence, in turn, can no longer be meaningful because it cannot find enduring embodiment in any of the four modes. Since Lifton equates his notions of symbolic immortality and experiential transcendence with the domain of ultimate concern, he is arguing that the nuclear peril persists because we have no access to infinitude. If he is correct, the field of psychology itself, having abandoned the domain of ultimate concern, both reflects and compounds the danger. For psychology, then, a renewed concern with ultimate concern would be a morally and politically significant act. This means that the psychology of religion now has a unique moral and political status, for psychology must involve itself above all with religious issues. Yet Lifton's own paradigm cannot respond effectively because it offers no possibility of transcending finitude. It leaves the psyche trapped in the nuclear predicament because it roots that predicament in the psyche's finitude, which it sees as inescapable. On this view, the nuclear threat stems from immutable facts of human nature. Perhaps this is why Lifton's writings, so rich in analyses of the problem, are relatively poor in specific remedies.

Yet an adequate theory of psychic numbing must be able to generate possibilities for political response that break through the numbing. If Lifton is right, this requires a paradigm that really does bring psychology into the domain of ultimate concern. If Laing is right, it requires a paradigm focussed on ontological concerns. Tillich's thought forms an obvious bridge between these two requirements, and Lifton himself implies that Tillich should be introduced more directly into the mainstream of psychology. Tillich's language presents a major obstacle, however. Outside the circle of religious believers, it is difficult today to find adequate language to talk about experiences of infinite or perfect reality. For empirical psychologists, professional philosophers, and others dedicated to pinning down precise meanings, such notions may seem hopelessly vague.

Even psychologists who share Tillich's concerns may well be frustrated at the imprecision of his formulations. In psychological discourse terms like *perfect reality* and *infinitude* can refer only to qualities of human experience, not to any ontological reality that exists apart from human experience. Even as qualities of experience, however, they must be rendered more concrete and more "psychological" if they are to be useful. Lifton's own paradigm offers the resources for one such psychological reading of Tillich's ontological and religious conceptions. With some reinterpretation, it can bring psychology into the domain of ultimate concern. And, in concert with the thought of Tillich and others, it can suggest a theory of psychic numbing that meets the criteria for an adequate understanding of the nuclear age.

Lifton's Paradigm: A Reinterpretation

Lifton's paradigm of psychic life is trapped within the domain of finitude defined by the conflict between the two basic psychic processes: the filtering process that strives to exclude stimuli and the symbolic growth process that continually opens itself to stimuli. If this conflict can never be permanently resolved, then it is impossible to answer his own guiding question: What is the singular motivating principle for psychic action? But if the paradigm is reinterpreted it can escape this dilemma.

Infinitude enters Lifton's paradigm with the claim that the desire for vitalizing images is the psyche's ultimate concern; since no other desire can supercede or circumscribe it, this desire must be unconditional and limitless. Since it is generated by a compound psychic process, though, both its components must be understood as limitless. In other words, every psychic image must drive simultaneously toward infinitude in two dimensions: toward both maximum and minimum openness, toward perfectly immutable structure and perfectly endless change. So the single motive for all psychic action must be a quest for a paradoxical state in which these basic opposites of psychic life both function without limit and the psyche is free of the need to choose between them.

In Tillich's understanding of religion, something very much like this paradoxical state is the essence of religious experience. He contends that religious experience is always mediated by a symbol which is itself finite and remains finite. The symbol thus demands a total focus upon a particular structure of stimuli. In Lifton's terms, this implies that the psyche's filtering process is totally unimpeded. All psychosomatic energy is devoted to the interaction between self and world mediated by this structure, which is therefore experienced as the centering structure for the individual's existence. All external stimuli and all inner images seem linked to this center and gain their meaning from their relationship to it, so both external and intrapsychic worlds are harmonized in one mutually reinforcing and all-encompassing structure. There seems to be nothing outside this unity that could threaten it. In Tillich's terms, the distinction between subject and object is transcended.

Secure in this apparently inviolable structure, the psyche can drop its defensive need to filter stimuli. It need not refuse any stimuli, nor need it diminish the intensity of any stimuli. Thus the symbol opens up the dimension of infinitude, mediating a conviction that all limits have been transcended. All intrapsychic possibilities for thought, feeling, and imagination, and all possibilities in external reality, seem equally accessible—even those that form logically contradictory pairs of opposites. Admitting apparently limitless stimuli, the self feels perfectly 'full-filled' with reality. It feels limitlessly secure in its continued existence because it feels limitlessly alive in endless growth—and it can accept the prospect of endless growth because it feels perfectly secure.

Neither a subject nor an object can actually be infinite. But this interpretation of Lifton's paradigm suggests that a human experience can seem infinite if the image mediating the relationship becomes no longer a shield against the world but a transparent window onto the world. An image that plays this role (and in principle any image could play this role) should be called a religious image, not because of its content but solely because of its function in a particular relationship. Since every image could become a religious image and every image aims at the two purposes that meet only in the religious image, it seems fair to say that every image wants to become a religious image. If there is a "central motivating principle for psychic action," it is the self's quest not for its own vitality but for self-transcendence in seemingly infinite structured interactions with a seemingly infinite world. This is not to prejudge the possibility of ever attaining this goal; it may remain a purely hypothetical ideal. Nevertheless, the closer the self approaches to this (perhaps unattainable) limit, the more genuinely alive it feels. The self's sense of vitality is a by-product of a formative process aiming at something beyond its own vitality.

Anxiety and Finitude

If all psychic images aspire to infinitude, then the greatest threat to the self and its vitality is the psyche's own finitude, which is experienced psychologically as anxiety. "Anxiety is a sense of foreboding stemming from threatened vitality and anticipated breakdown of the integrity of the self. . . . The motivational element that is countered or even overwhelmed by the threat is the self's impulse toward integrity and vitality and the formative energy behind that impulse."[14] Although Lifton speaks here as if the impulse to integrity and vitality were a single impulse, his own theory indicates that there are two distinct impulses inherent in every psychic image: one to the integrity of structure and the other to the vitality of growth. Each of these impulses, being finite, has a limited capacity to reach its goal on its own. If either impulse were to cease altogether, leaving the other to function by itself without limit, the result would be cessation of the formative process, through either total rigidity, the Scylla of no stimuli at all, or endless change, the Charybdis of too many discrete, rapidly fading stimuli. Both portend an end to structured interactions with the world—a formlessness that would be the psychological extinction of the self. Since the psyche must always feel driven toward infinitude yet know that all its images are limited and self-contradictory, it must always fear that its formative process might lead to this abyss of infinite unreality, a reality so drastically limited that it is reduced to nothing at all.

The psyche cannot escape the anxiety inherent in its finitude. But it can come to terms with both finitude and anxiety if its formative process is grounded in a religious image. The religious image, by its very nature, forges a connection between finitude and infinitude, for it is necessarily a particular limited structure that nevertheless opens up the possibility of limitless growth within limitless structure. Thus it can give a meaningful form to the experience of finitude by putting it in the context of infinitude. If the formative process is grounded in a religious image, all of its images will be grounded in that central image and tend toward it as an ideal limit. Being so grounded, the self can feel truly alive.

If the psyche can find a religious image to give form to its experience of finitude, that image will also give form to its experience of anxiety. A religious image, by its very nature, harmonizes the two poles of infinite unreality—unlimited structure and unlimited change—in a permanent form that promises permanent interaction with the world. Insuring that neither pole need threaten the other, it makes the threat of formlessness endurable. As long as the self sees the possibility of moving toward its innate goal of religious imagery, it can accept its finitude and anxiety. It need not quest for vitality, since it feels assured of its vitality.

The essence of the religious image thus lies in its assurance that the formative process is never definitely closed. It offers a prospect of infinite openness merely by expressing the possibility of infinite openness. While the history of religions records individuals who have claimed to experience moments of total openness within perfect structure, most religious people may never have such an actual experience. They are religious because they affirm an image that expresses the possibility of such an experience; typically they affirm that this image always has and always will express such a possibility. For most people, then, the power of a religious image depends on its claim to permanent validity and its sense of infinite possibility—its promise of the potential for offering perfect openness to all stimuli within its enduring structure. So the religious image may be defined as an image of pure possibility within perfect structure. To be grounded, the psyche need not directly experience the perfection promised by the religious image. It need only affirm the image as a door that is always open, leading to the possibility of perfection.

This analysis seems to lead to a catch-22: in order to move along its innate path toward religious imagery, the formative process must already be grounded in religious imagery. This would mean that the formative process can only approach its goal if it has already attained its goal. But this conundrum can be resolved by recalling the role of the community in the formative process. No psyche grows alone. Everyone is born into a community that immediately sets about inculcating into the newborn specific responses to specific stimuli. The community aims to ingrain those responses so deeply that they seem to the individual innate and inevitable. In the religious sphere, the community may offer every individual a set of religious images, claiming (or insisting) that these images open up the possibility of simultaneous perfect structure and perfect openness. If the community succeeds, the individual's inborn tendency to believe in this possibility is attached to these particular images, which become the grounding for a continuing sense of vitality. A few rare individuals may spontaneously discover religious images that can ground their psychic lives, but the vast majority of us must rely upon our elders and our cultural traditions. With few exceptions, the attempt to construct a private religion is doomed to fail.

Formlessness and Trauma

This revision of Lifton's paradigm leads to a reconsideration of the problem of death. If the self inherently aspires to the infinite reality mediated by religious images, then its fundamental fear is not physical death but finitude and finitude's threat of pure formlessness. Lifton himself suggests that death must be understood in the context of a wider psychological category: psychic trauma. While at times he seems to equate trauma with a death encounter, he indicates that the crucial element in trauma is not physical death but an experience of "death equivalents."[15] This point is especially important for understanding psychic numbing, since Lifton asserts an intimate link between trauma and numbing in his interpretation of depression, which he calls "the core condition for psychiatric disorder. . . . Depression, then, is inseparable from many forms of numbing in massive psychic trauma. But depression probably has more to do with death equivalents than with actual death."[16] Lifton restricts the "death equivalents" to separation, disintegration, and stasis. But if the critical problem for the psyche is not physical death but formlessness, then any experience that opens up the possibility of formlessness can become a death equivalent—even experiences of excessive connection, integration, and movement. In fact massive trauma could be defined as an intense experience of imminent formlessness; it always involves the threat of either a sudden immersion in overwhelming stimuli or a sudden deprivation of stimuli.

Lifton identifies loss as a central element in depression, trauma, and psychic numbing: "One can only lose that which one believes one has previously possessed. At issue is not so much the loss of an object but the loss of a state or mode of existence.... The mimetic deadness of the depressive stance is a response not only to the loss of connection with the sources of vitality but to the *loss of expectation of vitalizing experience.*"[17] The mode of existence lost in trauma is the assured capacity to give form to experiences of finitude by grounding them in religious images. The psyche innately expects to grow toward religious imagery; this is the mode of existence it has previously possessed. And a sense of possibility is an essential feature of this mode of existence. The crucial loss in trauma, then, is the loss of this sense of the possibility of religious images, on which the feeling of vitality depends. This loss is the psyche's greatest fear.

Although Lifton writes that "motivation revolves around life and death imagery, often experienced, respectively, as form and formlessness,"[18] the truth would seem to be the other way around. The sense of being alive is a function of form. Similarly, behind the encounter with physical death stands the more traumatic encounter with the possibility of psychic death, the death of meaningful forms. Physical death is a sort of metaphor for total formlessness, the clearest sign of the psyche's finitude and a perpetual reminder that the psyche lives only because its images are constantly changing and dying.

When the formative process seeks a form for physical death, it is using the search as a means to an end, seeking a form for its awareness of its finitude and the possibility that radical finitude may open the door to absolute formlessness. If the formative process can solve this larger problem, it will at the same time give a meaningful form to physical death. If it cannot solve this problem, the self will remain trapped in its feeling of finitude, unable to face its anxiety courageously, no matter what form physical death receives. And this problem can only be solved if the formative process is grounded in a religious image. So death must be given meaning in the wider context of the quest for religious images if the self's sense of reality and vitality are to be sustained. From this perspective, religious imagery rather than symbolic immortality is the key to psychic vitality.

Psychic Numbing: A Reinterpretation

When there is no grounding in religious images, the possibility of open-ended growth is blocked, and the psyche sees no way that its loss of vitality might be reversed in the future. It sees only two paths open to it, one leading to dissolution in overwhelming stimuli and the other to a total absence of stimuli. But the terminus of both paths is the same state of formlessness, a prospect that evokes intolerable traumatic anxiety. One possible response to this anxiety is the fanatical adherence to specific images that Lifton calls "totalism." Though the change that triggers totalism may be linked to a massive death threat, it need not be. However it always represents a trauma. The concept of totalism is one more indication that it is not death but a traumatic "death equivalent" that is the key to numbing. (Since Lifton interprets totalism largely in relation to threats of physical death, however, he places the concept outside the domain of ultimate concern.)

Another possible response to intolerable anxiety is psychic numbing. In light of this reinterpretation of Lifton's paradigm, numbing must also be understood somewhat differently from Lifton's own interpretation. It must be seen as an attempt to escape the threat of limitless filtering and limitless openness by resisting all movement along either path. The psyche hopes that by immobility, by avoiding all change, it can avoid impending unreality. The growth process is numbed to stave off the danger of stimulus overload. The filtering function is numbed to stave off the danger of stimulus starvation. In the former case, resisting new possibilities, the psyche denies its inherent aspiration to ever-expanding symbolic forms. In the latter case, resisting the filtering of stimuli, it denies its inherent aspiration to all-encompassing structure. Thus the conflict latent within every psychic image is magnified.

From both sides the numbed psyche denies its inherent desire to grow toward the religious imagery that could harmonize the two; it denies its inherent aspiration to infinitude. Numbing confines the self to purely finite images. These finite images define the self and its world, giving the impression of a highly structured and therefore secure reality. But no images are allowed to give form to finitude's threat of formlessness, since that would carry the psyche beyond the bounds of its finitude and compel it to recognize the anxiety of finitude as its ultimate problem.

As numbing denies the very possibility of religious imagery, it denies the gap between the psyche's present finitude and its possible infinitude. Once this gap disappears from awareness, awareness of finitude also disappears (since finitude is only a meaningful category when contrasted with that which transcends it). To deny infinitude is to deny finitude and its anxiety as well. So numbing can be seen as a strategy for avoiding the threat of infinite unreality by avoiding awareness of both one's potential infinitude and one's actual finitude (with its attendant mortality).

While this strategy may seem to make anxiety disappear, in fact it merely compounds the trauma that created the anxiety. No amount of numbing can make one's finitude or one's desire for infinitude disappear. Numbing can only remove the infinite grounding that gives form to finitude. But the loss of this grounding is itself the source of trauma. As long as a religious image holds out the possibility of perfect structure and unending growth, the psyche can continue to feel secure in its vitality. But when all images are finite, every image is an encounter with one's own finitude, which generates further traumatic anxiety. Once the innate tendency to move toward religious imagery is lost, every experience raises the threat of total formlessness. Numbing responds to this loss by ensuring that the loss will be permanent. Since harmonization of the two psychic processes seems impossible, the conflict inherent in images seems permanent, and permanent psychic numbing appears to be the only viable defense against the spiral of traumatic anxiety. The result is death in life: the desire to preserve life generates an equally intense desire for psychic death.

No mode of symbolic immortality can solve this problem unless it is formulated in the larger context of a religious image. Psychic numbing requires a religious solution because it is essentially a response to a religious threat. The numbed self may dimly sense this truth. In attempting to flee its own finitude, it is expressing its innate aspiration to the infinitude of religious imagery. In numbing itself, it is trying to deny what it still most longs for. But without grounding in a religious image, the psyche can only see this longing as a threat of infinite unreality. So it must remain ambivalent to its innate aspiration and repress the intrapsychic conflict by ever more strenuous numbing.

Correlations

This reinterpretation of Lifton's paradigm is one way of fulfilling Lifton's own aim: to bring psychology, and psychic numbing in particular, into the domain of ultimate concern. At the same time, it provides a language that can combine the insights of Lifton, Tillich, Laing, and Hillman in a comprehensive theoretical model for interpreting the nuclear age. Laing and Tillich agree that the ultimate concern of every human life is the quest for ontological security. So a psychology that enters the domain of ultimate concern must become an ontological psychology.

In ontological terms the self's quest for vitality is its quest for ontological security; to feel really alive is to feel genuinely real. Since each of the psyche's two impulses has a limited reality and each is in conflict with the other, the self must feel less than fully real. But the self can feel secure in its reality as long as it feels that the formative process is free to follow its innate path toward religious imagery. Ontological security thus depends on experiencing the endless freedom of the image-making process, which is our own most genuine reality, or what Laing calls the true self: "our personal idiom of experiencing . . . imagination, dreams, fantasy, and beyond that to ever further reaches of experience."[19] So security requires that imagination be grounded in a religious image, which can give form to the possibility of pure formlessness. The self must be able to look into pure possibility, which portends the abyss of unreality, within an immutably real structure and see pure possibility as the promise of perfect reality (even if that promise remains an unrealized ideal).

When there is no grounding in a religious image, the formative process seems unable to continue its innate path toward religious imagery. The psyche feels trapped in its limited reality. Yet, since it has no form for the prospect of formlessness, the pure possibility of that prospect can be experienced only as the threat of imminent unreality. This is the state that Laing calls ontological insecurity. Psychic numbing must be understood in ontological terms as a response to this crisis.

Psychic numbing displays the same psychodynamics described by Laing as the 'schizoid strategy' and by Tillich as 'neurosis.' In fact the schizoid strategy can best be understood as a particular manifestation (or perhaps a more precise description) of what Tillich calls neurosis. The schizoid fantasies that Laing discovered parallel the neurotic's nightmare images described by Tillich. Engulfment and implosion images clearly represent the formless void, while petrification images reflect a sense of being trapped. These images represent the threat of losing one's personal reality. In Lifton's terms, schizoids are caught in the conflict inherent in every psychic image. They are afraid of being overwhelmed by stimuli, afraid that their filtering process will cease to function altogether. Yet the only alternative that they can imagine is an equally total cessation of the growth function, which will cut them off from all stimuli.

Since schizoids see no middle ground between the trap of self-absorption and the void of absorption in all there is, any relationship of world and self seems doomed to lead to the unreality of formlessness. Their response is to try to avoid that fate by avoiding the limitless possibilities of the changing world. Creating a false self as a barrier between self and world, they shut off both the filtering and growth processes, refusing to admit external stimuli as real. Cut off from outside reality, they deny real dangers while nourishing unrealistic fears, all of which mirror their basic fears of limitless filtering and limitless openness. Yet sheltering behind the deterrent shield of the false self, schizoids merely replicate the image of the threat itself, for all that they can see in the world are their own entrapment and the sole alternative, the void.

Since each image threatens total formlessness, each demands pursuit of its opposite; each must be embraced in limitless measure as the antidote to the limitless threat of the other. Each time schizoids evoke the void that they fear, they feel compelled to make their inner trap more rigid and narrow, driving them back to the brink of the void, and vice versa. Attempting to escape this dilemma, they embrace each psychic process in limitless measure to forestall and ward off the threat of its own limitlessness; they do unto themselves before others do unto them. Of course this only ensures that each process will remain limited by the other. Unable to give form to the threat of formlessness, schizoids are permanently divided against themselves in a life of increasingly radical finitude. They take what Tillich calls the way of avoiding nonbeing by avoiding being, or, in the language of Lifton's paradigm, the way of avoiding formlessness by avoiding the limitless possibilities of the formative process. Their lives become an unending trauma, and the only remaining defense is to remain dead in life.

Modernity as a Schizoid Strategy

If Lifton is right in seeing psychic numbing as the fundamental source of the nuclear dilemma, then this numbing must be pervading our society. If so, then the pathologies he views as equivalent to numbing—Laing's schizoid strategy and Tillich's neurotic anxiety—must be pervading our society. But if Tillich, Laing, and Hillman are right, the schizoid was a prototype of everyman and everywoman in the modern West well before the nuclear age.

In every culture, the process of identity formation may do some violence to the individual's unique patterns of experience. But modernity demands an unprecedented level of falsification, distortion, and unreality, for it demands that we deny our most essential possibility: the possibility of moving toward infinite, perfect reality through grounding in a religious image. This falsification makes ontological insecurity the norm; formlessness and unreality seem to threaten at every turn. So the societal false self system of modernity is uniquely laden with unreality and is a uniquely powerful stimulus to psychic numbing. The formative process cannot feel free to discover what its own unique possibilities might be. It can only cope with its traumatic anxiety by restricting itself to the narrow confines of the heroic ego, clinging compulsively to the collection of fantasies that society calls "the real world."

The ego's most powerful tool for preserving its finitude is literalism. Since literalism imposes a single meaning upon each reality, and attempts to experience each in isolation from all others, it obviously contravenes the psyche's inherent desire to grow through multiple symbolic meanings and complex associations. Thus it raises the prospect of diminishing vitality and a loss of personal reality. It might seem wisest to counter this threat by clinging to the familiar psychic forms and filtering out as much changing reality as possible. As ontological insecurity grows, though, there is growing doubt that the familiar forms can continue to filter out stimuli in dependable patterns. In a state of heightened insecurity, it may seem too dangerous to invoke any psychic form, even a familiar one, to cope with new stimuli. And even if these forms did function dependably, they would still point to the possibility of filtering out all stimuli and losing touch with reality completely.

So there are good reasons to abandon the search for familiar forms and numb the filtering function along with the growth function. Literalism achieves this numbing by stopping the filtering process at its very first stages. It aims to isolate individual stimuli and focus on the narrowest possible pattern of meaning. Single-minded exclusion is its goal, and a strict curb on the intensity and range of interaction of stimuli is a crucial means to that end. Literalism thus counteracts the filtering process' ultimate aim: to organize stimuli in all-inclusive, ever-expanding, orderly patterns that can safely admit endless future stimuli.

Ultimately, then, literalism aims to limit the movement toward religious imagery by numbing both psychic processes simultaneously. It aims to deny the sense of infinite possibility that opens up the psyche's essential reality. The result of this literalizing radical finitude is a society that acts like a schizoid. Defining its greatest public concerns in images of freedom and security through stasis and isolation (the trap) and annihilation through total absorption (the void), it sets the two psychic processes permanently against each other. Since the numbing of each psychic process opens up the possibility that the other might function without limit, the conflict between them is not numbed but intensified. The heroic ego is constantly in search of more unified static structures to strengthen its illusion of control, which it calls security. But since the ego must numb the filtering process that provides structure as strenuously as it numbs the growth process that creates change, it is compelled to undermine whatever structures it can discover or create. The quest for stable meaningful forms to support genuine freedom and security is endless because it endlessly defeats itself.

Trapped in the insecurity of the schizoid strategy, the social nexus, like the individual, makes its own numbing its ultimate concern and dedicates itself to maintaining the radically finite fantasies of the false self system. This ultimate concern shapes every aspect of public life, including politics and international relations. Public political life thus becomes an unending, because impossible, quest for freedom and security. Every step toward genuine freedom and security is negated by the overriding demand of death in life: the desire to preserve life by embracing death.

The schizoid pattern may well have characterized Western society long before 1945. But public life in the nuclear age offers a unique element that could not be created by the individual alone, nor by society as a whole before 1945: the indisputably literal existence of the Bomb and the array of nuclear images it has spawned. These images offer no middle ground between the trap and the void, nor between the ego's invulnerable omnipotence and the threat of nuclear annihilation. So all our literalized nuclear images end up exacerbating rather than harmonizing the conflict between the two processes.

Modernity cannot abolish the innate desire to move toward religious imagery and its possibility of perfect reality. Indeed, the Bomb may be accepted, and even embraced, just because we aspire to transcend the psychic conflict and attain grounding in religious images. Since nuclear images do reflect the two conflicting psychic processes, the Bomb might be seen as a caricature of a religious image. But the Bomb simultaneously insures, more certainly than anything else, that the aspiration to religious imagery cannot be fulfilled. Although it seems to carry us beyond our finitude and harmonize all opposites, it actually fixes us in the radical finitude of our shared fantasy. As our predominant public image of the desire for infinitude, it usurps the role once played by religious images and prevents us from finding, or even searching for, any other publicly shared religious images. Therefore the Bomb and its images prevent us from finding, or even searching for, a meaningful form for the threat of formlessness that it poses. In other words, it locks us into the psychic numbing that continually leads us back to images of nuclear annihilation. Under the reign of nuclear terror, we literalize our death in life; because we are literally terrified of losing our lives, we are drawn irresistibly toward literalizing our fantasies of self-provoked death.

These correlations indicate that a theoretical model based on the work of Lifton, Tillich, Laing, and Hillman responds to most of the questions that an adequate theory of psychic numbing must answer. It shows how psychology, by taking up ontological issues and entering the domain of ultimate concern, can explain pervasive numbing as an institutionalized societal process. It shows how publicly shared images can flourish and nevertheless exacerbate numbing. It accounts for the self-perpetuating, self-destructive cycle of numbing as a public phenomenon, and it accounts for the physical self-destruction at the center of our public images.

This model clearly indicates that numbing has roots going back long before the first atomic explosions of 1945. It also clarifies the unique qualities of nuclear numbing as well as of nuclear imagery. If the Bomb is in some sense a symptom of an old and deep disturbance, it is certainly the most virulent symptom, virulent enough to change not just the intensity but the very nature of the disease. There is a striking similarity here to a pattern that Laing traces in *The Divided Self*. When the self-destructive pressure of the schizoid strategy reaches a certain intensity, schizoid neurosis can transform itself into a qualitatively different phenomenon: the psychosis of schizophrenia.

There is one more question that an adequate interpretation of nuclear numbing must answer: How can we generate new responses and new images to break through numbing? It would seem that we need a publicly shared religious image to begin this process. Yet it is hard to see what image might be proposed. One possible solution to this problem lies in a surprising direction—the direction charted by Laing's *The Divided Self*. Perhaps the nuclear age should be understood not only through the metaphor of the schizoid society but through the more radical metaphor of the schizophrenic society. Popular intuition sensed the aptness of this comparison long ago, when the phrase *nuclear madness* became a commonplace of our cultural vocabulary. The following pages will explore the implications of this popular image for diagnosing and responding to the nuclear dilemma.

Part II
Nuclear Madness

6

Nuclear Madness: A Model

Among all the new images spawned by the Bomb, one of the most familiar and perhaps the most disturbing is the image of nuclear madness. Sometimes this phrase is just a rhetorical flourish. Sometimes it is a shorthand symbol for particular irrationalities surrounding nuclear weapons. And sometimes it is just a vexed expression of inarticulate bewilderment.[1] But Robert Jay Lifton implies more than this when he asserts that "the external threat of contemporary nuclear weapons approaches the terrain of schizophrenia."[2] Lifton certainly does not mean that we are all literally schizophrenic today. Nor does he mean that a whole society can be schizophrenic in the same way that an individual can be. But he does suggest that schizophrenia can offer a useful model for a new understanding of the nuclear age.

In Lifton's paradigm, models are central to every experience, for a mental image always functions as a model. It guides us in selecting, organizing, and interpreting stimuli; it tells us that a new stimulus is in some ways like a familiar one, and thus it shapes our response. Before we can begin to explain anything, we must accept one or more models. Yet a model is not itself an explanation. It does not claim to prove how one thing causes another (though it may use the language of "because" metaphorically). Nor does it claim to present objective truths that can be empirically proven or disproven by accumulating facts (though facts can help support its plausibility). Rather, a model proposes an extended metaphor that endows the formlessness of empirical reality with a humanly created form. A model proves its worth when it provides a broader framework that makes sense out of phenomena previously seen as disparate and senseless. It is validated when it generates new possibilities for response in thought and action.

The idea of nuclear madness should be approached, then, as a model. To approach the nuclear arms race as a form of madness is to claim that we gain a valuable new perspective on the nuclear age if we view it through the metaphor of madness—as a madness to which we can ascribe method and therefore meaning. The interpretation of nuclear madness I shall offer here aims to give the phrase a substantive meaning by extending Lifton's ideas in more explicit terms, using schizophrenia as the prototype of modern madness. It relies extensively on Laing's view of schizophrenia, while also drawing on the work of Tillich and Hillman. Since it is a model of schizophrenia, it does not make any judgments about the ultimate origin of the disease (which may be genetic or biochemical as recent research suggests). The model only offers a phenomenological description of the psychodynamics of the disease once it has appeared and applies that description to the nuclear age.

A Model of Madness

According to Lifton, schizophrenics are the most ontologically insecure of all people. For whatever reason, they feel an acute threat of imminent psychic annihilation. To defend themselves, schizophrenics employ the ultimate form of psychic numbing: they cut off all meaningful relationships with the world and frequently believe themselves to be mere lifeless objects. "Since I am already dead, I need not fear death," seems to be their motto. At the same time, however, schizophrenics "often seem to show the very opposite of numbing—a kind of nonstop responsiveness to every possible stimulus. They create a confused collage of half-formed ideas and image-feelings. This 'overinclusion' involves 'inability to *exclude* the nonessential and to abstract the essential.' . . . In this sense the numbing is also fundamental, but is simply not working"[3]—as the emotional pain of madness attests. Lifton's understanding of schizophrenia thus includes the same "uneasy duality" that he finds in totalism: numbing is somehow counteracted by an inherent impulse to revitalization that generates new images. Yet, as in his theory of totalism, the "somehow" remains unexplained. If there is an impulse to revitalization, it can not be assumed as a given; it must be explained in terms of the larger paradigm. And that explanation must show how revitalization efforts actually end up not counteracting but reinforcing numbing.

In describing this process, Lifton alludes to Laing's views: "What Laing calls 'the false self' I prefer to call the dead self."[4] For Laing, however, it is essential to distinguish between the deadened false self of the nonpsychotic schizoid and the fate of the true self in schizophrenia. The schizoid state is always marked by the duality of true and false selves and the attempt to keep the former alive behind the latter. But when the effort to maintain this duality becomes too great and the welter of contradictory fantasies becomes too threatening, the schizoid may give it all up in one of two ways: "1. He may decide to be 'himself' despite everything, or 2. He may attempt to murder his self."[5] By one route, outer reality and the false self are abandoned. By the other route, inner reality and the true self are given up. The end result is the same in either case, however. The interaction between inner and outer, the prerequisite for reality testing and sanity, is gone.

Laing's interpretation suggests a new way to approach the problem of madness in terms of Lifton's paradigm. It suggests that madness can be understood as a double-edged response to the double-edged threat of psychic annihilation through either limitless filtering or limitless openness to stimuli, the same threat that spawns neurosis and the schizoid strategy. When those defenses fail, more extreme measures are called forth. Fearing that they will be overwhelmed by stimuli (both external and internal), schizophrenics detach themselves from reality altogether. They try to filter out all stimuli, to shut off the symbolizing process that mediates between self and world, to make themselves totally unresponsive, and to become inert nonentities. The authentic self once so compulsively guarded in the schizoid state is now murdered.

Since schizophrenics are equally afraid that they will be completely cut off from reality, they must simultaneously open themselves unreservedly to all stimuli. The protective false self of the schizoid state is discarded so that the true self can be revealed. But when the schizoid finally lets himself be "himself"—when he acts out his most hidden fantasies—they inevitably include fantasies of self-destruction. So the true self exposes itself to all stimuli, with no filtering at all. It exposes itself to the very danger it fears: perishing in an overwhelming flood of stimuli. The decision to reveal the true self is thus a decision to kill the true self. The strategies of self-murder and self-revelation are logically contradictory. Each strategy embraces as its chief weapon the very danger that the other strategy aims to ward off. But they can be pursued simultaneously because they produce the same result. They both leave the schizophrenic beyond all structured interactions with the world, beyond the prerequisite for a meaningful sense of personal reality. They form a pair of contradictory yet compatible paths to the murder of self and world.

Of course the schizophrenic is still caught in the contradiction of death in life, trying to ward off the onslaught of the world while simultaneously embracing it. The only possible defense against an overwhelming world is to intensify fantasies of world-destruction. As the self drains itself of reality, immuring itself even more firmly in a world of pure fantasy, it must immure others equally firmly in that fantasy, draining them of their reality too. But this only intensifies the crisis. Imagining themselves without self or world, schizophrenics feel totally bereft of reality and in more imminent danger of extinction. The obvious solution is to create a new self and world, which are wholly controllable because they are created wholly out of one's own imagination. A private reality must be created because the public reality is too dangerous, both in its power to overwhelm and in its power to starve the self of reality.

Yet the private reality turns out to be even more terrifying than the public. Schizophrenic imagination draws on innumerable imaginative forms and structures, each having meaning from one standpoint. But it takes all these various standpoints simultaneously and combines them all seemingly at random in what Lifton calls a "confused collage of half-formed images." Laing calls this collage a "word-salad": "a number of quasi-autonomous partial systems striving to give expression to themselves out of the same mouth at the same time. . . . Each partial system seemed to have within it its own focus or centre of awareness; it had its own very limited memory schemata and limited ways of structuring perceptions; its own tendency to preserve its autonomy, and special dangers which threatened its autonomy."[6]

This fragmented reality reflects what Lifton calls the "impulse to revitalization," and it reveals the source of that impulse: the conflicting psychic demands for perfect filtering and perfect openness to stimuli. Each process is invoked without limit to save the self. But since each aims to stave off the other, the two processes are set at war with each other. The structures produced by the filtering process constantly confine and congeal the products of imagination, while imagination constantly explodes and fragments mental structures. Since the radical limiting of each psychic process opens up the possibility that the other might function without limit, each must numb the other even more strenuously, which merely perpetuates the cycle. Shutting off the symbolizing growth process of the psyche, schizophrenics deaden their capacity to respond to, or find meaning in, either external or internal reality. Shutting off the filtering process, they deaden their capacity to find coherence in reality. So they find themselves inundated by an ever-widening circle of meaningless, disconnected, deadening images. This endless chaotic stream is the "overinclusion" that Lifton describes.

The impulse to revitalization thus ends up intensifying the schzophrenic's numbing and fantasies of self-murder. But schizophrenics also feel that the imaginary world has now become an uncontrollable enemy, so it deserves to die as much as did the uncontrollable external world. Indeed it may have no choice but to die. Immersion in an imaginary world totally erases the boundary line between inner and outer reality; if the inner self must be murdered to escape the threat of death, then the imaginary reality spun out of the self must necessarily die with it.

How can schizophrenics kill their world along with their own selves? They hope to do both deeds by experiencing their images—including their images of self-destruction—completely literally. The crucial challenge for schizophrenics is to be totally open to stimuli while remaining totally dead in life. Literalism seems to meet this challenge with its promise that endless streams of new stimuli can be admitted without risk because they are formless and lifeless. If all images are apprehended as discrete inert objects, while the self is experienced as literally lifeless too, then no images can affect the self or call forth any response. If all images are experienced as disconnected from all others, then none can join with others and turn against the self. The goal is a perception of all realities as rigidly inert, purely mechanistic, and therefore safe.

This attempt at ontological security is inevitably self-defeating. Since literalism perpetuates the war between the two psychic processes, it must undermine any overarching form or comprehensive meaning for its formless explosion of images. Above all, it must deny a meaningful form for the threat of formlessness itself; it must deny the religious images that might harmonize the conflicting psychic needs. As formlessness spins out of control, the reality of both self and world, and meaningful interactions between the two, are increasingly undermined. The flow of psychosomatic energy diminishes radically. Thoughts, values, feelings, and sensations take on the same hollowness as the dead hollow self. Reality becomes a chaotic "image-salad"—a random collection of disjointed stimuli that constantly threaten to overwhelm the self.

Self-Defeat and Self-Destruction

Striving to ward off chaos by numbing their psychic openness, schizophrenics end up opening themselves even wider to overwhelming streams of stimuli. Striving to numb their psychic filtering capacities and open themselves to chaos, they end up closing themselves even tighter to the impact of all stimuli. As each path drives its victim into the other, the two work together to lead to the mutually agreed upon goal: a self-destruction that also entails world-destruction. In Laing's words:

> Without an open two-way circuit between phantasy and reality anything becomes possible in phantasy. . . . Destructiveness in phantasy can thus rage on, unchecked, until the world and the self are reduced, in phantasy, to dust and ashes. In the schizophrenic state the world is in ruins, and the self is (apparently) dead. No amount of frantic activity seems to have the power to bring back life again.[7]

However both Laing and Lifton point out that schizophrenics imagine themselves already dead and thus invulnerable. As Laing says: "One no longer fears being crushed, engulfed, overwhelmed by realness and aliveness (whether they arise in other people, in 'inner' feelings or emotions, etc.) since one is already dead. Being dead, one cannot die."[8] With all their imaginings literalized, schizophrenics naturally assume that they are literally invulnerable and immune to the effects of the literal cosmic catastrophe they envision. In their fantasies they are immortal; they can live on, despite their own death, as the only survivor in a dead world. So their collage of images can easily include, and in fact must include, images of world- and self-annihilation alongside images of perfect security and absolute invulnerability to annihilation. Schizophrenia, then, is a literalized death in life—a desire literally to protect one's life that generates a literalized desire for death as well as endless life. What began as a flight from the anxiety of infinitude into a racially finite life ends up as a flight from the inescapable mark of finitude—the inevitability of death—into a literally fantasied infinitude of life.

Lifton summarizes this process and recalls its ultimate source: "Immortality must be literalized—and therefore rendered delusional—because it cannot be symbolized (rendered psychically real). Behind both experiential deadness and literalized immortality is . . . something close to perpetual dread of annihilation."[9] Of course this culmination of schizophrenia is just as self-defeating as every step leading up to it. A belief in oneself as the only survivor of a self-induced world destruction clearly signals a total detachment from reality—the very fate that schizophrenia hopes to avoid. So every experience becomes a trauma that conjures up visions of impending formlessness. Since schizophrenics can have no psychic form for this state, though, they can only embrace the problem—the psychic death of pure formlessness—as the solution. Their trap seems to have no exit.

Yet Laing asserts that the trap can provide its own exit. He endorses the opinion of Gregory Bateson that the schizophrenic "is, as it were, embarked upon a voyage of discovery which is only completed by his return to the normal world. . . . Once begun, a schizophrenic episode would appear to have as definite a course as an initiation ceremony—a death and rebirth."[10] Laing claims that some of his schizophrenic patients, when allowed to act out their fantasies with minimal interference, demonstrated the truth of this view. So the death and survival fantasies that Lifton describes may reflect not only the fears and pains but also the aspirations inherent in madness (aspirations that echo the death and resurrection implicit in Lifton's concept of experiential transcendence). And all of these reflect the complexities of schizophrenic imagination.

The fears, pains, and aspirations are all spun from the victim's own imagination, of course. The process of schizophrenia begins when a person throws off the mask of publicly defined roles and routines—the finitude of the false self—and confronts the authentic inner self, whose essence is the power of imagination. Madness itself is an imagining of the rigidified ego falling apart and murdering the infinite possibilities of imagination in self-defense. It is an imagining of a world and a life without imagination. Through literalism the imagination tries to murder itself.

This project is inevitably in vain, for the repressed images merely return, albeit in literal form. Madness thus actually nourishes imagination in spite of itself, for it is simultaneously an imagining of the imagination overwhelming the self. It is an imagining of the self being totally open, as well as totally closed, to inner as well as outer stimuli. Schizophrenics replace the literal with the imaginary and then imagine it all as literal. Since they know no boundary between inner thought and outer action, they imagine themselves literally omnipotent and invulnerable. For schizophrenics, as for dreamers, all things are possible. So they end up immersed in the realm of infinite possibility, which is where they both long and dread to be.

The essence of madness lies in its awareness of imagination as unlimited possibility—an awareness that the schizoid strategy sought to avoid—and in its ambivalence to this encounter with limitlessness. Schizophrenics may give up their defense against infinitude not only because they are fleeing the pain of keeping up that defense but also because they are lured to what lies beyond it. They embrace what they fear because they desire what they fear: not endless unreality, but endlessness itself, the quality that allows reality to be experienced as perfect. The inner self, having starved itself behind the inert mask of the false self, now asserts its deepest need: the need to be filled with its own life, which is the life of imagination. In this sense, madness may well be an immersion in formlessness motivated by a hope for new form and revitalized life, a life founded on an experience of infinite possibility. The false self and its pure finitude may be discarded not only as an act of desperation but also as the only possible act of integrity.

Madness may be understood, then, as an abortive quest for religious images. Schizophrenics desire both limitless filtering and limitless openness, the two paths that meet in a religious image. They recognize the threat of limitless unreality that every experience of limitlessness entails. But they are not grounded in the religious image needed to endure the infinite possibility they crave. Consequently they feel compelled to frustrate their own desire by radically limiting both psychic processes. The infinite possibilities released by revealing the true self must be experienced as literalized finite realities, each aiming to destroy the others. Every experience thus becomes a traumatic encounter with the self's finitude, which evokes the threat of total formlessness; every impulse to form and revitalization becomes a spur to deeper psychic numbing.

This model is not meant to romanticize madness. Because we so easily romanticize imagination, we can equally easily romanticize madness as a quest for imagination. In fact, though, it appears to be a terrifying trap that shuts its victim in a psychic isolation cell of despair whose walls are inexorably closing in. What could be more painful or less romantic? But this trap offers an illusion of security that may be more comforting than the risk of anxiety demanded by the psyche's innate movement toward religious images. And Laing, at least, insists that those who are allowed to dwell in the trap with minimal interference and generous support may eventually find their own way out.

Modernity and the Fantasies of Madness

Can this model of madness be legitimately applied to a whole society, or, more specifically, to our whole society in the nuclear age? If, as Lifton and Laing claim, the phenomenology of schizophrenia centers on ontological insecurity, then our society does seem to share the same foundation as madness. The idea that our existence is tenuous because it is not fully or genuinely real has long been familiar territory to modern artists and thinkers. Many have described modernity in terms of the 'mass man', the faceless digit in the lonely crowd whose existence seems to make no difference. Many have explored the individual's feeling of having no roots in, or intrinsic connection with, reality. Death, like birth, seems a random affair that may strike at any moment for no reason. With death stripped of all meaning, life is experienced as a brief moment that comes out of nothingness and constantly teeters on the brink of nothingness.

When meaninglessness and absurdity grow to such proportions, the world's events come to seem unreal. But if the world is unreal, then the self must be unreal too. This conviction is confirmed for many people by a feeling of inner emptiness. Experience grows pale and one-dimensional, leaving a constant dissatisfaction. The sense that there must be more to life engenders a similar sense that there must be more to the self; i.e., that no one is all they could or should be. But this constant desire to be something more (often spurred on by commercial forces) is foiled by the conviction that no one can be more than just another unreal, rootless, faceless digit in the lonely crowd. All these hallmarks of modernity are manifestations of ontological insecurity.[11] All are easily recognized by every student of contemporary culture. Most of the twentieth century's major writings and artworks deal with themes such as these.

But it is less widely recognized that these themes are all directly tied to secularization—the blocking of the psyche's innate movement toward religious images. Since our publicly agreed ultimate concern is the avoidance of an ultimate concern, the public and private realms conspire to deny the possibility of grounding in religious images. We must experience all reality and all possibility, including our own, as necessarily and inevitably limited. Each encounter thus becomes a trauma, convincing us further that our own reality is wholly limited and opening up the prospect of total formlessness. Without religious imagery we can have no meaningful form for formlessness, and without a meaningful form for formlessness we can have no religious imagery. As a result, we can only fear the limitless unreality inherent in every religious image; we can only take refuge in the radical finitude of psychic numbing, refusing the movement toward religious images altogether. But this flight from infinite unreality merely intensifies the primal fear of unreality that is the foundation of madness.

Obviously we are not all mad in the same way that clinical schizophrenics are mad. The concept of schizophrenia developed by Laing and Lifton can not be applied literally to an entire culture. But it can be used to develop a concept of 'public madness,' a category that must be distinguished from individual madness, even though the phenomenology of the latter holds the key to understanding the former. Public madness may be just as real as its private analogue, even if the two are not precisely the same pathology. The common occurrence of the phrase *nuclear madness* and the empirical fact of continuing technologies of self-destruction, coupled with the theoretical considerations developed here, point toward the concept of public madness as a hypothesis that is worth exploring.

Nuclear Madness: A Model

Public madness must be distinguished from its private analogue because the vast majority of us live quite sanely and reasonably in ordinary reality, and we generally cope with that reality quite efficiently. In fact, we cope with reality much more efficiently than did our ancestors of centuries past. But our efficiency in manipulating the things—and the people—of our world betrays a central element of public madness, for it is rooted in our massively literal mindset. We get the job done so quickly and effectively only because we focus so single-mindedly on the concrete task at hand. No questions of the larger context of meaning are permitted to intrude. In other words, we take for granted the same concretizing and fragmenting mindset that schizophrenics bring to their fantasies.

When a whole society approaches the terrain of schizophrenia, however, it transforms that terrain too. An individual enters into madness by one of two portals: either the false self is abandoned or the true self is destroyed. But when a whole society commits itself to this form of literalizing madness, it finds a new way to go mad by entering both portals at once. Neither the schizoid fantasies of the inner self nor the petrified forms of the social false self need be rejected, because we act out our deepest hidden fantasies in the shared forms of public life. The inner self's fantasies flourish without restraint because they need no longer hide behind and vie with the everyday facade of "normal" life. Rather, they now constitute "normal" life.

By merging the inner and outer realms we also discover a new way to murder the self: we petrify it by projecting it into the numbed rigidity of the public fantasy system. Eventually the inner self disappears altogether, for it is completely absorbed by the rational ego. This reinforces our conviction of the ego's absolute control over the world, which in fact no longer exists except insofar as the ego lets it exist. The ego recreates the world in the image of its fantasies quite literally through technology. The external world and all its threats are destroyed, not merely in schizophrenic fantasy but in material reality, by replacing them with a purely artificial world created from human imagination. We seem to avoid the pain of a purely private fantasy world because we all share the same fantasy and turn it into ordinary empirical reality.

We sustain our shared fantasy with an endless stream of new images, objects, and people treated as objects. These ever-growing collections of random possessions seem to fill our lives with the reality we crave, but they also confirm our radical finitude and the deadness of our world. We hope that by inundating our homes and our lives with ever-new realities we can simultaneously overwhelm ourselves with and protect ourselves against reality. Like individual schizophrenics, we hope to block out all stimuli while remaining open to limitless stimuli. So we cling tenaciously to the manifold literalized structures of the everyday world, hoping to find perfect security in them. And we look to the heroic ego to create ever more stable and secure structures in the battle against formlessness. But at the same time we refuse the very unifying impulse that the monotheistic ego imposes upon us. We embrace structures that are constantly shifting and dissolving, and we refuse to admit, or even seek, an overarching structure of meaning in our public life. Above all we refuse any meaningful form for the formlessness we share. So we are reassured that the formative process is permanently frozen; we can be inundated by endless stimuli while remaining numb to all stimuli.

Ultimately we are refusing the essence of our personal reality: the limitless possibilities of our own imagination. We feel safe in indulging imagination because we believe that our finitizing literalism has stripped it of its threat, which lies in its limitlessness. So we need not choose for or against imagination. We can let it overwhelm us while all the time denying that it is "really real." We know no reality outside our web of shared fantasy, so we have no standpoint from which it can be judged a fantasy. Should anyone ever suggest that our ordinary reality might actually be a tissue of imaginings, we have televisions, newspapers, billboards, supermarkets, and shopping malls around every corner to convince us that nothing could be more unalterably real than our everyday lives. So there is no point in desiring, or even imagining, any fundamental change.

The State of Nuclear Madness

These elements of madness may have existed long before 1945, although the explosions of that year revealed them in a glaring new light. But if much stayed the same, there was also a radical change in 1945: the elements of madness were fused, like the sands of Alamogordo, into a full-blown and inescapable public madness. Technology was turned back upon the world it had forged. Now, for the first time, we had a machine that could literally enact the fantasy of destroying the world we had spun from imagination—a fantasy that entailed destroying the national self and every individual self as well. This literal vision of universal destruction, and the equally literal vision of survival that it spawned, became the foundation of our publicly shared everyday reality. The distinction between private fantasy and public reality disappeared forever, along with the distinction between true and false self. No longer were annihilation and invulnerable omnipotence merely inner fantasies hidden behind the mask of the false self. As in every passage from schizoid neurosis to schizophrenic psychosis, the mask was dropped and the deepest imaginings were now played out in full public view.

Ever since 1945, the Bomb has been the guardian, the clearest sign, the driving force, and the ultimate enforcer of modernity's madness. As Laing puts it:

> In the context of our present pervasive madness that we call normality, sanity, freedom, all our frames of reference are ambiguous and equivocal. . . . A little girl of seventeen in a mental hospital told me she was terrified because the Atom Bomb was inside her. That is a delusion. The statesmen of the world who boast and threaten that they have Doomsday weapons are far more dangerous, and far more estranged from "reality" than many of the people on whom the label "psychotic" is affixed.[12]

In the rich imagery of nuclear policy and the nuclear threat, the schizoid patterns of modernity are not abandoned but affirmed ever more vigorously. Installing the heroic ego in place of the inner self, we maintain the apparent security of the false self system while acting out the deepest fantasies of the inner self: the fantasies of controlling the world—destroying it and remaking it at will—without any risk. Nuclear madness allows us, and indeed compels us, to act out our mutually reinforcing fantasies of invulnerable omnipotence and annihilation—the trap and the void—on the most public of stages, the political and technological stages. The most distorted fantasies are embodied in socially sanctioned national security policies, which meld private fantasy with official public attitudes.[13] Even the "mad scientist" is ultimately working for the good of all, as long as he is working for the state.

The Bomb-possessing nation-state is the vehicle that propagates and enacts the fantasies of nuclear madness. The state (i.e., the interlocking combine of all principal economic, social, and cultural institutions, coordinated by the government) determines both the shape of our filtering of stimuli and the limits of our openness to stimuli. It sets strict bounds upon individual and societal experience and points toward a total closing off of all experience. At the same time its fragmented literalized fantasies open up visions of unlimited possibility. Like the God of monotheism, it lays down irrefutable limits while seemingly transcending all limits. The state is the heroic ego writ large, repressing imagination precisely because it evokes it so powerfully, and vice versa. So it seems fruitless to challenge the collective false self that the state supports, even if it were desirable.

It rarely seems desirable, however. We identify with the state because it allows us each to enact its heroic ego fantasies so literally and because it promises national security. The measure of the state's progress toward the fantasy of perfect control is its capacity to protect us from "the enemy." Some enemy is necessary to give this fantasy literal form and credibility. But it matters little just what form this enemy takes. At times it may be another nation; at times it may be a technology such as the Bomb.[14] At all times, though, the enemy is a palpable embodiment of "instability": the uncontrollable dimension of reality that brings with it the risk of annihilation. Since the state's *raison d'être* is protection against this enemy, the state must propagate and control official fantasies of both annihilation and invulnerable omnipotence. As in all madness, each of these sets of fantasies must generate the other in an unending cycle. The state must act out its official fantasies of perfect security because it propagates fantasies of violent destruction. Yet these security fantasies detach us ever further from reality and thus generate ever greater fantasies of violent destruction—which require us to enact increasingly unrealistic fantasies of fending off violent destruction.

The nuclear-armed state monopolizes our violence fantasies, just as it monopolizes all other fantasies, and installs them in the shared fantasy system. When these fantasies center on nuclear war fighting, Cold War rivalry, and the threat of enemy nations, they exhibit clear parallels to the paranoia sometimes found in individual schizophrenics. The state's power turns our public schizophrenia into an irredeemably paranoid schizophrenia, and then the state proffers its invincible might as our only refuge.[15] When overtly paranoid imagery is eclipsed by images of disarmament, international cooperation, and the "safe Bomb," the formal structures of public madness remain the same. The public false self system becomes even more effective in repressing the shadow side of the public psyche because the state as heroic ego manifests itself not through its martial courage but through its rationality and technical expertise. The "safe Bomb" images of secure structure, as fragmentary and illusory as they are, effectively mask the countervailing imagery of world disintegration.

Most of the time, of course, paranoid Cold War fantasies and optimistic détente fantasies are acted out simultaneously in ever-changing permutations. Paranoia and optimism are so readily compatible because they are merely two different manifestations of the same dynamic of madness: in both cases, images of world- and self-destruction make it not only possible but necessary to imagine ourselves invulnerable and omnipotent through the agencies of the state. In both cases, images of annihilation and images of perfect security flourish side by side because each fosters the other.

The two sets of nuclear fantasies are also compatible because madness allows contradictions without number. Public madness, mediated through the state's national security policies, lets us live out the most contradictory fantasies without doubting our own sanity. Logically incompatible ideas, aims, and behaviors are maintained side by side quite comfortably, simply because everyone else maintains them too. Confronting the nuclear threat, the public madness clings to several "quasi-autonomous partial systems." It insists that only a madman bent on suicide would start a nuclear war; but in the next breath it insists that we must retain the right of first use and have enough weapons to defeat the enemy. It affirms military strength as the highest virtue; but in the next breath it decries "the military-industrial complex" for sapping the nation's economy. It praises the Bomb as the "umbrella" that keeps us out of war; but in the next breath it yearns for the simplicity and security of the prenuclear era. It praises the technology that builds ever more sophisticated weapons; but in the next breath it curses that technology as an ineffable danger. It is thankful that the danger of nuclear confrontation is past; but in the next breath it laments having to live in a world that is "falling apart."

Each of these views is the basis for some piece of our declaratory or actual nuclear policy. And each may seem reasonable enough within its own framework of belief. But there is no coherence among the various frameworks. Pieces of ideology and imagery from any one system can be juxtaposed with pieces from any others without clear rhyme or reason. Public discourse on the nuclear issue thus becomes just the sort of "word-salad" found in schizophrenia, and public policies are enacted out of this "word-salad" and the "image-salad" that goes along with it. The ego, despite its desire for unifying structure, accepts such chaos as ordinary reality because the chaos protects its numbing. And the superpower state, while claiming to protect us with its structures of "national security," preserves the chaos by monopolizing violence and images of violence. In the fantasy world of madness, only an omnipotent superpower can stave off the threat—a threat that is constantly perpetuated by the public fantasies of the superpower.

Nuclear Fears

Nuclear madness lets annihilation imagery live comfortably side by side with invulnerability imagery because the feeling of danger, which depends on imagination, is radically repressed. Images of nuclear violence can flourish in full public view (and may be heightened to stress the need for disarmament) because they seem so safe as long as they are framed in purely literal "realistic" terms. But, as in all madness, these images of formlessness are denied any meaningful form. We can go on forever, it seems, possessing the technology for world-destruction yet remaining immune to its meaning and its violence—as long as we place our trust in the state. Given the immensity of the threat and the state's self-proclaimed success in controlling it, what other choice do we have but trust?

This is not to say that we never worry. On the contrary, we worry a lot, not only about the Bomb but about the many terrors of a world apparently out of control. Lifton has called attention to this widespread capacity for living on two levels—one of awareness of impending threat and another of numbed disregard—and he has related it to the phenomenon he calls "doubling": the development of two autonomous personalities in the same individual.[16] This doubling, which is most apparent in those who plan nuclear policy and strategy,[17] is one way of managing the "quasi-autonomous partial systems" without entering clinical schizophrenia (although it calls up the popular, if somewhat misleading, Jekyll-and-Hyde image of the schizophrenic as a "split personality"). In Lifton's view, the average person is caught in a less intense version of doubling, capable of feeling anxiety over the nuclear threat yet driven by the intensity of the anxiety to detach from reality and live as if the threat did not exist.

But there is good reason to believe that even our anxieties about nuclear and other threats are elements of the public madness that numbs us. The state (through its public voice, the news media) feeds our worries, filling our daily lives with reports of the latest deaths and dangers. These reports reinforce the ubiquitous images of uncontrollable violence that fill our entertainment media. We consume violent images so greedily because they reflect the repressed imaginings spawned by madness. Our private fantasies become artifacts of public culture incorporated into the social false self system. When Cold War rages these fantasies are attached to the Bomb. When there is a thaw images of annihilation, being repressed, grow more insistent, so they are projected more insistently into other realms, both fictional and empirical. But in every era public images of violence, confirming our fearful sense of the world as both threatening and disintegrating, help justify madness as a necessary form of self-defense.

As we watch the news on TV, each item can seem perfectly reasonable (though deeper probing might unmask this seeming). But the ensemble has no coherence. The nuclear threat, along with all our largest public concerns, is reduced to the same status as the latest billboard advertisement or weather report; all are just so many disjointed stimuli in the ever-widening "image-salad." Our natural response in the face of this daily onslaught is to feel helpless, incapable of response, and therefore not responsible. So we sink back into the reassuring belief that questions of ultimate significance must be pursued (if they can be pursued at all) in our individual private lives. Yet as long as events in the public realm seem to have no ultimate meaning, the lethal terrors perpetrated in that realm do not genuinely touch us.

The state and its media also insure that the problems that do occupy us are stripped of their threatening aspect. By defining our world for us—by telling us what counts as a "real" problem—they help us destroy the real world and replace it with an imaginary world; we lose touch with the genuine reality of our problems, and they become in some sense unreal. Since the media insist that its fantasy images are the only literal reality, those images seem more compellingly real. In fact, though, they compound our sense of unreality. Denying the roots of our problems in imagination, we deny their capacity to touch the imagination and their capacity to truly terrify us. They paradoxically end up strengthening the ego's fantasy of total control. All problems are turned into a series of discrete literal problems that can and presumably will be solved by the state's technical means. Indeed the problems are defined in such a way that only the agencies of the state could possibly solve them. So every "real" problem is framed by the official annihilation and omnipotence fantasies propagated by the state.

Nuclear discourse exemplifies this process. Couched wholly in the language of the experts, it offers an alternative reality whose verisimilitude, complexity, and drama are often bewitchingly fascinating. We are inundated with passionate debates about the need for this or that particular missile, the legitimacy of first-strike or second-strike policies, the viability of space-based defenses, the impact of various disarmament options on our relations with allies, and so on. But all of this discourse refers only to the world it has itself created; it has no necessary or consistent relationship with the empirical reality that it claims to represent so faithfully. So the nuclear discussion takes us to the extreme terminus of the neurotic trait of ignoring real dangers. Detaching ourselves from the reality of the danger becomes one more way of embracing it; it increases the likelihood that the danger will eventually materialize in literal form.

Each time we worry about the Bomb and the other "real" problems of the day, we lose touch with reality, affirm the state and its madness as the answer, deepen our psychic numbing, and immerse ourselves once again in the chaotic kaleidoscope of stimuli constantly, yet apparently harmlessly, bombarding us. So the part of us that does worry may be just as numb as the part that refuses to worry. All the "quasi-autonomous partial systems" of the individual, as of the society, join together to affirm our true common purpose: to deny anxiety by denying any ultimate concern; to maintain fragmentation, meaninglessness, and radical finitude. This is the state's ultimate ideal, the ultimate security that it offers.

The Insecurity of National Security

In fact, though, our loyalty to the state and its ideals makes us constantly less secure. Every public madness, like every private madness, is a strategy for enhancing ontological security that actually undermines feelings of personal reality and therefore steadily diminishes the sense of security. The ultimate question for a mad society, as for a mad individual, is how to immerse in limitless stimuli—in the limitless possibilities of imagination—while yet shutting out all stimuli and all possibilities. The ultimate answer, for an individual or a society bereft of religious images, is to cling to a fixed set of fantasies taken absolutely literally, fantasies of world- and self-destruction that somehow render us invulnerable and omnipotent. This is obviously a first and major step into a loss of contact with reality.

Moreover this answer turns out to be no answer at all, for it leaves its victims trapped in a world of infinite possibility and trapped in ambivalence to that world, still needing to be both open to it and closed off from it. In schizophrenic fantasies, as in dreams, all things are literally possible: the most unspeakable violence and destruction, even the destruction of the world, even the simultaneous destruction and survival of the self in a destroyed world. In the nuclear age, all things seem literally possible because the means to enact our fantasies are so indubitably literal. The Bomb, like all our technological artifacts and images, breaks down the boundary between imagination and literal fact by literalizing our imaginings, immersing us in the realm of limitless possibility. So it is a constant reminder that we are drawn to what we fear. Nuclear madness, like all madness, only compounds our ambivalence toward the power of imagination, a power that seems to be irresistible. Without religious imagery to resolve this ambivalence, ontological insecurity and the resort to radical finitude are inescapable.

A public madness exacerbates this dilemma in a unique way. In a private madness, one hopes to survive by detaching oneself from external reality; the threat of formlessness comes only from one's own imaginings. A public madness, however, depends on a tacit agreement not only to literalize all images but to act them out together in the external world. So it attaches us more firmly to the ever-changing world and its ever-expanding waves of stimuli. The more external stimuli there are, the greater the need to filter them out and replace them with imagination. But the greater the flow of imagination, the greater the need to deny its limitless possibilities by enacting it in a material world ruled by the heroic ego. The more we try to deaden imagination by immersing ourselves in a dead world of pure objectivity, the more we feel robbed of reality and compelled to fill the empty external world with our own artifacts and imaginings. So every attempt to block out stimuli engulfs us in ever more external stimuli and ever more imagination; as the distinction between the two dissolves, ontological insecurity grows.

When we embrace nuclear madness as an escape route from this dilemma, we insure that we will continue to feel less real. Under the reign of radical finitude, we remain trapped in the insecurity of an ever-tightening circle of public madness. Since this trap is built from national security policies founded on the Bomb and its public images, it appears to be a brilliant solution to an insoluble problem: how to escape from ontological insecurity into madness without suffering the isolation and pain of madness. But this solution is hardly as successful as it seems. Behind its facade of normalcy and sanity, the heroic ego inevitably senses its increasing insecurity, emptiness, and loss of reality.

Responding to this crisis of security, the ego projects the ontological threat onto an enemy. Its fears are installed in the inertness of the objective world and the false self, and thus they are stripped of at least some of their terror. But the safety of this defense mechanism is predictably illusory. Projection merely ensnares us more firmly in the threatening external world and in the social fantasy of the heroic ego. The ego, feeling more ontologically impoverished and threatened, tries to defend itself in the characteristic way of madness: it acts out its fantasies of embracing the dangers it fears most. On the one hand it hopes to defend itself by cutting itself off from reality, filtering out all stimuli, petrifying itself, and making itself nothing. On the other hand it hopes to defend itself by being filled with the reality that exists elsewhere, opening itself to all stimuli, and having itself imploded and engulfed. Both routes converge in literal enactment of nuclear fantasies.

When we "stand firm" in the name of "stability"—whether in the war room or at the negotiating table—we enact our fantasies of petrifying ourselves in a risk-free static world. Acting as perfectly rational egos, we render ourselves as inert as our world and reduce ourselves to nothing at all. At the same time, though, we court the risk of literally imploding and engulfing ourselves. In eras of Cold War confrontation, our commitment to the state's official fantasies means a commitment to the state's manipulative behavior, which may provoke other nations into manipulations and provocations of their own. In such times, every encounter implies a potential conflict, and every conflict implies a threat of engulfment or implosion by the other. This kind of provocation may, in fact, be the secret purpose of the manipulations of schizophrenics and superpowers. Since the schizophrenic experiences reality as "always there, never here," one must provoke the other to engulf or invade the self and fill the empty self with reality.

When Cold War tensions are relaxed, our commitment to the state's official fantasies means a commitment to visions of a "safe Bomb." We may convince ourselves that the Bomb is now safely tucked away in a remote corner of the world where we need not worry about it. Yet behind this screen of apparent security nuclear arsenals are still deployed, new weapons programs proceed virtually unabated, and detailed plans for the use of these weapons remain in place. Major changes in political images create relatively minor changes in military realities.[18] And we still preserve our images of nuclear annihilation, though they are now framed within countervailing images of a perfectly secure global balance.

When we choose the "safe Bomb" rather than the Cold War route to nuclear madness, we confirm ourselves in a fantasy that cuts us off even further from reality. So we may feel even more compelled to court danger in hopes of filling ourselves with the reality that is "always there, never here." But now the Bomb itself becomes the enemy and thus the source of the reality that we crave, the reality that we must provoke to implode and engulf us. We may provoke the literal triggering of unforeseen danger simply by acting as if the danger no longer existed. This may now be the ultimate goal of the nation's nuclear policy.

At all times we nurture fantasies of engulfment and implosion that are simultaneously fantasies of making ourselves forever nothing at all. We project those fantasies into the public realm so effortlessly because nuclear technology makes it so easy to imagine them acted out literally. Thus we embrace the essence of madness. The logic of madness always drives it toward increasingly literal enactments of both total openness to all stimuli and total absence of stimuli—total engulfment or implosion and a simultaneous shrinking away to nothingness. The logic of nuclear madness puts us on the same twofold path toward a literalized state of pure formlessness. At the same time nuclear madness, like all madness, offers us images of invulnerable omnipotence in the midst of our annihilation images. The Bomb seduces us into its illusory vision of security by mirroring all these fantasies of madness, promising to make all come true simultaneously. It embodies our twin desires for literally endless life and literal death in the most concrete form. So its promise of "national security" necessarily brings with it a promise of literal world- and self-destruction.

This model of nuclear madness is a speculation. It predicts that nuclear madness will continue as long as nuclear weapons exist to literalize our fantasies of annihilation. It predicts that as long as we literalize those fantasies we will move ever closer to acting them out on a limitless scale of destruction. And it predicts that, as long as nuclear madness continues, all of us will share the ontological insecurity that lies at the core of schizophrenia. We are "normal" only because our strategies for dealing with insecurity reflect the public false self system, while the clinical schizophrenic's do not. Yet our "normal" state is a national security state whose promises of security only intensify our insecurity.

There can be no genuine national security (nor any other kind of security) without ontological security, and there can be no ontological security as long as our public and private lives deny the psyche's inherent drive toward religious images. The death in life of psychic numbing is at the root of our march toward self-destruction, as Robert Jay Lifton contends. Numbing reaches its zenith in the nuclear age, however, not because of the immensity of the threat of death and not because of a lack of images, but because the social fantasy system, with its literal instrument of mass annihilation, has now totally denied the authentic need of the self for religious images.

As a speculation, this model is not meant to be proven or disproven by any data. Rather it is meant to offer a new way to organize and interpret the data. Its value depends on its capacity to bring greater intelligibility to events that seem more or less unintelligible. Many events in the nuclear age still seem more or less unintelligible. So the value of this model may best be tested by using it to review and reinterpret the history of the nuclear age.

7

Nuclear Madness: The Cold War Era

On August 6, 1945, newscaster Don Goddard opened his noon broadcast with "the story of a new bomb, so powerful that only the imagination of a trained scientist could dream of its existence. Without qualification, the President said that Allied scientists have now harnessed the basic power of the universe."[1] Later that day, newscaster H. V. Kaltenborn boasted: "Anglo-Saxon science has developed a new explosive 2,000 times as destructive as any known before."[2] In the days that followed, *Life* reported that Hiroshima had been "blown off the face of the earth" and Nagasaki "disemboweled."[3] The *New York Times* warned that this was but a sample of the future bombs that could be "dropped on Japan at any time our military leaders chose,"[4] and *Newsweek* warned that "the Jap must choose between surrender and annihilation."[5] Many newspapers carried President Truman's proclamation that "America is now the most powerful nation in the world—the most powerful nation perhaps in all history."[6]

But there was also a very different kind of immediate response to the dawn of the nuclear age. H. V. Kaltenborn tempered his boast with a warning: "For all we know, we have created a Frankenstein. We must assume that with the passage of only a little time, an improved form of the new weapon we use today can be turned against us."[7] On August 7, the *New York Herald Tribune* editorialized: "[One] forgets the effect on Japan as one senses the foundations of one's own universe trembling."[8] Later that week columnist James Reston wrote: "In that terrible flash 10,000 miles away, men here have seen not only the fate of Japan, but have glimpsed the future of America,"[9] while Edward R. Murrow reported: "Seldom, if ever, has a war ended leaving the victors with such a sense of uncertainty and fear, with such a realization that the future is obscure and that survival is not assured."[10] When he reported the surrender of Japan, Kaltenborn repeated his warning: "Let us think of the mass murder which will come with World War III."[11]

From the very beginning, then, the American media responded to the fact of nuclear weapons with a creative outpouring of nuclear images. The history of nuclear policies ever since 1945 can be understood as a history of shifting ambivalent images and as a search for a unfying image that all Americans could share. Throughout this history, however, the cardinal rule of madness has always been observed: the Bomb and all the images used to interpret its meaning had to reinforce the quest for destruction and the death in life of psychic numbing. Every potentially unifying image had to yield to the inescapable spiral of insecurity, fragmentation, and formlessness.

The Imagery of Annihilation

The media reports of August 1945, taken as a whole, both shaped and reflected a national response compounded of celebration and dread. It is easy enough to understand the celebration. In 1945, Americans affirmed that "our way of life," representing the best of modern technology, culture, and morality, had proven itself invulnerable to even the most massive assault. Because the power of imagination had been preempted by "trained scientists" (as reporter Goddard put it), we had seen our dreams of omnipotence come true.

Why, then, should images of dread be so abundant? Taken at face value, they were surely exaggerated. No other country possessed nuclear weapons, nor was there any public evidence that any other country could obtain them. There was not even any public evidence that the U.S. would or could produce more (though perhaps fantasies of technological omnipotence demanded this assumption). Yet somehow it seemed natural to assume that both we and our future enemies would build nuclear arsenals. It did not seem natural to assume that nations would cooperate voluntarily to renounce nuclear weapons.

It might be argued, of course, that these were reasonable assumptions grounded in empirical observation of the modern past. But this merely shows that modernity was already moving inexorably toward self-destruction. And it leaves crucial factors unexplained. Given that some apprehension was reasonable, one would still expect that at the moment of victory, after half a decade of total war, the excitement of certain triumph would far overshadow the fear of an uncertain future. In fact, though, the nation could not articulate its excitement without an equal measure of fear; the two responses seem to have been interdependent. Moreover, the actual nuclear destruction of August 1945 was quite small by contemporary standards. There was no empirical reason to believe that much more destructive weapons would some day be built. Yet America's fantasies filled the future with innumerable Bombs of unlimited potency raining down infinite destruction.

Spencer Weart has shown that for most people the news of the atomic bomb was shaped by "myths that had grown up long before the first bomb burst."[12] These myths originated among early scientific investigators of radioactivity, whose minds were filled with ancient alchemical imaginings of dissolution, transmutation, and new creation. Journalists such as William L. Laurence were the intermediaries who passed these images on to the public. Yet Weart notes that only "a small minority of the public"[13] was familiar with their journalistic accounts before August, 1945. Why, then, were these images of dread so universally, enthusiastically, and immediately embraced?

The model of madness suggests that the dreadful fantasies, just as much as the triumphal fantasies, already existed in latent form and had eventually to be literally actualized. Modernity demands that the goal of death in life generate its own concrete images of that state. Perhaps, then, it was inevitable that modernity would use the discoveries of theoretical physics to produce a publicly visible embodiment of the fantasied threat that it is constantly fleeing. The Bomb certainly filled this role. The essence of the earliest annihilation fantasies, as of all subsequent nuclear annihilation fantasies, is summed up in an image that might be called "the big whoosh," an image of an instantaneous planetary explosion that would simply "blow up the world."[14] This phrase entered readily into common parlance, not because it reflected the empirical reality of what the first atomic bombs could actually do, but because it mirrored the fantasies of our shared madness. Laing's description of the schizophrenic process is perfectly apt here: "Destructiveness in phantasy can thus rage on until the world and the self are reduced in phantasy to dust and ashes."[15]

The nuclear "dust and ashes" fantasy is an image of formlessness that represents the terminus of both paths in the schizophrenic process. Nearly all images of a nuclear holocaust denote a world disintegrated into an endless stream of the smallest possible pieces—a world overwhelmed with finite stimuli thrown together in a meaningless chaos. Yet they also denote ubiquitous instantaneous death: selves suddenly meeting the ultimate sign of finitude, deprived of all stimuli and all structured interaction with the world. Both tracks of this imagery lead to the same infinite unreality. The dimension of infinitude is clearly present, for these images, like religious images, incorporate both limitless filtering of and limitless openness to external and internal stimuli. But both aspects are riddled with a radical finitude that denies the possibility of infinite reality. Both claim plausibility only because they can come to pass quite literally through finite technological means. And both are expressed in image fragments that deny the possibility of giving a unified meaning to universal formlessness. So images of nuclear holocaust must pit the two psychic processes against each other, leaving each in dread of annihilation at the hands of the other.

The same psychodynamics are at work in the popular images of a postholocaust world. Many early images show a static empty wasteland where no meaningful stimuli exist to be received and no responses are given or possible. Yet the survivors are pictured as totally overwhelmed, bewildered, and lacking consistent structures to cope with their environment. Inundated with, yet deprived of, stimuli, these imagined survivors "would not so much envy as, inwardly and outwardly, resemble the dead" (in the words of Robert Lifton and Kai Erikson.)[16] Again, the two components of religious images are brought together here. But these survivors are hemmed in on every side by a radical finitude that opens only into infinite unreality.

These are the prospects that Americans had to face (often unconsciously, but surprisingly often in graphic media images) in the early years of nuclear imagery. The Bomb gave tangible grounding to fantasies of literal annihilation that had flourished long before it. It made ontological insecurity seem a perfectly reasonable, perhaps even inevitable, response to an inescapable literal reality. Suspending a constant threat of formlessness over our lives, it insured that our every moment would have a traumatic quality. The Bomb locked the nation in to the schizophrenic's root problem.

The Psychodynamics of the Cold War

Inevitably, then, the Bomb also locked us in to the schizophrenic's fantasied solution. As the danger became undeniably literal, the search for protection turned exclusively toward literal thinking. Since the danger came from a machine, the search turned especially toward a machine that could save us. The machine threatened only because it had infinite power, so we had to find an equally powerful machine to pit against it. But the machine was uniquely threatening because it was uniquely powerful. Since there could be no other like it, our only alternative was to follow the schizophrenic strategy and embrace the very danger we most feared. We had to fantasize the Bomb as the only possible protection against the threat that it had itself made inescapable.

Once the Bomb was defined as our protector, the threat had to be projected onto "the enemy." Through its media, the state aimed to define the problem of the Bomb in purely political terms, so that only the state and its Bomb could be the solution. It wanted every nuclear image to point to one central message: the state must become and remain a superpower.[17] State-sponsored madness is inevitably suffused with paranoia and violence, so the Bomb created another set of fantasies that anticipated later reality. Even before the Axis powers were defeated, America prepared for the next struggle for world supremacy.[18] Again, it is curious that American fantasy did not foresee total American control of "the winning weapon." But Cold War imagery was not meant to eclipse annihilation fantasies. Rather, it aimed to simultaneously affirm and deny them by giving them a secure place in the nation's shared fantasy. The vision of a nuclear-armed enemy was necessary to solve this problem of both affirming and denying annihilation. The nation's rational ego had to deny the inner source of its annihilation fantasies. Like all paranoid fantasies, they had to be literalized and externalized.

In 1949 the Soviet Union fulfilled American fantasies by producing a very literal Bomb of its own. If Our Bomb was a protector, destruction could only come from Their Bomb. Literalized images of "the enemy threat" were easily absorbed into the regnant societal fantasy because Their Bomb made such images seem undeniably realistic and appropriate. Once absorbed, they committed our society more firmly to a paranoid madness. Taking on the Cold War fantasy, Americans no longer had to dread or feel responsible for the threat of nuclear annihilation. It was now easy enough to insist that only the Soviets would initiate an annihilating war (since the moral pretensions of our national heroic ego could not admit to our own aggression fantasies).

By 1950, the Soviet threat had encompassed the nuclear threat.[19] "The Bomb" and "the Communists" virtually merged in the public mind as twin symbols of a single chaotic force that had to be vanquished. Yet Americans could believe that they had nothing to fear, since modernity's madness and the recent events of World War II combined to legitimate the fantasy of invulnerable omnipotence. Images of survival were just as necessary to nuclear madness as images of global catastrophe, and they flourished just as readily. The rhetoric of the Cold War offered literal images of apocalyptic world destruction, with the triumphant national self surviving as omnipotent ruler of a purified regenerated reality.

Life, one of the most influential news media of the day, vividly illustrated these fantasies at the outset of the Cold War in General H. H. ("Hap") Arnold's article, "The 36-Hour War." To illustrate the General's facile summary of an all-out nuclear exchange, large cartoon drawings showed missiles streaking back and forth across the globe like something out of a Tom Swift story. On the last page, New York's 5th Avenue was drawn as a heap of rubble, with only the Public Library's guardian lions surviving, standing sentinel over the nothingness. Somehow, America's leonine courage and superiority would prevail; after depicting nearly total mutual destruction, the text inexplicably concluded: "The United States wins the war."[20]

In the early years of the Cold War, as in schizophrenia, anything was possible, and the more fantastic the better. The Bomb, as the absolute destroying and saving machine, reinforced our fantasy of absolute control and our tendency to equate freedom with omnipotence. Freedom now meant that we could do anything, that anything was possible for us. Our passion for perfect freedom mirrored the schizophrenic's hope of preserving life through constant change and unlimited psychic openness. For a superpower, this goal seemed perfectly reasonable and literally attainable, as long as we had the biggest nuclear arsenal.

Because the Bomb promised to protect our perfect freedom, it became the cornerstone of national security. But security now meant just the opposite of freedom: permanent life preserved through immutable structure and unfettered psychic filtering. As in schizophrenia, there could be no middle ground between security and risk. Every risk of change became a risk of absolute extinction. Once the enemy became a superpower, its threat also had to appear absolute; we could only assume that it shared our madness and sought the same omnipotence. So we looked to the absolute destroyer for absolute safety, and the decision to build "the super" (the hydrogen Bomb) was accepted as inevitable.[21] We fantasized an apocalyptic victory so absolute that "the enemy threat" would simply disappear from the face of the earth. And we insisted upon an absolutely literal, technologically guaranteed victory. For a superpower, perfect security seemed as perfectly reasonable and literally attainable as perfect freedom.

The Bomb led modernity deeper into madness because its absolute power demanded thinking in these kinds of absolutes. It demanded that all nuclear fantasies be held with unprecedented literalism and absolute rigidity—a rigidity characteristic of schizophrenia. And it united all these absolutized fantasies in a single object. Freedom and security came to depend completely on the centralized state and its unique all-powerful machine. The heroic ego's monotheistic values and fantasies, enshrined in the social false self, seemed uniquely true; the deadening hand of technological literalism seemed uniquely triumphant. More than ever before, freedom and security were equated with a desperate clinging to the numbed status quo. If the Bomb left us too immured in, and too petrified by, our madness to resist or even question it, that merely reaffirmed its promise to make our freedom and security absolute.

Modernity thus cast the Bomb into a God-like role as ultimate destroyer and savior. The nation felt compelled to cling to the Bomb in both its roles and to the fantasies spawned by both, for both were demanded by nuclear madness. The nothingness of nuclear catastrophe promised the murder of the self. But it also promised a transcendence of all finite reality. Its images of technology gone wild offered a release of the infinite possibilities once concealed in the innermost self. The Bomb made it possible, and indeed necessary, to act out every facet of madness in empirical reality. It framed all issues of security and survival between its demand for radical finitude and its threat of total formlessness. So it turned every moment of life into a trauma that required the refuge of deepening madness. Yet this transformation seemed easy enough, and even reassuring: so many of the Bomb's trauma-laden paradoxes were the familiar paradoxes of modernity. Even its images of annihilation were familiar. The Bomb merely brought them from the realm of fiction, religious tradition, and arcane scientific reporting into the center of "realistic" public discourse.

In the Cold War era, annihilation fantasies were accepted, and sometimes avidly pursued, because they were placed in the context of state guarantees of invulnerable omnipotence. Indeed the state and its media propagated such lurid fantasies in order to make state-sponsored "superpower" fantasies seem indispensable. In this context, radically finite images of total formlessness became weapons in modernity's campaign to wipe out formlessness. Again, *Life* illustrates this vividly. An article headlined "The elemental fact of 1950: The enemy of the free world is implacably determined to destroy the free world," was followed by another titled "The Soul-Searchers Find No Answer: In the face of world crisis and the H-Bomb they foresee annihilation but not how to forestall it." This article gave the last word to a teenager's essay: "The word he used was the one that underlay the thinking of all [the scientists and statesmen]. The soul-searchers tidily tripped around it, but the schoolboy boldly picked it up and swung it like a sledge hammer. 'The hydrogen bomb reeks with death. Death, death of thousands. A burning, searing death. The most horrible death man has invented, the destroying, annihilating death of atomic energy. The poisoning, killing, destroying death. Death of the ages, of man. The lasting death.' "[22]

The Cold War's Contradictions

For nearly a decade the Bomb's literal and emotional menace were contained by the numbing power of the public false self system, which seemed to satisfy the ego's demand for the simplicity and security of a unified structure of images. Eventually, though, these efforts to enhance national security were bound to unravel, for they only exacerbated the nation's ontological insecurity. Beneath the nuclear "umbrella," the contradictions that plague every madness multiplied. The contradiction of combatting and embracing annihilation fantasies is just one obvious example.

Another example is the psychological symbiosis of annihilation and omnipotence. In madness the two sets of fantasies must go hand in hand; as each undermines ontological security, each generates the other. And the Bomb concretized both in equal measure. As the nation took refuge in the Bomb and its literalized fantasies of omnipotence, it drained itself of reality and demanded more fantasies of world- and self-destruction, which in turn had to be literalized. The more they were literalized, the more terrifying they became. When the Bomb offered itself as the omnipotent answer, it only sowed the seeds of new and more vivid annihilation fantasies and insured that this schizophrenic cycle would continue to turn.

A less obvious contradiction was hidden within the omnipotence fantasies themselves. These fantasies promised security and freedom through nuclear armament. Under the absolutizing reign of the Bomb, however, security could mean only limitless psychic filtering while freedom meant limitless psychic openness. So the two seemingly compatible values actually reflected the fundamental dynamic of madness: each was imagined as warding off the threat inherent in the other, and the two were set at war with each other. Nuclear madness aimed to resolve this conflict with its grab bag of literalized images that could be combined and recombined in any convenient way. The contradictions between security and freedom, and between annihilation and omnipotence, were papered over in the prevailing fantasy system, which provided a superficially coherent rationality as long as its constituent fantasies were accepted without question.

Beneath the surface, however, the overall conviction of growing formlessness had to be maintained. The fragmentation of images perpetuated the madness and made a literal image of annihilation even more indispensable. This literalism had to be affirmed for psychological reasons. Yet it had to be denied because its product, the Bomb, was so terrifying. So the superpowers renounced the heat of literal war in favor of a literalized Cold War. Traditional martial images were now used to numb rather than inflame conscious imagination, deepening the sense of unreality. The Cold War as a psychological stratagem shifted competition from the literal to the symbolic level. The state used its Bomb essentially as a token to stir up responses in the enemy's imagination—to "send a message to the other side."[23]

The public discourse on nuclear weapons readily acknowledged this symbolic function. But it insisted that all messages subserve the goal of literal protection. So it obscured the Bomb's primary role of sending messages to ourselves. The Bomb virtually shouted all the fantasies of madness at us every day. It surrounded us with the most extravagant imaginings. Yet we could deny their status as imaginings because they seemed so literally plausible. The classic schizophrenic paradox—trying to escape imagination by an upheaval of imagination—was raised to new heights by the literal possibility of nuclear annihilation.

But the Bomb threatened our psychic numbing with more than just an explosion of images. It surrounded us especially with Western civilization's most vivid kind of imagination: the traditional religious imagining of the end of the world. "Spiritual Armageddon Is Here—Now," Bernard Baruch warned. "The situation demands self-denial and sacrifice," he exhorted. "No outside enemy can defeat us. We *can* defeat ourselves. Yours is the decision."[24] The model of madness suggests that Baruch was quite right to say that we can defeat ourselves, though for far different reasons than he believed. In nuclear weapons the religious domain of limitless possibility had become a literal reality, and the nation pinned all its plans and hopes upon that reality. Images of perfect freedom and security, of transcendence and total transformation, were now indelibly inscribed in the social false self system, in external as well as internal reality. So the infinitude of the Bomb's destructive power threatened not only our continued existence but also the radical finitude at the root of our numbing.

As the Bomb brought the need for religious images to the surface and raised the prospect of limitless unreality, it evoked a stronger insistence on radical finitude. Perhaps people sensed "the foundations of one's own universe trembling" (as the *Herald Tribune* put it) less because their physical universe might some day vanish than because the psychological universe of modernity's finitude was already vanishing.[25] This was indeed an essentially spiritual situation, and it did demand self-denial and sacrifice—of the most basic spiritual need. It was an occasion for defeating ourselves. No matter what decision Americans made, however, we were bound to go on defeating ourselves, because all the options had to be cast within the framework of modernity's radical finitude to ward off their genuinely religious possibilities.

The Cold War itself typifies this response to the religious problematic of the nuclear age. It can be understood as a strategy for institutionalizing all of modernity's schizophrenic fantasies within a finite framework of shared fantasy. The essence of the Cold War was a vision of reality as permanently split into opposites and therefore finitized. The U.S. and the U.S.S.R. would be forever at war, even though they met each other at the Iron Curtain. Similarly, nuclear images of total openness and total filtering, and the threat and promise inherent in each, had to remain at war with each other, even though they appeared side by side. Indeed the Iron Curtain served as a necessary guarantee that all these images could be indulged at will without threatening the reign of finitude. Even when overtly religious images were used, they had to serve political, military, or economic aims. All images had to point back to technical problems that the experts, armed with hard facts, were on the way to solving. All had to support the false self system and the heroic ego. As long as they did, the Bomb seemed to make the world safe for immersion in unfettered fantasy.

In fact, though, nuclear fantasies also undermined the protective shelter of the social false self system. That system offers, above all, the reassurance that we are living in "normal" objective reality rather than in a solipsistic fantasy. But the Bomb, fusing religious imagination and literalism, blurred the boundary between fantasy and empirical reality beyond recognition and removed the last slim possibility of reality testing. Having "harnessed the power of the atom," we could no longer say where humanly crafted power ended and nature's power began. Nor could we say with certainty where scientific reality ended and imagination's fiction began. Human technology now stood at the very center of the most far-reaching product of imagination: the fantasy of provoking and surviving the end of the world. By creating its unique blend of literalism and imagination, the Bomb reaffirmed this schizophrenic fantasy as the foundation of modernity. As early as 1946, psychiatrist Edward Glover recognized this as the central truth of the Bomb: "The first promise of the atomic age is that it can make some of our nightmares come true. The capacity so painfully acquired by normal men to distinguish between sleep, delusion, hallucination, and the objective reality of waking life has for the first time in human history been seriously weakened."[26]

Loss of reality testing is normally the defining mark of an individual's entry into madness. But it plays a more complex role in a public madness, which demands belief in an absolute distinction between fantasy and reality. That distinction is a prerequisite to the social fantasy system and its conviction of the ego's absolute control. So the prerequisite for all our fantasy was a conscious insistence that it was science, not fiction. By undermining reality testing, the Bomb simultaneously undermined our control fantasy and made that fantasy absolutely necessary. Precisely because it made us feel less secure in our shared fantasy, as well as less ontologically secure, the Bomb compelled us to depend on it for security. Once the line between literal and imaginary reality was gone, the line between security and insecurity was bound to disappear as well.

All the other boundaries that normally mark sanity and the false self system were equally blurred. With everyone always on the "front line," the distinctions between war and peace and between public and private life began to vanish. The line dividing the responsible from the unresponsible was also hard to find. The state's decision makers and managers were no more or less at risk than the most humble citizen. Fantasies of omnipotent control gave everyone an imagined sense of full responsibility. But fantasies of the Bomb as an alien, God-like power denied any possibility of responsible control. It was no longer clear whether humans or machines were in charge; indeed the difference between human and mechanical action was increasingly hard to find. And if humans were in charge, it was no longer clear whether they were sane or mad. With all these fundamental distinctions in question, the viability of the social fantasy system itself could no longer be assured.

From every direction, then, the Cold War images that claimed to offer security left the nation feeling less ontologically secure than ever. Eventually the structures holding together annihilation and omnipotence fantasies had to begin to erode. The dominance of the latter had to be challenged by a resurgent sense of imminent formlessness. The possibility of a meaningful overarching form had to be undermined by images of fragmentation and "blowing the world to bits."

Omnipotence versus Annihilation

The confident structures of Cold War imagery began to erode in the late 1950s. To be sure, renewed nuclear fears were fed by realistic and appropriate responses to empirical facts about radioactive fallout. But the model of madness suggests that the psychological reality was paramount. The dreadful and chaotic side of nuclear imagery, which had receded for nearly a decade, was bound to emerge again. If the facts about fallout had not appeared, the need for images of self-destruction and the need to undermine all unifying forms would have attached themselves to some other objective phenomena. The essential point, as always, was to find a way to literalize the fantasies of madness. Madness, when threatened, can only take refuge in intensified madness.

The old pattern was played out with a new psychological twist, however. For the first time, fictional treatments of the issue became popular. While novels and films such as *Fail-Safe* and *On the Beach* catered to the need for literal visions of catastrophe, other artists tried to undermine this literal approach through satire and science fiction (most notably in Stanley Kubrick's *Dr. Strangelove* and Walter Miller, Jr.'s *A Canticle for Leibowitz*). These works drew upon the innate vividness of nuclear fantasies; their popularity demonstrated the deep roots of these fantasies in the wellsprings of psychic imagery. Holding up the mirror to imagination, they threatened to pierce the numbing literalism of Cold War ideology and imagery.

But since all these fictions fell in the category of "mere entertainment," they could not be apprehended as "really real." For many people, they domesticated the Bomb as a familiar prop on the stage of popular culture. At best, they might be taken as calls to action in the literal realm. So they became merely more fragments of stimuli added to the nation's growing collection. Their real message—that the true danger lay beyond the reach of literal reality—could not be heard. Renewed fears of the Bomb thus remained within the orbit of madness. They represented just the next phase in the cycle of schizophrenic images. So the cycle was bound to turn once more. Concretized fears of annihilation inevitably generated more intense apocalyptic fantasies of Cold War triumph. Invulnerable omnipotence had to be affirmed once again as a literal technological possibility. When Herman Kahn urged

Thinking About the Unthinkable, it was more a symptom than a cause of this reaffirmation.

A more significant symptom was the "missile gap" of the late fifties and early sixties, a fabrication promoted by various groups for political purposes.[27] The important point is not the dishonesty of the fiction, but how successful it was. Americans wanted to believe, in the absence of any empirical evidence, that the Soviet Union had a nuclear arsenal stronger than our own. We wanted a graphic literal image of the Bomb's immense danger, but we also wanted to be convinced that we were not responsible for that danger. We wanted to be reassured that the Bomb and the Soviets were still interwoven strands of the same threat, on which the public paranoid fantasy of the Cold War could be strung. The nation's commitment to closing the "missile gap" offered an inviting way to both affirm and deny our fantasies of impending annihilation.

The "missile gap" paved the way for the most memorable nuclear fantasy of the early sixties: the bomb shelter craze. While this too (like all Cold War scenarios) may have been orchestrated by the government and its media supporters,[28] the crucial point once again is that it found such enthusiastic (albeit short-lived) acceptance across the nation. One need only descend below the earth for a brief time, advocates claimed, while the twin evils of fallout and Communism (long merged in the public mind) were disappearing. Then one could emerge into a cleansed, renewed world where America's triumphant power and goodness would be forever unchallenged. The religious overtones of this imagery underscored the nature of our madness. It bid us enter into the earth, the nothingness of pure potentiality from which we came, trapped in a little box. The funereal imagery here implied both sides of schizophrenia—limitless openness and limitless closing off—joined in a literal image of surviving the end of the world. Yet the shelter craze created no coherent or unified form. Though it "drove home the idea of nuclear war as an indescribable catastrophe, while reinforcing murky associations with fantasies of victimization and survival," Weart notes, "it did little to bring the vague imagery into focus."[29]

Perhaps it is no accident that the shelter craze died out at the time of the Cuban missile crisis, when fantasy threatened to act itself out in all too real empirical terms. The missile crisis was the first hint of reality testing to intrude upon nuclear fantasy. But fantasies are not necessarily given up because a disconfirming reality appears. They have a life, and sometimes a death, of their own. The nation as a whole was already deeply ambivalent about the shelter craze. Even many supporters came to doubt its wisdom. Yet firm opponents of the shelter-building movement could not help being fascinated as well as repelled by its seductive promise, and the shelter fantasy has never disappeared.[30]

This ambivalence was just part of a growing national ambivalence toward all nuclear fantasies. In the late fifties and early sixties, terrifying and reassuring nuclear images, pitted against each other in broad public view, were more pervasive than ever. As each fostered the other, the contradictions inherent in all of them multiplied and became harder to hide—or to hide from. In the typical way of madness, each image, taken in its own context, offered an appealing and coherent point of view. But since each undermined the viability of the others, all fell under the shadow of suspicion.

The conjunction of shelter craze and missile crisis may have focussed more attention on these contradictions. The antinuclear activism of the early sixties may have done the same. This activism could not resolve the contradictions, nor could it get the nation to grapple with them, because it could not itself escape them. It became merely another force for literalizing schizophrenic fantasies and another piece in the collage of nuclear images. Yet it also played a key role in bringing the crisis of conflicting imagery closer to a head. It gave a public voice to the growing doubts about the prevailing Cold War fantasies. And it gave a public voice to the end product of fragmented imagination: the typical schizophrenic sense of a world falling apart.[31]

The nuclear imagery of the early sixties made it harder than ever to sustain the social fantasy system. There was a growing feeling that the nuclear age had undermined every fantasy of security. The agencies of the state and all the other familiar structures that had once nurtured the hope of perfect psychic filtering were now called into doubt. The possibility of absolute formlessness hung over every future day, so every change betokened a movement toward trauma. Thus the Bomb told us that we could not risk the freedom of perfect openness to all stimuli. We looked to our nuclear arsenal to fulfill literally our fantasies of perfect security and freedom. But the unique qualities of the Bomb inevitably rendered those fantasies as frightening as they were impossible to fulfill.

These forebodings filled the air with a sense of urgency. The collective fantasy was hard pressed to make room for all its nuclear images; it seemed increasingly difficult, but increasingly necessary, to choose among them. Yet proponents of all positions on the nuclear issue shared an apocalyptic feeling that the world itself was facing some cataclysmic change. From every side, this imagery stressed rapid and radical movement. Madness is inherently ambivalent about such movement. While it wants images that change rapidly merely for the sake of novelty, it also hopes that the changes will stay within its fantasy system. The threat of total transformation—an end of its world—is as frightening as it is enticing. Perhaps, then, nuclear imagery had reached a point where its inherent tensions and apocalyptic implications were threatening too radical a transformation.

The nation may have recognized that it was trapped in a web of contradictory nuclear fantasies, but it saw no way out. It seemed that images of annihilation and omnipotence could only evoke and undermine each other in a ladder of escalation that had no end—except, perhaps, at the top rung on the ladder of literal nuclear escalation. But the schizophrenic knows no refuge from such contradictions except to burrow deeper into madness. When madness is shared throughout society and defined as sanity, the refuge of madness seems even more inviting. The nation's response was not, therefore, to question nuclear madness but merely to question the particular images it had created. The collective fantasy system could be sustained only by finding a new image that could attach itself to changing historical events and shift the focus of attention while reaffirming our loyalty to the state and its nuclear madness.

The model of madness suggests that this new image had to meet numerous requirements. It had to represent an even greater level of destruction. Ontological insecurity had grown to unprecedented dimensions, and images of limitless filtering and limitless openness now existed in the external world as well as in imagination. So it seemed more necessary than ever to destroy both world and self without limit. Yet radical finitude also had to be maintained in the face of the nuclear threat to its reign. The new image had to both sustain and mask the heightened appeal of, and ambivalence toward, religious imagination.

This image also had to reinforce psychic numbing and silence doubts about the viability of both individual and collective false self. To accomplish this, it had to resolve various tensions: between annihilation and omnipotence, freedom and security, numbing and imagery, choice and necessity. Most importantly, perhaps, it had to ease the schizophrenic's classic fear that reality is in permanent flux—that its rapid change, portending radical transformation, is out of control. To meet all these requirements, the new image had to harmonize more symbolic meanings than ever while expressing them all more strictly literally and technologically than ever. It had to image more destruction than before while hiding itself more effectively than before.

8

Nuclear Madness: Deterrence, Détente, and Disarmament

The search for a new image led first to the quintessential image of the nuclear age, the one whose very name betrayed the deepest meaning of the Bomb: MAD. One hardly ever wrote the full name, Mutually Assured Destruction, without appending this abbreviation. The whole world was now encompassed in an immense fantasy of total destruction that seemed quite literally plausible, given the widespread belief in the "missile gap" and the Soviet nuclear menace.

MAD and Deterrence

The new MAD image produced a major change in the Bomb's perceived purpose. During the 1960s, the public came to believe that it was no longer possible to win a nuclear war in any meaningful sense. Now deterring nuclear war (which meant deterring a Soviet attack), rather than winning nuclear war, became the center of the nation's declaratory nuclear policy. Whether it has ever been at the center of actual policy is an open question.[1] But ever since the mid-sixties, the public image of nuclear weapons has been based on the assumption that this declaratory policy was the nation's actual policy as well. Psychologically, the significant point is how quickly people abandoned the tension of annihilation and omnipotence fantasies to embrace deterrence.

The persuasive image of a deterrent "wall" (or "shield" or "canopy" or "umbrella") automatically warding off every threat is just the kind of false self image that schizoids cherish most dearly. The individual who moves into schizophrenia must abandon that image. But a whole society can deepen its madness while deepening its trust in the protection of the communal false self. This is the primary effect of MAD. It gives the impression that the rational ego has taken control again, facing reality and rejecting the dangerous fantasies of the past, while it actually propagates the psychodynamics of madness.

MAD pictures the world living forever on the brink of annihilation, and for that very reason forever safe. Both sides are frozen in a stalemate because each is too petrified of the other to make a move. So it says that we need not, should not, and in fact dare not ask either ourselves or our enemy to give up omnicidal arsenals. The Bomb's devastating power, ordained as the only possible protection against its own threat, is institutionalized as a necessary and permanent foundation of our lives. As Winston Churchill summed up the essence of MADness: "Safety will be the sturdy child of terror, and survival the twin brother of annihilation."[2] Schizophrenics do embrace annihilation and its terror in hopes of survival and safety. This is the essential fantasy of madness: to be threatened by the power of total destruction yet retain total control of that power; to believe that all options have vanished, taking all personal responsibility with them; to see reality as frozen in an immutable, destruction-filled, yet ultimately safe stasis.

Unfortunately the safety is more illusory than sturdy, as the MAD policy illustrates. Deterrence theory must assume that each side will be in rational control of its actions and act in its reasonable self-interest. Without these assumptions there is no reason to believe that even the threat of total annihilation will deter anyone from anything. So the great enemy is not the presumably predictable "other side," but rather "instability"; i.e., anything that is unpredictable and therefore uncontrollable. Yet deterrence, like madness, inevitably increases instability. Schizophrenics fear the stasis of total filtering as much as they crave it, so they are driven to make their lives a chaos of ever new, ever changing, unpredictable stimuli. They make themselves unstable in order to fight against instability. Of course they deny that this is what they are doing.

Deterrence theorists go one step further: they recognize this truth yet ignore what they know. They admit that each side is best deterred when it cannot absolutely predict the other side's response. As the influential theorist Thomas Schelling put it, the brink of nuclear annihilation is "a curved slope that one can stand on with some risk of slipping. Brinksmanship involves getting onto the slope where one may fall in spite of his own best efforts to save himself, dragging his adversary with him."[3] Moreover, deterrence requires that the other side believe that retaliation will follow an attack, no matter how pointless and irrational retaliation seems. Another influential deterrence theorist, Herman Kahn, concluded that "a pretense of unreason is not reliable, and that one must *really intend to do it.*'"[4] Kahn called this policy "the rationality of irrationality." Henry Kissinger understood this; he planned to title a Harvard seminar on nuclear policy "The Political Uses of Madness."[5] These thoughts went beyond the realm of theory at least once, when President Nixon contemplated using his "Madman Theory": he would frighten the Vietnamese into submission by convincing them that he was a reckless madman who would even use nuclear weapons to win the war.[6] Despite this necessary dose of madness, deterrence theory has largely conquered the American mind because its practitioners declare it to be incontestably reasonable.

The supposed rationality of nuclear deterrence also undermines itself because it must immerse the nation in the most fabulous imaginings. The MAD policy has little to do with either side's actual capabilities. It aims to deter only by creating the appearance of a "credible threat" of retaliation under any circumstances, even when it seems mad. Under MAD, the weapons are renounced as a means of attaining victory. Instead they become, more than ever before, symbols to communicate a message of "firmness" and "resolve," underscoring the society's heroic ego fantasies of unyielding all-conquering strength.

So MAD's annihilation fantasy leads the nation to enlarge its fantasy of invulnerable omnipotence while convincing itself that it is doing just the opposite. Both these fantasies, and their unrealistic denial, detach society further from reality, increasing its fears of—and therefore its fantasies of—annihilation. But since deterrence policies obviate the need to choose between omnipotence and annihilation fantasies while promising permanent safety, they create a broad political consensus. And, as always, society can deepen its numbing by acting out and apprehending these public fantasies absolutely literally. It can convince itself even more firmly that nothing need be done, since there is nothing to fear.

The Disarmament Fantasy

Shortly after the Cuban missile crisis and the enunciation of the MAD doctrine in the early sixties, the nation did enter a long period of intense numbing on the nuclear issue, some fifteen years when it was tacitly agreed that little need be done or even said about the subject.[7] In addition to the crisis and the doctrine, a third factor may have contributed significantly to this spell of silence: the confidence generated by disarmament hopes and arms control negotiations. The Limited Test Ban Treaty of 1963 was the first of a long line of treaties that gave the appearance of increasing cooperation between the superpowers. Each of these treaties was hailed as a step toward greater security. On the face of it, this claim seems reasonable; two enemies are less likely to attack each other if they are talking to each other and setting mutual limits on their weaponry. But the model of madness suggests that disarmament and arms control imagery should be seen as one more twist in the nation's nuclear fantasies.

How did the arms control process contribute to security? Not by actually reducing the number or danger of nuclear weapons; in fact, the superpowers' arsenals were much larger and more volatile in the late 1970s, after a series of treaties, than they were in 1962. Rather, arms control helped sustain a fantasy of security. In madness, feelings of security have little relationship to empirical reality; they depend on a fantasy of the self as omnipotent controller of a dead world. The essence of disarmament, when implemented through the arms control process, is to foster a similar image. The forces of annihilation are not removed. But they are declared inert, manipulable, and incapable of acting back upon us. So the word *disarmament* loses its original meaning of "removing weapons" and becomes synonymous with "arms control"; i.e., with retaining and controlling weapons. The problem of survival is thus reduced to a long series of radically finite political and technical problems, and the rational ego, in the person of the experts, is said to be on the way to surmounting every challenge. The whole process ultimately aims at perfect parity—the same mutually petrifying balance that is imaged in deterrence theory.

Over time, the movement toward disarmament has generated its own fantasy world, with no necessary correspondence or relation to ordinary reality. It has become a sort of game, with its own rules, appropriate moves, aims, and rewards. In this game all the fantasies of madness are brought together in apparent harmony. Disarmament is always in the news, and the outcome is always in doubt, yet its fundamental structure remains the same. In the overall scheme of our lives, even the most impressive achievement in arms control becomes just one more piece of news, one more stimulus to add to the collection. In media reports the same key phrases of disarmament jargon, repeated over and over again, became something like ritual incantations, underscoring the sense of static structure that gives the process its greatest appeal. Many of these terms remind us that we are watching a play: the actors take center stage and deliver their lines, all of which must contribute to a show (usually of "firm resolve"). We feel more secure because the Bomb has been removed from ordinary reality and installed in this show, this alternative world filled with immensely confusing stimuli. Yet the media insist, and we generally believe, that the show is a literal reality that has (at least for the experts) some comprehensible order.

At the heart of this apparent order lies a paradox. On the one hand, the disarmament play is a team sport, a contest between Us and Them. Its rhetoric is filled with terms taken from the chess table, the ball field, and the battle field: the players strategize, make their deadly gambits, score points, wait for the opponent to make the next move, and try for the winning move (or the kill) that will outwit the opponent and avoid stalemate or defeat. All this contributes to the air of unreality that surrounds the process. But its primary function is to sustain the social false self system, with its unbridgeable gulf between Us and Them. A chief U.S. arms negotiator once chastized his predecessors because they "continued to believe that the Russians would or could think like us. . . . Unfortunately it is strength alone that the Soviets understand."[8] Every time "we bargain from strength" and "stand up to them," we literalize our fantasies of the enemy: the annihilating threat coming solely from the enemy, our unyielding omnipotence in the face of the enemy, and our ability to stay safely untouched by the enemy.

At the same time, though, the disarmament play acts out the fantasy of tearing down the boundaries between self and other. Both sides join together in moving toward a wholly inert and controllable world, implicitly agreeing that the true enemy is "instability." As long as both sides are playing the game, neither can lose, because this enemy is always on the run. The game can apparently go on indefinitely with no danger to either side. The annihilating power of the Bomb, controlled by the numbing power of technology, is once again confirmed as the only protection against its own threat. No response is required from the average person except passive viewing. Yet the average person feels genuinely more secure, simply because the game is being played.

The disarmament play, which is so widely hailed as the only way out of nuclear madness, seems to be merely another form of that madness. Its apparent rationality hides a web of contradictions as rich as any schizophrenic's. As long as we join the universal chorus of praise for disarmament and arms control, we remain immersed in instability yet convinced that our control has created stability. The world seems excitingly alive, while it is treated as a collection of safely dead objects. The threat of annihilation seems to recede even as it grows. The firm lines dividing Us from Them are demolished yet simultaneously built higher and stronger than ever. The lines dividing fantasy from empirical reality are equally blurred, as we build a world out of our fantasies and then apprehend this world purely literally. So the disarmament process doubly detaches us from reality and fixes us in our psychic numbing. It is a path to "national security" that only leads deeper into ontological insecurity.

The Dual Track and Its Contradictions

Historically, deterrence and disarmament have always gone together. Both became central in American policy during the Kennedy and Johnson administrations. Both came under sharp criticism by opponents of Carter administration policies. Both were first questioned and then affirmed together by the Reagan administration, when the term *dual track* became current to symbolize the natural pairing of the two.[9] Psychologically, the two form a natural dual track as well. Both appear to be reasonable constructive responses to realistic fears. The fears are quite genuine and they are responses to a very real danger. But under the reign of madness, perceptions of danger and the fears they engender are both distorted. The threat of physical and social destruction can be apprehended only in terms of the threat of infinite unreality, so the fears reflect the dual track of madness: total formlessness through either drowning in limitless stimuli or being starved of all stimuli.

The dual track is so appealing because it offers an image of these twin fears that avoids the perceived pitfalls of the classic Cold War imagery. It could eclipse Cold War imagery so rapidly because it solved the problem of the early sixties: to find a new image of madness that would embody more destruction than ever, while masking that destruction by promising safety both for the individual and for the social false self system. It resolves the tension of annihilation versus omnipotence by denying the need to choose between them. It offers assured stasis in the midst of constant novelty. It reaffirms the state and state-sponsored technology as the source of all security. Its all-encompassing imagery offers a rich immersion in imagination while strengthening the numbing power of the heroic ego and its literalizing control.

But the deepest appeal of the dual track may be its capacity to mimic religious images, turning the twin fears of nuclear madness into a twin promise of salvation without breaking the bounds of radical finitude. Its vision of static balance mimics the perfect filtering of religious images. The supposed safety of that vision mimics the perfect openness of religious images. The dual track fantasy plunges us into a world of pure imagination, where everything is possible. It allows all nuclear images to be entertained simultaneously; apparently none need be filtered out or tested for coherence with each other or with empirical reality. Images of a permanently divided world live side by side with images of a unified world where former enemies join together to create a single global order. Images of a resolute national ego prepared for the final battle merge easily with images of a life-affirming national morality always seeking a just compromise.

The dual track is much like a religious ritual. It offers a permanent humanly controlled form that can open up all the endless realities of imagination within enduring structures and thus make anxiety endurable. As a condition of this offer it demands, like all rituals, that it be repeated regularly with no doubts about its efficacy. Yet in popular consciousness the religous and ritual dimension of the process is strictly denied. Madness must continually evoke and then thwart the power of religious imagination. It must also evoke and then thwart imagination's power to create unifying forms. All the dual track images seem held together in a form whose unity creates a broad political consensus. Yet beneath the surface these contradictory images remain disjointed pieces of an "image-salad" intended to stave off, rather than give meaning to, thoughts of impending universal formlessness.

The dual track can only be a caricature of religious ritual and religious imagery. Consequently, the security it provides can only be a caricature of genuine security. In fact, like every madness, it must lead deeper into insecurity. When the dual track superseded the Cold War image, it took on the Cold War's role: it became the new strategy for institutionalizing modernity's schizophrenic fantasies within a rigidly finitized structure. Therefore the dual track repeats the Cold War's psychological pattern. It offers a seductive illusion of protective form for the threat of formlessness while actually compounding our feelings of unreality and thus undermining the very security it claims to provide.

But the dual track adds its own distinctive contribution to this undermining. Promising to save us not through apocalyptic change but through immutable balance, the dual track precludes the possibility of finding any form at all for universal formlessness. The Bomb's destructive power now becomes even more ontologically threatening, for it is nothing but inimical "instability," to be fought without quarter. Our ambivalence toward annihilation, which was once expressed in apocalyptic Cold War imagery, simply disappears from sight. Yet the dual track unwittingly resurrects another ancient religious image: the timelessness and perfect balance of universal stasis. In the context of madness, this image only reinforces our sense of numbed petrification and the ontological threat it implies.

Exchanging one kind of image for another, the dual track approach leads us even deeper into the trap of trying to use the fantasies of religious imagination in order to escape religious imagination. In fact the rigidly rational technological fantasies of the dual track do hide their fantasy quality much better than the Cold War images they replaced. We live more completely and undisturbedly in a fantasy world, convinced that we are "hard-headed realists." In deterrence, nothing matters more to the public than statistical comparisons; in disarmament, nothing is more important than foolproof verification procedures. All this confusion between empiricism and imagination immerses us deeper in fantasy, which evokes a stronger unconscious need to deny fantasy and insist on purely literal reality, further masking the fantasy. The dual track thus erases the line between fantasy and empirical reality even more than earlier images, numbs us even more, and leaves us more bereft of any sense of genuine relationship with reality.

The dual track erases other lines as well. Images of separation and division are now merged with images of cooperation and unification. Choice merges with necessity, for the dual track claims to be the only option open to rational people. Its technological imperatives take responsibility more totally out of human hands, blurring the distinction between human and computerized decision making. Most importantly, the dual track cancels out the difference between order and disorder. It must embrace what it most fears, building its hopes for order upon our prime symbol and agent of disorder, the Bomb.

The dual track may soothe our conscious fears of losing security and freedom because its static images persuade us that no fundamental change is possible. But its inner contradictions remove us ever further from structured reality; they intensify our unconscious intimations that the Bomb will destroy the very value structure it is supposed to protect. Since the dual track is apparently a successful all-encompassing and static structure, it satisfies the psychic demand for adequate filtering of stimuli. But within the framework of madness this raises the possibility of limitless filtering, which creates a countervailing demand for the chaos of limitless openness to stimuli. In the nuclear age, this demand is easily met by images of impending nuclear formlessness, which intensify our psychic numbing. So the dual track leaves us feeling ever more petrified—stuck in an ontologically perilous impasse. By the logic of madness, images of invulnerable omnipotence become fantasies of entrapment that generate fantasies of escape into the endless void.

Historically as well as psychologically, the dual track has served to undermine security and perpetuate the threat of annihilation. Deterrence demands that we have a nuclear arsenal and an element of uncertainty about its uses. Arms control has historically supported nuclear arsenals, calling for more weapons if only as "bargaining chips" and spurring research on new weapons technologies. Yet arms control also threatens to breach the wall of the social false self with its suggestion that "the enemy" may not be such an enemy after all. This suggestion, though welcomed as a hope for security, also raises questions that many would rather not face. Such issues were especially disturbing to the nation during the Vietnam war, when for the first time many Americans began to question the fantasy system that undergirded our wars.

For both historical and psychological reasons, then, the dual track fantasy could not be sustained. It appeared to be our best chance for security because it was the one image that could embrace all others and thus forge a broad political consensus. It promised the psychological security of a social fantasy free from challenge and change. But, like all schizophrenic fantasies, it was bound to undermine itself and evoke a new set of images that would challenge it.

Omnipotence, Annihilation, and the Dual Track Revisited

When a challenge to the dual track policy first surfaced within the government in the early 1970s it went largely unnoticed by the public. Even the announcement of the new "flexible options" policy in 1974 caused little stir, though it was actually a rejection of MAD and a foundation for returning to a "nuclear war fighting" policy.[10] By the late seventies, however, there was a considerable wave of public support for this change, generated largely by the work of the Committee on the Present Danger (CPD), which counted Ronald Reagan, George Bush, and many top officials of their future administrations among its members. The CPD called for a return to "traditional American values," and it stressed the Cold War images of invulnerable omnipotence as the highest symbols of those values.[11]

"Victory Is Possible" proclaimed one of the most influential statements of the CPD campaign.[12] Richard Pipes, a leading CPD theorist, argued that in nuclear war "victory is quite feasible exactly as it is in any military conflict."[13] This return to warfighting scenarios brought with it a renewed fantasy of the social false self system as an absolute and impermeable barrier between Us and Them. All threats of formlessness had to be projected onto the other side. This was accomplished by claiming that Americans' concerns about nuclear catastrophe were manipulated, and perhaps even originated, in Moscow. Pipes, for example, contended that nuclear anxiety was generated by the Soviet Union as part of its plan for global hegemony: "It is designed to translate the natural dread that most people have of war in general and nuclear war in particular into an overwhelming anxiety that paralyzes thought and will."[14] Both omnipotence fantasies and ontological insecurity were projected together onto "the enemy."

This campaign brought the traditional Cold War images of world catastrophe, survival, and renewal back to center stage as literally as ever. But now the scope of that catastrophe was much more immense, since the era of détente had seen a huge expansion of nuclear weaponry. Fantasies of omnipotence were therefore much more satisfying, since there was so much more destructive power to be controlled. Nuclear theory had become as sophisticated as weaponry. The relatively crude fantasies of the fifties were replaced by the dry complex logic of the defense intellectuals in government decision making and (to a lesser extent) in the public media. The rational ego seemed more in control than ever. Beneath it all, however, this revival movement offered a return to familiar collective fantasies of nuclear madness whose enduring appeal was now potentiated by many magnitudes of power.

The enthusiastic response to the CPD campaign, which culminated in the election of Ronald Reagan in 1980, was soon met by an equally intense opposition. In the early eighties, a reinvigorated antinuclear movement publicized the horrors of nuclear holocaust and demanded immediate total nuclear disarmament as the only way to avoid it. The movement cast itself as the agent of reality working against the madness—concretizing the nation's anxieties, giving them empirical grounding, and compelling us to look into the abyss we had so long denied. As a result of this political polarization the nation became as divided over nuclear imagery as it had been in the early sixties or in August 1945. The debate over nuclear policy, fueled by revived images of omnipotence and annihilation, dominated much of public life.

Since the two sides in this debate seemed so bitterly opposed to each other, it was rarely noticed that they shared much in common, for both framed the debate in images rooted in traditional religious apocalypticism (as their predecessors had in the early sixties). Both agreed that the global battle of good against evil created an inherently unstable situation that could not continue forever. Both agreed that this battle necessarily generated an impending crisis of worldwide proportions. Both agreed that the resolution of this crisis would have to lead to a fundamental global political transformation, which would cleanse the world of its greatest moral evil. Both agreed that only two options existed: either absolute nuclear superiority or absolute nuclear disarmament. Finally, both tacitly agreed, for their own political reasons, not to mention the fact that they shared this common ground.

The era of renewed nuclear apocalypticism was short-lived. It did not become highly visible until late 1981, and by early 1984 it was fading from the headlines. Many explanations for this quick decline might be suggested.[15] The Reagan administration, which had spurred nuclear fears with its Cold War rhetoric, acted quickly to undercut those fears. During 1983 it backed away from its talk of controlling and winning a nuclear war, focussing instead on the more moderate dual track image. The disarmament movement could take much of the credit for forcing this change, but ironically it helped the nation retreat into the apparent comfort of numbed indifference. To some extent, disarmament activism was bound to enhance numbing; renewed images of nuclear holocaust threatened to break through the wall of numbing and therefore had to be quickly shunted aside in favor of renewed commitment to the dual track. Added to the fear of holocaust was an equally strong fear of the absolute transformation (whether through war or total disarmament) that both sides seemed to demand. As in the early sixties, the demand for fundamental change made every change seem massively traumatic.

There was also something about the particular character of the antinuclear movement itself that helps to account for the waning of nuclear concern. During the early eighties, the movement quickly translated its demand for total disarmament into a series of specific political programs: a bilateral freeze, removal of Pershing and Cruise missiles from Europe, cancellation of the MX missile program, defeat of Ronald Reagan in 1984, and others. As it gained political skill, it achieved a series of successes. When the US and the USSR agreed to ban intermediate nuclear forces in 1987, disarmament activists once again justly claimed credit for forcing the Reagan administration to change its policies.

The movement paid a high price for this success, however. Just as Mr. Reagan embraced Mr. Gorbachev, the leader of the former "evil empire," so disarmament activists actually embraced their former archenemy, Mr. Reagan, when they proclaimed his INF treaty as a great victory for them. This reconciliation symbolized a dramatic shift in the antinuclear movement. Entering into mainstream politics, it had to abandon the appearance of radical opposition and downplay the horrifying images of global holocaust that had been its central focus. The movement did combat overt fantasies of invulnerable omnipotence, especially in its continuing battle against the Strategic Defense Initiative or "Star Wars" plan. But implicitly (and sometimes explicitly) it accepted the same dual track image that the Reaganites advocated, disagreeing only about precisely where the track ought to be laid. So it joined the Reaganites in turning from images of sudden apocalyptic transformation to images of gradual progress toward a static balance. Its absolute demands for total immediate disarmament were distinctly muted and in some cases inaudible, as it focussed on specific short-term goals. Total disarmament became a distant goal with little relevance to the present situation.

The move into mainstream politics, with its radically limited goals and gains, happened gradually, seemingly effortlessly, and in many minds inevitably. It was accomplished in a very few years with hardly any public agony or even significant debate. If the antinuclear outburst of the early eighties was an attempt to break the bonds of nuclear madness, it fell back into those bonds rather quickly. This raises some questions: Did the antinuclear movement ever really step beyond nuclear madness? Did it bring the nation face to face with nuclear anxieties by forcing it to look directly into the abyss of formlessness? Or was it always confined within the mold of nuclear madness? Did it perhaps offer not a radical challenge to the madness but merely another set of fantasies within it?

Disarmament and Radical Finitude

One way to approach these questions is to look at the movement's two most representative texts of the early eighties, Jonathan Schell's book *The Fate of the Earth* and Nicholas Meyer's film *The Day After*. Both of these texts struggled to make Americans confront the possibility of infinite unreality, and both relied heavily on metaphoric images. In this sense they went beyond the conventional approach of the disarmament movement, which tends to rely on empirical facts and logical arguments. The work of Schell and Meyer was so important, and gained such wide audiences,[16] largely because it evoked images to give three-dimensional reality to the facts. Ultimately, though, their work remained within the limits of radical finitude.

Meyer's images create a depiction of both pre- and postholocaust reality defined by the models of modernity. The preholocaust segment of *The Day After* portrays the collective fantasy at its Hollywood best. The private realm of family life and love is seen as America's sole concern, with the public fact of the Bomb at first little more than background noise. Eventually the public fact explodes into private life, with a long lurid montage of explosions and incinerations. But many viewers saw this climactic sequence as just a variation on a familiar Hollywood theme: the disaster film, which is perennially popular because it offers a shared schizophrenic fantasy of a world in dust and ashes.[17]

The days after a nuclear cataclysm would be filled with much the same modernity as the days before, according to *The Day After*. The possibility of reconstructing public life is left open, but dubious. The viewer is directed firmly to the private realm as the sole arena where meaningful renewal might take place. At the film's end, the preholocaust fantasies of love and family are reaffirmed. A pregnant woman, whose hopelessness had prevented her baby's birth, finally gives birth and smiles tearfully. Two young lovers, who foolishly left their apparently protective bomb shelter, join hands despite the acute radiation poisoning and vow to "go home." In the final sequence, two sick old men embrace amidst the rubble, and then there is only darkness, with a voice asking: "Is anyone there? Anyone at all?" The existentialist dramas of Pirandello and Beckett could hardly have depicted our present, preholocaust ontological insecurity any better. At best, then, *The Day After*'s rain of nuclear terror just exchanges one perspective on the present for another; it gives hardly a glimpse into the future abyss of nuclear extinction. And the elaborate media buildup surrounding the film, which cast it almost exclusively as a political event with emotional titillation, insured its domestication within the familiar framework of modernity's finitude.

Jonathan Schell's work attempts to confront the abyss that Meyer skirts. He assembles copious scientific evidence to describe the "radical nothingness"[18] of nuclear extinction. More than this, he asserts that, "strange as it may seem, we may have to teach ourselves to think about extinction in a meaningful way."[19] But then he offers a subtle logical analysis of the psychological barriers to this project: above all, there is simply nothing to imagine. So he concludes that we can find the meaning of future extinction only by examining the effects of the nuclear threat on our present lives. Schell sees the Bomb principally as a threat to our trust in future life and the endless chain of generations. His debt to Lifton's thought is great (though largely unacknowledged). He adds a deep concern for the "common world" of shared, historical, public life, linking public and private values in a positive way that Meyer's work lacks.

But Schell does not recognize that both the "common world" and the chain of generations might be bound within a radically finite realm of experience, because his own thought is bound within that realm. His highest value is endless continuation of human biological and social life. Posing the issue as endless life versus universal nuclear death, he offers a series of logical arguments to enlist our aid on the side of life. He shows little psychological sensitivity to the meaning of, and perhaps need for, extinction imagery. This is not surprising, because Schell is a spokesman for the rational ego, and the ego must stop short when there is simply nothing to imagine. It can not teach us how to imagine nothing, nor can it find a reason for learning that lesson. The need to face formlessness as a dimension of infinitude is beyond its ken. Much of Schell's great appeal lies in his urgent apocalyptic tone—his echo of traditional religious images that once gave universal formlessness a meaningful place in life. He can not develop this deeper significance of his own work, however. He can find no meaning for extinction because he approaches the nuclear threat in purely logical, not psychological, terms.

Although both Schell and Meyer are masters of symbolic imagery, acutely aware of the power that imagery carries, neither confronts the Bomb and its attendant images as symbolic realities. Both use their own imaginative resources only to grapple with the Bomb's literal threat. For both, the underlying premise is the struggle between physical life and death. Infinite unreality remains the enemy to be fought at all costs precisely because, reduced to purely finite physical terms, it is meaningless and absurd. Neither author can find meaning in absolute formlessness, and neither sees the need to look for such meaning. Focussing only on the nuclear threat, as if it could be disengaged from its cultural matrix, neither can address the Bomb as the emblem of modernity's madness. Neither can bring the nation any closer to finding a form for the threat of future formlessness, nor for the reality of present finitude. It is hardly surprising, then, that the disarmament movement as a whole remained deaf to the symbolic message of the Bomb. So it was carried along in the tide of nuclear madness, readily following the state and its media in the transition from apocalyptic to dual track imagery, because it was never able to understand and thereby challenge the roots of the madness.

The Late 1980s

During the mid-eighties both the left and right moved toward the center on nuclear policy issues because the center was where political success lay. For most Americans, the dual track image had an irresistible appeal. Neither the Cold War fantasies of invulnerable omnipotence nor the reciprocal fantasies of total disarmament could compete, for the dual track offered the best of both with no need to choose between them. It offered a highly satisfying set of images consonant with madness and most conducive to deeper psychic numbing. During the 1980s the nation reprised the first three decades of the nuclear age and reaffirmed the dual track, with its image of static rational balance, as the best of all possible nuclear worlds.

In the late eighties, two notable developments in nuclear imagery helped to strengthen the grip of this consensus. American public opinion saw the Soviet Union as significantly more conciliatory in its nuclear weapons policies and negotiating stances. In the media the image of "the enemy who only understands strength" was replaced by "the enemy that we can do business with" or even "the new friend," and there was widespread talk about "the end of the Cold War." In addition to this, nuclear fears were focussed primarily on the environmental damage caused by the weapons production process. The growing nuclear consensus merged with the growing interest in environmental concerns to create strong political support for "cleaning up" domestic weapons production facilities.

Both of these developments represented new permutations of old images. The "end of the Cold War" recalled the era of détente some two decades earlier. Perhaps it was an effort to resolve the tension inherent in disarmament imagery: the opponent as simultaneously enemy and ally. There were still voices warning that the apparent changes in the Soviet Union's policies were temporary or even illusory (though in the mainstream media these voices were generally perceived as marginal by the decade's end). But even most of the skeptics were urging us to use Our Bomb principally to compel the Soviets to control Their Bomb. So everyone agreed on the most essential points: "instability" was the enemy, and regardless of its source it could be contained by reasonable people acting reasonably. From any point of view, there seemed little reason for a sense of urgency.[20]

The concern about environmental problems also echoed an earlier era: the fallout controversy of the late 1950s. Although the details were different, the central image of radiation as an insidious invisible poison was the same. Yet this renewed concern did not show signs of generating new antinuclear activism, as it did in the fifties. Rather, the prevailing image from the outset was one of government and concerned citizens working together to insure that nuclear weapons would be made cleanly and safely. The question was not whether this goal could be achieved, but only when and how it would be achieved. Both major developments of the late eighties thus symbolized the triumph of the dual track policy's premise that nuclear weapons should, and could, be made safe and safely—that (as Churchill put it) survival should and could be the twin brother of annihilation because we could have a safe Bomb. Regardless of the source of threat, there was little doubt that our expertise coupled with resolute will would make us invulnerable to and omnipotent over it.

The Bush administration expressed the same sense of omnipotence during its first year in office. It acknowledged the need for cooperation with the Soviet Union and for environmental reforms. Yet it embraced virtually all the existing and proposed weapons systems that it inherited from its predecessor, and it continued revising the Single Integrated Operating Plan for nuclear war. Its decisions were justified principally in the name of "modernizing" American nuclear forces to keep up with a purported Soviet modernization program.[21] These matters were duly reported in the media but generated relatively little controversy. On the whole, the nuclear issue was not a primary concern of either the government or the public during the first year of the Bush administration.[22] It appeared in the media almost exclusively as an appendage to concerns about environmental reforms or the political changes in the Soviet Union and eastern Europe, which seemed to confirm the "end of the Cold War" and bring the "safe Bomb" fantasy closer to reality. The modernization image, with its implication of technological progress moving toward a perfectly static balance, fit quite readily into the prevailing "safe Bomb" imagery.

Indeed many Americans believed that we were ushering in a brand new era, an era of cooperation that would make nuclear weapons unnecessary and obsolete. This perception of radical political change seemed to make the apocalyptic mood of the Cold War era equally obsolete. Yet there was a paradox here. The rapidity and scale of the shift in American thinking certainly outpaced the actual events.[23] It was a sort of inverse image of 1945, when Americans were so quick to believe in imminent threat, although the available facts hardly dictated such a belief. In the late 1980s, as in 1945, Americans showed an eagerness to believe in radical global transformation—a transformation of apocalyptic magnitude. So what looked like a rejection of apocalyptic thinking in the late eighties may actually have been just exchanging one kind of apocalyptic scenario for another.

Of course this new scenario was especially appealing to Americans because it harmonized so well with the prevailing image of static balance. All of the apocalyptic destruction was confined to the other side of the Iron Curtain. Most Americans saw the tearing down of that Curtain as part of a much larger destruction: "the crumbling of the Communist empire." Images of apocalypse, American omnipotence, and perfect security were therefore intimately linked. Similarly, environmental concerns were expressed in images of global decay, defilement, and disintegration, which are typical of traditional apocalyptic rhetoric. The issue was sometimes seen as the challenge of "saving the planet." Yet this apocalypticism, too, was rendered tolerable and even welcome because it was framed within a vision of the triumph of the heroic ego's technical expertise—a triumph that would cleanse the earth and redeem it forever from its peril.

Retrospect and Prospect

Looking back over the history of images in the nuclear age, a pattern begins to emerge. The era began with a battle between images of the new Bomb as savior and as destroyer. For about a decade (late forties to late fifties) the savior theme was dominant, then for about half a decade the battle of images was fought out again. For nearly twenty years, therefore, all nuclear perceptions assumed that some sort of apocalyptic transformation—whether through war or total disarmament—was imminent. The tensions inherent in this assumption were resolved by the dual track image and its promise of a safe Bomb, which has prevailed ever since, except for the brief renewal of the battle of images in the late seventies and early eighties. (It seems that the nation can endure the battle of opposing apocalyptic images for only about three to five years at a time.) The conventional view that the nation must choose between pro- and antinuclear stances is thus somewhat misleading. Since the mid-sixties at least, the true choice has been between the apocalyptic assumption that the Bomb must bring a radical transformation and the alternative dual track position, which denies that any radical change is either necessary or desirable. Both of these positions, with all their ever-changing permutations, have been pressed into the numbing service of nuclear madness.

By the end of the 1980s, however, nuclear madness had reached a new stage. The dual track image had encompassed apocalypticism and found an apparently safe place for it in the prevailing "image-salad"; it had created the image of a risk-free apocalypse that did not threaten but rather enhanced "stability." For the time being, at least, it seemed as if the drive toward a unified form for nuclear imagery had finally attained its goal.[24] The heroic ego itself provided the foundation for the comprehensive structure it sought—a structure that seemed to be unchallengeable and therefore immutable. A vision of slow, steady, technological progress toward perfect stasis prevailed. With images of transformation successfully domesticated, a radical transformation of the social and political structure now seemed not merely undesirable but unthinkable.

This success meant the most perfect fulfillment yet of the model of madness—the most perfect integration yet of images of global destruction and images of invulnerable omnipotence. So the essential elements of apocalyptic imagery had not disappeared. They had merely been drawn into the all-encompassing orbit of the communal false self system. Following the logic of a public madness, the fantasies of absolute change once harbored within the true self had been absorbed and deadened by the public false self; their sense of risk and the madness they betoken had been effectively masked, for the time being at least.

But the logic of madness also dictates that this new form will bring greater ontological insecurity. Not only does it detach the nation from the reality of continued weapons production and nuclear threat, it also locks the nation more firmly into the vicious spiral of psychic numbing, petrification fantasies, and a deepening threat of unreality. And precisely because the inherently dynamic, unstable, and foreboding qualities of apocalyptic images are repressed, they are more likely to flourish unseen and eventually return in literal form to generate new avenues of nuclear madness. If the political consensus of the late eighties suggested the possibility of a coherent form for the threat of formlessness, it also portended, by the logic of madness, the need for a new wave of imagery to dissolve the illusion of secure structure and a new vision of total transformation to dissolve the illusion of immutable stasis.

What might follow the dual track image is hard to say. Perhaps the pendulum will swing back toward Cold War imagery (as in the late 1970s) and then again toward the dual track, as each generates a desire for the other. If so, then some revival of a more apocalyptic perception is to be expected (perhaps fueled by the approaching end of the millennium). It may turn out, though, that the reprise of Cold War imagery under the Reaganites was its swansong—a brief retesting of images once found wanting, which confirmed again that dual track imagery was indeed the preferable option. If so, then the dual track will eventually have to be eclipsed by some new version of nuclear imagery.

A New Nuclear Image?

At the beginning of the 1990s, one new image was beginning to suggest itself, albeit very tentatively. With the apparent "end of the Cold War," some public images began to picture the Bomb as an irrelevant anachronism, like old guns in the basement that should be thrown away because the children might get hurt playing with them. At the same time, environmental concerns brought to the fore an image of "cleaning up the mess." These two sets of images could easily combine into a persuasive image of nuclear weapons as a kind of litter or rubbish. We might easily tell ourselves that, like the old guns in the basement, we are definitely planning to get rid of them soon, but we just haven't gotten around to it yet (and anyway no one has gotten hurt so far).

In such an image the Bomb is no longer seen as the fulcrum of planetary political balance; indeed it has no political function at all. If the Cold War is really over, then it seems that the Bomb can not be used. Removed from the arena of dynamic human conflict, detached from the vagaries of human decision making, it is seen as totally inert. It is treated like a gun with no bullets, like mere matter, or perhaps like dirt waiting to be washed away. So the Bomb becomes more than ever a purely technical problem to be cleaned up by the experts; it becomes a target for the heroic ego and its vision of progress. This would naturally heighten the ego's fantasy of security through perfect control. Since progress means slow, steady, careful work (with perfect verification at every step) any lingering hint of urgency is taken out of the whole issue.

If this image were to come to prominence, it would give the Bomb yet another unconsciously maintained religious meaning. The Bomb would retain its apocalyptic dimension, though now merged into the general category of planet-threatening pollution. In many religious traditions there is a great concern for polluting impurity, which is often treated as if it were an almost material dirt. Cleansing may mean restoring natural or social order—a token of the perfect structure that every psychic image seeks. Some traditions (including Christianity) give impurity a philosophical interpretation as a mark of human finitude and mortality (the stain of sin). To wash it away is to gain, or regain, a sacred status beyond finitude—the limitless openness that every psychic image seeks. Indeed the whole Western apocalyptic tradition has sometimes been interpreted as an image of cleansing the world. But in this tradition the stain of sin, far from being an inert object of manipulation, is the mark of that very dynamic and religiously charged character, the devil.

An image of the Bomb as polluting rubbish would therefore intensify its dynamic apocalyptic symbolism, while at the same time reducing it to an inert stasis that undermines that symbolism, especially when it is treated in purely literal terms. The

Bomb's imagery of annihilation would be heightened. Therefore it would be more insistently repressed, effectively rendered unreal, and treated as if it did not exist. Once again, the Bomb would mimic the two elements of a religious image while negating its religious meaning; the quest for perfect reality would once again be evoked and simultaneously denied.

The appeal of this new image would be considerable, for it would satisfy all the requirements of any new nuclear image. It would confirm the social false self system in its illusion of omnipotence, as the heroic ego takes upon itself the power to destroy the most powerful reality ever known. It would therefore generate a greater imagery of global destruction while offering an even more convincing assurance of survival, and it would do all this in absolutely literal technological terms. The new image would also harmonize easily with existing images. The arms control process could be understood as a "clean up," and it would seem perfectly logical to keep a deterrent force "just in case." The abolition of nuclear weapons would therefore be postponed indefinitely, and the acutalities of nuclear policy and production would simply be swept under the rug. So the threat of unreality would mount and ontological insecurity would grow, as would the threat of annihilation. The unifying form, denying any meaning to this impending formlessness, would harbor the seeds of its own undoing. An image of the Bomb as rubbish would fulfill the prediction of the model of madness: that every new nuclear image will lead us more deeply into nuclear madness.

It is easy to imagine the nuclear debate of the early 1990s framed between two competing images: the Bomb as rubbish and the Bomb as a high-tech gadget requiring constant modernization. Since both these images reinforce the prevailing "safe Bomb" fantasy and its hope for immutable static balance, neither would challenge the foundations on which the dual track is laid.

The Dilemma of the Disarmament Movement

This raises a critical question for the nuclear disarmament movement: Can it offer a meaningful alternative to this madness? Most disarmament activists now tacitly embrace the general principles of the dual track approach. When they oppose particular nuclear weapons policies, they usually argue either that the policies endanger the strategic balance and chances for arms control, or that the weapons are unnecessary for deterrence and therefore redundant. The apparent rationality of the dual track is so convincing that no alternative can be imagined. Moreover, it seems to be working; most disarmament activists have also embraced the general mood of optimism abroad in the land and look forward to participating in "cleaning up the mess." So their apocalyptic imagery and absolute demands for immediate disarmament, which had growing political appeal just a few years earlier, are now virtually forgotten. Accepting the political mainstream's promise of a new era of global harmony and peace, they have joined in forging the comprehensive form that strips apocalypticism of its dynamism in the name of gradual progress toward perfect stasis.

At the same time, though, they are beginning to suspect that things may not be what they seem. The actual progress toward reducing nuclear armaments is agonizingly slow; activists may wonder whether this is due, in part, to some reluctance on the part of their government to match rhetoric with policy changes. And there is little evidence that actual policy for using the existing and planned weapons systems has changed significantly at all.[25] The disarmament movement has difficulty seeing these ambiguities, and when it sees them it cannot explain them. It remains stymied because it does not recognize that its analysis of past and present and its policies for the future are founded on the same basic premises as the conventional wisdom offered by the state: moral resolve and enlightened rationality.

Antinuclear activists cast their appeals largely in moral terms, proclaiming that "if you love this planet" (or "humanity," or "your children," or any one of several other moral values) you should convert to the antinuclear cause. At the same time, they advocate literal knowledge of literal facts, assuming that enough accurate facts combined with clear logical thinking can produce the moral conversion they seek. Behind this approach is the prior assumption that all people are logical and can eventually be shown the logical convergence of morality and self-interest. Yet the movement's limited success to date casts doubt on the pragmatic value of this approach and on the fruitfulness of its assumptions. The movement's apparent successes (such as the popularity of arms control negotiations) only indicate how easily it is absorbed into the fantasy system that numbs the nation and propagates the nuclear threat.

Indeed it seems that the antinuclear movement is asking the public to root itself more firmly in the same cultural milieu that produces nuclear madness. So it poses no challenge to the fundamental structures of the culture. It does sometimes challenge the technological "quick fix" fantasy, but it mounts that challenge in the technical terms dictated by those who produce and deploy the weapons. And its alternative is another fantasy (which James Hillman would call another monotheistic fantasy) of reason and will mobilized to vanquish moral evil. The essential image remains: "the winning weapon" could defeat the enemy's threat of annihilation, if only we had the will to use it. The rational ego might have to use a different tool, but it does not have to abandon its belief in its own total control. Nor does it have to abandon the radical finitude of its literalizing "hard-headed realism."

The antinuclear movement, treating the fantasy world of the nuclear experts as the only true reality, pushes the nation further toward unreality. It helps to repress the fantasy images of nuclear madness because it fails to engage those images as fantasies. Repression inevitably makes images more fascinating, more compelling, and perhaps more indispensable. Even most of the activists themselves seem bewitched by the undeniable richness, intricacy, glamour, and sheer power of nuclear imagery. To judge from their literature, which is filled with the most detailed journeys into this imagery, they are generally content to explore new byways within its familiar boundaries.[26] They seem caught in the grip of the unique quality that is "absolutely essential to the notion of archetypes: their emotional possessive effect, their bedazzlement of consciousness so that it becomes blind to its own stance."[27] When archetypal fantasies seem to be so literally real, so eminently reasonable, and so dedicated to a safe Bomb, they are all the more difficult to resist.

Refusing to recognize the role of fantasy in nuclear politics, the disarmament movement cannot see the struggle over nuclear policy as essentially a struggle over fantasy images. So it cannot see the link between its former apocalyptic imagery and its former place in the national headlines. It cannot see that apocalyptic images, by their very nature, created a demand for immediate and drastic movement that propelled support for total disarmament. Nor can it see the link between its present support for incremental arms control and the perpetuation of the nuclear threat. It believes that it is working to end reliance on the Bomb in the only logical way. In fact, though, its policies work psychologically to foster reliance on the Bomb, because they reinforce the nation's commitment to the dual track and its "safe Bomb" fantasies. Every arms control agreement and every cleaned up weapons factory is viewed by the public as simply another step toward a risk-free nuclear arsenal. The nuclear fantasies of the early nineties all converge on an image of stasis that offers no motive for, and perhaps no possibility of, a transformation as radical as the abolition of nuclear weapons.

This is obviously not what the disarmament movement intends; its conscious aim is to persuade us that we will not be safe as long as we have the Bomb. But it cannot see the counterproductive consequences of its day-to-day activities because, in its pursuit of "hard-headed realism," it cannot see the psychological facts that are so central to the nuclear age. Failing to distinguish between dynamic and static images, the movement cannot even consider what kind of images it should foster. It cannot understand how its embrace of static imagery represses the desire for genuine change. It cannot understand how the desire for change, deprived of any conscious political expression, can only express itself in the psychological underworld of madness. And it cannot consider what the antidote to nuclear madness might be, for it has no theoretical conception of that public disorder at all.

The antinuclear movement might be able to offer a truly alternative analysis if it approached the issue in psychological terms. Yet it has generally relegated psychology and the role of images to the periphery of its concerns. Even when antinuclear thought does attain psychological sophistication and acknowledges the centrality of imagination—as in the work of Robert Jay Lifton—it remains caught in the bonds of radical finitude. Lifton recognizes that the nuclear dilemma has religious roots, and on occasion he looks to religious sources to confront the dilemma. He advocates "imagining the real," borrowing a phrase from the religious philosopher Martin Buber. For Buber, such imagining is a key to the I-Thou relationship, which opens one up to a sense of infinitude.[28] But for Lifton it seems to mean only a literal mental reconstruction of a literalized future scenario. Similarly, Lifton has touched on religion's capacity to form eschatological images of nothingness and world renewal, suggesting that a parallel capacity is necessary today. But again he advises literalized imagination: "Nuclear nothingness [is] literal nothingness. . . . Literal nothingness may be a contradiction in terms. Yet nothingness can be suggested, approached."[29] The implication here is that the more literally it is approached, the better (even though on the very next page Lifton notes that when eschatological imagery is literalized it comes disturbingly close to the terrain of schizophrenia).

So disarmament activists still stand within the bounds of radical finitude and therefore within nuclear madness, which remains in its essentials unchallenged. From inside that madness, nuclear proponents and opponents appear to stand at the two ends of the political spectrum. But an observer looking in from the outside might see the two groups standing just slightly to the left and right of the center of the spectrum. As long as the debate remains so essentially fraternal, there is little likelihood that the prevailing assumptions can be challenged. This is precisely the numbing effect of literalism: its power to bind us to the given and blind us to alternatives. Despite the political successes of the antinuclear movement and the popular success of works like *The Day After* and *The Fate of the Earth*, disarmament images can still be swallowed up into the potpourri of public fantasy because they fit so easily into that fantasy.

The antinuclear movement thus has no foundation for opposing the essential premise of the state's national security policies, which is also the essential premise of madness: to keep on propagating ever-new and ever-changing images of annihilation while insisting on our own invulnerable omnipotence to the growing threat. With everyone except the so-called lunatic fringe agreeing on the dual track as the only reasonable course, its irrationalities are buried deeper than ever, and so are the seeds of anxiety hidden within it. The broad political consensus nourishing those seeds leads the nation further away from reality and deeper into the ontological insecurity of nuclear madness.

The model of nuclear madness leads to a rather pessimistic vision of the future. This pessimism may be tempered a bit, however, by its inability to predict the specific shape of our madness. Modernity and the nuclear age are historical phenomena, constantly subject to unpredictable changes. Just as they began in specific historical conditions, so we can imagine other conditions bringing them to an end. R. D. Laing contends that madness, too, is a historical process—an initiatory journey through death to new life. Once begun, he says, the journey must be followed through to its end. If he is correct, then we cannot simply choose to throw off our madness. Laing's view holds out the possibility of a radically new kind of madness, consciously acted out in a public form. But it is not clear what that new form might be. One way to explore this possibility is to return the psychology of nuclear madness to the domain of ultimate concern and deal directly with the religious meaning of the Bomb by looking at it through the eyes of a historian of religions. Perhaps it will turn out that merely interpreting the religious aspirations hidden in nuclear madness will open a path to both a new form of madness and a new, more peaceful, life.

Part III
Madness and Transformation

9

The Meaning of the End of the World

Few historians of religion have been as influential or as controversial as Mircea Eliade. The controversy centers principally on the question of method in studying the history of religions. For Eliade, the history of religions as an academic discipline entailed not only recounting specific religious developments, but also uncovering universal and unvarying patterns of religious experience, which he believed hold the key to the essential structures of all human experience. This emphasis on universal patterns has often been criticized. Other historians of religion have little difficulty finding errors in Eliade's treatment of their own special areas. Some suggest that Eliade molded (or perhaps even distorted) the data to fit his schema—a schema that did not arise inductively from the data, these critics contend. So there is some doubt whether his studies lead us to the historical, objectively verifiable truth about the world's religions.

There is little doubt, though, that Eliade created an imaginative and thought-provoking model of what he called *homo religiosus*—humanity in its unvarying religious dimension. As a model, it can be neither verified nor falsified by empirical research. It may be best understood as a mythical being sprung from a great scholar's imaginative encounter with the world's religions. But homo religiosus is equally a product of Eliade's encounter with modern Western culture. In Eliade's work there is always a sharp distinction between homo religiosus and modern man—so sharp that the image of homo religiosus often seems drawn largely in the service of a cultural critique. This is not surprising, since Eliade's early career was dominated by his passionate quest for the "new man" who would live a spiritually richer and more genuinely human life than Western modernity would allow.[1]

So the terms *homo religiosus* and *modern man* may both be taken as ideal types. Eliade's depiction of modern man sums up the shortcomings he found in the urban bourgeois society of his youth. Homo religiosus is essentially his vision of an alternative to that society, illustrated by but not necessarily derived from his study of the history of religions. Understood as hypothetical constructs rather than objective realities, both these concepts can be useful tools for delving further into nuclear madness, and especially for understanding nuclear madness as an initiatory journey.

The Human Situation

Eliade's images of homo religiosus and modern man are grounded in a philosophical and psychological analysis of the foundations of human existence. For Eliade, as for Tillich and Laing, the critical issue of life is the problem of limited personal reality. This problem is articulated, he contends, in the ubiquitous myths that speak of humanity's fall from a primordial state of perfect reality in which all opposites were harmoniously united. Mortal, sexed, and condemned to work, humanity now recognizes its condition as a limited existence bound within a network of opposites: body and spirit, life and death, time and eternity, up and down, near and far, order and confusion. Realizing that we are limited by—and condemned to choose between—dualities, we recognize that our own reality, like every specific reality, is less than the sum total of all possible reality. To counter this sense of limited reality, we identify ourselves with the sum total of the given reality that we can comprehend; i.e., we see ourselves as part of a cosmos. As long as that cosmos maintains its reality, our own reality feels secure.

But the reality of the cosmos itself is never perfectly secure. We always sense that there is something more, something not included in our present cosmos. So we experience life as a tension of what is now real—the cosmos—against what might possibly be real but is now unreal. The unreal is by definition unknown and uncosmicized; it is formless chaos. The tension between reality and unreality is manifest in society as a conflict between "our world" and "their world." "Our world" is always the familiar cosmos in which we can orient ourselves and find meaning and value. "Their world" and its inhabitants always embody the universal threat of absolute formlessness. No threat is more fearsome, for it is not only one's own existence but reality itself that is at stake. Every human being, whether consciously or unconsciously, "thirsts for *being*. His terror of the chaos that surrounds his inhabited world corresponds to his terror of nothingness.... If by some evil chance, he strays into it, he feels emptied of his ontic sustance, as if he were dissolving in Chaos."[1a]

The cosmos/chaos polarity is the root cause of the one mark of the human condition that Eliade stresses above all others: our awareness of temporality. If there were either perfectly static order or perfectly complete disorder, there would be no change, and thus no awareness of time. As long as there is both cosmos and chaos, however, "our world" is constantly (though usually quite slowly) being undermined by, and slipping into, unreality, which transforms it into a new reality. So it is the cosmos/chaos dynamic, not time itself, that wears away all realities, causing suffering and anxiety. Beneath a human being's existential concern about temporality and the contingency of the self lies a deeper concern about unreality and the contingency of the cosmos.

The threat of chaos is generally manageable as long as the cosmos has relatively stable structures to defend against chaos. There are times, however, when these structures, and the viability of the cosmos itself, are called radically into question. According to Eliade, such an "existential crisis... puts in question both the reality of the world and man's presence in the world."[2] Although acute existential crises may be rare, an existential crisis is always latent in human existence, simply because we are temporal beings who always face the threat of incipient chaos. Eliade also invokes Freud to affirm that every individual unconsciously remembers an ideal state of perfect reality as a personal experience—"the 'human primordial,' earliest childhood. The child lives in a mythical, paradise time."[3] Compared to this primordial perfect reality, every moment of present existence, marked by the conflict between cosmos and chaos, can only appear relatively unreal. Thus some sense of unreality is with us all the time. When the structures of our cosmos, our buffers against unreality, are seriously threatened, this latent crisis breaks out into the open.

What every human being desires, naturally, is some guarantee of a permanent reality that is immune to all change; i.e., a reality that transcends time. The cosmos itself cannot offer such a guarantee because there is always chaos beyond its border portending the possibility (and usually the actuality) of conflict, change, and time. A permanent reality must therefore encompass both cosmos and chaos and reconcile the conflict between them; it must embrace both the existing reality and the unreality of pure possibility. And it must reconcile these polarities on a universal scale. Any image of reality that excludes chaos, or includes only a limited part of the chaotic realm, leaves reality polarized between cosmos and chaos and allows the threat of greater chaos to continue. Thus it leaves the door open to change and temporality. Only in the universal harmonizing of cosmos and chaos can time be transcended and one's personal reality assured.

Cosmos versus Chaos: The World of Modern Man

The essence of modernity, Eliade believes, is that it lacks any effective means to satisfy this fundamental human desire for permanent reality. Modern man[4] asserts that only those events taking place within the flow of historical time are real. Indeed he knows no other time. So he remains unaware of any eternal, "really real" reality that might offer a secure grounding for his own evanescent reality. His ignorance of his existential plight makes that plight all the more desperate.

The crux of the problem is that modern man cannot find any positive meaning in experiences of chaos because he does not accept the possibility of a coincidence of opposites. Therefore when his reality is threatened he can only seek to defend his world by fighting against chaos. The possibility of a coincidence of opposites can only appear to him as a further threat to his world, since the order of that world seems to depend on radical resistance to chaos. This radical resistance is evident not only in overtly military wars against foreign nations, but in all the wars that modern man fights: the war against nature, the war against disease, the war against drugs, the war against poverty, and all the other wars, all modelled on the traditional image of war against a foreign nation. Whenever he is faced with the possibility of disorder, modern man raises the wall higher and wider between his cosmos and everything outside it. In this unending state of conflict the gap between cosmos and chaos grows ever wider, the coincidence of opposites becomes ever more unthinkable, and the possibility of any transcendence of time vanishes.

Modern man's problem is compounded because he confronts the question of the meaning of chaos, if he confronts it at all, in purely private terms. He apprehends his imaginings only as individual attempts to correlate order and disorder in his own inner life. Upon entering the public realm of work, education, politics, and the like, he must leave all questions of ultimate meaning behind. Because he always understands his crises as crises of the individual self, he cannot apprehend his inner images as implicating all of reality. He lives without consciously affirmed images to reconcile cosmos and chaos on a universal scale. So his attempts to stave off the unreality of chaos leave him unable to secure his own sense of reality. Feeling increasingly drained of personal reality and vulnerable to chaos, he evokes the existential crisis that he fears.

Modern man values his secular life, nevertheless, because it seems to guarantee him individual freedom and collective progress as he "makes history." But Eliade questions both of these apparent values. History today, he asserts, "tends to be made by an increasingly smaller number of men"[5] who impose their will upon the masses. The protagonist of Eliade's novel *The Forbidden Forest* (living through the same historical crises as the author himself) says: "All Europe's behaving like a monstrous robot set in motion by the news . . . We're slaves of history. . . . In the long run it's sterile. . . . It enriches no one; we discover nothing really worth being discovered. . . . History is invigorating and fertile only for those who make it, not for those who endure it."[6]

Ultimately, though, Eliade questions whether anyone today is really free to make genuine changes in the world. Genuine changes require a willingness to accept the death of the status quo. But modern man's fear of chaos means a refusal of all death: "In the modern world, Death is emptied of its religious meaning; that is why it is assimilated to Nothingness; and before Nothingness modern man is paralyzed."[7] For modern man the disappearance of any structure threatens the dissolution of all structure. Consequently he clings to every structure that now exists in his world. He rigidly opposes truly transformative change—i.e., total change—even as he seems to embrace constant change. His passion for tiny incremental changes, which he calls progress, is part of his defense against total transformation. Movement in any direction seems more dangerous than stasis. The status quo, no matter how dangerous, is affirmed simply because it is the status quo.

For Eliade, Mephistopheles, not Faust, is the paradigmatic modern man. Mephistopheles stands for the numbing which is death in life: "In place of movement and Life he tries to impose rest, immobility, death. For whatever ceases to change and transform itself decays and perishes. This 'death in Life' can be translated as spiritual sterility; it is, taken all in all, damnation."[8] Since modern man lives constantly in the face of nothingness, he is condemned to be constantly paralyzed. So his belief in both freedom and progress are illusory. In his paralysis, he can do no more than fulfill his biological needs and material desires, like a robot endlessly repeating rote actions. He can do no more than live like an ant. "I see man crushed, asphyxiated, diminished by industrial civilization. . . . After a long mythological period, and a short historical period, we are on the threshold of a biological (economic) period. Man will be reduced to the condition of a termite, an ant. . . . For several generations, or, perhaps, several thousand years, men will live like ants."[9]

For Eliade, the tragedy may extend beyond human life. One of his fictional characters speculates that "all of cosmic life suffers and withers because of the indifference of man toward the essential problem. By forgetting to ask the right question, by wasting our time on futilities or frivolous questions, we not only kill ourselves, we also sterilize a portion of the Cosmos and cause it to die a slow death."[10] And the "right question" for our time would seem to be: What is the meaning of the end of the world? Because we fail to ask this question, we and our world remain inert: "We are paralyzed because we are missing the meaning of the end of the world. Like Seneca, the men of today believe that 'after death there is nothing'—that death itself is nothing"[11]—nothing but our own private and utter extinction.

As moderns, we cannot ask the right question because we have forgotten how to ask any questions of universal meaning. The paralysis of our death in life is a compound of our failure to find meaning in chaos and our failure of imagination; much of the richness of Eliade's critique of modernity lies in the connection between these two failures. Our questions now reduce the world to literal material reality, he contends, because we are at war with uncertainty and instability: "The explanation of the world by a series of reductions has this aim in view: to rid the world of extra-mundane values. It is a systematic banalization of the World undertaken for the purpose of conquering and mastering it. . . . It is an idiosyncrasy of Western man.'"[12] Imagination reveals our innermost images as ambiguous, nonrational, and uncontrollable. It reveals the unreality we fear welling up inside ourselves. For those who do not understand its structures, it appears to be a confusing chaos; a religious image especially "seems absurd when one takes it in the literal sense."[13]

Since our commitment to controllable structure is so extreme, we can see no positive value in imaginative, multivalent representations of a multidimensional reality. We can only experience them as the threatening not-yet-real of pure possibility. So we literalize. We demand a single, conscious, rationally consistent meaning for each image, a meaning that is partial and incomplete and therefore, Eliade contends, necessarily false. The symbol cannot reveal its true meaning in modernity because the whole person—body, feelings, and imagination as well as conscious thought—is debarred from grasping it as a whole. Confining us to limited realities, this literalism confines us to a world of inert materiality, pure temporality, and irreconcilable conflict between opposites. It rules out the harmonization of cosmos and chaos that could allow us to imagine perfectly secure reality. Our literalism is thus an intrinsic part of our rigid stance toward reality, our war against disorder, which may be at root a war against the pure possibility of imagination. But this war only compounds our dread of chaos as an omnipresent threat and makes existential crisis our daily norm. All our attempts at coping turn out to be self-defeating attempts that exacerbate the problem, because we do not consciously know what the problem really is.

Cosmos and Chaos: The World of Homo Religiosus

What alternative is there to the dilemma of modernity? Eliade's studies in the history of religions can all be understood as a response to this question. All invite the reader to imagine a radically alternative way of life, which Eliade ascribes to homo religiosus. For Eliade, to be sure, homo religiosus is premodern man—a historical reality confirmed by empirical data. But his own critique of literalism should warn his readers not to take this picture on its own literal terms. It should be accepted as a hypothetical construct, a creative image of a possible way of life rather than a depiction of the historical past.

The existential situation of homo religiosus is defined by the same threat of chaotic unreality that faces modern man. But homo religiosus, as Eliade imagines him, can consciously acknowledge, confront, and withstand the existential crisis, in both its latent and acute forms, because his way of life is based on the exercise of religious imagination.

"Most of the products of imagination have a 'religious' significance. That is to say, they have related to primordial *excellence* a religious dimension."[14] Imagination always tends to have religious meaning, Eliade points out, because imaginative acts, like religious images, create an ideal realm (an "excellence") that transcends the givens of empirical reality. Imagination can comprehend logical opposites in a paradoxical unity and thereby make the impossible appear possible. Their sense of unlimited possibility resembles a primordial chaos, but the very fact that imagination shapes possibility and gives structure to the chaos of mental flux endows imagination with cosmogonic powers. An imaginative act, in short, founds a new world, which is why imagination opens up a "primordial excellence." In this new world, the formlessness of pure possibility is harmonized with the emergence of an enduring structure.

Not all imaginative acts have a fully religious dimension, however, in Eliade's view. An image of primordial excellence becomes a religious symbol only when it "*imitates* the exemplary models—the Images—reproduces, reactualises and repeats them without end. To have [religious] imagination is to be able to see the world in its totality."[15] "Religion is the exemplary solution of every existential crisis. Religion 'begins' when and where there is a total revelation of reality. . . . The sacred is the exemplary in the sense that it establishes patterns to be followed: by being transcendent and exemplary it compels the religious man to come out of personal situations, to surpass the contingent and the particular and to comply with general values, with the universal."[16] For homo religiosus every reality that does not imitate a paradigmatic pattern is precarious and evanescent. Only the eternal patterns, repeating the creative events of the "timeless time" before profane historical time began, are genuinely real. These sacred events are narrated in myths. Repeating the myths, homo religiosus reenters the enduring era of origins. He reaffirms the reality of his cosmos as sacred and eternal because it is founded on the paradigmatic and universal.

If this affirmation is to endure existential crises, however, it must give a meaningful place to chaos in paradigmatic and universal terms as well. A "total revelation of reality" must transcend all time and change. Therefore it must embrace both total cosmos and total chaos simultaneously. Of course religious imagination can not simply wish away the radical difference between cosmos and chaos. Homo religiosus knows that their conflict, and the change it brings, are inescapable—that every reality must come to an end because it is worn down by time. And he believes that "life cannot be *repaired*, it can only be *re-created* by a return to its sources."[17] But those sources always involve some form of chaos. So chaotic formlessness can take on positive meaning as the prelude to totally new life.

> Any form whatever, by the mere fact that it exists as such and endures, necessarily loses vigor and becomes worn; to recover vigor, it must be reabsorbed into the formless if only for an instant; it must be restored to the primordial unity from which it issued; in other words, it must return to "chaos."[18]
>
> We can talk of the positive value of periods of shadow, of times of large-scale decadence and disintegration. . . . Just as death represents a positive value in itself, so do they; it is the same symbolism as that of larvae in the dark, of hibernation, of seeds bursting apart in the earth so that a new form can appear.[19]
>
> The Water of Death is preeminently killing: it dissolves, it abolishes all forms. That is just why it is rich in creative "seeds."[20]

As all forms dissolve into chaos they pass their "energy" into the chaotic state, which embodies the limitless possibility that existed in the beginning, offering an infusion of novelty, growth, and regeneration. So every creative, renewing, or healing act must begin by returning to the unreality of chaos. But this dissolution of forms can only be religiously meaningful if it is imagined on a universal scale; the reality of the cosmos can be guaranteed only by the end of the world.

The Meaning of the End of the World

The possibility of the world's end is neither new nor shocking to homo religiosus, for he acts it out periodically in his rituals. At the New Year festival and other critical times, he annuls the effects of time and history by symbolically returning to the primordial chaos and then reenacting the birth of a new world—a paradise where perfect order is guaranteed yet all things are possible.

> These myths of the End of the World implying, as they do in clearer or darker fashion, the re-creation of a new Universe, express the same archaic and extremely widespread idea of the progressive "degradation" of a cosmos, necessitating its periodical destruction and re-creation. . . . The essential thing is not the fact of the *End*, but the certainty of a *new beginning*. Now, this rebeginning is, properly speaking, the counterpart to the absolute beginning, the cosmogony. . . . It was possible to accept the idea of the apocalyptic destruction of the World because the cosmogony—that is, the "secret" of the origin of the World—was known.[21]

In religious terms the expectation of the end of the world is, above all, an affirmation that things need not remain the way they are—that the sins, sufferings, and weariness brought by time can always be abolished because time itself can be transcended and thereby regenerated. Since the origin of the world is a timeless reality enshrined in timeless myth, the birth of a new world is an eternally available possibility. So, in describing a myth about the periodic world-destroying fire, Eliade speaks of the "optimistic character of these ideas. In fact, this optimism can be reduced to a consciousness of the normality of the cyclical catastrophe, to the certainty that it has a meaning, and, above all, that it is never final."[22] Homo religiosus knows that universal chaos is a necessary part of a cosmic or historical pattern and that his myths and rituals are essential to the pattern. "In the final instance, the religious man comes to *feel himself responsible for the renewal of the World.*"[23]

For homo religiosus "the terror of the end of the world has never . . . succeeded in paralyzing either Life or culture,"[24] nor is the threat of death paralyzing. Since death is homologous with the end of the world, it implies an opening onto the pure possibility that enables the birth of a new world of perfect reality. So death represents the freedom for total transformation—the freedom to transcend time, death, and the human condition and experience the possibility of a paradisal mode of existence. For homo religiosus this is the only true freedom. As

Anisie, the old sage who represents the outlook of homo religiosus in *The Forbidden Forest*, puts it: "All the other rights that history struggles to gain definitively—liberty, for instance, or respect for the individual—are just a preamble to the only right that is truly inviolable, the right to immortality. . . . We have to hope that someday, here, we shall recover the primordial Adamic condition, that we shall live not only in Time but also in Eternity."[25]

The price of recovering eternity is to endure—and evoke, if necessary—the end of the world. This is never an easy price to pay. Chaos remains for homo religiosus the daunting realm of absolute unreality, the nothingness where one would lose one's ontic substance and die if not rescued by the ordering powers of cosmos. Cosmos and chaos thus have a complex dialectic relationship in Eliade's system: they oppose each other yet each is the prerequisite for the other and so they generate each other, in a never-ending cycle. Homo religiosus is understandably ambivalent to both cosmos and chaos. But his ultimate ideal is always the *coincidentia oppositorum*, the harmonizing of opposites that would allow him to transcend temporality altogether.

A sacred symbol offers a resolution to existential crisis precisely because it embodies all the contradictions of cosmos and chaos, and the resolution of those contradictions, on a universal scale. Ontologically, a sacred symbol must express a vision of absolute formlessness as a universal possibility. Psychologically, it depends on an exercise of religious imagination: an experience of one's most genuine psychic reality, which simultaneously demands an experience of the not-yet-real of pure possibility. Only such an immersion in unreality can dissolve all existing structures and enable the emergence of a new world. Only the risk of psychic chaos, experienced in universal ontological terms and understood as the means of transformation to new cosmos, can harmonize cosmos and chaos on a universal scale.

This is the basic paradox of religious imagination: the existential crisis must be intensified to its utmost if it is to be resolved; the feeling of relative unreality must be made absolute before it can be transcended; to transcend one's innate sense of unreality means not to escape it but to accept it and give it meaning. Thus homo religiosus is at one with modern man in having to face the perpetual threat of existential crisis. The essential difference between the two is that homo religiosus consciously expresses and responds to the immutable facts of the human condition in his religious life. Modern man is homo religiosus totally unconscious of himself, his proper mode of being, and the potentially religious meaning of his images.

As moderns, lacking all conscious access to religious imagination, we know no possibility of an absolute ontological transmutation. We do not know that the unreality of pure possibility can serve as a prelude to the perfect reality of paradisal freedom. We cannot endow chaos with universal meaning because we have shut ourselves off from religious imagination. But we refuse to open the gates of religious imagination because we are afraid of the chaos that seems to await us there. For Eliade, modernity is an existential crisis defined by this circular trap. It may be fruitless to ask which came first: the fear of chaos, the desire for control, or the closing off of religious imagination. All are interdependent strands of a single web. Today we remain largely unaware, on the conscious level, of this web, and so we deepen the existential crisis.

The Ambiguities of the Bomb

Although Eliade rarely made public judgments on specific political issues he did offer many observations on contemporary affairs, always interpreting them in terms of the tension between modern man and homo religiosus. The importance of nuclear weapons did not escape his notice. In his journal he recorded these remarks of a colleague:

> Eric Heller was telling us about the depressing impression that he got at a conference of microphysicists he attended last summer. These scientists find no meaning in the creation or in existence. Life, according to them, is nothing but simple randomness. Hence according to Heller, their unconscious desire to put an end to life on earth; they feel guilty for having reached this point, for having completely "demystified" the whole creation, and they want to expiate their sins by destroying the whole world with a few superbombs. If nothing has any meaning, it's just as well to end it definitively.[26]

If the nuclear scientist is indeed the paradigmatic person of modernity, then these remarks might be valid for modern man in general.

Eliade did not lay all blame at the door of science and technology, however. Another journal entry at about the same time notes: "Cosmic cataclysms (floods, earthquakes, fires) are also known in other religions. The cataclysm provoked by man, as a *historical being*, is the contribution of our civilization. The destruction, it is true, will be possible only thanks to the extraordinary development of Western science. But the *cause* or *pretext* of the cataclysm is found in man's decision to 'make history.'"[27] But in Eliade's theory modern science and the decision to make history both grow from the same root—the loss of religious meaning for both cosmos and chaos when the two are permanently sundered.

In an interview nearly twenty years later, when asked to respond to the chaos, the cruelty, and the "terrible myths of modern man," Eliade replied: "The transcendent values are now absent. The horror is multiplied, and the collective slaughter is also rendered 'useless,' by the fact that it no longer has any meaning. That is why such a hell is a true hell: its cruelty is pure and absurd cruelty."[28] He saw this destruction of meaning as a direct parallel to nuclear destruction: "It is very possible that our heritage . . . may be despised, ignored, and even destroyed. It goes without saying that atomic bombs can destroy libraries, museums, and even whole cities in a very real way. But a particular ideology, or ideologies, can annihilate them equally well. Perhaps that is the truly great crime against the spirit."[29] Eliade's thought suggests that world-destroying weapons are only a symptom of modernity's world-destroying ideology: the paralyzing ideology of individualism and material progress that pits cosmos unalterably against chaos and therefore demands to be taken literally.

In at least one place, Eliade suggested explicitly that the nuclear threat should be understood in the context not only of meaninglessness and cruelty but of madness. In *The Forbidden Forest*, Anisie contends that contemporary history is "the quintessence of zoological cruelty. And this new cruelty, this historic cruelty, doesn't even have the excuse that animal cruelty has—that of being committed by instinct. So if you would be objective you wouldn't be too saddened by the fate awaiting humanity. Because it is 'humanity' only in name. In reality, it's a zoological species driven mad by its so-called freedom to fashion its own destiny."[30] Stefan, Eliade's alter ego, asks: "Are we doomed to death because the world is guided today by a handful of ambitious madmen?" Anisie replies: "The flaw is more ancient. Our downfall began long ago, very long ago in fact. Hitler, Stalin, and the others are just agents through whom the disintegration hastens its own process. If it were not they, there would be others." Here, as in Eric Heller's comments cited by Eliade, there is a disturbing theme of crime and punishment introduced into the discussion of nuclear holocaust. If modern man is nothing but a vicious mad animal, does he really deserve to die? If Anisie, who speaks on behalf of homo religiosus, also speaks for Eliade, this would seem to be the latter's view.

Even more disturbing is Anisie's apparent indifference to the prospect. He tells Stefan that the immediate future "promises a devastating series of wars and catastrophes destined to reduce to dust everything that history has built in the last several thousand years." For modern man, committed to history, this is "undoubtedly catastrophic. But there exists another kind of humanity besides the humanity that creates history. There exists, for instance, the humanity that has inhabited the ahistoric paradises . . . the world that we encounter at the beginning of any cycle, the world which creates myths." Anisie, speaking for this ahistoric humanity, concludes optimistically: "I have every reason to hope that the annihilation of our civilization, the beginning of which we are witnessing already, will definitely close the present cycle. . . . Perhaps such annihilation will allow the other type of humanity to reappear. . . . Only what comes after is important. . . . The few who survive will recover the true dignity of man." Does this mean that Eliade, in championing his vision of homo religiosus, actually accepts or even welcomes nuclear catastrophe?

The matter is not so simple, for he expresses another view through Stefan, who objects to Anisie's opinion: "I too dream of escaping from time, from history, someday. But not at the price of the catastrophe you forecast. . . . I believe—I even hope—that an exit from time is possible even in our historic world." Stefan's words point to the specifically Christian type of homo religiosus, as Eliade understands it: Christians believe that the world and its history should be preserved because "historical experience is capable of reaching the perfection and bliss of the Kingdom of God."[31] But if the end of history should come, Christians can accept it in largely the same optimistic terms as the "pagan" Anisie. Eliade recounts this incident in his journal: "Last week, to the 'Fireside' students who were questioning me about the atomic bomb, I replied: A Christian shouldn't fear the bomb too much. For him, the end of the world would have a meaning. That would be the Last Judgment."[32] Christians must preserve the world and its history precisely because they are waiting hopefully for the end of the world and its history. These two dimensions of Christian faith, mirrored in the dialogue between Stefan and Anisie, probably reflect Eliade's own inner dialogue, wavering between hope and dread at the prospect of nuclear catastrophe.

This inner dialogue was clearly expressed during an informal seminar in 1982.[33] Asked to respond to the nuclear threat, Eliade stressed the wide dissemination of myths about world destruction and renewal. He commented that a historian of religions "must be optimistic" for two reasons: first, because his source materials are filled with images of regeneration, and second, because these images and their endless reinterpretations testify to the inexhaustible creativity and freedom of human imagination. He noted the parallel between this optimistic mythic vision and the widespread belief that some people would survive a nuclear holocaust.

Yet he commented cryptically: "Personally I don't believe this." And he stressed that a historian of religions must work to prevent everything that endangers human historical existence, precisely because the historian of religions has such unique awareness of the great achievements of human imagination. Eliade also voiced the opinion that the greatest threat might come not from nuclear catastrophe, which is avoidable, but from technology's destruction of the environment. This possibility troubled Eliade deeply, not only because it might be unavoidable, but because it has no apparent echo in religious traditions. In contrast to the image of sudden apocalyptic disaster, it seems to elude imagination's capacity to bestow meaning. As always, Eliade's primary concern was for the question of trans-historical meaning in historical events.

This persistent concern for religious imagination may be the key to Eliade's seemingly ambiguous responses to the nuclear threat. As a literal possibility, the image of nuclear catastrophe no doubt caused him to feel dread. Yet his responses often seem detached, as if he were considering the whole issue from a perspective beyond history and its suffering, as if he were somehow exempt from that suffering. Like Anisie, Eliade did not confront the threat of the end of human history in literal terms, for he saw literalism as itself the source of the threat. He felt compelled to become a spokesman for homo religiosus, to look constantly beyond the literal and always ask the "right question": the question of symbolic meaning, and especially of the symbolic meaning of the end of the world.

In Eliade's views the ancient flaw that has reduced us to a zoological madness—the fall into secular time and the banality of technological literalism—prevents us from asking this question. Thus it robs us of our true dignity, which consists in creating and comprehending the trans-historical meanings that spring from the deepest recesses of imagination. So we remain paralyzed in the face of the nuclear threat because we are missing the meaning of the Bomb—the meaning of the end of the world—and, as inveterate literalists, mistake the concrete symptom for the disease. Eliade hoped that we might eventually learn (in part by studying the history of religions) to exercise religious imagination, gain a new sensitivity to symbolic meaning, and thereby open up a trans-historical perspective, the only perspective that could save us from the deadly consequences of modernity.

Correlations

Eliade did not develop a specific psychological theory to correlate with his analysis of cultural phenomena. But his theoretical model does incorporate all the central elements drawn from Lifton, Tillich, Laing, and Hillman to create the model of nuclear madness presented here. In fact his work recapitulates those elements quite conveniently. Homo religiosus' need to live in a perfectly secure sacred cosmos reflects the innate psychic desire for perfect filtering, while his need to immerse in chaos reflects the desire for perfect openness to all stimuli. He recognizes that either of these desires fulfilled without the other can lead to pure formlessness. Yet he feels ontologically secure enough to open himself to his own most genuine reality—his religious imagination—and take its inherent risk of formlessness. He can endure the anxiety of this risk because he believes it possible for all his desires to be harmonized in the hierophanies that ground his life in publicly shared religious images of infinite reality. These hierophanies provide a meaningful form for universal formlessness, integrating chaos in a cosmic structure that can support, rather than cripple, the formative process. They assure him that the formative process is never permanently blocked on its path toward religious images.

Modern man, on the other hand, is caught between the inescapable desires for cosmos and chaos because he can not reconcile them. Like the schizoid, he sees the trap as the only alternative to the void. So he traps himself in the increasingly rigid structures of the social false self system and its radical finitude. Although Eliade does not use the term "radical finitude," it is clearly congenial to his analysis, which sees modernity reducing the infinite possibilities of imagination to the very limited possibilities of the ego's technological literalism. Yet, as Eliade indicates, modern man's war against the void leads him to embrace the unreality he fears in its most literal form—the Bomb.

This is the psychodynamic that is acted out in nuclear madness, as schizoid fantasy turned public policy becomes our only reality. The schizophrenic is surprisingly akin to homo religiosus. Both desire a perfect structure that can open up the limitless possibilities of imagination. Both are irresistibly drawn to this realm of infinitude and both experience it, with all its desires and risks, on a universal scale; both identify the possibility of their own formlessness with universal formlessness. Unlike homo religiosus, however, schizophrenics cannot give meaningful form to universal formlessness. They have no symbolic means to acknowledge what their true desire is, so they do not dare open themselves to the formlessness of pure possibility that they secretly crave. The more they fight against the imagination's threat of unreality the more unreal they feel, and the further they retreat into numbing fantasy. They are paralyzed because they are missing the meaning of the end of the world.

With no grounding in religious images, we are caught in the same kind of self-destructive pattern as the clinical schizophrenic. In Eliade's opinion, all the images of schizophrenic fantasy are equally valid images of our "normal" lives: endless openness, engulfment, implosion, invasion, disintegration, entrapment, desolation, and petrification. He sees us trapped in the annihilating narrowness of our own limited world. He consistently speaks of the world of time and history, the only world we know, as a "closed" world; without "an 'opening-out' into the transcendent, one would ultimately become suffocated in any culture."[34] And he suggests that we feel crushed and asphyxiated by industrial civilization. Yet because our world is built on such ontologically insecure foundations, we feel thrown into a chaotic void, engulfed by a world disintegrating beyond our control, and left desolate. We fear imminent invasion from unknown terrors, yet we are too petrified to contemplate fundamental change. Eliade's fictional alter ego explicitly expresses his fear of suffering this paralyzing fate: "I don't want to grow old, to turn into a mineral spiritually, and then one day to die."[35] Yet this is just the path that Western culture has entered, in Eliade's view. And, like schizophrenics, we experience this as the path not only of our individual lives but of the entire world. We experience the annihilation of our own reality as the literal annihilation of the world.

As Eliade restates the essentials of the model of madness in his own terms, he also adds a crucial insight about the meaning of the madness. The homo religiosus that he imagines does more than just accept the risk of formlessness in opening up religious imagination. He recognizes that the formative process, in moving toward religious imagery, requires periodic experiences of pure formlessness. Eliade's theoretical model can accept Lifton's view of psychic forms and images as inherently unstable. The struggle between cosmos and chaos is reflected in the struggle enacted within every image between the desires for limitless filtering and limitless openness. Periodically this struggle threatens to overwhelm the psyche with either totally rigid structures or a total lack of structures.

But homo religiosus believes that psychic images, like life itself, can not be repaired. They can only be destroyed and created anew by opening up religious imagination, where anything is possible, and immersing in formlessness. As long as this process is grounded in a religious image that affords a universal pattern, it unfolds within the context of infinitude and avoids the dangers of neurosis and madness. Since homo religiosus is "continually dying countless deaths in order to be reborn to something else," immortality and the perfection of eternity "ought to be conceived as a limiting situation, an ideal situation towards which man is straining with his whole being, and that he strives to attain by dying and resurrecting continually."[36] On this view, the movement of the formative process is not a steady progress. Rather it is an endless cycle of dissolutions and new creations.

These continual transformations harmonize cosmos and chaos, giving a glimpse of the ideal of perfect openness within perfect structure. They lead to a trust in the possibility of a new experiential state, beyond time and the tensions that mark the human condition. (This seems to be what Lifton is seeking, though not attaining, with his notions of grounding, symbolic immortality, and experiential transcendence.) For Eliade, all the pathological images cited by Tillich and Laing, which reflect our shared existential crisis, can also be signs of such a religious transformation if they are grounded in a religious image. In his studies of initiation[37] all the fantasy images of impending formlessness appear as symbols of the coincidence of opposites that the schizophrenic seeks: a universal death that promises permanent life. We distort these images into madness, however, because we cannot consciously apprehend them as religious symbols.

Secularization and Shamanic Initiation

In his journal, Eliade described modernity's plight in these terms: "The ugliness, the boredom . . . are, with nihilism in philosophy, anarchism in social ethics, and violence in political activity, the expressions of a single, specific existential situation of man in Western societies. The unprecedented success of hallucinogenic drugs among the young illustrates the same syndrome."[38] The relevance of hallucinogenic drugs in this context is not immediately apparent. It was explained in a lecture, "Waiting for the Dawn," which catalogued many examples of contemporary fear of impending nuclear, technological, and environmental doom. But Eliade also catalogued counterexamples of an optimistic faith in technology's ability to transform life drastically for the better. The essential point, he maintained, was not the literal accuracy of any of these predictions but the message shared by all: the world as we know it, "our world," cannot continue as it is, so it must soon come to an end. Some sort of global transformation—for better or worse—must be in the offing. Taking the viewpoint of homo religiosus, Eliade saw us clinging to and acting out images of annihilation precisely because of their unacknowledged messages of spiritual renovation.

The interest in hallucinogens is one such unacknowledged message, in Eliade's opinion. Another is the growing interest in studying the values and experiences of homo religiosus. He saw the "most *creative* encounter" with homo religiosus, at least in the United States, in "the recent discovery of Shamanism by artists and the youth-culture. . . . Probably such interest was incited in great part by the fascination of the youth-culture with hallucinogens, especially LSD. . . . A part of contemporary youth tries to reactualize an archaic, prehistoric technique, even if the results are, medically speaking, more or less disastrous."[39]

The shaman's experience can be equally disastrous, by modern medical standards. In the course of learning his techniques of ecstasy, the shaman must suffer much the same tortures as today's schizophrenics. He may have to descend to hell and be entombed, burned, cut up, frozen, and the like, and he will insist that these things happened quite literally. But when the shaman is seen as a prototype of homo religiosus, "his physical pains and psychomental disorders represent a series of initiatory ordeals; his symbolic death is always followed by a 'resurrection' or a 'rebirth,' manifested by his radical cure and by the appearance of a new, more structured, stronger personality."[40] The shaman's mind, dissolving so that it can be renewed, clearly imitates the paradigmatic model of all disease and healing: "The 'return to chaos' is, for a man of the archaic culture, equivalent to the preparation for a new 'Creation.' *Now, the same symbolism is discernible in the 'madness' of the future shamans, in their 'psychic chaos'; it is a sign that the profane man is on the way to dissolution, and that a new personality is about to be born.*"[41]

Through his madness, the shaman emerges mentally stronger and wiser. Since the initiatory descent into Hell

> symbolizes regression into Cosmic Night as well as into the Darkness of "madness" where all personality is dissolved . . . then we understand why Darkness also symbolizes Wisdom, why the future shamans ought to first know "madness," why creativity is always in relation to a certain "madness" or "orgy," unifying the symbolism of death and Darkness. . . . The sacred science is only accessible in the course of or following the process of spiritual regeneration achieved by the initiatory death and rebirth.[42]

The shaman does not gain his vocation merely because he "goes mad," however, but because he uses religious imagination to endow his madness with meaning—because he apprehends madness in terms of a universal exemplary pattern and is thereby healed. He is regenerated and acquires the sacred science because he understands the meaning of his own death and rebirth as a reflection of the meaning of the death and rebirth of the world.

In "Waiting for the Dawn" Eliade suggested that the contemporary interest in shamanism and hallucinogens could be understood in this context of homo religiosus' fundamental desire for initiation: "Such an 'existential' interest in shamanism and the awareness of the psycho-mental risks involved in hallucinogens, may have another consequence in the near future: helping contemporary Western man undergo sickness (both physiological and psycho-mental) as a series of *initiatory ordeals.* In other words, any affliction could be considered and 'realized' as an 'occasion' for the integration of personality and spiritual transformation: that is to say, the contemporary equivalent of traditional initiation."[43]

From the perspective of homo religiosus, the interest in hallucinogens, along with nihilism, anarchy, violence, and the images of schizophrenic fantasy, represent our existential situation because all bespeak our desire for perfect reality through dissolution and transformation. But when this dissolution is effected by madness it has a special meaning, as Eliade interprets it: it bespeaks a desire for shamanic descent into the wisdom of religious imagination, "the world in which *everything seems possible.*"[44] To those outside it, the road into this world of pure possibility can only look like the dead-end road of madness. To those who endow it with religious meaning, however, this road leads to the healing of madness.

In his interpretation of hallucinogens and shamanism the two lines of Eliade's critique of modernity converge. Madness, he implies, can be a road to meeting modern man's two great intertwined needs—access to religious imagination and a positive meaning for universal chaos—if we choose to adopt the standpoint of homo religiosus and grant it religious meaning. We can overcome our paralysis by consciously employing religious imagination to find symbolic meaning in our fears of, and preparations for, the end of the world. If this is the ultimate message in Eliade's thought, it is certainly a radical one. It calls for nothing less than dismantling the false self system of modernity and opening ourselves to the domain of the sacred, which is the domain of infinite possibility. In other words, it calls for the same kind of confrontation with imagination that occurs in schizophrenia. Ultimately it calls upon us to embrace our madness as a consciously chosen and consciously understood destruction of our cultural, social, and political world, in order to save our world and ourselves.

Secular Politics and Sacred Meaning

Is such a turn to religious imagination possible? Eliade offers both encouraging and discouraging responses. He is discouraging when he emphasizes modernity's radical lack of symbolic religious meanings. His analysis seems to lead to a catch-22: there can be no religious imagination unless we take the risk of entering into imagination's chaos, but we will not take that risk unless we find positive meaning in chaos, and we cannot find positive meaning unless we open up religious imagination. Perhaps this is why he has little to say explicitly about how these meanings might be regained, except through the study of humanity's religious past. He certainly did not imagine homo religiosus as a model that we might follow. Implicitly, though, he is encouraging when he asserts that religious imagination always generates new symbolic images in response to existential crises. His theory contends that the desire for perfect reality through religious images can be repressed or denied, but never eliminated. It predicts that as existential crisis grows, the imagination should produce copious images of a total religious solution to the crisis.

Eliade's interpretation of the data fulfills this prediction. He stresses the abundant initiatory imagery not only in modern dreams and daydreams, but also in private leisure pursuits and entertainments, where their religious meanings usually remain unnoticed. Yet he has also written that myth "will never disappear; in the collective life it sometimes reasserts itself with considerable force, in the form of a political myth."[45] "Certain 'religious' forms can easily fail to be recognized as such. . . . For example, it is possible that certain movements, apparently political on the surface, are coming into being now or are already expressing the desire for a certain profound liberty; such movements could be transpolitical, or could become so, but not be recognized as such."[46] This suggests that our public political images embody the same desire as our private images: homo religiosus' desire for absolute freedom through total transformation.

Moreover, the distinction between private entertainment and public politics has grown increasingly dubious in recent years. Most Americans get nearly all their experience of the political process, and indeed of the historical process in general, through the media. When Americans turn on the television to watch a recounting of the day's events, do they get "hard" news or mere entertainment, historical happenings or symbolic images? It is difficult to say, for the line between the two is becoming more and more obscure. The anchormen who bring history into our homes every evening sit almost like divinities, enthroned above all mundane events. Their ironic Olympian style invites (and perhaps compels) us to share their attitude, which paints a rich coating of imagination upon every event and casts doubt on the meaning, and even the reality, of all they report. Television's growing trend toward "infotainment" shows, which treat the most serious subjects in the most entertaining manner, makes the distinction between news and entertainment even more dubious. And as politicians rely more and more on TV images shaped by advertising agencies and media consultants, are they offering political discourse or entertainment? Again, it is difficult to say.

These transformations of the political-historical process by entertainment's mythic qualities provide one avenue for approaching the perspective of homo religiosus in the public realm. Perhaps our perception of supposedly secular events has always had a mythic dimension. But in the nuclear age, when our historical existence itself rests on a weapon that seems to most people so fantastically unreal, the mythicizing of history has reached new heights. Eliade's thought suggests that we can and should apprehend our political life from the perspective of homo religiosus. We can and should find profound religious meanings hidden in the public political phenomena of the nuclear age.

Eliade often speaks as though those meanings already exist in our minds, affecting us unconsciously and waiting to be rediscovered consciously (which he sees as the primary task of historians of religions). This claim is a hypothetical assumption that can never be empirically proven. Historians of religion can only prove that a specific image has had a certain meaning for some people in the past and therefore is able in principle to convey that meaning. Eliade himself suggests this alternative view when he says: "All we need to do is specify what a hierophany *could mean* or could not mean."[47] On this view the unconscious can be seen as a reservoir of possible—rather than inevitable—religious meanings. The religious meaning of a phenomenon is neither objective nor subjective; it is a potentiality inherent in the relationship between subject and object.

Historians of religions can surely demonstrate, for example, that madness has symbolized universal chaos to some people at some time. They can also demonstrate that on certain occasions of existential crisis this symbolism has offered a resolution by harmonizing the conflict between structure and disintegration. This hardly entitles them to assume that madness must unconsciously function the same way today. But it does reveal a previously unrecognized symbolic meaning that madness could have—if we consciously choose to embrace that meaning.

Most of Eliade's own interpretations of contemporary phenomena (like most of his studies in the history of religions) rest on the questionable hypothesis of universally valid unconscious meanings. Yet his studies and interpretations are a rich resource for new understanding, since they demonstrate what each phenomenon has meant at some time and therefore "*could mean*" again. So his more extreme theory of universal invariant meanings can serve as a creative tool even if viewed as a useful fiction. It can help create very variable but potentially religious meanings that can exist today. The following chapter will adopt Eliade's methodology in this spirit to explore the symbolic meanings of nuclear weapons.

Approaching the Bomb and nuclear madness as religious symbols need not deny or diminish their empirical political and social meanings. In the dialectic of the sacred, a profane phenomenon that becomes a religious symbol retains all its ordinary qualities while it is simultaneously charged with extraordinary meaning. Nor does this line of interpretation necessarily redeem these phenomena of the nuclear age. They remain as destructive as ever. If Eliade is right, though, viewing them from the perspective of homo religiosus as if they were religious symbols may be a way to redeem ourselves from the destruction they portend, for this is a way to open up religious imagination and allow us to bestow meaning upon our images of the end of the world. The first step on this way is to do what homo religiosus always does when the end of the world is at hand: to recite and reflect upon the story of the beginning.

10

The Myth of Nuclear Origins

Homo religiosus seeks the religious meaning of every phenomenon by asking about its origin. He finds the answer to this question in a myth. A myth, in Eliade's view, is essentially a story about how things came to be. Current political views and the news reports that feed them are also shaped by mythic stories. Perhaps we, too, yearn to know about the time of origins, the time when things were brand new and therefore freshest, purest, strongest, and most real.[1] When Americans consider the nuclear age, the time of beginnings—the years around 1945—certainly exercise the greatest fascination. Probably more has been written about that era than about all the other years of the nuclear age combined.[2]

The Text of the Myth

Is there a prevailing myth of nuclear origins, a consensus about what happened at that original time? There are surely many disagreements about details, but it seems likely that most Americans would generally agree with the following broad sketch:

It all began when Hitler's demonic forces set out to conquer the world. Had they succeeded, many lives would have been lost, but more importantly democracy and freedom would have been lost. Indeed the demonic forces would have undone the work of enlightened civilization; the world as we know it, governed by the rule of law and basic norms of morality, would have disappeared. So we committed all our energies to an all-out war against the Nazis.

It so happened that just at this time technological progress had reached the brink of a dramatic breakthrough: the possibility of releasing the energy bound up in the nucleus of the atom.

This possibility was as yet known only to a handful of scientists and government leaders. It was clear to them that whichever side in the war first achieved this breakthrough might very well become invincible. It was absolutely vital that we achieve it first, no matter what the cost. So a secret city was built in a remote wilderness, and the nation's leading scientists were gathered there to pursue a single mission: to build an atomic Bomb before the enemy could do the same.

As it turned out, the Nazis never came close to building an atomic Bomb of their own, and by the time our Bomb was ready for use the war against Germany had already been won. Yet the war against Japan raged on, and the Japanese appeared to be even more barbaric and dangerous than the Germans. It seemed that only a full-scale invasion of Japan could insure the extermination of evil, but this invasion would cost millions of lives. The bombs dropped on Hiroshima and Nagasaki saved those millions of lives and secured the victory of democratic civilization over its most potent enemies. To insure the fruits of this victory the allies created the United Nations, an organization intended to reconcile opposing political forces, thereby uniting the world in peace and freedom.

Yet the end of the war did not bring an end to the threat, for a new demonic force arose to replace those that had just been defeated. And as soon as the secret of the Bomb became public, it was clear to all that an unprecedented new danger was now part of our life—a threat of massive nuclear destruction that could some day be turned against our own nation. So the victory of good over evil brought joy mixed with, and often overshadowed by, uncertainty and fear of another war, one that might very well mean the end of civilization as we know it, the end of "our world."

This story can be understood in terms of its basic themes: the context of war against the enemy; the overriding motive of saving lives and saving the values of our civilization; the technological prodigy of a weapon of unprecedented power; the secrecy surrounding the weapon; the hope of unifying the world peacefully under a single political structure; the foreboding sense of doom and the possibility of the end of the world. These themes have remained central in our perceptions of the Bomb throughout the nuclear age. Other themes have arisen, but these few continue to form the context in which those others find their place. Most Americans still believe that some form of nuclear arsenal is necessary because of enemies who might threaten our civilization. Of course the war against those enemies has been a Cold War, and in that most Americans see lives and our civilization being saved; there is a widespread belief that nuclear weapons have prevented a major "hot" war from erupting. Nuclear technology remains almost as awesome, remote, and secretive as it was in 1945. There is a continuing hope for political arrangements that will permanently avert the threat of "hot" war. Yet the sense of fear and impending doom certainly remains. So the myth of nuclear origins does provide a key to understanding public attitudes in the nuclear age.

This myth is, to all appearances, a story of a well-intentioned effort that produced unintended consequences. Our total devotion to saving life and noble values has somehow, by a cruel twist of fate, placed both values and life itself in peril. This is surely how the myth is usually understood. But Eliade suggests that we can understand the deeper meaning of our own myths only by following a three-step process of careful analysis. First, each element of the myth must be examined in terms of the universal symbolic structures underlying it. Second, each element must be set in its cultural-historical context, to see how the universal structures interact with unique historical events. Third, these findings must be linked together to provide an overall interpretation of the meaning of the myth. This three-step process will yield a deeper understanding of the myth of nuclear origins.

War and Warriors

The story of the Bomb begins in the midst of a global war. The religious meaning of war appears most clearly, Eliade suggests, when war is seen as a form of ritual hunting. Warriors commonly perceive their enemies as animals, both nonhuman and charged with demonic power. More importantly, perhaps, warriors assimilate themselves to animals, drawing on the hunter's experience of "mystical solidarity" with his prey. Traditional warriors, like hunters, often wear animal masks to signify their transformation, to show that they have been initiated into the secrets of their trade and raised to a higher spiritual state. As they go out to war, they leave ordinary profane time behind and return to the time of origins. They imitate the primal deeds of a divinity or mythic hero—often the slaying of a dragon or monster—and thereby establish a new, pure world. Offering up their victims as a sacrifice, warriors renew life with a bloodshed that sacralizes both their world and themselves. They feel that they live in a perfected reality, freed from the weaknesses and limitations imposed by the human condition. This religious meaning of war persists in large measure for the losers as much as for the winners. War is actually a meeting of two bands of wild animals; the battlefield slaughter is actually an immense animal sacrifice in which both sides cooperate in offering up the blood that renews the world.

Both sides also cooperate in generating creative heat. Acting like wild animals, they work themselves into a frenzy and develop a furious heat that is the special mark of their superhuman status. Heat, for homo religiosus, is a creative force that brings new life. The more fiercely the enemies compete, the more heat is given off by their clash. But this clash need not be with lethal weapons. Sacred wars can be fought by many means, even with words alone. Every contest, whether a duel, a race, or a battle of epic poets, stimulates sacred power and revitalizes life.

Nevertheless the two sides are opponents and must remain so if there is to be a war. War is a confrontation that plunges the world into the depths of chaos—of bloodshed and social frenzy—yet in the process evokes the experience of a new and perfect cosmos. The very act of evoking chaos is simultaneously the act of protecting cosmos against the forces of chaos. The act of identifying oneself with the enemy one kills is an initiation that generates greater life. War thus mirrors the intricate interplay, and ultimately the union, of cosmos and chaos more readily than perhaps any other human pursuit. Where else as well as in war can we act out our ambivalent feelings toward both cosmos and chaos in a single experience that renders all our feelings a meaningful unity?

Mythic Meaning in World War II

According to Eliade's theory, the modern secular warrior ought to experience these religious meanings of war only unconsciously. But there is evidence that elements of this religious symbolism survive even in conscious public perceptions. World War II was surely seen as a battle of cosmos against chaos, and often enough as a task of hunting down wild animals. The Germans, reduced in public imagination to subhuman "Huns," were often depicted as dogs, wolves, or other kinds of wild beasts. The Japanese were even more totally stripped of their humanity. The ubiquitous term "Jap" became almost synonymous with some form of animal (most often in images of monkeys, snakes, rodents, and vermin), and Americans commonly spoke of the war in the Pacific as a hunting expedition.[3] President Truman wrote to a critic of the Hiroshima bombing: "When you have to deal with a beast you have to treat him as a beast. It is most regrettable but nevertheless true."[4]

During World War II America, like all nations at war, justified its actions by the hunter's principle that one must become a beast in order to kill a beast. This principle helped plunge the whole world into apparent chaos. Yet American troops received the blessing of all the nation's religious denominations. The soldier had a special sacred status that was sometimes explicitly articulated but always implicitly present. The average GI was widely praised as emulating heroic models from the pioneers and the colonial Minutemen to the medieval crusaders and (in the case of the war dead) the early Christian martyrs and their prototype, Jesus Christ. Americans often voiced their feeling that the nation had been lifted out of its ordinary profane existence into a time of heightened intensity in which the world's destiny hung in the balance.[5]

In all these ways, the historical event was interpreted in terms of universal religious and mythic categories. An assimilation of unique events to eternal archetypes is common enough in the life of homo religiosus; it is perhaps the most effective way to deny the ultimate reality of change and escape the effects of profane time. The historian of religions recognizes a dialectic at work here, however. When a new event is interpreted as if it were merely a repetition of an old event, the meaning of the old event is enriched, enlarged, and to some degree transformed. This process of application guarantees that myths and symbols will continue to grow in meaning.

For example, while World War II was understood as a religious ordeal, the religious meaning of war was enriched by the novel qualities of World War II. Most notably, the innovation of large-scale aerial bombing broke down the line separating civilian from soldier and created "total war" in its distinctively modern sense. For the first time, war's aim was not so much to defeat the enemy's army as to destroy the enemy's industrial capacity and civilian morale by bombing large cities. War was no longer a matter of army against army but nation against nation. The entire enemy nation therefore became the animal to be hunted down, and correspondingly civilians in our own nation felt their status transformed as well (though perhaps not quite as much as those who actually donned the uniform).

Since the war seemed to be everywhere, and everyone was called on to contribute to the war effort, every act was charged with new meaning. In terms of homo religiosus' worldview, the world was changed into a chaotic battlefield filled with warring packs of wild animals, making every act, whether of soldier or civilian, religiously meaningful as an animal sacrifice. Advances in global communications further extended this sense of the whole world plunged into chaos, for World War II was the first truly global war.

Yet precisely because the chaos seemed total, the perception of "our world" as morally good and the enemy as morally evil was equally total. Total chaos was now evoked in the service of a radically dualistic struggle for immutable order. And the hope generated by the war was a hope for total renewal, an eschatological purification of the whole world. Dwight Eisenhower spoke for most Americans when he called the enemy "a completely evil conspiracy with which no compromise could be tolerated. Because only by the utter destruction of the Axis was a decent world possible, the war became for me a crusade in the traditional sense of that often misused word."[6]

Here was another fundamental change in the religious meaning of war: the "mystical solidarity" between hunter and victim was consciously denied, the hunter's traditional concern that the victim be able to regenerate itself was forgotten, and unconditional surrender—the total extermination of chaos—became the goal. Perhaps the rapid post-war turnaround, in which the United States befriended its enemies and helped them regenerate economically, indicates that the mystical solidarity had never actually disappeared. But the changes wrought by World War II have certainly affected popular thinking about war throughout the postwar era.

World War II as Paradigm

Just as World War II was assimilated to a mythic paradigm, so it became the paradigm repeated in the Cold War, concretizing the religious meanings of war for our own time. World War II is often nostalgically recalled as the end of an era: "the last good war," the last time that good and evil were clearly delineated and good triumphed decisively over evil, so that "our world" could be saved and renewed. But in another sense 1945 seems to be a beginning: the year in which "our world" was first created, the year we would like to relive continually.

Certainly the postwar era was a time of unprecedented American hegemony, so the war itself could be seen as the chaos prerequisite to the assumption of sovereignty and the founding of a new world order (symbolized by the formation of the United Nations). In this new world the Russian bear and its allies have often been depicted as dreaded monsters to be hunted down. But the hunt is still viewed as a sacrifice that must be offered if we are to retain a living connection with the pristine time when our postwar world was born. The World War II paradigm teaches us that only unreserved sacrifice—always of national resources and sometimes of lives—offers the possibility of unlimited victory. It also teaches us that the war must be fought through to unlimited victory, for the outcome must be either perfect world order or total chaos. There can be no thought of a relatively stable yet permanently unpredictable political situation.

The advent of huge nuclear arsenals, nuclear parity, and Mutually Assured Destruction have radically changed the meaning of victory and therefore of war itself, however. Since we hesitate to carry out the hunt directly with weapons of war, other means of competition have been found. Primary among them is that ubiquitous image of the nuclear age, the arms race—the head-to-head competition that forms a common paradigm for the arousal of "magical heat" in religious ritual. There are also other races: the struggle for economic supremacy, the battle for influence in the Third World, the many diplomatic and political wars of words, the contests at the negotiating table, etc. Indeed every facet of life has become a potential political battleground.

The need to find other forms of competition has intensified the new meaning of war arising from World War II. With the line between soldier and civilian erased, the front is everywhere, and everyone is on it at all times. When Cold War rages, it is even more global than the "hot" war it emulates. Since every act can contribute to defeating the enemy, the line between war and peace is erased too. The Cold War becomes a ubiquitous fact of life, and the nation willingly accepts a permanent national security state. War thus becomes a hunting expedition involving the entire nation every hour of every day. Any act by any citizen can contribute to its success and therefore be charged with religious meaning and power. This expedition brandishes its weapons at will,[7] but it has so far refrained from launching them, recognizing that the consequences might well be "mutual suicide."

This restraint in using the weapons suggests that we now fear the chaos of war as much as we fear the chaos of the enemy. In other words, both war and enemy now have the same symbolic meaning. So our war against the enemy can easily become a self-proclaimed virtuous struggle against war itself, waged in the name of peace as well as "our way of life." In fact, the outcome of this process of symbolic change is that peace has become synonymous with "our way of life" in public rhetoric. When Cold War tensions are relaxed, the war against the enemy can just as easily be transformed into a war against war itself. The destructive power of the Bomb has directed the nation's aspirations more than ever to a new world order purified of the evil of war. War has thus taken on a new cultural meaning; perhaps never before has war itself been proclaimed the enemy in such forthright terms, for never before have the stakes been perceived as so high.

If the recognition of war as "mutual suicide" creates a new symbolic meaning for war, it also leads back to the original sense of war as a hunt in which the hunter and hunted are bound together in a mystical solidarity. Once again, the hunting expedition comes to see the use of its weapons as a form of mutual sacrifice. As we turn to other forms of competition to avoid this ultimate sacrifice, the enemy joins us in a mystical solidarity of mutual confrontation mingled with varying degrees of cooperation, which generates immense amounts of political heat—just as the technological aspects of the arms race quite literally generate heat through fission and fusion. Do we expect any creativity or renewal of life to come from all these forms of heat? Many Americans see our stiffened resolve to defend our country as a renewal of patriotic values and the "American spirit," which means in religious terms a renewal of the cosmos. Many see valuable technological and economic progress stimulated by military competition. Many proclaim an unprecedented era of world peace brought on by the weapons whose very destructiveness (they trust) renders them unusable. And for many, "the end of the Cold War" means the crumbling of "the evil empire," a victory of the West over the Soviet Union, and a realization of 1945's promise of global American hegemony.

Finally, there is a persistent belief in some quarters that if the ultimate heat of the arms race were detonated, we could survive, begin anew, and very possibly build a purified reinvigorated world. This belief persists, in part, because it is fueled by the World War II paradigm. If the bloody sacrifices of World War II regenerated the world, should not the "mutual suicide" of World War III do the same? Indeed, since the chaos of World War III would be incomparably greater, should it not lead to a grander and more completely new creation? The very term *World War III*, so commonly applied to a war between the nuclear superpowers, inevitably evokes cosmogonic hope. Even when used by those who consciously eschew nuclear weapons, it cannot fail to suggest unconscious associations with all the symbolic meanings of World War II (and World War I, which was also charged with eschatological hope, at least for Americans). Every reference to a nuclear cataclysm as World War III implies that we need not refrain from using these weapons forever. World War III, like its forerunners, might be just the mutually generated heat we need for a global renewal.

Eliade's view of war suggests that there is no essential difference, on the level of religious meaning, between "hot" war, Cold War, and "the end of the Cold War." Disarmament negotiations, the arms race, the various forms of nonmilitary competition, and the hostile firing of nuclear weapons should all be seen as so many different forms of martial hunt. We are generally reluctant to take this view, for we hope that all the aspects of the Cold War, and certainly "the end of the Cold War," will protect us against chaos, while the firing of nuclear weapons seems to promise only the total chaos of World War III. Yet Eliade opens up a new perspective, in which at all levels the desire for order is interpenetrated by a desire for chaos. The path to order is through chaos, and the ultimate goal of war and hunt, as of every religious rite, is a union of the two. The Bomb symbolically effects this coincidence of opposites precisely because it ties its life-giving promise in the present to its death-dealing promise for the future. The paradox of MAD—that the weapons remain unusable only as long as we are sincerely willing to use them—illustrates this intermingling of cosmos and chaos.

MAD also illustrates another important coincidence of opposites: having bound ourselves to our enemy in a joint suicide pact, we have brought the enemy into our cosmos and simultaneously put ourselves at the mercy of the enemy's chaos; the line dividing cosmos from chaos is as sharp as ever yet irretrievably blurred. Is this not emblematic of our ambivalence toward both cosmos and chaos? Yet it also reflects the hunter's age-old intuition that only by binding oneself to the enemy—the wild beast, the forces of chaos—can one be free of human limitations and the weight of time. This religious renewal has always been the ultimate goal of the interpenetration of cosmos and chaos, and every human culture has found some symbolic way to enact it. The very fact that so little of any practical value could be gained by using nuclear weapons points to the symbolic realm as the source of their enduring appeal. And that symbolic appeal seems to have something to do with the renewal sought by every warrior and every hunter.

In the nuclear age we can experience a mystical solidarity with the enemy equally well by an arms race or by disarmament efforts. When we support "our side" and champion any form of competitive program, whether of armament or disarmament, we step into a primordial religious stance, one validated for us by the heroic warriors of World War II. We emerge from our petty world of everyday concerns into a realm of global and even cosmic consequence, and we find ourselves renewed as every enactor of a mythic scenario is renewed. We touch the point at which life and death compete—and commingle—on a global and even cosmic scale, a point at which we sense, however dimly, a fundamental rock-bottom reality that promises total transformation.

The more intense the contest and the more precarious the risk, the greater the immersion in power and fundamental reality. So we may insist on keeping up some form of nuclear competition primarily to keep the contest and risk alive, to maintain our contact with the sacrality embodied in the Bomb, and to keep alive that auroral age of beginnings that culminated in 1945. As our thoughts about war, peace, and political conflict turn persistently (if unconsciously) back to 1945, the beginning of "our world" and therefore its mythic paradigm, we are actually seeking a return to a timeless set of values and experiences embodied in all war.

Technology and Weaponry

Nineteen forty-five seems to mark the creation of a new world less because of the war's end than because of the new weapon that (according to the prevailing myth) brought the war to an end. The religious meaning of weapons, in Eliade's view, derives largely from the fact that they are humanly created objects. Every human creation "implies a superabundance of reality, in other words, an eruption of the Sacred into the world. It follows that all construction or fabrication has the cosmogony as an exemplary model. The creation of the world became the archetype of each creative human activity."[8] Every artisan or builder, having transformed nature by artifice, brings a new mode of existence—a new world—into being and thus forges a new point of contact between this world and the divine. To create or construct means to halt the flow of profane time and return to the eternal realm of mythic origins. Every repetition of the cosmogony demands an encounter with primal chaos, however. In many cultures, builders put this principle into practice by immolating a sacrificial victim on the site of each new construction. The victim is believed to live on in the building and impart its sacred vitality, just as, according to many myths, the world itself was produced and sustained by a primordial divine sacrifice. Sometimes this myth is reenacted in a human sacrifice.

These religious meanings are evident in every form of technology. But modern technology, in Eliade's opinion, has its roots especially in the religious traditions surrounding metalworking. Homo religiosus views the earth as a maternal womb and metals as embryos slowly gestating within it. All metals, given enough time, would grow into the perfect metal—gold. The miner removes the metal in its embryonic stage. Then the metallurgist, by smelting and refining, continues the gestation process, doing above ground the work that time and nature together would have done below. Metallurgists seem to speed up the processes of nature at its deepest geological level; their craft takes the place of time itself. Moreover, they can produce alloys that do not exist in nature.

Since they seem able to work faster and better than nature, they inevitably enter into that "very old dream of *homo faber*: collaboration in the perfection of nature while at the same time securing perfection of himself."[9] Doing the work once reserved for the gods, revealing the sacrality previously hidden in nature, they appear to be as perfect as gods.

Yet the respect accorded these wondrous workers is hedged with numinous dread and ritual tabus. "There is above all the feeling that one is meddling with the natural order of things ruled by some higher law and intervening in a secret and sacred process."[10] Since miners must descend into the depths and work with subterranean materials, they take on the sinister sacrality of the depths. The blood sacrifice—sometimes human sacrifice—often offered by metalworkers underscores the demonic side of their craft. To enter their ranks is to be initiated into the darkest but most potent secrets of human creativity, to transcend ordinary human limits, to penetrate and reveal the most hidden layers of sacrality.

Metalworkers therefore possess "a terrible, inordinate, supernatural power. . . . But all [their] techniques have their origin and their point of support in the mastery of fire, the apanage of shamans and magicians before it becomes the secret of potters, metallurgists, and smiths."[11] Fire is the key to the secret of transforming metals. Itself palpable yet nonmaterial, fire destroys matter but in doing so purifies it, renders it spirit, and leads to a new material creation. Every work with fire is therefore a work of initiatory transformation, signifying freedom from the human condition and access to a higher state. Smiths and metallurgists reenact the initiatory scenario whenever they work with their fire. Like shamans and magicians, they take on the qualities inherent in fire: "At many levels, fire, flame, dazzling light, inner heat, express spiritual experiences, the incarnation of the sacred, the proximity of God."[12]

In one common mythic motif, the smith forges a magical weapon with which the warrior slays the dragon or monster; here the warrior's "magical heat" merges with the smith's mastery of fire. The weapon is often symbolically equated with the fiery lightning-bolt and its thunderous roar. Fire is thus the central thread tying together this whole symbolic complex: the smith masters fire on his forge, enabling him to make a weapon ostensibly of metal but actually constituted of fire itself, which is passed on to the warrior who masters the weapon's fire and generates a comparable fire within himself. Since the fire is charged with sacred ambivalence, the metallic weapon inspires both awe and dread.

Weapons take on a richer religious meaning when they are projectiles. As an instantaneous killer, the projectile seems to be unnatural, beyond time, and so akin to the divine lightning-bolt or the demonic curse. As a killer from a distance, it gives human beings a mastery over space, which also represents a transcendence of the human condition. Because it flies, it invokes a large symbolic complex related to magical flight and ascension to the heavens. At the center of this complex is the universal human aspiration to transcendence and freedom, especially from the spatial limitations of gravity. When the metalworker's mastery over time is combined with the projectile weapon's mastery over space, both time and space are abolished. In religious terms, the meaning of the weapon fuses with the symbolic import of those who forge and wield it. The warrior, like the smith, passes into a state of perfection. Sharing in the weapon's power and initiated into its secrets, these privileged humans are thereby renewed and transformed. They embody the perfect union of cosmos and chaos, life and death, construction and destruction, matter and spirit, humanity and the divine, time and eternity.

Nuclear Technology and Nuclear Weaponry

How does this rich symbolism of technology and weaponry illuminate our situation in the nuclear age? Eliade points out that the religious world of homo faber has achieved its greatest triumph, paradoxically, in the secularizing success of modern Western technology. The growing commitment of the whole world to that technology cannot be explained solely in terms of the creature comforts gained. There is also an enticing, if largely unconscious, level of religious meaning at work. "The visionary's myth of the perfection, or more accurately, of the redemption of Nature survives, in camouflaged form, in the pathetic programme of the industrial societies whose aim is the total transmutation of Nature, its transformation into 'energy'. . . . Man succeeds in supplanting Time. His desire to accelerate the natural tempo of things by an ever more rapid and efficient exploitation of mines, coalfields and petrol deposits, begins to come true."[13] Thus arises the myth of infinite progress, which triumphs "where there is faith in the limitless possibilities of homo faber; everywhere where the eschatological significance of labour, technology and the scientific exploration of Nature reveals itself."[14]

Ultimately the transformation of nature into artifice and energy may be speeded up so much that time itself will disappear. This hope for eternity, the perpetual goal of homo religiosus, may also be the deepest wellspring of the modern faith in technology. But since modern man pursues this hope by taking the place of time, he has paradoxically ended up identified with and therefore immersed in time. Nowhere is a wholly secular, time-bound existence more evident today than in the specific world of homo faber, the world of work, which no longer affords access to any conscious sense of eternal meaning. "The secularization of work is like an open wound in the body of modern society."[15] In secularized work "man feels the implacable nature of temporal duration, its full weight and slowness. . . . The temporality assumed and experienced by man is translated, on the philosophical plane, into the tragic awareness of the vanity of all human existence."[16]

Modern man's feeling that all is in vain may stem directly from another profound paradox of modern technology: "Scientific and technological progress has made it possible to prolong and periodically to regenerate human life (with such indefinite regeneration corresponding to a secularized expression of immortality) as well as to destroy human collectivities, even the whole of humankind."[17] The apotheosis of homo faber, the desire of homo religiosus to experience sacrality wholly through matter and work, culminates in the twentieth century in the discovery that nature can be transformed into energy on a limitless, and hence limitlessly destructive, scale. The release of immense energy is always one mark of sacrality; the sacred always shows itself as strikingly powerful and efficacious as well as permanently or "really" real. But the religious meaning of power depends on its particular historical context and symbolic expression. So it is not enough to say that nuclear weapons may strike us as sacred simply because of their overwhelming power. We must look more closely at their twofold significance as technological prodigy and lethal weapon of war. On both counts, Eliade's analysis suggests that the Bomb is steeped in religious meaning. Indeed virtually every facet of his account of technology and weaponry is readily manifest in the most common nuclear images.

If 1945 marks the beginning of a new world primarily because it marks the beginning of the nuclear age, the nuclear scientists who created the Bomb are more responsible than anyone else for this radical renewal. Today's nuclear scientists and technicians are merely repeating the world-founding creative acts of the Manhattan Project team that serves as their paradigm. But the participants in the Manhattan Project were themselves returning to the origins of human technology, repeating the paradigmatic gestures of the first metallurgists. More importantly, they were returning to the origins of the universe itself, as they "unlocked the secret of the atom," the basic building block of every natural process, and "harnessed the basic power of the universe."[18] Nuclear scientists, more than any other technological experts, symbolize in the public mind humanity's newfound ability to touch the very origin of all tangible reality. Therefore they are credited (albeit unconsciously) with stopping the flow of profane time, discovering a new access to sacrality, allowing the superabundance of reality to flow into human life, and thereby founding a center from which a new world springs.

More than this, they are our chief symbol of humanity's ability to intervene in nature's fundamental processes and control tangible reality at its deepest level. This symbolic meaning is most evident in the process of obtaining nuclear fuel. Uranium must be mined from the earth and then transformed, sometimes into other uranium isotopes and sometimes into another element altogether (plutonium), by technological means that are nothing short of magical to the general public. Nuclear scientists speak of "breeding" plutonium in "breeder" reactors, as if the plutonium were an embryo needing a midwife to bring it to birth. But every aspect of nuclear technology exhibits the same basic symbolic meaning: the Bomb is our prime example of the triumph of modern science, its astonishing capacity to plumb nature's secrets, release the energy trapped in matter, and transform nature for human purposes. This is widely seen as a quantum leap in our ability to tamper with the life of nature at the deepest geological levels, opening up access to an awe- and dread-inspiring realm that had previously been closed to human experience. If this door can be opened, then perhaps no doors are permanently closed; the Bomb symbolizes modern technology's eschatological promise of limitless possibility.

Not only can we improve upon nature now, but we can obviously work more quickly as well; we can release in an instant energy that would otherwise have seeped out over thousands of years. This amazingly rapid transformation seems to mirror the equally rapid transformation of our lives wrought by nuclear technology. In terms of the whole history of humankind, the years since 1945 mark a change that feels as instantaneous as it is radical. The temporal process has been speeded up to a point where time itself is on the verge of vanishing—as it apparently does in a nuclear explosion. Every nuclear explosion reminds us of the Bomb's ultimate threat: to put an end to history and thus to time itself. But this threat is also an eschatological promise, for redemption always implies an escape from our bondage to time. The ultimate religious hope hidden in nuclear technology, as in every technology, is the hope for eternity and immortality.[19]

If the deepest meaning of technology is the urge to transcend time, to perfect nature, and thereby to perfect the self, then nuclear scientists stand closer than anyone to the contemporary vision of technological perfection. Like the ancient metallurgists and their divine prototypes, however, they are perceived as wielding an uncanny, ambivalent, magical, and ultimately terrible power. Their efforts to turn the earth into paradise are tainted with sinister threats, for those efforts, too, intervene with the most secret processes of the cosmos. The ambivalence of the scientists is most evident in the widespread belief that they are the only ones who can save us from the weapon they have created; nearly everyone today believes that disarmament efforts depend largely on the technical experts' ability to solve technical problems. So the scientists' visions of a saving transformation are counterbalanced in public imagination by the possibility of destructive transmutation—especially the mutations caused by radiation. As masters of the fiery heat of radioactivity, they can cause death just as easily as they can prevent it. It was more than mere metaphor, then, when Norman Moss titled his book about these scientists *Men Who Play God*.[20]

Those who work with nuclear technology might well object that their reputation is unfairly tarnished when all attention is focussed on their weapon-making talents. They might want to stress their contributions to arms control and their nonmilitary accomplishments. In the popular mind, however, the links tying technology and disarmament to armament and war seem ineradicable. Perhaps that is because, among all artificial creations, none is more potent or memorable than the weapon of war. In any event, the nuclear scientists of our own day must live with the image, deserved or not, of "Bomb makers." At the same time the military has become so dependent on modern technology that it is hard to distinguish between the soldier and the technology, hard to know whether the soldier wields the weapon or vice versa. Thus the religious meanings of war and technology have enriched each other in roughly equal measure in modern times.

This process of mutual influence is certainly very old. But it was greatly accelerated in the two World Wars and then reached unparalleled heights in the nuclear age. The Bomb, those who make it and therefore could defuse it, and those who could wield it in war now form a single unit in popular imagination. This is the same unity reflected in the myths of magical weapons, smiths, and warriors. Perhaps never in recorded history has this mythic scenario been played out as vividly as in our own time. Never before has the magical weapon so palpably contained the infinite fire, heat, and light that are emblematic of divinity. Never before has a projectile weapon been forged that can kill so many so instantly at such globe-circling distances. The military and the nuclear scientists join together in sharing this aura of transcendence. Their power appears to be infinite. As their weapon represents a mode of existence beyond the ordinary human condition, so they too seem to step beyond that condition into a supernatural status.

Nuclear Shamans

With their "mastery of fire" and "magical heat," the nuclear warrior and smith emulate the figure whom Eliade considers the religious virtuoso *par excellence*: the shaman. As their aerial weapons free them from the constraints of space and time, they also take on the shaman's "celestial" virtues: the ability to leave the earth, behave like a spirit, link the earth and humanity with the divine celestial realm, and thereby return to the perfection of the era of beginnings. These shamanic qualities associated with the Bomb point to other dimensions of meaning in the nuclear myth. Shamans are pre-eminently the anti-demonic champions .... The military elements that are of great importance in certain types of Asian shamanism (lance, cuirass, bow, sword, etc.) are accounted for by the requirements of war against the demons, the true enemies of humanity. In a general way, it can be said that shamanism defends life, health, fertility, the world of "light," against death, diseases, sterility, and the world of "darkness".... Men are sure that *one of them* is able to help them in the critical circumstances produced by the inhabitants of the invisible world.[21]

It might be said, then, that the scientists who make the Bomb and the warriors who wield it serve a shamanic role in our day, protecting us against the foreign "demons" who threaten "our world." Just as shamans see an invisible world, so the scientists see the invisible world of the atom, and the government's intelligence agencies see the secret doings of enemy nations. When these nuclear experts turn their efforts toward disarmament, they show themselves more than ever to be indispensable masters of the Bomb and its secret knowledge, though the Bomb itself becomes the demon against which they defend us.

In order to master the apparently magical weapon, the shaman and his modern nuclear successors must also master a secret language known only to initiates. In this secret language they speak of, and to, the inhabitants of the secret world, giving that world a concrete form.[22] This means that they must rely heavily on the powers of imagination; they must create a world so convincing that the average person accepts it as irrefutably real and terrifying. The more compelling their imaginings are, the more indispensable their protective services appear. Ultimately, though, these portrayals of the demonic realm make that realm less terrifying, for they give chaos a visible, structured, and eventually familiar place within the cosmos; they defend the cosmos by enlarging it. To achieve this goal, shamans and nuclear specialists both rely heavily upon public ceremony and dramatic spectacle as well as their secretive private activities.

All the shaman's spectacles and magic powers combine to "stimulate and feed the imagination, demolish the barriers between dream and present reality," and create a world "in which *everything seems possible*, where the dead return to life and the living die only to live again ... where the 'laws of nature' are abolished, and a certain superhuman 'freedom' is exemplified and made dazzlingly *present*."[23] Perhaps this is the freedom that our nuclear arsenal is really aimed at preserving. Surely the wonders of nuclear technology have made it seem that today all things are possible. But those who make and control the weapons assure us that their true goal is a world at peace, a world in which the weapons cannot under any circumstances be used. They express their ardent desire to return to an earlier time, a time without danger or anxiety. The shaman also returns to such a time, the era of primordial paradise when heaven and earth were in intimate contact and perfect harmony reigned. Perhaps the nuclear specialists, hoping to bring earth and skies under their control through both armament and disarmament programs, are driven by the same nostalgia for a perfectly secure past, the world of 1945 when the demons had been utterly subdued.[24]

Like the shamans, the nuclear scientists are an elite with privileged access to the most recondite secrets of the cosmos. Nuclear research has been "top secret" from the beginning largely because of its potential military uses. Even if this research had no military applications, its complexity alone would have demanded some kind of initiation into arcane secrets. So the nuclear scientists, upon taking up their work, would have inevitably felt some sense of entering a new life and leaving the old behind. Their mastery of the fire that can destroy and recreate the world would have symbolized this initiatory transformation, as it has for all their predecessors. But the special dimension of secrecy attendant on weapons research has surely intensified this whole aspect of their experience.

Here again the Manhattan Project, carried out in a remote wilderness with elaborate security precautions,[25] serves as a paradigm for all later nuclear technology. Los Alamos still thrives as a research center today, and other nuclear facilities were placed in areas as remote as Hanford, Washington and Oak Ridge, Tennessee. Even installations near metropolitan centers are on the fringes of those centers (e.g., the Lawrence Laboratories in Livermore, California; the Rocky Flats plant near Denver, Colorado; the Pantex plant outside of Amarillo, Texas). Public consternation over spying and other breaches in the nuclear security cordon has been a continuing trait of the nuclear age. In the 1970s and 1980s there was a tendency to classify ever greater domains of research as "secret" and to encourage classified research on university campuses.[26] And of course the military installations where Bombs are actually deployed remain as remote and secret as ever. So there is a continuing demarcation between the realm of ordinary life and the hidden realm of the Bomb.

Initiations, especially those into secret societies, have usually been carried out in remote wilderness spaces, under the strict supervision of initiatory masters who often forbid the noninitiates from even approaching the sacred space. Initiates are commonly forbidden to divulge any details of their experience to the uninitiated. More importantly, they are forbidden to divulge any of the secret wisdom they have learned, for the imparting of secret wisdom is a nearly universal feature of initiatory rituals. One becomes a new person in large part because one has been made privy to sacred secrets and hence raised above the ordinary human condition. Those who work with the Bomb, whether scientists or warriors, surely fit this description in the popular imagery of the nuclear age; the security clearance has become the modern equivalent of the initiatory ordeal. Like all initiates, though, they must suffer a symbolic death to attain their privileged new life. Not only must they offer a total dedication of self to their work, they must also give up the candor and open discourse with others that marked their previous life and take on the stigma of bearing a power as demonic as it is awesome. And they must run the risk of being overwhelmed by that power, succumbing to its demonism, and becoming the "mad scientist" of popular imagination. For the nuclear expert, as for the shaman, madness is an inescapable shadow lurking in the secret depths.

The Nuclear State

The whole ambiguous structure of symbolic meanings related to magical power, secrecy, and initiatory death and rebirth is recapitulated in the shamanic image of the "mastery of fire." But this image has even more complex meanings in the nuclear age, for these modern masters have gone beyond the achievements of the shamans and smiths of old; the fire they have mastered is the fire of nuclear fusion that fuels the sun and creates life on earth. The "magical heat" that they can generate is thus the heat of the sun, and the dazzling light they produce has been described as "brighter than a thousand suns."[27]

These references to the sun indicate that the religious meaning of technology has taken on new dimensions in the nuclear age. In Eliade's view, the sun as a religious symbol represents the creative fertilizing power of life. Solar symbolism also has close connections with secret societies and social elites. But the sun's most distinctive connection is with political elites. "It could be said that where 'history is on the march', thanks to kings, heroes, or empires, the sun is supreme. . . . The hero 'saves' the world, renews it, opens a new era which sometimes even amounts to a new organization of the universe."[28] The heroic sovereign reenacts the sun's mythic role as demiurge, carrying on the creative pattern first begun by the divine creator. He dispenses life to those whom he deems deserving, those who have been initiated or passed his test.

The Bomb's rich solar symbolism points to the sovereign state as the true master of the nuclear fire. Its mastery was obtained in the thick of a battle for global supremacy, where "history is on the march." So it is now the state (represented in the public's mind by the government) that completes the scientists' creative work by imposing a new cosmic structure that "saves" the world. This work, whether it be war or the avoidance of war, is claimed to be in accordance with a divine mandate. The state thus takes on a new aura of religious meaning, more all-embracing than its previous symbolic significance. It maintains the elite, secret, magical power inherent in all sovereignty. It reserves for itself the sole right of reorganizing the world. In pursuit of this aim, it assumes the warrior hero's cosmogonic role (using the magical weapon to slay the chaotic monster) as well as all the shamanic virtues associated with the cosmogonic weapon. The nuclear state reinforces its powers through the technological wizardry it controls, drawing on the distinctive Western tradition of the sun as the sign of Apollonian rationality. It takes control of space and time—in fact it replaces time—as it takes control of nature as well as history.

All these powers are brought together in the service of the sovereign's traditional goal: the quest for a new world order, most often through his own global hegemony. At the outset of the nuclear age, President Truman summed up the solar values afforded by the Bomb in his typically blunt way: "Get plenty of atomic bombs on hand—drop one on Stalin, put the United Nations to work, and eventually set up a free world."[29] But if the Bomb has the same symbolic meaning as the sun, then Truman (and his successors) may have been driven by an unrecognized religious motive: a desire for perfection akin to homo faber's dream of self-perfection. This dream has been symbolized by the alchemists' project of transmuting lead into gold; gold, in religious symbolism, represents the sun. In the nuclear age, then, the state has become, in the human realm, what gold is below the earth and the sun is above the earth: the focal point and symbolic repository of all perfection.

The symbolism of the sun is even more complex than this: "Though immortal, the sun descends nightly to the kingdom of the dead; it can, therefore, take men with it and, by setting, put them to death; but it can also, on the other hand, guide souls through the lower regions and bring them back next day with its light."[30] The sun is the sign of elites because they are perceived as initiates who have followed the sun through death and rebirth into some kind of immortality. Rulers frequently cast themselves as mythic heroes whose passage through dark mortal danger leads to shining salvation. They hold up this passage as a model, dispensing life only to those who prove themselves worthy by enduring the threat of chaos. Hence they are always shadowed by the sun's power to kill. This lethal power can take on cosmic meaning. There is a widely attested fear that during the solstice the sun might keep moving away from its equinoctial setting point and never return. Sometimes "this state of alarm is expressed in apocalyptic visions: the falling or the darkening of the sun becomes one of the signs of the coming end of the world."[31]

The state has gained unique power in the nuclear age because it is the sole possessor of a weapon that can bring the world to an end. Taking on the role of sovereign, scientist, shaman, and warrior all in one, it must take on the sun's ambivalence too, for all these roles represent a coincidence of opposites. All allot a place to death as well as life, to chaos as well as cosmos, to destruction as well as construction. And all, as modes of religious experience, harmonize these opposites in an overarching unity, seeing the dark side as a necessary prelude to the renewal of life and light. This is the sacred solar wisdom that holds the key to every quest for perfection. The state would seem to understand this wisdom, for it has taken as its symbol of perfect order its prime symbol of the end of the world.

Acting upon this wisdom, "religious man comes to *feel himself responsible for the renewal of the world.* And it is in this responsibility of a religious order that one must look for the origins of all forms of politics."[31a] Perhaps nuclear politics originate in the same sense of responsibility. The superpower state declares itself responsible for dispensing life by controlling nuclear weaponry, harmonizing political conflicts, and thereby preventing nuclear annihilation. But it demands as the price of its efforts a willingness to endure as much threat of nuclear chaos as it deems necessary. All opposites merge in the state; it monopolizes the power of peaceful life as well as the power of death and dispenses each however it chooses. And its efforts to peacefully reorganize the world may sometimes be a subterfuge whose true aim is world domination. Ultimately, though, the state as sovereign must strive for a global initiatory transformation, one way or another. So it may also feel responsible for destroying the world in order to recreate it.

The Meaning of the Myth

Eliade's method of interpretation does not lead to any objectively verifiable "truth" about the myth of nuclear origins or the meaning of nuclear weapons. When used as a heuristic device to open up religious imagination, however, it does lead to an understanding of the myth—and therefore of the weapons—that is quite different from the one held by the state and the public. The myth is commonly taken as a story about the unconditional surrender of the forces of chaos to the forces of order, since its climax is our victory over Germany and Japan and our hope for permanent peace through the United Nations. It seems to give no positive meaning to the possibility of world destruction inherent in the weapons. That possibility is apparently nothing but an unwelcome accident. Appearances can be deceiving, however, and Eliade contends that those who live out a myth are not necessarily the best interpreters of its deeper meaning. A synthesizing interpretation of the myth within its cultural context may offer a very different view of the significance of the whole myth and especially of its anomalous ending.

The war between cosmos and chaos is certainly one important component of the myth of nuclear origins. While the myth feeds our traditional desire for total victory in war, its ending also suggests radically new images of war that introduce equally new relationships between cosmos and chaos: on the one hand an endless conflict between cosmos and chaos—a war without any winner, or universal conflict as a permanent state of affairs; on the other hand an end to conflict forever—the necessarily permanent abolition of war. This sense of a novel situation dominates the myth; it is essentially a story not about the defeat of enemies but about the origin of the nuclear age.

In religious terms the beginning of a new era is always the birth of a new world, and every new world demands the death of the old. Just as the hunter and warrior kill in order to regenerate life, so homo faber often animates a construction that founds a new world with a sacrifice of life. Both take responsibility for creative murders that transform the world and open up the prospect of a perfect reality in which structure is immutable yet everything is possible. The nuclear myth states quite explicitly that the new world founded by the Bomb was initiated by a sacrifice of life. And the agents responsible for that sacrifice were not only the nuclear scientists, but also the airborne warriors who hunted down the people of Hiroshima and Nagasaki. The scientists' and warriors' conviction that they were serving the cause of life, not death, only confirms the religious meaning of their act.

As long as nuclear weapons are produced and deployed (and negotiated and debated) the average citizen can participate in the mythic drama of creative killing committed by the paradigmatic warriors, scientists, and sovereigns of World War II. All these roles offer a mode of religious transformation. They all possess a magical power that can dissolve our world and create a more perfect world, because they have been initiated into a secret wisdom. But their creative acts all repeat the tragic message of this wisdom: transformation always demands a prior death for which the initiate must assume responsibility. As we repeat the paradigmatic acts narrated in this myth, acting them out on all the great and small stages of nuclear politics, we are lifted out of our circumscribed profane lives into the timeless era of beginnings, whose eternally valid events are charged with cosmic saving power.

Although the myth is actually acted out only by a chosen few who work in and for the secret circles of government, the government serves here as the representative agency it was designed to be. Western democracy has afforded the average person a substantial sense of (or illusion of) participation in the heroic exploits of the political elite for two centuries or more. But only in the nuclear age has this sense of participation become so compelling, for only now are we so clearly linked, from the greatest to the smallest, by a common danger and a common fate. The elite's capacity to destroy the world affords us all an unprecedented opportunity to participate in religious experiences that had previously been reserved for the elite alone. And now, for the first time, the elite figure of homo faber as technological wizard has stepped into the center of the myth of world destruction. Nuclear weapons offer us all a way to share in this figure's sacred gesture: completing nature's and time's geological work—exhausting the full spectrum of possibilities of the earth's life—in one convulsive instant of global cataclysm.

We are understandably ambivalent about this gesture; the traditional ambivalence of weapons has now been raised to its ultimate cosmic level. We want to share in the privileges that come with being responsible for the Bomb. At the same time, we declare ourselves, and honestly believe ourselves, to be horrified by its potential consequences. But our efforts to escape from it lead back to dependence on the same shamanic figures: the state, its warriors, and its experts. So the ambivalence of those who make and wield nuclear weapons has been raised to new heights too. This intensification makes us more eager to participate in their transformed status, which means participating in the ongoing life of the Bomb itself, with its ambivalent power to redeem by destroying. Ultimately we want to be rid of the Bomb while still retaining it; we want to be rid of responsibility for it while still retaining control over it. Consequently, in popular imagery, the weapon is given a life of its own while yet remaining in the hands of divine or human heroes. Since the magical heat that is the essence of the weapon is shared by all who come in contact with it, the distinction between weapon and wielder may be irrelevant anyway.

Our ambivalence toward the Bomb reflects our twofold stance toward the physical world. On the one hand, since we find our characteristically modern sacrality in matter and its manipulations, we hope to preserve the world. On the other hand, we embrace a particular kind of myth of world-destruction, one that expects a total annihilation of matter. In religious terms this reflects a conviction that matter itself, the arena of science's greatest triumphs, is evil and must be destroyed. Our distinctively modern myth of the end of the world is not, therefore, simply a myth of escaping from matter. Its ultimate meaning seems to be the ultimate achievement of homo faber: perfecting matter by totally transmuting it into spirit. And behind this stands a vision of total human renovation projected on a global scale.

A key to understanding this renovation lies in the figure of the shaman, whose distinctive trait is his capacity to link this world and the celestial realm, the material and the spiritual. All his unique powers work toward this end, including the mastery of fire. Fire itself appears to be both material and nonmaterial, so mastery of fire always bespeaks a transformation from the material to the spiritual mode of existence, which is the same transformation attained in the shaman's madness. Today, nuclear destruction and nuclear madness symbolize to us the etherialization of the world—raising it up in fire and smoke and freeing it from the bonds of the material condition, which is the human condition.

This hope for transformation, a new world born out of the ashes of the old, is apparently the deepest meaning of our myth.[32] The Bomb holds us in its power because it seems to resolve all our ambivalent feelings toward the human condition—toward matter and spirit, sanity and madness, life and death, cosmos and chaos—with its coincidence of opposites. But the price it demands for this resolution is its promise to destroy the past with all its faults, to destroy time itself, to etherialize matter, to fuse all reality in a unified mass, to restore the primeval chaos. If nuclear images are modern man's only avenue to initiatory rebirth, then we cannot escape these promises even if we sincerely want to. Consciously we may commit ourselves to eliminating chaos throughout the world by instituting a new global order of immutably static peaceful balance. Or we may commit ourselves to unleashing chaos only upon the enemy, in order to impose "our world" upon the whole world. Unconsciously, though, what we desire is a new cosmos for ourselves that includes the possibility of all the modes of perfection symbolized by the scientific, military, and political elites—a cosmos grounded in religious images and imbued with religious meaning.

We can only fulfill this desire by embracing the chaos that we fear. Unconsciously, then, we must take responsibility for destroying and recreating our world and ourselves. If we wish to share in the privileges of the elite, we must also share in their initiatory confrontation with nothingness. Like the shaman who must endure the chaos of madness, we must descend ever deeper into nuclear madness; we must all take on the uncanny power and lethal terror of the "mad scientist." We must therefore accept nuclear madness and approach the end of the world optimistically. We must take the path that leads to global death because we still hope for global renewal and the possibility of infinite life.

We have taken the first step toward such an initiation with the ubiquitous mechanization, sterilization, and subhumanization of our world and ourselves. But death in life is just a first step. In the imagery of nuclear annihilation we see the only way our literalizing consciousness knows to complete the process of destroying the world, wiping the slate clean, and bringing a new world into being. We demand literal death as well as literal life. All the particular images of transformation that run through the myth of nuclear origins thus find their consummation in the image of the Bomb as literal world-destroyer. This is the other side of the coin that shines like the solar disk, reflecting the quest for perfection that produced the light like a thousand suns. Without it, the myth could not speak of universal religious transformation.

The Meaning of a Meaningless End

This interpretation still leaves unexplained the puzzling anomaly of the myth's end. If the myth's central theme is homo religiosus' desire to live in a reborn cosmos, we would expect the story to narrate the destruction of the world and then to describe, at its end, the birth of a new, perfectly cosmicized world. Homo religiosus normally describes the end of the world in a state of certainty, assured that the end will lead to a new beginning. Our myth gives us no such assurance, for it tells of a securing of perfect order that is simultaneously a reemergence of universally threatening chaos: the battle against the enemy rages on, it is still fought with weapons that can destroy the world, and the outcome is wholly unpredictable. The world born in 1945, the world whose origin we are constantly reenacting, hopes for immutable cosmos yet remains on the verge of chaos.

This open-ended situation can not be written off as an incidental element. It is the one distinctive feature that colors the entire myth and sets it apart from all other myths about the end of the world. Nor can it be argued that historical facts demand this particular ending. Homo religiosus knows that myth, not history, reveals the essential facts; our behaviors are fundamentally determined by the myths we enact, not by the historical circumstances in which we enact them. It is easy enough to imagine our society choosing another myth and then acting upon that myth to try to change the facts of history. We could have chosen a myth that ends with one superpower conquering another, replicating the great conquests of 1945. We could have chosen a myth that ends with the superpowers agreeing to eliminate all weapons of mass destruction and joining together to rule the world, or renouncing the concept of world rule. We could have chosen a myth that ends with a new, more flexible, risk-laden political arrangement for the world. These alternatives were all suggested at the outset of the atomic age.[33] Instead, though, we chose a myth with no definite ending at all. This choice holds the key to our distinctively modern interpretation of the age-old vision of the end of the world. If myths reflect the existential situations assumed by their creators, then our existential situation is clearly the insecurity of a great global question mark.

The question mark surely has something to do with modern man's total immersion in time and history. Homo religiosus can approach the world's end with a feeling of certainty because for him the whole process is a timeless mythic event, already accomplished either in fact or in divine promise. Modern man has no such assurance. He must approach the end with intense uncertainty because for him the event can take place only in a literal historical future. The myth's insecurity reflects modern man's futurity, his feeling of standing on a historical brink, and his uncertain hope that the risk of destruction will lead to renewal. But modern man's radical temporality is only one facet of his existential situation. At the root of that situation lies the radical dualism of cosmos against chaos and the lack of a positive meaning for chaos.

The key to understanding the nuclear myth and its unique ending lies in modernity's two contradictory responses to the meaninglessness of chaos. Unconsciously we accept the wisdom of homo religiosus—the need for world destruction. We must immerse in the madness of chaos, we dimly sense, and this immersion must be total if it is to be totally regenerating. But any genuine encounter with chaos must be unpredictable; unpredictability is the essence of chaos. So the insecurity of our global question mark is a function not so much of our temporality as of our desire to transcend temporality by destroying the world, with its time and history, and reverting to universal chaos.

Consciously, however, we remain deaf to the whole dimension of symbolic meaning. We avoid its call by insisting on our other response to the meaninglessness of chaos: the war against chaos. As we repeat the myth of nuclear origins in words and deeds, we tell ourselves that we are striving to stave off the end of the world by defeating chaos as utterly as we did in 1945, whether through preparations for a war to end all wars or through a new world order of disarmament and peace. To insure the success of our evasion, we project our symbolic desires into literal realities. The engulfment we consciously fear may be engulfment by the "Red tide" or by the mushroom cloud; the annihilating narrowness we fear may be the oppression of "Communist totalitarianism" or of the nuclear cage; the implosion we fear in either case is the attack of enemy nuclear missiles. As pure literalists, we can only act out a transhistorical hope in the realm of history, politics, and technology.

When apocalypticism, whether of the Cold Warriors or the antinuclearists, threatens to pierce the veil of literalism with its symbolic images of chaos, we turn to the apparent security of the immutable balance offered by the dual track image. Although elements of the dual track also point back to the mythic era of 1945 and the desire for global transformation, it is the most successful mask of that desire to date. So we evade the responsibility of knowing the initiatory meaning of our chaos.

This is the existential situation enshrined in the myth of nuclear origins, the situation we reenact every day. We feel that we must tell a story about the triggering of universal chaos. We also feel that we must tell a story about the universal defeat of chaos. So we choose a story that tells of both. The myth of nuclear origins is thus, as its deepest level, a story about the conflict between modern man and homo religiosus—between what we are and what we would become, if only we knew how. It tells of the innate desire of every psychic image to attain perfect reality through perfect filtering of stimuli and perfect openness to stimuli. In both its content and its literalizing form, however, it also tells of the radical finitude that leaves us unable to unify these two fundamental desires in a religious image. So it reflects the schizophrenic paralysis of nuclear madness. We cannot heed the voice of religious imagination, nor can we silence it. We cannot accept responsibility for the end of the world, nor can we avoid it. We cannot resist the lure of global madness, death, and rebirth, but the only death we know is a literal death that would allow no rebirth. So we are paralyzed, unable to respond to either symbolic need or literal threat, because we are missing the meaning of the end of our world.

We are stuck in the middle of an initiatory journey. But every movement toward completion—toward a conscious discovery of the infinite possibilities of religious meaning—threatens to plunge us into a new kind of formlessness whose unpredictability and apparent meaninglessness terrify us. We would rather live with the madness we know—the madness given structure in our nuclear-age cosmos—than risk the madness we know not. To avoid risking the unknown, we refuse to acknowledge the meaning of the formlessness we have embraced. We feel compelled to fight against it, which only perpetuates its grip upon us and leaves us feeling ever more threatened by unreality. This self-defeating pattern is inescapable, for the existential crisis that provokes the battle against chaos also evokes the initiatory images that modernity fights against. The greater the sense of crisis, the stronger the lure as well as the dread of religious imagination and its symbols of initiatory chaos. We are wedded perforce to our most dreaded enemy; madness seems to hold our only hope for the transformation that leads to the possibility of limitless reality. So every step toward order and clarity becomes a step deeper into madness.

The myth's anomalous ending reflects this paradox: when we try to tell a paradigmatic story about the triumph of world order, we end up in disorder, contradicting and confusing ourselves. The myth tells us that this insoluble crisis is the existential situation we have chosen. But the more desperate the crisis, the more ardent the hope for renewal. So we continue to reenact the myth and perpetuate the madness, hoping that the

Bomb can somehow give us both immersion in and triumph over chaos. The Bomb and all those who wield it thus compound our sense of omnipresent chaotic unreality, deepening the ontological insecurity of modernity and compelling us to renew the impossible battle.

The Appeal of Chaos

Perhaps we recognize, at some deeply buried level, that the battle against chaos is in vain. Perhaps we recognize that the confusion of the myth's ending is the essence of the story we choose to reenact. But this need not vitiate the myth's value for us, since the myth also harbors another religious meaning: a desire to live permanently in chaos. This meaning arises in part from the unique situation of secular modernity. Because we consciously deny the possibility of a coincidence of opposites, we can think only in terms of mutually exclusive alternatives. This attitude is so deeply ingrained that it permeates our unconscious thoughts and images as well. So our unacknowledged symbols of chaos as the prelude to new cosmos simultaneously evoke doubt about harmonizing these opposites.

Under the shadow of this doubt, the only alternative to cosmos seems to be permanent chaos. So an unconscious hope for the end of our cosmos must conjure up images of endless chaos. If we want to transcend our secular literalism, the only alternative we can imagine is to be overwhelmed by the power of religious imagination, which we identify with chaos and madness. By now we may collectively despair of finding any meaningful structure that can incorporate the infinite possibility of imagination. With no vision of new structure rising out of our madness, we believe that our only alternatives are to try to live in the dying structure of modernity, which seems no longer viable, or to let that structure—and all structure—simply disappear.

Yet even in this radical either/or attitude, permanent chaos still has profound religious meaning as the polar opposite of both our profane existence and the strictures of the human condition. Homo religiosus recognizes this meaning too. Although he trusts that chaos will give way to new cosmos, he also retains an ambivalent longing to live in chaos. When he emulates the experience of the warrior, smith, sovereign, and shaman, he transcends the burdensome rigidifying structures of the cosmos. He enters the time before cosmos and time began—that infinitely fertile realm where nothing is binding and everything is possible—and thus embodies in himself a universal union of all possibilities. Chaotic madness draws him not only as a means to new cosmos, but also as a paradoxical good in itself.

Perhaps we, too, are drawn to that paradoxical good, embodied in its uniquely modern form, the Bomb. Where else can we find any publicly shared tangible symbol of religious meaning? Even if the Bomb is a dangerous, perverse, or self-destructive caricature of a religious image, at least it has a meaning that speaks to the deepest unconscious levels of the psyche, where religious imagination has its home. At those levels, the Bomb speaks not only of chaos, but of going beyond all limits, transcending the human condition, and glimpsing an opening to infinite possibility and perfect reality. If Eliade is correct, the modern West was yearning for such a symbol long before 1945. Only in that year, however, did we find the concrete image we desired. Bereft of all other religious meanings, we may cling to the new reality created in 1945 as our only hope.

Unconsciously, then, we may embrace the global question mark at the end of the nuclear myth as a gamble that we can not lose. We are profoundly unsure whether our present chaos will lead to a new cosmos or not. Whether we see these opposites as conjoined or disjoined, however, we can be sure that the sterile death in life of modernity's cosmos has been ended by the chaos of nuclear madness. So we are just as loathe to turn back the clock of history to its prenuclear situation as we are to step forward into a radically new world of religious meaning.

Mircea Eliade's perspective shows the popular understanding of the myth of nuclear origins to be superficial. The risk of world destruction is neither incidental nor accidental. Rather it is the key to deciphering the meaning of the myth, which, in turn, holds the key to the meaning of our behavior and our madness. Nuclear madness is more than just a defense against ontological insecurity. It also grows out of a positive longing to immerse ourselves in infinite possibility, experience a total transformation, and open a psychic path toward perfect openness within perfect structure. Without any grounding in a religious image, however, we must go on, like the schizophrenic, ambivalently thwarting our own deepest desire. So we remain paralyzed in the midst of impending chaos.

This interpretation of the myth of nuclear origins is, like the model of nuclear madness, a speculation. It can not be verified by empirical data. Nor does it rest on a theoretical model that can be empirically verified. It derives its validity from its capacity to afford a new viewpoint on the nuclear dilemma: the viewpoint of homo religiosus. That viewpoint, in turn, is valid to the extent that Eliade's philosophical and psychological reflections on modernity have a convincing power. If our greatest need now is to open ourselves to religious imagination, Eliade's method of interpretation affords one step in that direction. The Bomb may offer a surprising opportunity to actualize the values of homo religiosus by consciously acknowledging and embracing the religious meaning of our personal, societal, and global madness. Interpreting the myth of nuclear origins is only one of many ways that religious imagination can be rekindled in the nuclear age. The question that remains is how this transformation might be accomplished as a public political act. One clue toward an answer may lie in a further consideration of the thought of James Hillman.

11

The Hell and Renaissance of Madness

For James Hillman, the psychopathology of schizophrenia and the sociopathology of nuclear madness meet in the mythic home of all madness: Hades. Hillman's archetypal psychology views all psychological disease as an enactment of a pathologizing fantasy. In madness, the fantasy is one of "split personality," "cracking up," "falling apart," and "going to hell." A very similar fantasy pervades our public life. However "it's all invisible psychopathy today. Very successful and very adapted and you can't see it,"[1] because the line that once separated the psychopathic from the normal has been erased. Household appliances and national economies are falling apart, inner cities and suburban marriages are going to hell, and "death lurks in things: asbestos and food additives, acid rain and tampons, insecticides and pharmaceuticals."[2]

Above all, though, death lurks in the Bomb, the ultimate embodiment of our pathological fantasies. Hillman agrees with Mircea Eliade that the chaos of nuclear madness may point to a hope for transformation and rebirth, for Hades is the home not only of madness and death, but also of the infinite possibilities of imagination. Hilman also agrees with Eliade that, although a nuclear hell may be imagined as a way station to new life, it need not be; hell can also be evoked as a final resting place, a chaotic end in itself. But Hillman suggests a third alternative: nuclear madness may be endowed with a religious meaning that embraces both interpretations offered by Eliade's thought. In fact Hillman's thought leads to the conclusion that both interpretations must be embraced as complementary, rather than contradictory, possibilities if there is to be any hope for peace.

The Bomb and the Descent to the Underworld

To understand the meaning of modern fantasies (whether

private or public), Hillman seeks their prototypes in classical Greek mythology. The Greek conception of Hades, as he understands it, certainly shares much in common with the prevalent images of nuclear holocaust; nuclear madness evokes images of turning the world into a living hell. The Bomb's impact upon the living is often described in terms of invasion, penetration, violation, and rape (like the mythic rape that brought Persephone down to Hades). It removes the solid ground from under our feet as it twists, distorts, and tears apart the natural environment. Yet it simultaneously fuses together things that are by nature separate. What it leaves is a dark, confused, unnatural void. Its characteristic elements are ice, smoke, filth, intolerable heat, and unbearable cold. (Christianity adds to these Greek images another characteristic element of nuclear war's hell—endless fire.)

The people in this hell must suffer the pain and degradation of sickness, plague, and ever-present reminders of death. But they are not really people in the full sense; they are shades, one-dimensional remnants of human beings, deprived of flesh and blood. (As Robert Jay Lifton and Kai Erikson have put it, the survivors of a nuclear holocaust "would not so much envy as, inwardly and outwardly, resemble the dead.")[3] The cold chill we feel when the thought of nuclear war flits for an instant across our consciousness is like the core of ice at the deepest level of hell. There everything is frozen and immobilized. There is no hope because there is no future. Time and change have come to a stop; the urge to perfect stasis has achieved its final victory.

But one need not look to a fantasy of nuclear weapons unleashed in order to find images of Hades in contemporary life. The very existence of these weapons brings the underworld to our doorstep. The confusion and complexity of a world destroyed is only slightly greater than our present confusion as we try to unravel the complexities of the nuclear dilemma. The moral standards that guide other dimensions of life seem irrelevant here. Much is obscure and hidden, especially intentions; we strive to keep it that way with our passion for nuclear secrecy. The children of the goddess Night, who include Strife, Deceit, Envy, Lamentation, and Doom, are as active in the nuclear age as they are in Hades. Whether planning "warfighting" strategies or riding the dual track of deterrence and disarmament, the heroic ego seeks to accomplish the task of the river Styx, guardian of the underworld: "The ego here becomes Styx's instrument, a Child of Hatred, icily preserving itself against all enemies, the greatest of which will be warmth. . . . Hatred uses the ego to destroy pain. Each of us becomes a child of Styx when we embark on the pain-killing course, justifying our victories and zeal in destruction in terms of 'self-preservation' and 'ego-development.' "[4]

The pain-destroying river is just one image of Hades that recalls the dominant feature of our psychological landscape: psychic numbing. The road to Hades leads not only to the river Styx but also to the waters of Lethe, the river of forgetfulness. Hades is the realm of sleep, where the cares and dangers of the everyday world are cast aside. The shades in the underworld are as devoid of every emotion as they are devoid of hope; they are static, abstract, one-dimensional beings. If there is one emotion that survives the journey downward, it is depression. As Hillman describes depression, he seems to be talking precisely about our cultural paralysis in the face of the Bomb: "We feel ourselves caught in hatefulness, cold, numbed, and drawn downward out of life by a force we cannot see, against which we would flee, distractedly thrashing about for naturalistic explanations and comforts for what is happening so darkly. We feel invaded from below, assaulted, and we think of death."[5]

What earthly reason could we have for creating and perpetuating such an unearthly world? Hillman has devoted one essay specifically to this question, finding in the Bomb a futureless apocalyptic fantasy of absolute ending and total destruction.[6] As a totally abstract reality, it cannot engender heightened sensation or emotion, but only numbed stupefaction at its power. Its emblematic image is fire: "It evokes the apocalyptic transformation of the world into fire, earth ascending in a pillar of cloud."[7] Hillman traces the Bomb's apocalyptic imagery, as well as its heroic ego imagery, back to classical mythology and the origins of Christianity. Both ancient Greeks and early Christians believed that the hero (whether Hercules or Christ) must descend to the underworld to subdue the dark powers of evil so that the virtues of goodness and light could flourish. In Christian apocalyptic imagery, this triumph was understood as a global death and resurrection. For Hillman, the ego is bound to this resurrection fantasy whenever it approaches death and the shadow side of the psyche. So our nuclear fantasies must betray the same desire for death and rebirth.

Americans have traditionally seen their martial heroes in terms of a similar fantasy. American soldiers have always been reminded that their heroism was in the name of Christian ideals—that there was something Christ-like about their willingness to go into war's hell and make the ultimate sacrifice in order to rid the world of evil.[8] Today it is the nuclear warrior, buried in a war room or missile silo deep beneath the earth, who imitates Christ's descent to the underworld. This is the obvious irony in all myths of the conquest of Hades: one can conquer it only by descending to it. The ego must leave its enlightened literal clarity to surround itself with the nebulous shades far below. It must experience itself as at least temporarily burned up in hellfire: "In the end, Hercules goes up in fire."[9]

The image of fire links the apocalypse and conquest-of-Hades myths, for in the Christian context there is only one way to complete the conquest of Hades: the whole world must imitate Christ by descending to hell so that it can be raised to Heaven. Fire must fight fire. Only when all things are on fire can the heroic ego win its apocalyptic victory. The Christian myth thus projects the conquest-of-Hades myth onto a cosmic scale, but the two share an essentially similar Herculean structure. This is the same structure that frames our nuclear madness, with its vivid images of descending into a fiery hell. Like all good monotheists, though, we want something concrete that we can literally grapple with. So we evoke the underworld in the only way we know how—in the concrete literalism of technological and political reality.

The Underside of Nuclear Fantasies

Hillman's theoretical model bids us look for the underside—the repressed images of the shadow side—in every social pathology. In the nuclear arms race, then, we should expect to find a fantasy not sanctioned by the daylight consciousness of the modern West. Our daylight consciousness may sanction the descent into Hades as an apocalyptic journey leading to resurrection. But it does not sanction another image that Hillman points up in his essay on the Bomb when he writes: "The nuclear epiphany unveils the apocalyptic God, a God of extinction, the God-is-dead God, an epiphany of Nihilism."[10] This passage conflates the two meanings of the underworld's chaos suggested by Eliade's perspective: apocalypse (formlessness as the infinite possibility that enables transformation) and nihilistic extinction (formlessness as an end in itself). Both of these meanings are evident in the imagery of a nuclear hell, but they should be kept conceptually distinct, for modernity cannot consciously validate images of nihilism and extinction; it cannot admit that the fire of nuclear apocalypse and hell may be a nihilistic end in itself. Yet this journey into destruction for its own sake is precisely the blind alley where the heroic ego has ended up, in Hillman's view. This is the underside of our nuclear fantasies.

There has always been some public suspicion that nuclear weapons can only produce this sort of dead-end descent. One part of the Bomb's message has always been the message posted at the gate of Hades: "Abandon all hope ye who enter here." During the early years of the nuclear age, this message was repressed by fantasies of civil defense and nuclear rebirth. Now it is more likely to be repressed by the dual track and its "safe Bomb" fantasy. One way or another, the public ego denies its own shadow side by believing that it aims to purify the world of every evil "shadow." The ego represses its fantasy of the journey down to the depths as a journey of no return.

This journey could well be the terminus of all our thinking and not thinking, about the Bomb and everything else. Yet we do not turn back. Apparently we will permit the Bomb to lead us down into the underworld. Why? Hillman notes that apocalyptic fantasies "announce the end of the world. As with suicide fantasies we must ask them precisely what world is coming to its end. . . . The fantasies of the literal end of the world announce," he contends, "the end of this literalist world, the dead, objective world. . . . That vast insensate edifice—the doctrine of a soulless world—now streaked with acid rain and stained by graffiti has in our fantasies already exploded into dust."[11]

Through its apocalyptic fantasies the public ego can admit its need for its own breakdown—the same breakdown it complains of as it looks despairingly at its appliances, its cities, its families, and its world. It can experience (in a comfortingly familiar form) the full intensity of its desire to fall apart, destroy itself, and go to hell. This desire is fully understandable, and indeed inevitable, from the perspective of archetypal psychology. The psyche can never be satisfied with monotheistic consciousness. It can never accept its reduction to the single fantasy of the literalized heroic ego. It must seek those myriad fantasy images that have been repressed. Every such image has its source in Hades, the prime metaphor for the endless depth of metaphorical connections and transformations in every image.

The death that Hades portends is not literal but metaphorical death, the demise of the ego's preeminence: "Hades' realm refers to the archetypal perspective that is wholly psychological, where the considerations of human life—the emotions, organic needs, social connections of humanistic psychology—no longer apply. In Hades' realm *psyche* alone exists."[12] If the psyche descends to Hades on a journey of no return, it is seeking its authentic reality, the reality of archetypal imagination, as an end desirable in itself. This is just what Hillman sees happening in our public pathologies: "The sickness fantasy is now so dominant that one sees disintegration, pollution, insanities, cancerous growth, and decay wherever one looks. . . . It seems the psyche itself insists on pathologizing the strong ego and all its supportive models, disintegrating the 'I' with images of psychopathic hollowness in public life . . . opening it to the Underworld of psychic being."[13] If nuclear madness is a desire to return to Hades then it is a hidden desire to be healed and a hidden intuition of where the healing can be found. Its terminus is the termination of the literalizing world of modernity; it aims to move beyond destruction to a renewal of imagination; its hidden purpose is to heal the underlying pathology of modernity.

This psychological perspective on social problems may explain why the problems are so intractable. Just as in Hades, so in imagination there is no pursuit of progress. To the ego this feels like acting out the same old mistakes in apparently pointless repetitions—as we seem to do on the repetitive treadmill of the nuclear arms race. It appears to be a form of psychic numbing, an inability to respond to changing problems with creatively changing solutions. "But is the solution to these problems as problems what the soul seeks? . . . The psyche seems more interested in the movement of its ideas than in the resolution of problems. . . . Psyche's obstinate problems offer focus for fantasy."[14]

So the psyche may be especially drawn to the dual track that always leads back to the Bomb just because the Bomb is so richly evocative of multivalent imagery. We may feel compelled to continue along that track, despite its dangers, for the same reason that we must dream: to be nourished by the images repressed in daylight life. Confronting nuclear weapons we inevitably lose the distinction between literal and imaginal, between day world and night world. The Bomb and its effects elude our literalizing grasp every time. Scientific research confirms our intuition that no amount of empirical data can ever fully predict the consequences of a large-scale nuclear "exchange." Even if science could attain perfect accuracy, it is doubtful that we would be able to accept its findings on a purely literal level. The Bomb, like Hades, is saturated with mythic meanings and symbolic imagery that we can never escape.

But as long as we literalize every image in order to avoid dealing with its deeper mythic meaning, we must also literalize Hades and perceive it only as literal extinction. We must act like waking people dealing with our nuclear images, which are largely the stuff of dreams. Is it any wonder, then, that we act like sleepers when faced with the very real daylight threat of catastrophe? In the classical Hades, imagery opposed and overcame psychic numbing. Hades was sundered from the literal material world, so its timeless stasis opened up a unique space for the archetypes of imaginal reality. But when Hades literally invades life, as in the nuclear age, its tide of archetypes appears to be only an epiphany of nihilistic extinction—a numbed death in life that closes off imagination.

In our nuclear hell imagery and numbing are not opposites but embracing partners. Whether we think about the Bomb's present impact and possible future use, or refuse to think about them, we enter a realm that bears a striking resemblance to Hades. We seem to be stuck in a rut that negates the power of new fantasies as it generates them and thus offers no healing. And the more we literalize—the more we repress our nuclear fantasies—the more they press for return in literal form and call forth more strenuous efforts of literalizing repression. As a result of this vicious cycle, the public psyche is drawn ever more firmly down toward the underworld and the underworld is drawn up into public life. Hades-in-life becomes our goal.

Polytheism, Monotheism, and Dualism

Hillman's conflation of apocalypse and extinction imagery brings together the two sides of the myth of nuclear origins revealed by Eliade's thought: the Bomb's chaos as a prelude to new birth and as an end in itself. It shows both those sides as expressions of a single overriding myth: the descent to the underworld—to an acknowledgement and conscious experience of the psyche's archetypal images. But our desire to go to hell is dreadfully distorted because it has been captured by the singleness of our monotheistic consciousness. The solution to our problems would seem to begin, then, with a turn to polytheistic consciousness, to a conscious encounter with the multivalent fantasy images of the psyche. We not only want but need to choose together to go to hell.

But a rush into long-repressed images might exacerbate rather than heal our madness: "To let the depths rise without our systems of protection is what psychiatry calls psychosis: the images and voices and energies invading the emptied cities of reason which have been depersonified and demythologized and so have *no containers to receive the divine influxes.*"[15] Our lack of an adequate container, like our literalizing, turns Hades into pure formlessness and nothing else. Clearly this is not the kind of descent to the underworld that Hillman would promulgate. It is not difficult to find seemingly constructive mythic containers for nuclear madness, even within the Western tradition. It might be seen as a painful odyssey, or a walk through the valley of the shadow of death, or even a crucifixion. And the disarmament movement's vision of an end to the nuclear threat might be imagined in terms of homecoming, salvation, or even resurrection to a life of perpetual peace. Certainly, as Hillman himself suggests, the nuclear age can easily be interpreted in apocalyptic terms as a descent into hell, and total nuclear disarmament could be seen as an apocalyptic triumph of antinuclear politics.

These images of initiatory transformation all represent the kind of symbolic meaning that Eliade advocates. Yet for Hillman they merely compound the root of the problem, for all are monotheistic fantasies. It is too dangerous, Hillman argues, to imagine the Bomb and its vicissitudes in terms of death and resurrection. What is the alternative? Apparently it is only to deepen the fantasy of world destruction—of turning the world permanently into Hades—understood purely as fantasy. Yet how can the disarmament movement ignore the initiatory images that Eliade's analysis offers? How can it refuse to provide a fantasy of hope for a better future? How can it dispense with images of a Bomb-free future as the light at the end of the tunnel?

Perhaps Hillman's theoretical model seems unable to answer these questions because it casts the alternatives too starkly. Like Eliade's model, it seems to offer either resurrection fantasy or endless Hades fantasy—either monotheism or polytheism—as mutually exclusive alternatives. Ironically, Hillman identifies dualism as a feature of the monotheistic consciousness he so strenuously opposes. He sees dualism reflecting a devotion to singleness because its motto is "divide and conquer." (In some cases it may be "an *extreme metaphor*, a radical way of saying one thing as though it were two violently different things in sharp war with itself." The dualism of today's left and right wing politics is a case in point, he claims; both share the same monotheistic literalizing attitude.)[16]

But does he perhaps employ this very divide and conquer strategy? On the first page of his fullest programmatic statement, *Re-Visioning Psychology*, stands this categorical declaration, in the singular: "The human adventure is . . . for the sake of making soul. . . . The purpose of life is to make psyche of it."[17] Hillman's archetypal psychology rarely deviates from this unitary foundation, and he mounts his attack on monotheistic consciousness and its resurrection fantasy precisely in the service of this single goal. He has admitted the irony in this but claimed that it is inescapable for historical reasons: "Arguments between 'the One and the Many' play themselves out in an arena already set up by monotheistic consciousness. . . . Because the opposition of monotheism to polytheism is so much the baggage of this culture, it is deep in the collective unconscious of each of us."[18]

Hillman's dualism may have a deeper significance, though. He is, by his own admission, out to kill the monotheistic God: "The revolution fermenting in the soul of northern monotheism which has occasioned the belief in the death of its God must also be taking place in psychology. It, too, must be afflicted by the death of this same god."[19] Yet the gods, he asserts, do not want to be killed. They want to be served by being remembered. When forgotten, they force their appearance upon us in the most concrete ways, bedazzling us with a power that can blind us to their presence. Has Hillman himself perhaps forgotten that the omnipotent All-Father of Judaism and Christianity is also one of the gods, one whose claim to sole existence is intrinsic to his archetypal nature? Is Hillman somewhat bedazzled by the God-Devil dualism in the resurrection fantasy he so strenuously opposes? Has the forgotten deity taken his revenge (which, by all traditional accounts, we should surely expect him to do) in the dualistic cleavage that runs down the middle of archetypal psychology?

If so, then archetypal psychology is acting out the same ambivalence it ascribes to the nuclear age. Our desire to return to Hades and transform our existence demands the death of monotheism's God the Father. Yet our myths of apocalyptic Herculean transformation show the heroic ego clinging to the monotheistic divinity, postponing the death sentence indefinitely (as evidenced most clearly in the resurgence of literalizing fundamentalism). The ambiguous meanings of our nuclear myths suggest that, as Nietzsche prophesied over a century ago, we want to do the deed of deicide but deny the doing. Having repressed the deed, we are condemned to act it out literally on the stage of world politics. Nuclear and antinuclear policies both aim to destroy the power of the devil, whether it be the Cold Warrior's "Red devil" or the antinuclearist's diabolical weapon of omnicide. Yet both sides may actually be aiming their destruction at God himself, for the devil is God's shadow, and "the shadow is not a separated archetype. . . . Each God contains shadow."[20] The "light" and "dark" side of an archetype form a psychological unity; God's health and very life depend on his incorporating his shadow, the devil. "If God has died, it was because of his own good health; he had lost touch with the intrinsic *infirmitas* of the archetype."[21]

If nuclear politics is driven by a repressed deicidal impulse, the intended victim certainly does take his revenge. Those who would kill monotheism's God by literally destroying the "Red devil" end up so bedazzled by God that they must cling to his characteristically literal weapon—the Bomb—to do the deed. Those who would kill monotheism's God by literally destroying the diabolical weapon end up so bedazzled by God that they often forget their ultimate aim in their rush to score more political victories by serving the heroic ego. So nuclear politics joins archetypal psychology in testifying that the resurrecting God of the Bible, like all gods, demands to be remembered. He demands that we face our ambivalence toward him honestly, lest he take his literally lethal revenge by compelling us to act out his apocalyptic drama literally.

This does not vitiate the value of Hillman's insights. If there is danger in forgetting the resurrection fantasy, there is equal danger in clinging to it exclusively. We must also remember the gods of polytheism in order to escape the nuclear dilemma; we must acknowledge our desire to dwell permanently in the polyvalent image-world of Hades. So we must find a way to blend both rememberings. Hillman has occasionally alluded to such a possibility. In *Re-Visioning Psychology* he refers to "an unworried blending of polytheistic and monotheistic styles" (although two central statements along these lines are relegated to footnotes).[23] But it is not clear what this blending might look like.

Hillman offers one concrete description in his discussion of another basic form of the death and rebirth fantasy in Western tradition: the Italian Renaissance. For Hillman, the Renaissance offers just the kind of container that we need for an upsurge of archetypal fantasies, a container that goes beyond the traditional Western images of death and rebirth. Renaissance is a "movement of rebirth from natural existence to psychological existence [that] requires a preceding or a simultaneous dying. Fantasies of rebirth occur together with death fantasies; Renaissance and death belong together. . . . I believe the God of the Renaissance and of *all psychological renascences* to be Hades. . . . [In Renaissance] rebirth is coupled with defeat, failure is its precondition, Hades is its deepest secret."[23] For Hillman the renaissance fantasy is quite different from the apocalyptic vision of resurrection. While resurrection is the ego's journey through formlessness, undertaken in order to attain a world of pure eternal form, renaissance is the soul's journey away from dualism into a world of permanently entwined form and formlessness.

Dualism persists, however, even in Hillman's treatment of the Italian Renaissance. He calls it an expression of a southern sensibility, wholly opposed to the northern sensibility of the Reformation. He contrasts it sharply with the medieval Christendom that preceded it and the Cartesian modernity that followed it. Perhaps this dualism, too, is the paradoxical result of a one-sided view. While the Renaissance made a place for imaginal death, it surely gave a central place to images of resurrection as well. Its Christian symbols and Neoplatonic philosophies inevitably carried overtones of monotheistic wholeness. Its manifold images of light and spirit testify that it embraced death as a springboard to transcend death. As Hillman says: "Renaissance psychology does not end in death—it only begins there. From this position comes the leap into life and the embrace of shadow and soul."[24] It seems, then, that a proper understanding of rebirth as renaissance must be taken beyond dualism (as the nature of renaissance demands). As a container for our fantasies, it must illustrate an unworried blending of monotheism and polytheism. In renaissance, the two sides of our nuclear myths—chaos as a prelude to resurrection and chaos as an end in itself—meet, and both are affirmed as fantasies necessary for the soul.

Nuclear Suicide and the Soul

Can this notion of renaissance be applied to fantasies of individual healing, or to societal healing in the nuclear age? Hillman suggests an affirmative answer in one of his earliest books, which is of special interest here for two reasons. First, he wrote it before setting himself so squarely against monotheistic consciousness. Thus it reflects an incipient sense of polytheistic imagining while still honoring the monotheistic psychological tradition. Second, it goes to the heart of our subject—the threat of human self-destruction—for it is called *Suicide and the Soul*.

In this book the meaning of suicide is clearly set forth: it is "a demand for an encounter with absolute reality, a demand for a fuller life through the death experience."[25] In this "attempt to enter another level of reality . . . one level is wiped out for another. *Suicide is the attempt to move from one realm to another by force through death.* . . . Death appears in order to make way for transformation. The flower withers around its swelling pod, the snake sheds its skin, and the adult puts off his childish ways. The creative force kills as it produces the new. . . . *Then suicide is the urge for hasty transformation.*"[26] One could hardly find a theory of suicide more marked by the fantasy of death and resurrection.

At one point Hillman uses an explicitly monotheistic image to describe this fantasy: suicide "demands that God reveal Himself. . . . Suicide offers immersion in, and possible regeneration through, the dark side of God. It would confront the last, or worst, truth in God, His own hidden negativity."[27] In other words, we may feel driven to destroy ourselves in order to meet the diabolical side of God, to reunite God and his shadow. Yet precisely because they have been so radically separated we may see no way to this goal but literal self-inflicted death. Hillman claims that the potential suicide has confused the inner with the outer, the needs of the imagination with the literal physical dimension of life. Resisting the psyche's demand to immerse in the formlessness of imagination and undergo an imaginal death experience, the suicide ends up making the urge to formlessness more compelling and literalizes it as physical death.

Is it fair to take these speculations about individual suicide and apply them to the nuclear destruction that has been called "mutual suicide"? Hillman thinks it is fair, at least in some measure, for he devotes a dense paragraph to the issue, in which he says:

> If suicide is a transformative impulse, we can regard today's concern with mass suicide through the Bomb as an attempt of the collective psyche at renewal by ridding itself of the binds of history and the weight of its material accumulations. . . . Through the Bomb we live in the shadow of death. . . . *The more imminent the death experience, the more possibility for transformation.* . . . What must occur if the actual suicide does not come is a transformation in the collective psyche."[28]

In light of the later archetypal psychology, the nature of this transformation is clear: from materialism and literalism to imagination, from the dualism of matter and spirit to the innate polytheism of the psyche. But in its own context, this text does not define the transformation so specifically; it merely implies that some fundamental change in public values is needed. So it concludes: "The Bomb may thus be God's dark hand which He has shown before to Noah and the peoples of the Cities of the Plain, urging not death, but a radical transformation in our souls."[29] Here again the shadow side of the biblical monotheistic God is invoked, not as a distinct devil figure but as a necessary part of the archetype.

This discussion of the Bomb as suicidal transformer, like the whole vision of suicide as transformative urge, shows Hillman's thought preparing for the leap to archetypal psychology. But one foot remains firmly planted in a more conventional style of thinking. So *Suicide and the Soul* is itself a blend—an apparently unworried blend—of monotheistic and polytheistic psychology. As such, it is also a blend of endorsement and criticism toward monotheism's resurrection fantasy. This is most clear when Hillman comes to discuss the therapist's responsibility toward the suicidal patient. The therapist's first duty is not to prevent suicide by resurrecting the patient's spirit or giving the patient hope for resurrection. In fact, such efforts are counterproductive, for what the patient needs most is to allow nothingness and despair into life's midst, to recognize the urge to literal death as a metaphor masking the genuine need to accept psychic formlessness. "An analysis leads up to this moment and by constellating this despair lets free the suicidal impulse. . . . Transformation begins at this point where there is no hope. Despair produces the cry for salvation."[30]

But Hillman chooses a most telling historical example of the despairing cry for salvation: "It was not with a voice of hope that Jesus called, '*Eli, Eli, lama sabachtani*?' [My God, my God, why have you forsaken me?] . . . Despair ushers in the death experience and is at the same time the requirement for resurrection."[31] This is the same author who would later call Christianity "that organization of the mind which makes our culture sick"[32] and condemn the resurrection fantasy in the harshest terms for its claim that all suffering is good and heroic, the prelude to a better day. Perhaps Hillman became so bedazzled by Christianity as his opponent that he lost sight of his earlier positive vision of resurrection. Having discovered how the heroic ego captures the soul's desire for rebirth and turns it into a fantasy of conquering literal death, he seems to have forgotten his earlier insight that the soul needs its own resurrection fantasy as part of its acceptance of imaginal death.

Hillman's insistence that the repressed always returns suggests that this forgetting was more than just the passion of a partisan. Every rebirth fantasy, no matter what its theological context, must contain some positive role for suffering, some sense of victory over death, some hope for a better day, and in general some measure of heroic ego virtues. So the soul's need for rebirth must contain a monotheistic dimension, as the Renaissance recognized. This repressed monotheistic dimension comes back in Hillman's thought as a dualistic attack on monotheism's narrowly defined egoic resurrection fantasy. If archetypal psychology aims at a blending of monotheism and polytheism, it must recognize the soul's desire for a rebirth fantasy that blends monotheism and polytheism, resurrection and Hades.

This desire suggests another approach to the nuclear age's apocalypse and descent-to-Hades myths. They both speak of our conscious aspiration to vanquish chaos and death, viewing annihilation as the means to resurrection and a life eternally beyond death. They both speak of our unconscious desire to remain immersed in chaos and death, thereby destroying the literal and returning to the healing power of the imaginal. But there is a third way to read these myths: perhaps they are both suicide myths secretly spoken by the soul. Perhaps they speak of the soul's aspiration to renaissance, a rebirth that renews life not by conquering Hades nor by literally immersing in it, but by embracing Hades permanently in imagination. If so, we need not choose between the two interpretations of the myth of nuclear origins suggested by Eliade's method: chaos as a prelude to resurrection and an end in itself. Indeed only when chaos as imaginal death—the formlessness of infinite possibility—is accepted as an end in itself can life be preserved, enhanced, and raised beyond the threat of literal death.

Under the rule of the heroic ego, however, the soul cannot understand its need in terms of renaissance. It can only translate its need into fantasies of literal self-destruction. The ego can feel its impulses to annihilation and to resurrection only as mutually exclusive alternatives; death as an end in itself can be seen only as the polar opposite of life. So archetypal psychology can fruitfully view Western civilization as a suicidal patient caught in a deadly psychic conflict. On the one hand, there is a compelling urge to destroy the old life quite literally so that a new life can be born. On the other hand, there is a sense that it is too late for transformation, that no new life is possible, that death is the only alternative. And this vision of death must be literalized because the soul's desire for imaginative death is denied.

Modernity's suicidal ego is caught between its desire to conquer its enemies and its desire to extinguish itself, its desire to serve its All-Father and its desire to murder him, its desire to maintain its monotheistic consciousness at all costs and its desire to be pulled down—or blown up—to the riches of polytheistic consciousness. But these two apparently contradictory sets of meanings lead to the same vision of literal extinction. Failing to give a place to our ambivalent needs in imagination, we are compelled to act out both sides literally.

The Bomb is the perfect container, the perfect kettle for this sociopathic stew. It replaces God the Father as the center of our cultural structure, for it is greater than that traditional image of God. It enshrines all the complexities of his monotheistic consciousness. But it simultneously harbors our desire to destroy that consciousness in the name of our polytheistic birthright. And it embodies our suicidally literalized hope for an unworried blending of monotheistic and polytheistic consciousness. All these fantasies, along with their endless permutations and combinations, are fragments of our pervasive madness. Like every madness, the Bomb opens up the realm of infinite possibility only to shut it down again.

Renaissance and Madness

The lethal power of our suicidal fantasies might yet be disarmed if the patient were treated by a sensitive therapist who could help constellate global annihilation in the imagination, thus releasing the literalizing compulsion and allowing for personal and societal renaissance. For society, as for the individual, constellating annihilation means forging a fantasy of renaissance. Renaissance fantasies must entwine formlessness with form, death with resurrection, the gods with the One God. And they must do so on a universal scale. They must give imaginal form to the end of the world as a global descent into hell that is a journey of no return, while paradoxically retaining hope for a more perfect future. This is the transformation in the collective psyche that must occur, according to Hillman, if the actual suicide is to be averted. But how can a whole society accomplish this when it has no therapist to turn to, when each can only turn to the others in a shared pathology?

Hillman hints at an answer when he quotes the words of Heraclitus: "Hades and Dionysus are the same, no matter how much they go mad and rave celebrating bacchic rites in honour of the latter."[33] A universal descent to Hades means universal madness, universal immersion in unlimited imagination. Renaissance, too, means universal madness. Oddly enough, although Hillman links Hades and the Renaissance so closely and parallels Renaissance pathology with our own[34], he does not focus specifically on the madness of the Renaissance. However Michel Foucault, beginning his *Madness and Civilization* with a discussion of the Renaissance, suggests its relevance for the nuclear age: "If the end was near, it was to the degree that madness, become universal, would be one and the same with death itself.... It is man's insanity that invokes and makes necessary the world's end."[35]

Hillman sees in this foreboding of the end the very source of the Renaissance: "Revival emerges from the threat to survival and is not a choice of something preferable. Revival is forced upon us by the dire pathologizing of psychic necessities. A renaissance comes out of the corner, out of the black plague and its rats, and the shades of death within the shadow."[36] That shadow is the shadow of Hades, the shadow of archetypal imagination. So renaissance and madness are intertwined because both are propelled by the same need—the psyche's irrepressible need to claim the fullness of its own imaginal reality. When the psyche feels itself sufficiently drained of reality, its very nature compels it to seek renaissance along the hellish road of madness, the road on which the world comes to an end because all things are possible. But the psyche finds renaissance only when it accepts madness as an end in itself—as a permanent reflection of its reality—as well as a portal to new sanity and life.

The threads linking renaissance, madness, hell, and our contemporary predicament are evident. Today, the impending shadow of a nuclear end of the world is the strongest force compelling us toward renaissance. The impending shadow is also the clearest sign that, in the face of our ontological insecurity, we must seek renaissance through madness. The question is not whether to take the road down to madness, for we are already upon it. Nor is the question whether to continue on the road; madness, once begun, is an initiatory journey that must be carried through to its end. Hillman implicitly acknowledges this when he writes of the archetypal *senex*, the conservative old man who rules in and through the state: "Our senex order rests on senex madness. Our order itself is a madness.... The only protection is the dissolution of this fantasy of sanity, and in Joseph Conrad's language the recipe is 'immersion in the destructive element'.... To penetrate the riddle of senex destruction means to go to the heart of darkness."[37]

The question that faces us now is how we will understand and respond to the journey of madness. The answer to that question may well determine the nature of our journey and its end. For if Hades is Dionysus, then not every madness succeeds in descending to Hades or rising to renaissance. Dionysus presides over madness, Hillman contends, only when there is awareness of the archetypal meaning in the madness. Madness does not enter Hades or become renaissance unless its fantasy content is consciously constellated, understood as fantasy, and accepted as an enduring part of the self. Dionysian madness would require "remaining true to one's shadow-angel, true to one's own central madness which is as well the wisdom of nature that is unconscious of itself and cannot speak in words. It would mean a wholly new feeling of respect towards our own 'craziness.' "[38] Respect would mean breaking through our psychic numbing, opening ourselves to our own imagination, acknowledging our ambivalence, and affirming our longing to dwell in the realm of infinite possibility. It would also mean giving conscious form to our formlessness, bestowing a meaning upon the end of the world, and finding a container to structure our explosion of fantasy.

A renaissance of madness would therefore require a kind of politics that the disarmament movement does not yet understand. For Hillman, that movement embodies the archetypal *puer*, the young spiritual seeker who fights against the senex. But "puer consciousness does not see the madness of the [senex] archetype. It moves among the gods like beautiful Ganymede, serving ambrosia, carrying their messages but not reading the horror between the lines."[39] The puer may miss the madness because it is caught up in the same monotheistic literalizing as its elder.[40] Today's antinuclear puer may not read the horror because it is caught up in the same monotheistic dual track and "safe Bomb" fantasies as the senile state, failing to recognize those fantasies as fantasies. An antinuclear politics of renaissance would call upon the puer, first and foremost, to acknowledge its own madness, "to care for it as precious, as the one thing that he truly is. . . . The spirit needs witness to this madness. Or to put it another way, the puer takes its drive and goal literally unless there is reflection, which makes possible a metaphorical understanding of its drive and goal."[41]

If transformation is being forced upon us today from the darkest corner of all—from the shadow of the nuclear cloud—it must begin with a conscious recognition of and care for our nuclear madness within a new, consciously chosen container.

As a first step, we need to understand our drive toward war and destruction metaphorically. We need to open ourselves to the seductive power of the Bomb itself as a container for our fantasy images of universal death. Ultimately, of course, the Bomb and its false promises must be rejected altogether. Our transformation must also be what most of us assume it to be: a movement from the threat of world war to the reality of world peace. But the path to peace must lead into the valley of the shadow of madness. So we also need a new container that can preserve us on this path by peacefully constellating our suicidal fantasies. This container must afford a conscious shared understanding of our madness as a form of renaissance, a "creative breakdown"[42] that blends the hellish darkness of the schizophrenic trap with a journey toward the light at the end of the schizophrenic tunnel. Suicidal madness can be healed only when the two are experienced as inseparable.

Ultimately, then, the container that can heal the madness of "mutual suicide" must be found within the madness itself. Our renaissance can begin only when we affirm the desire for perfect openness within perfect structure—religious imagination's desire for perfect reality—that is caricatured in modernity's madness. So the container must be able to open up limitlessly variegated possibilities within a unifying, all-embracing, limitlessly secure structure. It must serve the same role as a religious image. When Hillman refers to the images rising from the psyche's depths as "divine influxes," he makes it clear that the power of imagination is ultimately a religious power. When he speaks of the archetypes as innate patterns shaping the products of imagination, he makes it clear that he seeks a radical openness to imagination within the confines of enduring structure. When he speaks of the need for a container, he makes it clear that there must be a single overarching structure within which the infinitude of archetypal structures can be safely experienced.

Our new container must, therefore, be itself a religious image that can ground our lives and support a new birth of religious imagination. It must satisfy the psyche's inherent need to move toward perfect reality, and its unifying form must provide a meaning for the absolute formlessness of the end of the world. What image might offer us such a container? Hillman's suggestion that the Italian Renaissance could serve the purpose hardly seems adequate. Since the problem is played out in the public arena of everyday life—since our pathology is now in our streets and our politics—the container must assume an equally publicly accessible and political form. The cure must come from the source of "dis-ease" itself. Perhaps the popular understanding of the political transformation we need—the popular desire for world peace—holds the answer. Perhaps we must understand our drive toward peace metaphorically as a drive into the seeming madness of religious imagination.

12

Madness and Peace

Any theorizing about the Bomb and the nuclear age must eventually respond to the question that is uppermost in everyone's mind: How can we move the world closer to peace? The desire for world peace seems to be nearly universal. Yet the precise nature of the peace we seek remains rather vaguely defined. While much careful attention is given to the problem of war today, there is noticeably less thinking about peace, for the nature of peace seems to present no problem. It is the opposite of war, we assume, and as such is clearly to be desired. The problem is apparently not how to define or conceptualize peace but how to get it. And that brings us back ever again to the problem of war.

War and Peace

The meaning of peace may not be as self-evident as it seems, however. In fact peace may not even be the opposite of war. *War* and *peace* are interpretive labels that we place on complicated situations; whenever these words are uttered, the speaker must impart a particular meaning to each one. But these meanings are necessarily grounded in the speaker's cultural worldview, which forms a single soil giving rise to the meaning of both terms. In this sense, war and peace are correlative, not opposite, concepts. Whenever one is used, it implies a particular meaning for the other.

This principle has always been true.[1] But it is especially evident in the nuclear age and its imagery. When the Bomb is seen as an apocalyptic tool for cleansing the world of evil, peace receives a correlative meaning: with the conflict between good and evil ended, no further change is possible, so peace means the inviolable structure of a perfect cosmos. When the Bomb is seen as a global annihilator, war between the superpowers is understood as an anachronism, since there can be no victor.[2] Peace therefore comes to mean the total abolition of war and the instituting of a radically new system of international relations—a system (often imagined as some form of world government) that prevents even the possibility of violent conflict. When both these views are rejected in favor of the dual track image, the Bomb becomes the global balancer. War is understood as irrational and terribly dangerous instability. So peace can only mean an immutable balance of power guaranteed by mutually beneficial negotiated agreements and by a continuing nuclear deterrent.

An individual can hold more than one of these views simultaneously. (Most of us probably do; perhaps that is one reason we find issues of war and peace so confusing.) They need not be mutually exclusive, because all share several essential features in common. Across the political spectrum, no matter what the particular conception of peace, it is rhetorically praised as the highest ideal. What political candidate or public speaker would deny that world peace is the number one goal of every American? Although other concerns might take precedence in our daily lives, the fervent wish for peace is always present as a horizon of ultimate concern, a distant hope for a global transformation that would somehow make our world a perfect place.

The rhetorical praise of peace implies an apocalyptic longing, although this remains largely unconscious outside the formal religious communities. Just as all views of war between the superpowers imply an end to the history of the world as we know it, so all the corresponding views of peace imply an end to the conflicts that drive history. All imagine peace in distinctly religious terms; they envision a perfect universal structure that would allow us to drop our defenses without risk. The religious dimensions of war and peace are therefore correlated: both are imagined as radical global transformations leading to immutable static structures. World peace, as the public imagines it, has the characteristics of a religious image.

Yet all our visions of peace undermine their potentially religious meaning because they are construed in purely literal terms. They nullify the potential dynamism of their images of transformation because they aim at a particular form of perfect stasis, literalize it, and call it peace. Contemporary aspirations to peace thus follow the same pattern as preparations for war. Images of the end of the world as we know it are juxtaposed with images of omnipotence or petrification. Religious imagination is, at the same moment, evoked and denied. The longing for transformation is repressed by the compulsive need for static structure. (The dual track vision and its images of gradual progress are especially effective in denying our desire for radical transformation; the dual track may be so appealing in part because it masks such a frightening desire.) In short, all our visions of peace, as of war, mirror the fundaments of nuclear madness. No amount of political activism, international negotiation, or moral good will can cure the madness because all these avenues toward peace replicate the madness.

If peace has become another form of madness, then it is not the opposite of war. As always, the two are merely different forms of the same psychosocial reality. It would seem, then, that whether we work for war or peace we are choosing to go deeper into madness. This is a reminder that the journey of madness demands completion. The religious images and needs at the heart of the madness will not go away. We cannot simply erase our longing for an apocalyptic immersion in chaos. Nor do we really want to, even though we are too petrified to admit our deepest desire.

This certainly does not mean that we literally want to die. Most Americans really do want to find a way out of the nuclear dilemma and into world peace. The problem is that we can not distinguish literal from imaginal desires or fulfillments. Madness is the existental situation we have chosen and continue to choose. Whatever our position on the nuclear issue, we all want to fulfill our desires for both madness and peace. What we need, then, is an understanding of peace correlated with the contemporary meaning of war as madness. And we need to acknowledge that the basis of peace, as of war, lies not in the literal facts but in our imagination. So we need to imagine peace as a form of madness.

Peace as Madness

How might we imagine peace as madness? One answer is suggested by another commonality between apparently opposing visions of peace. Proponents of a continuing nuclear capability remind us that there can be no peace unless the nation is free and secure against its enemies. For nuclear abolitionists, on the other hand, peace depends on an informed public demanding moral national policies that serve the best interests of all humanity. The conflict between these two perspectives often inhibits unified national efforts toward peace. But the two meet in their common desire for greater security. Indeed the nuclear debate continues only because all parties agree that we need to be more secure than we are now.

Few seem to recognize, though, that the security they seek is actually ontological security. All feelings of genuine freedom and national security derive from a sense of full and enduring reality. Ontological security is also the key to public support for antinuclear policies. The powerful interests supporting nuclear arms will not yield their position easily. Only when ordinary citizens break through their psychic numbing can they mobilize the immense energy needed to demand a share in the state's decision-making process. But psychic numbing will persist as long as ontological insecurity pervades our lives. All political viewpoints can agree, then, that ontological security is the prerequisite for peace.

This prerequisite is a psychological state that depends upon the fundamental psychological freedom: the psyche's freedom to transcend radical finitude and pursue its innate path toward religious images. All the theorists contributing to the model of nuclear madness would agree with Tillich that religious images, like all symbolic images, cannot be produced intentionally. "They grow out of the individual or collective unconscious and cannot function without being accepted by the unconscious dimension of our being."[3] But if they are to ground the psyche in a vision of perfect reality, they must also be accepted, to some degree at least, by the conscious dimension of our being. Ontological insecurity, which is the primary obstacle to peace, begins when this essential process is repressed and compelled to remain wholly unconscious.

Depth psychologists have long recognized that individual conflict is a function of repression and that the release of repression can bring the individual greater peace. The same equation holds true, in a metaphoric but very real sense, for social conflict and peace. As long as life is bound by the strictures of the social false self system, the heroic ego rules supreme. The ego, striving to repress all movement toward religious imagery, sees absolute dualism, conflict, and constant threat as the universal law of life. The desire for the harmony of religious imagery persists nonetheless. But as long as the ego contradicts this desire we are "divided selves," at war with ourselves and therefore insecure and at war with each other. The ego and its repressions are the barrier laid across society's path to security and peace.

This barrier is only removed when the ego removes its blinders and consciously recognizes a new possibility: the self's death and rebirth, its immersion in the religious image's promise—and threat—of infinite possibility. When the ego imagines itself stepping aside and removing all its repressive finitizing structures, it releases an endless myriad of perspectives. It recognizes its dichotomizing and literalizing as just one among these many, one that must renounce its claim to primacy for the sake of security and peace. Only when the self is open to all its imaginings can it feel "full-filled" by its most genuine reality, end its inner conflict, and therefore feel securely at peace. In a world where madness prevails, however, the imaginings of madness are the essence of each person's genuine reality. So each ego can get beyond radical finitude to ontological security and peace only by accepting this reality, ceasing its struggle against madness, and letting itself be "full-filled" with madness. This is the truth in the popular slogan that world peace begins within every individual.

This slogan is only partially true, however. In its renaissance, the self discovers that its problems and processes can claim universal meaning because all are rooted in unconscious fantasies, which know no limits. It discovers that there is no absolute dichotomy between self and world; self and world are two complementary perspectives on a single reality. If world peace depends on removing repression, it must begin with simultaneous changes in both individual and society. Political, economic, and social oppression can not be eliminated until psychological repression is transcended in public as well as private life (just as an end to repression requires an end to oppression). No individual can be genuinely free until all are free from the artificial repressive limits of the social false self system.

Depth psychologists know how frightening it is for an individual to begin to lift repression. In unconscious thoughts and desires, all things are possible. Immersion in this sense of pure possibility can quickly turn to overwhelming anxiety. With the rigid walls between unconscious and conscious thoughts, self and world, inner and outer, and fantasy and empirical reality all crumbling, there is a genuine risk that reality as we know it will be dissolved. This is the dissolution we seek to evoke yet evade with the Bomb. It is the risk that we unconsciously long for, yet consciously fear, whether we confront or refuse to confront the Bomb.

It would be even more terrifying to confront our collective madness and acknowledge the longing for infinite possibility hidden in that madness. Admitting the dimension of infinitude into our public life would open the floodgates of religious imagination. Madness and its shadow-side images might seem to be everywhere as public realities. But the terror could be relieved if a common understanding of it were shared with everyone around us. If world peace begins with the release of repression, it must be grounded in a public structure—what James Hillman calls a "container"—strong enough to bear the burden of that release. Only a communally shared religious image can sustain an individual or a society facing the threat of madness.

What image might play this role in our own day? Just as the public long ago intuited the diagnosis of nuclear madness, so it has begun to intuit the cure by speaking of world peace in religious and apocalyptic terms. We already imagine peace as a total transformation from fragmentation and conflict to the perfect structure of one harmonious world. World peace imagined as madness would mean a vision of this perfectly secure structure allowing us to be perfectly open to the infinite possibilities of imagination. It would mean holding our finite conceptions of political reconciliation as symbols that point beyond themselves to the infinite peace of unrepressed religious imagination.

If we were to go beyond our literal conceptions and embrace this image of world peace as madness, we could begin to experience the grounding that a religious image offers. We could consciously attain the opening to infinite reality that our madness now unconsciously seeks, yet find in it a beginning of the healing of our madness. If society can endorse this mad notion of peace, it can give a meaningful form, on a universal scale, to nuclear madness and the Bomb's threat of the end of the world. It can see its plunge into chaos as the initiation of a global renaissance—as both an end in itself and a path to lasting peace.

Work and Play in War and Peace

The meaning of peace as madness can be enriched by considering another commonality among apparently opposing conceptions of war and peace. All sides in the current political scene assume that war, however it is understood, is a means that nations use to gain some desired end. This can be called the concept of war as work. The nuclear debate is essentially a debate about what kinds of jobs the Bomb can reasonably be used to accomplish. Those who see the Bomb as a savior expect it to let us prevail over the enemy. Those who see it as a balancer claim that it can deter aggression, hasten negotiated agreements, and perhaps even compel genuine cooperation between adversaries. For those who see the Bomb as an annihilator, these supposedly rational purposes are illusory. They say that the Bomb cannot have any use, since every proposed purpose leads to the destruction of the nation and all its purposes. Perhaps they are right, if war is always a rational enterprise undertaken to change the world.

There is another side to war, however, one not often acknowledged in modern Western culture but readily apparent in other cultures. War can be undertaken as an end in itself. It can aim not to change the world but to act out and thereby confirm or reestablish some enduring pattern in the world. In this case the very act of going to war benefits the nation, regardless of the outcome, as long as it fights in conformity with the received pattern. War then becomes a form of play, both as a dramatic representation and as a ritual game.[4]

The notion of war as play opens up a new perspective for those who are baffled by the apparent irrationalities of nuclear policy. Why, some will ask, do we deploy weapons that cannot be used without destroying ourselves? Why do we continue to aim those weapons at the Soviet Union if the Cold War is over? The answer may be that the primary purpose of the weapons has always been, and remains, symbolic rather than pragmatic. Although the Bomb may never be a rational tool to get any job done, it can still be prized as an end in itself. The very process of producing, deploying, negotiating, and debating nuclear weapons acts out every strand of the pattern that we prize above all—the intricate web of modernity's madness. As long as the nuclear age continues, every presidential address, every six o'clock news report, and every disarmament newsletter reassures us that reality is just the way we want it to be: literal, radically finite, menacing, doomed to destruction, yet somehow survivable.

The success of the dual track image, with its vision of the Bomb as the great balancer, puts a special premium on the notion of war as play, for it affirms that an eternal structure is preferable to any change. It does not aim at any particular outcome but seeks simply to perpetuate the process of overcoming "instability." Each battle against "instability"—each new round of arms control talks, each new wrinkle in deterrence strategy, each new weapons system developed as a deterrent and a "bargaining chip"—assures us that the "stability" wrought by technical reason is constantly conquering chaos. Yet each battle legitimates and perpetuates the technology that can unleash global chaos. Thus we play out all our ambivalences toward chaos and structure within the overall pattern of nuclear madness.

Since our images of peace are images of numbing compatible with nuclear madness, each one and the political activity it generates is actually pure play too—a representation and reaffirmation of some fantasy of nuclear madness. However, although our engagement with both war and peace has become predominantly play, we continue to deny this momentous change. All parties to the nuclear debate still consciously assume that war is work, so all cooperate in masking the playful dynamic of the arms race, and the madness remains incurable. Even those who work fervently for peace serve this deception; all the currently debated images of peace are directly correlated with notions of war as work. This insistence on war as work confirms the modern worldview, for it sees human behavior only in terms of means-ends relationships, radical temporality, and the desire to control history by vanquishing chaos. When there is a war to be waged or to be prevented, it is always the heroic ego that sets to work.

Predictably, though, the ego undermines itself. The more the reality of war as play is denied, the more insistently the denied psychic needs demand to be played out. Since the nuclear play brings our ambivalence to imaginative possibility ever closer to the surface by enacting it literally, the play of imagination must be repressed more insistently. So the cycle of demand and repression is perpetuated endlessly. The only way to break the cycle is to admit that we are all playing out our shared madness, no matter what our political stance. Our vision of peace must include play as well as madness. We need to imagine a peaceful way to play out our madness. We need to imagine ourselves playing madly at peace.

Imagining the Mad Play of Peace

The renaissance we seek must be a form of play, for it must affirm both peace and madness as ends in themselves. In play, actions are not taken as a means to some supposed end (which is most often only a means to some other means); all are playful ends in themselves. There is constant change yet never any progress. When we "work for peace," on the other hand, we press it into a means-ends relationship, and its pure play falls back under the rule of radical finitude. So the peace process must become the process of madness, and the process, not the product, must become our ultimate concern. As a popular slogan puts it: "There is no way to peace. Peace is the way."

Peace as mad play does not mean an end to conflict. Indeed the ideal of peace as a static state would be abandoned in favor of a world that nourishes dynamic processes of endless change. In this new world imagination's inevitably conflicting offspring could be born, and borne, without limit because those conflicts need no longer be literalized. World peace as a religious image means a structure of shared understanding and shared desire that makes the world safe for the infinite interplay of chaotic images. It means a public life that unleashes the endless diversity of imagination yet embraces all possibilities in a polyphonous harmony. It means sharing our madness together and recognizing it as the renaissance we want and need. Acknowledging all our collective choices as forms of play, we could choose and enact our ends more freely, and perhaps discover the way to free ourselves from the play of nuclear madness, whose ending act we can so clearly predict.

It may seem like unrealistic utopian dreaming to advocate such a radical conception of peace. It is surely utopian, in the original meaning of the word: "u-topia," no place. Critics of utopianism often recall this meaning. But modern utopian thinkers and peace activists too often forget it, insisting on schemes and projects to carry out their fantasies in literal reality. As agents of the rational ego, they plan to build a world of eternal brightness, where no shadow can intrude. They forget that the true home of fantasies of perfect reality is in no literal place but rather in the pure play of imagination. Once handed over to literal thought, fantasies become symptoms of a crippling madness that distorts all of life. Allowed to flourish in their native soil, however, they bring healing by giving madness and its many shadows a meaningful place in the full spectrum of reality. If the source of our madness is the radical finitude that represses all images of perfect reality, then the therapy must address the level of images, where real healing can occur. Politics must become utopian, as C. Wright Mills clearly saw in *The Causes of World War III*: "We are at a curious juncture in the history of human insanity; in the name of reason, men are quite mad, and precisely what they call utopian is now the condition of human survival."[5]

Utopian political thinking is the way to bring the dimension of infinitude into our public life. It is a kind of public dreaming; as such it is inevitably unrealistic. To entertain utopian projects in strictly literal terms is insanely unrealistic. It is one more fantasy of nuclear madness. But to imagine the mad play of peace is a very different matter. By playing with images of the most unrealistic possibilities, we open up our imaginations to the realm of infinite possibility. We imagine ourselves transcending all limits and annihilating all the repressive structures of our radical finitude in the chaos of pure possibility.

Images of peace as playful madness are a way to this transcendence, as long as they are grounded in world peace as a religious image. Of course the image of world peace can only offer a structure to contain the madness of endless imagining if it, too, is consciously held as a playful fantasy. The initiatory transformation from nuclear madness to the mad play of peace must be constellated in imagination, not acted out literally, if it is to be the renaissance we desire. Nevertheless, it can have profound repercussions in literal reality. To escape literal destruction, we must publicly acknowledge our shared fantasies of madness as well as world peace. We must open the floodgates of imagination within a public container, to build a new order on the foundation of fantasy that already exists.

The new order must include new political arrangements. But those arrangements will not endure unless they are rooted in ontological security; political peace must be grounded in world peace as a religious image. Though the image may serve as a future historical goal, the future it images can only be created if it is understood as a symbol for the bewildering complexities of imagination that fill our present. If peace must be understood as a playful process of madness, affirmed as an end in itself, and if madness is an act of imagination, then the very act of imagining the process is the essence of the process. If madness can only become peace when grounded in a religious image, then the willingness to fantasize world peace as a religious image is the heart of the peace process.

The Peace Movement

This new understanding of peace demands a new direction for the peace movement. If the peace movement ultimately seeks nuclear abolition, it is not likely to attain its goal as long as it intends its actions and demands purely literally. By that route it only perpetuates the social fantasy system's static visions, whether they be of a *pax Americana* or a "safe Bomb." Construing war and peace primarily in symbolic terms is the paradoxical path to averting literal war and enhancing literal peace. Caring for the process rather than the goal is the paradoxical path to attaining the goal. So the movement should abandon its literalism and learn to see the world peace for which it strives primarily as a symbol for the infinitude of religious imagination. Relinquishing its "hard-headed realism," it would also relinquish its commitment to progress. Peace work could no longer be done as piece work, aiming at a perfectly static balance of disarmament agreements. Acting out the apocalyptic desire of madness for total transformation, the movement would have to become "unrealistic" and return to its former dynamic vision of immediate and total abolition.

A mass movement demanding radical change is certainly full of dangers. If it demands something as radical as public madness, the danger is only compounded. In the past demands like this have generally created only a minority bent on destroying the status quo and a majority compulsively defending it, with both sides literalizing their aims and ultimately resorting to violent means. The peace movement could avoid this danger by casting its message in non-literal forms. Yet the apparent security that most people find in the prevailing structure must be respected, while it is simultaneously exposed as illusory. The best way to achieve these goals may be to follow the example of traditional religions, which set aside ritual times, places, and routines for acting out proleptic images of a new, more perfect, reality, yet recognize that most people will want to return from these ritual excursions to the familiar routines of everyday life.

The peace movement could draw creatively on this model by recalling that peace is now a form of play and that ritual is the original form of theater. Nuclear weapons are unique because they are the first weapons that can destroy the theater in which the human play unfolds. War may be an inevitable act in that play. But it cannot go on if the theater is destroyed. So war between nuclear-armed superpowers may be obsolete, not because war lacks any rational purpose (since it is now play rather than work), but because it stands to destroy its own stage. The peace movement's most compelling slogan now is not "No more war!" but rather "The show must go on!"

This slogan should lead the peace movement to offer its own activities as ritualized realizations of the mad play of peace. This would mean that peace activism would become a form of play-acting; the movement would become a theater of the imagination, dedicated to the proposition that the show must go on. In play as in madness there is no significant distinction between imagining and acting, for there is no distinguishing fantasy from reality. Indeed the fantasy is the reality, so the imagining is the acting. If war is an inevitable act in the human play, it might even be necessary for the peace movement to wage war against the Bomb—a war fought out purely in imagination.[6] But each battle would be a fantasy of madness played out in full consciousness of its meaning.

Of course the demand for nuclear abolition is a very real one, since abolition remains the goal. So utopian imagining must enter into a creative dialectic with literal reality. Literal reality, like the God of monotheism, demands it rightful place in any renaissance. But imagination must maintain its independence too. This means that the literal reality must be engaged and transformed into a setting for another act in the play. The lobbying and letters to Congress, the speeches and symposia, the petitions and peace marches must all continue. But they should not be taken literally. They should be understood as just so many ways of playing out the fantasy of intellectual and moral crusade that is so central to our madness.

The learned debates about subtleties of nuclear strategy, weapons production, disarmament negotiations, and the like should also continue, but they too must be played as fantasy games (which means merely acknowledging what they already really are). A return to demands for immediate abolition might also imply returning to the former strategy of massive public actions in opposition to the ruling authorities. The madness of the crowd would become one (though certainly not the only one) of the movement's vehicles. But these mass actions would be understood as playacting—a ritual show rather than a show of brute political strength. As acts in the play of madness, they would become more like carnivals than political battles.[7]

To promote this perception of symbolic meanings, the peace movement must also learn to play with images of war, the Bomb, and nuclear madness. All its political tactics, learned debates, and mass actions could become such a play. As a society we must descend as deeply as we can into the psyche, dredging up our nuclear fantasies in all their intricate detail. Creative artists will have to play a central role in this effort. But we must also search out and interpret the potentially religious symbolism of nuclear imagery.[8] To imagine a renaissance that embraces both nuclear death and rebirth—a world destroyed by the Bomb and a world without the Bomb—may now be the most valuable form of antinuclear activism.[9] Understood in their full religious meaning, such imaginings would bring an honest awareness of the Bomb as a schizophrenic image of destruction and transformation. They would allow us to recognize all our contradictory desires and fulfill them in fantasy without needing to literalize any.

The peace movement's greatest responsibility is to create opportunities for, and examples of, the mad play of peace. Initiatory plunges into nuclear madness and peace as madness, acted out on ritual stages set apart from everyday life, can safely begin to open up the full reservoir of imagination's possibilities and lead us beyond our radical finitude. They can teach us to experience world peace in the present, as a process of imagination that is eternally available to us. Thus they can help us accept the open void, withstand our anxiety, and escape the narrow trap of madness that prevents nuclear abolition. If the peace movement is to live up to its name, its activities should become models for the renaissance of world peace. But the movement can only begin this play in earnest if it is grounded in world peace as a consciously held religious image.

Looking Back

If the peace movement chooses to embark on such a new direction, it need not begin from scratch. Some influential voices in that movement already understand peace as a dynamic process that has room for endless conflict. Some stress imagination as the key to creating visions of a more peaceful future. Some combine these perspectives and advise that a playful spirit is needed for both. These are all elements that can be used to build a religious image of world peace and a vision of peace as mad play. Yet they must be reinterpreted, for their ultimate aim now is almost exclusively the literal resolution of literal conflicts. The centrality of fantasy, and especially of fantasies of madness, is still largely unrecognized.

Outside the explicitly political arena, though, the culture of modernity has already immersed us in creative images of impending madness. Nuclear weapons may have destroyed the distinctions between reason and unreason, image and reality, waking and dreaming. But this process was underway long before August, 1945. The most influential artists of our time have proclaimed the line dividing inner from outer reality porous at best, and perhaps wholly illusory. The same discovery is at the foundation of much of modern physics and certainly of modern depth psychology. The various movements that call themselves postmodern all share a vision of reality reduced to a kaleidoscope of fragmented images, with logical coherence and unity only a nostalgic memory. Postmodernism and its deconstructions may be only a flowering and conscious recognition of the seeds of madness buried in modernity, which, when brought to fruition by the Bomb, demand an explosive end to modernity.

These modern and postmodern cultural developments have roots that go back at least to the *Sturm und Drang* and romanticism of the late eighteenth century. Modernity has seen such upheavals periodically. Each has been, in one form or another, a protest on behalf of imagination against the prevailing literalistic rationalism; each has been decried by rationalists as a harbinger of social disintegration and madness. Each has also articulated its own ideal of peace. But these articulations all suggest that unrepressed imagination is the key to peace. At least as far back as the Reformation thinker Theophrastus of Hohenheim (Paracelsus), there was an intellectual tradition developing this insight in complex ways. Under the influence of Paracelsus, the mystical theologian Jakob Boehme forged an apocalyptic vision of peace as a paradise of imagination, which was passed on to the poet William Blake, who wrote: "Art Degraded, Imagination Denied, War Governed the Nations." Blake warned of the "Hirelings in the Camp, the Court and the University, who would, if they could, for ever depress Mental and prolong Corporeal War." Against them he offered his vision of an eternal peace that has room for mental wars—"the Great Wars of Eternity, in fury of Poetic Inspiration, to build the Universe stupendous, Mental forms Creating."[10]

The cultural explorations of "the sixties" were merely the latest (and probably the most widespread) of these recurring protests on behalf of imagination and its hope for world peace. It hardly seems likely that they were the last. Another era of radical cultural change is bound to occur, perhaps on a larger scale than "the sixties," and it is bound to feel like a form of madness, as if all familiar reality were in danger of crumbling. It would not be too surprising if the year 2000, with its inevitably apocalyptic overtones, became the focal point of the next assault on modernity. But it is not at all clear whether that assault will be made by the forces of imagination or by the Bomb.

Looking Forward

History, culture, and above all the Bomb itself tell us that madness is inescapable. The question is not whether we should entertain fantasies of madness, but only what form the madness will take. To speculate about peace as madness is not, therefore, to advise an entry into madness. It is only to advise an acknowledgment and understanding of our madness, and a conscious responsibility for the attitude we take toward our madness and the shape we give it. We can interpret madness as a crippling disaster or as an unfolding opportunity, or as a renaissance that encompasses both. We can choose to fight, either for structure or for deconstruction, convinced that we possess the literal truth. Or we can recognize that the desires for structure and deconstruction demand equal respect, since both meet in infinite measure in our desire for the utopian perfection of religious images. Our choices will be intimately linked to the particular form we give to our madness—the particular game that we choose to play.

Every game has its promise and its risk. There are enormous risks in playing at, or even imagining, a total transformation of culture and worldview. The very idea of a whole society consciously acting out fantasies of a plunge into madness seems crazy, for it implies a total dissolution of the prevailing reality on a universal scale. There is no way to predict the forms these fantasies might take or the effects they might have; it is difficult to sketch out even a vague suggestion. Constant uncertainty, and the lack of control that comes with it, are of the essence of madness. But we can begin a conscious discourse about our choices for understanding and playing out our madness. We can nurture a madness that is shared, comprehensible, and responsible, even though unpredictable. And what is the alternative?

The prevailing official wisdom would have it that the alternative is to continue riding the dual track, making reasonable prudent progress in arms control while keeping up the minimum necessary deterrent safeguards, until a day comes when deterrence is no longer necessary and the last nuclear weapons can be disposed of, like rubbish. The prevailing wisdom may turn out to be correct. There are signs that a majority of the American public may understand the dangers of the Bomb and support rational measures to defuse it, such as the Intermediate Nuclear Forces treaty, strategic arms reduction, a comprehensive test ban, and cuts in SDI funding. Of course there are skeptics on each of these issues who argue that the apparent gains are illusory. Hopes for disarmament have been dashed before: the late 1940s, the 1960s, and the mid-1970s were all eras when reason seemed about to triumph over the Bomb. Each of these was followed by renewed nuclear militance. Perhaps this time is different; perhaps it is not. If we have truly reached "the end of the Cold War," then progress toward ending the nuclear age is inexplicably slow (though there is no way to predict what might occur between the time this book is completed and the time it is read).

As long as nuclear weapons do exist, even if their numbers are reduced and they are never used, the end of the world will still be the invisible center of our public imagination. We will remain trapped in nuclear madness unless we can find a model to endow the Bomb and its images of the end of the world with meaning. The model developed here presents one viable option. Even if nuclear weapons were speedily abolished, the present model would still merit consideration for several reasons. We can never forget how to make nuclear weapons, but more importantly we can never forget that we have made nuclear weapons in exorbitant numbers for at least half a century (and will probably do so much longer). The Bomb will remain in our imaginations as the essential emblem and symptom of the madness we have shared together. And we will need some interpretation of that madness. If a potential suicide walks away from the brink, we do not just give a sigh of relief and forget about it. Some therapy is indicated to uncover the causes of this near-miss and try to prevent it from happening again.

Moreover, even if all nuclear weapons were to disappear tomorrow, the conditions that spawned them would continue to spawn other self-destructive tendencies. Modernity's willingness to destroy the natural, social, and economic environments slowly, through pollution, squandered resources, squalid urbanization, and fiscal irresponsibility, must still be reckoned with. If the 1980s indeed marked the beginning of the end of nuclear weapons, that would surely be cause for celebration, even if modern rationality is the hero in the piece. But as long as self-destructive behavior continues in any area of society, we must have some model for understanding it.

Finally, regardless of the course of nuclear events, there is the likelihood that another time of social and cultural upheaval lies ahead. If society exchanges one form of madness fantasies for another (as perhaps occurred in the mid-sixties, when nuclear fantasies were temporarily set aside), it is still vital to give meaning to madness, especially when it is acted out in the streets. Shared conscious interpretations may be the only way to avert the destructive potentialities of such uncontrollable times. In James Hillman's terms, without containers our explosions of imagery will only engulf us in a more chaotic madness.

If our madness, whether nuclear, environmental, or sociocultural, insists on playing itself out in public, the appropriate containers for it must themselves be acted out in the basic communal processes. Madness must be understood as a political reality, and the containers we fashion must be political forms. So the conventional political approaches to understanding and solving the nuclear dilemma must continue, but they must be complemented by a new psychological and religious dimension. The peace movement must create a stage for playing out utopian fantasies grounded in religious imagery. It must demand ontological security, which is the only real security, and the freedom of infinite possibility, which is the only real freedom. Perhaps, as Mircea Eliade has hinted, we must see all of modernity's justly prized human rights as "a preamble to the only right that is truly inviolable, the right to . . . recover the primordial Adamic condition, [to] live not only in Time but in Eternity."[11] A politics grounded in the madness of world peace must be a utopian politics of perfection, a politics of paradise.

I offer these speculations in the spirit of peace as madness—as a piece of intellectual play. Playing around with five different theorists, and my own interpretations of their intellectual play, I have spun out some fantasies that I hope will stimulate a few fantasies in other minds. Thinking, studying, and imagining, as forms of play, are forms of action. And they are deadly serious, as all good play must be. There is no more serious occupation than spinning fantasies to interpret, and thereby recreate, the world. Surely if there has ever been a time for deadly serious action to change the world, it is now. Robert Jay Lifton, having had the first words here, may also have the last words, words whose meaning has been enriched, I hope, by my playing around with them: "The weapons are a product of human imagination, and human imagination is capable of getting rid of them."[12]

Notes

Introduction

1. Ira Chernus, *Dr. Strangegod: On the Symbolic Meaning of Nuclear Weapons* (Columbia, S.C.: University of South Carolina Press, 1986).

2. I have minimized the number of footnote references in this book. I do not mean to claim any false originality. The theoretical ideas about psychology, religion, and modern culture are all those of the individual theorists being explicated, unless otherwise indicated. The applications of theory to the nuclear issue and the resulting interpretations are my own, unless otherwise indicated. (Of course what I call my own is often just a new rearrangement of others' ideas; my unacknowledged debts here are many.) The examples of nuclear imagery are mostly familiar enough to need no sources cited. Two valuable works extensively documenting nuclear imagery are Spencer Weart, *Nuclear Fear: A History of Images* (Cambridge, Mass.: Harvard University Press, 1988) and Paul Boyer, *By the Bomb's Early Light: American Thought and Culture at the Dawn of the Atomic Age* (New York: Pantheon Books, 1985).

3. Some readers may find my continuing references to modernity throughout this book anachronistic at a time when there is so much talk about "the postmodern situation." Perhaps modernity has "objectively" come to an end. If so, I suspect that this has been internalized only in elite intellectual circles. In the Pentagon and the White House, and in the corporate boardrooms and suburban living rooms of America, beliefs and values are still firmly rooted in modernity (perhaps all the more firmly precisely because they are "objectively" threatened by postmodernity). These modern beliefs and values are the subject of this book. It may be, too, that postmodernism's "deconstructive turn" and "the end of the subject" are just another chapter of modernity (see a brief comment in chapter 12 below).

4. The Public Agenda Foundation, *Voter Options on Nuclear Arms Policy* (New York: The Public Agenda Foundation, 1984), p. 39.

Chapter 1. Numbing, Imagery, and the Schizoid Strategy

1. Robert Jay Lifton, *The Broken Connection* (New York: Simon & Schuster, 1979), p. 39.

2. Robert Jay Lifton and Richard Falk, *Indefensible Weapons* (New York: Basic Books, 1982), p. 101.

3. Robert Jay Lifton, *Death in Life: Survivors of Hiroshima* (New York: Random House, 1967), p. 500. See chapter 5, below, for a more detailed analysis of Lifton's theoretical model.

4. Lifton, *Broken Connection*, p. 180, citing Paul Tillich, *The Courage To Be* (New Haven: Yale University Press, 1952). p. 66.

5. Robert Jay Lifton, "The Image of the 'End of the World': A Psychohistorical View," *Michigan Quarterly Review* 24, no. 1 (Winter, 1980), p. 80. Cf. Lifton, *Broken Connection*, p. 416.

6. Lifton, *Broken Connection*, pp. 296–297.

7. Chapter 5, below, will show that Lifton's paradigm leaves the psyche trapped in the nuclear predicament because it roots that predicament in immutable facts of human nature.

8. R.D. Laing, *The Divided Self*, 2d ed. (Baltimore: Penguin Books, 1965), p. 39.

9. Ibid., p. 42.

10. Ibid., pp. 45–46.

11. Ibid., p. 90.

12. Ibid., p. 91.

13. Gregg Herken, *The Winning Weapon: The Atomic Bomb in the Cold War, 1945–1950* (New York: Alfred A. Knopf, 1980), especially pp. 113, 334–339; cf. Martin J. Sherwin, *A World Destroyed: Hiroshima and the Origins of the Arms Race*, 2d ed. (New York: Vintage Books, 1987), especially pp. 114, 194, 224–228, 238. According to Sherwin (p. 201), even advocates of nuclear cooperation like Leo Szilard and Henry L. Stimson "looked to the Bomb's power to persuade the Soviets to accept an American blueprint for world peace."

14. *Life*, August 20, 1945, p. 32.

15. Lifton and Falk, *Indefensible Weapons*, chapter 14; Daniel Ellsberg, "How We Use Our Nuclear Arsenal," in E.P. Thompson and Dan Smith, eds., *Protest and Survive* (New York: Monthly Review

Press, 1981); Richard Betts, *Nuclear Blackmail and Nuclear Balance* (Washington, D.C.: The Brookings Institution, 1987).

16. Spencer Weart, *Nuclear Fear: A History of Images* (Cambridge, Mass.: Harvard University Press, 1988), p. 138.

17. Colin Gray and Keith Payne, "Victory is Possible," *Foreign Policy* 39 (Summer, 1980), p. 21.

18. Peter Pringle and William Arkin, *SIOP: The Secret U.S. Plan for Nuclear War* (New York: W.W. Norton & Co., 1983); Michio Kaku and Daniel Axelrod, *To Win A Nuclear War: The Pentagon's War-Fighting Plan* (Boston: South End Press, 1987). Some analysts believe that the SIOP is designed primarily for a disarming first strike; see Robert C. Aldridge, *First Strike!* (Boston: South End Press, 1983) and *Nuclear Empire* (Vancouver: New Star Books, 1988). For recent revisions of the SIOP, see Robert Toth's front-page articles in the *Los Angeles Times*, July 23 and 24, 1989. Toth demonstrates that the concept of "winning a nuclear war" is still very meaningful to many government planners, especially in the military.

19. See, for example, one of the earliest influential psychological interpretations of the nuclear age, Jerome D. Frank's *Sanity and Survival* (New York: Random House, 1967), pp. 143–145.

20. Roger Molander, "How I Learned to Start Worrying and Hate the Bomb," *Washington Post*, March 21, 1982.

21. Laing, *Divided Self*, p. 47.

22. Ibid, p. 144.

23. Ibid, p. 145.

24. Ibid., p. 91.

25. Ibid., p. 51.

26. Ibid.

27. As political scientist Richard Barnet put it: "The entire purpose of the nuclear arsenal is to influence the behavior of six or seven Soviet leaders. As an educational system, it has the highest per-pupil cost of any in the world." (*Real Security: Restoring American Power in a Dangerous Decade* [New York: Simon & Schuster, 1981], p. 27).

28. Laing, *Divided Self*, p. 88.

29. Ibid., p. 113.

30. Herken, *Winning Weapon*; Sherwin, *World Destroyed*. For other psychological interpretations of nuclear secrecy, see Lifton, *Broken Connection*, pp. 354-358, and Weart, *Nuclear Fear*, pp. 55-59, 119-127.

31. Laing, *Divided Self*, p. 145.

Chapter 2. Numbing and Imagery as Social Fantasy

1. R.D. Laing, *The Self and Others*, 2d ed. (New York: Pantheon, 1969), p. 78.

2. R.D. Laing, *The Politics of Experience* (New York: Ballantine Books, 1967), p. 21.

3. Laing, *Self and Others*, p. 23.

4. R.D. Laing, *The Politics of the Family* (New York: Vintage Books, 1972), p. 121.

5. Laing, *Self and Others*, p. 27.

6. Ibid., p. 60.

7. Laing, *Politics of Family*, p. 14.

8. Laing, *Politics of Experience*, p. 93.

9. Ibid., pp. 87, 91.

10. Laing, *Politics of Family*, p. 95.

11. Laing, *Politics of Experience*, p. 84.

12. For a parallel argument from a sociological viewpoint, see Robert D. Benford and Lester R. Kurtz, "Performing the Nuclear Ceremony: The Arms Race as Ritual," in Ira Chernus and Edward T. Linenthal, eds., *A Shuddering Dawn: Religious Studies and the Nuclear Age* (Albany: SUNY Press, 1989).

13. Laing, *Politics of Family*, p. 95.

14. Ibid., p. 16.

15. Laing, *Politics of Experience*, p. 98.

16. Laing, *Politics of Family*, p. 124.

17. Laing, *Politics of Experience*, p. 88.

18. Laing, *Self and Others*, p. 68.

19. Laing, *Politics of Experience*, p. 57.

20. R.D. Laing, in Richard I. Evans, *R.D. Laing: The Man and His Ideas* (New York: Dutton & Co., 1976), p. 28.

21. There is a time-honored intermediate stage between the first and second phases of invalidation: the charge that protesters are "Communist dupes." For a classic example, see John Barron, "The KGB's Magical War for 'Peace,'" *Reader's Digest*, October, 1982, an article that was publicly praised by President Ronald Reagan when it first appeared. Compare the remarks of Richard Pipes quoted in chapter 8, note 14, below.

22. Laing, *Politics of Family*, p. 82.

23. Laing, *Politics of Experience*, p. 36.

24. Ibid., p. 95.

25. Laing, *Self and Others*, p. 90.

26. Laing, *Politics of Family*, p. 98.

27. Laing, *Self and Others*, p. 23.

28. Laing, *Politics of Experience*, p. 78.

Chapter 3. The Neurosis of Modernity

1. My approach here is to interpret the avowedly socialist culture criticism of Tillich's early years in light of his psychological theories, developed after he came to the United States in 1933. In this country Tillich muted his earlier socialist voice (see Ronald H. Stone, *Paul Tillich's Radical Social Thought* [Atlanta: John Knox Press, 1980]), so the relationship between these two aspects of his thought has rarely been examined.

2. Paul Tillich, *Dynamics of Faith*, (New York: Harper Torchbooks, 1957), pp. 9, 76.

3. Paul Tillich, *What Is Religion?*, ed. J.L. Adams (New York: Harper & Row, 1969), p. 162. Tillich recognizes the philosophical distinction between the unreality of the not-yet-real and the conceptual-

ly rather different unreality of absolute nonbeing. But he implies that in lived experience these two abstract categories merge, for both portend the abyss of personal unreality.

4. Paul Tillich, *Theology of Culture*, ed. R.C. Kimball (New York: Oxford University Press, 1959), pp. 7–8.

5. Paul Tillich, *The Courage To Be* (New Haven: Yale University Press, 1952), p. 66, cited in Robert Jay Lifton, *The Broken Connection* (New York: Simon & Schuster, 1979), p. 180.

6. Tillich, *Courage To Be*, pp. 66, 68.

7. Ibid., p. 62.

8. Ibid., pp. 69, 70.

9. Paul Tillich, *The Religious Situation*, trans. H.R. Niebuhr (New York: Henry Holt & Co., 1932), pp. 22–23.

10. Tillich, *Theology of Culture*, p. 46.

11. Tillich, *Courage To Be*, p. 49.

12. See, for example, Lloyd Dumas, ed., *The Political Economy of Arms Reduction: Reversing Economic Decay* (Boulder, Colo.: Westview Press, 1982), and William J. Weida and Frank L. Gertcher, *The Political Economy of National Defense* (Boulder, Colo.: Westview Press, 1987), chapter 5.

13. Quotations from *New York Times*, May 30, 1982, p. A1; ibid., June 4, 1982, p. A10. On actual U.S. policy, see the sources cited in chapter 1, note 18, above.

14. The Public Agenda Foundation, *Voter Options on Nuclear Arms Policy* (New York: The Public Agenda Foundation, 1984), p. 18.

15. See Ira Chernus, *Dr. Strangegod: On the Symbolic Meaning of Nuclear Weapons* (Columbia, S.C.: University of South Carolina Press, 1986), chapters 6, 7; and chapter 7, p. 158 below.

16. *Dr. Strangelove*, directed by Stanley Kubrick (1962) remains perhaps the most influential of all American antinuclear films. On Postal Service plans, see *Washington Post*, August 13, 1982, p. A1.

17. Tillich, *Courage To Be*, p. 63.

18. For some examples of ambiguous images of entrapment in the nuclear age, see Daniel C. Noel, "The Nuclear Horror and the Hounding of Nature: Listening to Images," in Ira Chernus and Edward T. Linenthal, eds., *A Shuddering Dawn: Religious Studies and the Nuclear Age* (Albany: SUNY Press, 1989).

19. See Chernus, *Dr. Strangegod*, for an extended discussion.

20. Gunther Anders, "Reflections on the H Bomb," trans. Norbert Guterman, *Dissent*, Spring, 1956, stresses the desire to escape infinitude as a central fact of the nuclear age and foreshadows a number of the issues raised in the present discussion. This early article should have initiated an important debate, but unfortunately it has received too little attention.

Chapter 4. Disarmament and the Modern Ego

1. R.D. Laing, *The Politics of Experience* (New York: Ballantine Books, 1967), p. 73.

2. R.D. Laing, *The Voice of Experience* (New York: Pantheon Books, 1982), p. 18.

3. Ibid., pp. 26, 14.

4. For numerous examples of this imagery of perfect balance, see the study of *Time*'s nuclear images in the early 1980s (which amounted to a full-blown doctrine of static rational balance) in Ira Chernus and Edward T. Linenthal, eds., *A Shuddering Dawn: Religious Studies and the Nuclear Age* (Albany: SUNY Press, 1989), chapter 3. On March 29, 1982, for example, *Time* (p. 26) told the nation that "the volatile human forces at work on the planet earth may be able to maintain their dynamic equilibrium indefinitely. That will unquestionably require ever increasing wisdom and skillful management, as well as luck." (The last phrase recalls Laing's claim that "the cold schizoid person may 'go for kicks,' court extreme thrills"; cf. chapter 1, note 31, above.)

5. R.D. Laing, *The Politics of the Family* (New York: Vintage Books, 1972), p. 16.

6. William Broad, "From Cold War to Nuclear Nostalgia," *New York Times*, Dec. 12, 1989, p. C1. In a similar vein, *Times* reporter Maureen Dowd flatly asserted that "the arms race is over." ("No. 1 Concerns: The New Dawn is Casting Some Things in a Bad Light," *New York Times*, March 4, 1990, p. IV:1).

7. Strobe Talbott, "Rethinking the Red Menace," *Time*, Jan. 1, 1990, p. 68. The administration confirmed Talbott's claim in its proposed FY 1991 budget by asking for "major spending increases for numerous strategic weapon systems" (*Washington Post*, Jan. 30, 1990, p. A1).

8. Gene R. La Rocque, "Prospects for Change in the U.S. and Soviet Military," *The Defense Monitor* 18, number 8, 1989.

9. *New York Times*, Sept. 13, 1989, p. A30. On Jan. 15, 1990, the *Washington Post* (p. A1) reported that a proposed treaty to eliminate mobile multiple-warhead missiles was receiving hardly any support in the Bush administration, largely because Secretary of Defense Cheney favors building more such missiles, since they provide "more bang for the buck" (the same rationale used for building the first nuclear-armed missiles in the 1950s). The administration has subsequently shown more flexibility on this issue.

10. The Bush administration's proposed FY 1991 budget included nearly a quadrupling of funds for research on a "new nuclear tipped tactical rocket" to be deployed in West Germany as a follow-on to the Lance missile, according to the *Washington Post*, Jan. 30, 1990, p. A1. Political pressure may curtail this project, however.

11. For example, Ron Hirschbein found at a 1988 arms control conference (sponsored by the American Association for the Advancement of Science) that "high ranking government officials, representatives of various think tanks, and the managers of military-industrial firms shared the view that arms reduction is a mandate to design more sophisticated weaponry." (Ron Hirschbein, *Newest Weapons/Oldest Psychology: The Dialectics of American Nuclear Strategy* [New York: Peter Lang, 1989], p. 250.) One can also develop new interpretations of treaties, as the Reagan administration did with the 1972 ABM treaty when it wanted to justify deploying antimissile weapons in space.

12. *Bulletin of the Atomic Scientists* 46: 1 (Jan./Feb., 1990), p. 49. However the number of nuclear warheads may not decrease. The Denver weekly *Westword* reported that the administration's proposed FY 1991 budget called for the Rocky Flats nuclear weapons plant to produce approximately 1430 actual bombs during the year, which is equal to or above reported production levels during the 1980s (Bryan Abas, "Rocky Flats is Back," *Westword*, March 21-27, 1990, p. 18).

13. *Washington Post*, June 29, 1989, p. A3.

14. *New York Times*, Nov. 10, 1989, p. A14; cf. ibid, Oct. 12, 1989, p. A1.

15. Abas, "Rocky Flats is Back," p. 18.

15a. *U.S. News and World Report*, Dec. 11, 1989, p. 23. In 1990 the Bush administration's public rhetoric began to focus on the claim that we must modernize our nuclear arsenal with new weapons, such as the Trident, in order to keep up with the Soviet Union's nuclear modernization program. This might best be understood as the 1990s version of the traditional "missile gap" argument. Compare this with Secretary of Defense Cheney's justification for new missiles cited in note 9 above. Both of these justifications have deep roots in traditional Cold War imagery.

16. Evan Thomas, "From Abyss to Brink: Will United States be More Interventionist in a Post-Cold-War World?", *Newsweek*, Jan. 8, 1990, p. 27. The article concludes by evoking typical schizoid fears of impending "instability" and annihilation: "History teaches that change breeds instability, and instability breeds war. Given all the weapons loose in the world, and the madmen who wield many of them, the battles of Bucharest and Panama City may one day seem like skirmishes, mere sparks before a greater conflagration."

17. Robert Toth, "U.S. Shifts Nuclear Response Strategy," *Los Angeles Times*, July 23, 1989, p. A1.

18. Robert Toth, "Planners Split on How to Meet Nuclear Threat," *Los Angeles Times*, July 24, 1989, p. A1. Perhaps it is significant in this context that the Air Force recently planned to buy 173 "nuclear-hardened" fax machines, at a cost of $421,000 each. (*Bulletin of the Atomic Scientists* 46: 1 [Jan./Feb. 1990], p. 48.)

19. *Bulletin of the Atomic Scientists* 45: 10 (Dec., 1989), p. 2.

20. Laing, *Politics of Experience*, p. 145.

21. James Hillman, *Re-Visioning Psychology* (New York: Harper & Row, 1975), p. 22.

22. Norman Moss, *Men Who Play God* (New York: Harper & Row, 1968), p. 54.

23. "Let's Prepare Shelters," *Life*, Oct. 13, 1961, p. 4. Cf. the related articles in *Life*, Sept. 15, 1961, pp. 95–108.

24. Secretary of Defense Harold Brown applied this salvific vision directly to nuclear weapons when he said: "Given our disadvantage in numbers, our technology is what will save us." ("Missiles, Missiles, Missiles," *Business Week*, Aug. 11, 1980, p. 81).

25. Hillman, *Re-Visioning Psychology*, p. 149.

26. Ibid., p. 6.

27. James Hillman with Laura Pozzo, *Inter Views* (New York: Harper & Row, 1983), p. 131.

28. Ibid., p. 46.

Chapter 5. The Theory of Psychic Numbing Reconsidered

1. Robert Jay Lifton, *The Broken Connection* (New York: Simon & Schuster, 1979), pp. 36–44.

2. Robert Jay Lifton, *The Life of the Self: Toward a New Psychology* (New York: Simon & Schuster, 1976), p. 36.

3. Lifton, *Broken Connection*, pp. 41, 42.

4. Lifton, *Life of the Self*, p. 75.

5. Robert Jay Lifton, *The Future of Immortality and Other Essays for a Nuclear Age* (New York: Basic Books, 1987), pp. 133–135.

6. Lifton, *Broken Connection*, pp. 38, 39.

7. Ibid., pp. 34, 24, 36.

8. Robert Jay Lifton and Richard Falk, *Indefensible Weapons* (New York: Basic Books, 1982), p. 63.

9. Lifton, *Broken Connection*, pp. 34–35.

10. Ibid., p. 340.

11. Paul Tillich, *Systematic Theology*, vol. III (Chicago: University of Chicago Press, 1963), pp. 409–410.

12. Lifton, *Future of Immortality*, p. 14.

13. Lifton, *Broken Connection*, p. 194.

14. Ibid., p. 128.

15. Ibid., p. 175.

16. Ibid., p. 181.

17. Ibid., p. 187.

18. Lifton, *Future of Immortality*, p. 175.

19. See chapter 2, note 2, above.

Chapter 6. Nuclear Madness: A Model

1. For a representative sampling of the ways in which influential psychologists and psychiatrists have used the phrase *nuclear madness*, see the sources cited by James G. Blight, "Toward a Policy-Relevant Psychology of Avoiding Nuclear War," *American Psychologist* 42, no. 1 (January, 1987), p. 15.

2. Robert Jay Lifton, *The Future of Immortality and Other Essays for a Nuclear Age* (New York: Basic Books, 1987), p. 155.

3. Robert Jay Lifton, *The Broken Connection* (New York: Simon & Schuster, 1979), pp. 416-417.

4. Ibid., p. 416. Cf. Robert Jay Lifton, "The Image of the 'End of the World': A Psychohistorical View," *Michigan Quarterly Review* 24, no. 1 (Winter 1985), p. 80.

5. R.D. Laing, *The Divided Self*, 2d ed. (Baltimore: Penguin Books, 1965), p. 147.

6. Ibid., pp. 196, 198.

7. Ibid., p. 85.

8. Ibid., p. 176.

9. Lifton, *Broken Connection*, p. 228.

10. R. D. Laing, *The Politics of Experience* (New York: Ballantine Books, 1967), pp. 117-118.

11. For a poignant example, see the suicide note penned by former Secretary of Defense James Forrestal, one of the first American officials charged with responsibility for planning to use the Bomb. Forrestal concluded that human beings "vanish from a world where they were of no consequence . . . where they left no sign that they ever existed." (Gregg Herken, *The Winning Weapon: The Atomic Bomb in the Cold War, 1945-1950* [New York: Alfred A. Knopf, 1980], p. 298).

12. Laing, *Politics of Experience*, pp. 11, 12.

13. Ron Hirschbein, *Newest Weapons/Oldest Psychology: The Dialectics of American Nuclear Strategy* (New York: Peter Lang, 1989), shows that nuclear policy is driven by a desire to resolve the tension between apocalyptic fantasies and the bureaucratic rationalization characteristic of the false self system. He relies on the argument of Jacob Talmon, *The Origins of Totalitarian Democracy* (London: Mercury, 1961), that this tension is fundamental to all modern Western politics. For Hirschbein, the civilian defense expert or "national security manager" in particular "seems to labor under the delusion that, as a member of the elect, he can control anything—even apocalyptic weaponry" (p. 37).

14. In recent years the "drug menace" has fulfilled this role. David R. Gergen, a former aide to President Ronald Reagan, exemplified the interchangeability of enemies when he wrote: "America must fight drugs the same way we have fought Communism: With a

consuming moral passion." (*U.S. News and World Report*, Dec. 18, 1989, p. 84).

15. Joel Kovel, *Against the State of Nuclear Terror* (Boston: South End Press, 1983) sees state-sponsored paranoia as the key to understanding the nuclear age.

16. Lifton, *Broken Connection*, p. 366, and *Future of Immortality*, p. 145.

17. Lifton, *Future of Immortality*, pp. 130–133. Lifton cites Stephen Kull's interviews with policymakers and strategists, now available in Stephen Kull, *Minds At War: Nuclear Reality and the Inner Conflicts of Defense Policymakers* (New York: Basic Books, 1988). Lifton's concept of "doubling," first developed in *The Nazi Doctors: Medical Killing and the Psychology of Genocide* (New York: Basic Books, 1986), is summarized in *Future of Immortality*, chapter 14.

18. See the discussion of "Disarmament Fantasies and Actualities" in chapter 4 above.

Chapter 7. Nuclear Madness: The Cold War Era

1. Paul Boyer, *By the Bomb's Early Light* (New York: Pantheon Books, 1985), p. 4.

2. Ibid., p. 5.

3. *Life*, August 20, 1945, p. 87B.

4. *New York Times*, August 7, 1945, p. 22.

5. *Newsweek*, August 13, 1945, p. 30.

6. See chapter 1, note 14, above.

7. Boyer, *Bomb's Early Light*, p. 5.

8. *New York Herald Tribune*, August 7, 1945, p. 22.

9. *New York Times*, August 12, 1945, "News of the Week in Review," p. 6.

10. Boyer, *Bomb's Early Light*, p. 7.

11. Ibid.

12. Spencer Weart, *Nuclear Fear: A History of Images* (Cambridge, Mass.: Harvard University Press, 1988), p. 103.

13. Ibid., p. 74.

14. See Ira Chernus, *Dr. Strangegod: On the Symbolic Meaning of Nuclear Weapons* (Columbia, S.C.: University of South Carolina Press, 1986), pp. 20-23, 130-132.

15. R.D. Laing, *The Divided Self*, 2d ed. (Baltimore: Penguin Books, 1965), p. 85.

16. Robert Jay Lifton and Kai Erikson, "Nuclear War's Effects on the Mind," in Robert Jay Lifton and Richard Falk, *Indefensible Weapons* (New York: Basic Books, 1982), p. 278.

17. See Boyer, *Bomb's Early Light*, chapter 27 for examples.

18. See Martin J. Sherwin, *A World Destroyed: Hiroshima and the Origins of the Arms Race*, 2d ed. (New York: Vintage Books, 1987). Sherwin (p. 62) quotes General Leslie Groves, military chief of the Manhattan Project: "There was never . . . any illusion on my part but that Russia was our enemy, and the Project was conducted on that basis."

19. Gregg Herken, *The Winning Weapon: The Atomic Bomb in the Cold War, 1945-1950* (New York: Alfred A. Knopf, 1980) details this process in political terms. Boyer, *Bomb's Early Light*, chapter 27, describes it on the level of popular culture.

20. *Life*, November 19, 1945, pp. 27-35.

21. See Herken, *Winning Weapon*, pp. 304-321. According to Ronald E. Powaski, *March to Armageddon* (New York: Oxford University Press, 1987), pp. 55-56, J. Robert Oppenheimer despaired of opposing the hydrogen Bomb because of the way it had "caught the imagination" of government and military leaders. President Truman "simply asked, 'Can the Russians do it?' When all heads nodded affirmatively, Truman responded, 'In that case, we have no choice. We'll go ahead.'"

22. *Life*, February 27, 1950, pp. 19-40.

23. Cf. Richard Barnet quoted in chapter 1, note 27, above.

24. Bernard Baruch, "Spiritual Armageddon is Here—Now," *Reader's Digest*, March 1951, pp. 59, 60.

25. This was recognized early in the nuclear age by Gunther Anders ("Reflections on the H Bomb," trans. Norbert Guterman, *Dissent*, Spring, 1956), who argues eloquently that our problem is defined

by the tension between our unwelcome infinitude of power and our nostalgic longing for our former finitude.

26. Edward Glover, *War, Sadism, and Pacifism* (London: Allen & Unwin, 1946), p. 274.

27. Edgar M. Bottome, *The Missile Gap: A Study of the Formulation of Military and Political Policy* (Rutherford, N.J.: Fairleigh Dickinson University Press, 1971).

28. Fred Kaplan, *The Wizards of Armageddon* (New York: Simon & Schuster, 1983), pp. 307–310; Weart, *Nuclear Fear*, pp. 254–258.

29. Weart, *Nuclear Fear*, p. 257.

30. See, for example, the federal government's 1977 pamphlet, "Protection in the Nuclear Age," which was still being distributed in the 1980s (at least in Boulder, Colorado). Its first page assures the reader that in case of nuclear attack, "the entire Nation would be mobilizing to repulse the attack, destroy the enemy, and hold down our own loss of life. Much assistance would be available to you." See Chernus, *Dr. Strangegod*, pp. 100–105.

31. According to Boyer, *Bomb's Early Light*, p. 354, themes of mutation and societal disintegration were especially common in the nuclear imagery of the early sixties.

Chapter 8. Nuclear Madness: Deterrence, Détente, and Disarmament

1. See Fred Kaplan, *The Wizards of Armageddon* (New York: Simon & Schuster, 1983), chapters 22, 25; Ron Hirschbein, *Newest Weapons/Oldest Psychology: The Dialectics of American Nuclear Strategy* (New York: Peter Lang, 1989), pp. 83–95; and the sources cited in chapter 1, notes 15 and 18, above.

2. Quoted in Spencer Weart, *Nuclear Fear: A History of Images*, (Cambridge, Mass.: Harvard University Press, 1988), p. 231.

3. Quoted in Jonathan Schell, *The Fate of the Earth* (New York: Avon Books, 1982), p. 205.

4. Ibid., p. 204.

5. Michio Kaku and Daniel Axelrod, *To Win A Nuclear War: The Pentagon's War-Fighting Plan* (Boston: South End Press, 1987), p. 123.

6. H.R. Haldeman with Joseph Dimona, *The End of Power* (New York: New York Times Books, 1978), p. 83.

7. For interpretations of this era, see Paul Boyer, "From Activism to Apathy: The American People and Nuclear Weapons, 1963-1980," *Journal of American History* 70 (March 1984); Robert Benford, "The Nuclear Disarmament Movement," in Lester Kurtz, *The Nuclear Cage: A Sociology of the Arms Race* (Englewood Cliffs, N.J.: Prentice Hall, 1988), pp. 247-249; Weart, *Nuclear Fear*, pp. 262-269.

8. Edward V. Rowny, "How Not to Negotiate With the Russians," *Reader's Digest*, June, 1981, p. 70.

9. On nuclear imagery during the Carter and Reagan administrations, see Ira Chernus and Edward T. Linenthal, eds., *A Shuddering Dawn: Religious Studies and the Nuclear Age* (Albany: SUNY Press, 1989), chapters 2, 3.

10. Gregg Herken, *Counsels of War* (New York: Alfred A. Knopf, 1985), pp. 259-265; Kaplan, *Wizards of Armageddon*, pp. 364-377.

11. Edward T. Linenthal, "Restoring America: Political Revivalism in the Nuclear Age," in Roland A. Sherrill, ed., *Religion in the Life of the Nation: American Recoveries* (Urbana, Ill.: University of Illinois Press, 1989); idem., in Chernus & Linenthal, eds., *Shuddering Dawn*, chapter 2.

12. See chapter 1, note 17, above.

13. Richard Pipes in Charles Tyroler II, ed., *Alerting America: The Papers of the Committee on the Present Danger* (Washington, D.C.: Pergamon-Brassey's, 1984), p. 34.

14. Richard Pipes, *Survival is Not Enough: Soviet Realities and America's Future* (New York: Simon & Schuster, 1984), p. 66; cf. chapter 2, note 21, above.

15. See Benford, "Nuclear Disarmament Movement," pp. 263-265.

16. *The Fate of the Earth* went through eleven printings as a mass-market paperback in its first six years. *The Day After* was shown on the ABC television network on November 20, 1983, to an audience estimated (perhaps somewhat excessively) at upwards of 100 million Americans. See *Los Angeles Times*, November 23, 1983, sec. VI, p. 1.

17. *Time* (December 5, 1983, p. 39), for example, contended that this blunted the film's impact, especially among children: "The special effects struck much of the *Star Wars* generation as tame."

18. Schell, *Fate of the Earth*, p. 119.

19. Ibid., p. 139.

20. According to Paul Boyer, college students now realize intellectually that there is still a danger from nuclear weapons, but they do not feel the reality of the danger emotionally. Boyer likens this to what he calls "the big sleep" of 1963-1980: "Arms Race as Sitcom Plot," *Bulletin of the Atomic Scientists* 45: 5 (June 1989).

21. For an overview of Bush's policy during his first year in office, see chapter 4 above. It may be worth recalling that as a vice presidential candidate in 1980 Bush endorsed the views of Colin Gray and Richard Pipes, cited above, that there can be a winner in a "nuclear exchange." See Robert Scheer, *With Enough Shovels* (New York: Random House, 1982), p. 12.

22. At the end of that first year *Newsweek* (Jan. 8, 1990, p. 26) said: "National security is undergoing a redefinition. In place of communism there are new evils: drugs, terrorism, environmental destruction." See chapter 6, note 14, above.

23. See chapter 4, on "Disarmament Fantasies and Actualities."

24. Hirschbein, *Newest Weapons/Oldest Psychology*, argues that a similar unification of apocalypticism and rational stability is the goal of the political and military elites who make nuclear policy; see chapter 6, note 13, above.

25. See the discussion in chapter 4 above.

26. According to Boyer (*Bomb's Early Light*, p. 364) and Weart (*Nuclear Fear*, p. 382), "nuclear winter" is the only image of the 1980s that was not familiar a generation or two earlier.

27. James Hillman, *Re-Visioning Psychology* (New York: Harper and Row, 1975), p. xiii. For an analogous critique of the disarmament movement's preoccupation with technical weapons issues, from a political rather than a psychological perspective, see William A. Schwartz, Charles Derber, et al., *The Nuclear Seduction* (Berkeley, Cal.: University of California Press, 1990).

28. Martin Buber, *The Knowledge of Man*, ed. Maurice Friedman (New York: Harper Torchbooks, 1966), p. 168.

29. Robert Jay Lifton, *The Future of Immortality and Other Essays for a Nuclear Age* (New York: Basic Books, 1987), p. 157.

Chapter 9. The Meaning of the End of the World

1. See Mac Linscott Ricketts, *Mircea Eliade: The Romanian Roots, 1907–1945*, 2 vols. (Boulder, Colo.: East European Monographs, 1988). Ricketts concludes (p. 1206) that even Eliade's "so-called 'scientific' works in the history of religions are, as he has freely acknowledged, really works of philosophy."

1a. Mircea Eliade, *The Sacred and the Profane*, trans. Willard R. Trask (New York: Harper Torchbooks, 1965), p. 64.

2. Ibid., p. 120.

3. Mircea Eliade, *Myth and Reality*, trans. Willard R. Trask (New York: Harper Torchbooks, 1968), p. 77.

4. Since I am treating *modern man* as a hypothetical construct created by Eliade, I follow his gender-biased usage, although it would have been preferable had he employed a gender-neutral terminology.

5. Mircea Eliade, *Cosmos and History: The Myth of the Eternal Return*, trans. Willard R. Trask (New York: Harper Torchbooks, 1959), p. 156.

6. Mircea Eliade, *The Forbidden Forest*, trans. Mac Linscott Ricketts and Mary Park Stevenson (Notre Dame, Ind.: University of Notre Dame Press, 1978), p. 250.

7. Mircea Eliade, *Myths, Dreams, and Mysteries*, trans. Phillip Mairet (New York: Harper Torchbooks, 1967), p. 243.

8. Mircea Eliade, *The Two and the One*, trans. J.M. Cohen (New York: Harper Torchbooks, 1969), p. 79.

9. Mircea Eliade, *No Souvenirs: Journal, 1957–1969*, trans. Fred H. Johnson, Jr. (New York: Harper & Row, 1977), pp. 80, 89.

10. Eliade, *Forbidden Forest*, pp. 317–318.

11. Eliade, *No Souvenirs*, p. 158.

12. Eliade, *Two and One*, pp. 156–157.

13. Eliade, *No Souvenirs*, p. 160.

14. Mircea Eliade, *Symbolism, the Sacred, and the Arts*, ed. Diana Apostolos-Cappadona (New York: Crossroad Publishing Co., 1985), pp. 164–165.

15. Mircea Eliade, *Images and Symbols*, trans. Phillip Mairet (New York: Sheed & Ward, 1961), p. 20.

16. Eliade, *Myths, Dreams, Mysteries*, p. 18.

17. Eliade, *Myth and Reality*, pp. 31, 30.

18. Eliade, *Cosmos and History*, p. 88.

19. Mircea Eliade, *Patterns in Comparative Religion*, trans. Rosemary Sheed (Cleveland: World Publishing Company, 1963), p. 184.

20. Eliade, *Images and Symbols*, p. 158.

21. Eliade, *Myth and Reality*, pp. 60, 75-76.

22. Eliade, *Cosmos and History*, p. 88.

23. Eliade, *Two and One*, p. 159.

24. Eliade, *Myths, Dreams, Mysteries*, p. 243.

25. Eliade, *Forbidden Forest*, p. 304.

26. Eliade, *No Souvenirs*, pp. 143-144.

27. Ibid., p. 145.

28. Mircea Eliade, *Ordeal by Labyrinth: Conversations with Claude-Henri Rocquet*, trans. Derek Coltman (Chicago: University of Chicago Press, 1982), p. 126.

29. Ibid., p. 67.

30. The dialogue between Anisie and Stefan discussed in this and the following two paragraphs appears in Eliade, *Forbidden Forest*, pp. 314-315.

31. Mircea Eliade, *A History of Religious Ideas*, vol. II, trans. Willard R. Trask (Chicago: University of Chicago Press, 1982), p. 361.

32. Eliade, *No Souvenirs*, p. 73.

33. This colloquium with Mircea Eliade and faculty members of the University of Colorado was held in Boulder, Colorado, on October 25, 1982. I am grateful to Professor David Carrasco for making audio tapes of the discussion available to me.

34. Eliade, *Images and Symbols*, p. 174.

35. Eliade, *Forbidden Forest*, p. 304.

36. Eliade, *Myths, Dreams, Mysteries*, pp. 227-228.

37. See especially Mircea Eliade, *Rites and Symbols of Initiation*, trans. Willard R. Trask (New York: Harper Torchbooks, 1965).

38. Eliade, *No Souvenirs*, pp. 317-318.

39. Mircea Eliade, "Waiting for the Dawn," in David Carrasco and Jane Marie Swanberg, eds., *Waiting for the Dawn: Mircea Eliade in Perspective* (Boulder, Colo.: Westview Press, 1985), pp. 13, 15.

40. Ibid., pp. 15-16.

41. Eliade, *Myths, Dreams, Mysteries*, p. 80.

42. Eliade, *Symbolism, Sacred, Arts*, p. 11.

43. Eliade, "Waiting for the Dawn," p. 16.

44. Mircea Eliade, *Shamanism: Archaic Techniques of Ecstasy*, trans. Willard R. Trask (Princeton: Princeton University Press, 1964), p. 511.

45. Eliade, *Myths, Dreams, Mysteries*, p. 38.

46. Eliade, *Ordeal by Labyrinth*, pp. 115-116.

47. Eliade, *Patterns*, p. 145.

Chapter 10. The Myth of Nuclear Origins

1. A desire for the new, fresh, and pure is especially characteristic of American culture, as Eliade points out in *The Quest* (Chicago: University of Chicago Press, 1969), pp. 90-101.

2. In 1986 author Richard Rhodes found the subject important enough to devote over 800 pages to it in *The Making of the Atomic Bomb* (New York: Simon & Schuster), a book that gained a Pulitzer Prize and widespread public recognition. Its bibliography fills fourteen closely printed pages.

3. John Dower, *War Without Mercy: Race and Power in the Pacific War* (New York: Pantheon Books, 1986), pp. 81-93.

4. Martin J. Sherwin, *A World Destroyed: Hiroshima and the Origin of the Arms Race*, 2d ed. (New York: Vintage Books, 1987), p. xvii.

5. See Edward T. Linenthal, *Changing Images of the Warrior Hero in America* (New York and Toronto: The Edwin Mellen Press, 1982), pp. 113-130.

6. Dwight Eisenhower, *Crusade in Europe*, quoted in J. Glenn Gray, *The Warriors* (New York: Harper Torchbooks, 1970), p. 147.

7. See the sources cited in chapter 1, note 15, above.

8. Mircea Eliade, *Symbolism, the Sacred, and the Arts*, ed. Diana Apostolos-Cappadona (New York: Crossroad Publishing Co., 1985), p. 112.

9. Mircea Eliade, *The Forge and the Crucible*, trans. Stephen Corrin (New York: Harper Torchbooks, 1971), p. 169.

10. Ibid., p. 56.

11. Mircea Eliade, *A History of Religious Ideas*, vol. I, trans. Willard R. Trask (Chicago: University of Chicago Press, 1978), p. 267.

12. Eliade, *Forge and Crucible*, p. 171.

13. Ibid., p. 172.

14. Ibid.

15. Ibid., p. 178.

16. Ibid., p. 176.

17. Mircea Eliade, "Homo Faber and Homo Religiosus," in Joseph Kitagawa and Gregory Alles, eds., *The History of Religions: Retrospect and Prospect* (Chicago: University of Chicago Press, 1986), p. 9.

18. The latter phrase was used by President Truman in announcing the bombing of Hiroshima (*New York Times*, August 7, 1945, p. 4).

19. Spencer Weart, *Nuclear Fear: A History of Images* (Cambridge, Mass.: Harvard University Press, 1988), demonstrates a direct historical link between the images of nuclear technology discussed here and traditional alchemical images centering on hopes for transformation, rebirth, and immortality. Eliade, *Forge and the Crucible*, demonstrates the historical roots of alchemy in metallurgical symbolism.

20. Norman Moss, *Men Who Play God* (New York: Harper & Row, 1968).

21. Mircea Eliade, *Shamanism: Archaic Techniques of Ecstasy*, trans. Willard R. Trask (Princeton: Princeton University Press, 1964), pp. 508–509.

22. There is a growing literature on the esoteric language of nuclear weapons. For an especially interesting view, see Carol Cohn, "Sex and Death in the Rational World of Defense Intellectuals," *Signs* 12, no. 4 (Summer, 1987).

23. Eliade, *Shamanism*, p. 511.

24. This nostalgia is one of the motives driving the Strategic Defense Initiative; see Edward T. Linenthal, *Symbolic Defense: The Cultural Significance of the Strategic Defense Initiative* (Urbana, Ill.: University of Illinois Press, 1989).

25. Rhodes, *Making of Atomic Bomb*, pp. 449–455.

26. This has been documented by John Shattuck and Muriel Morisey Spence in "Government Information Controls: Implications for Scholarship, Science, and Technology," a report prepared for the Association of American Universities in 1988. See the summary in *Science*, April 29, 1988, p. 595. Cf. Morton H. Halperin, "Secrecy and National Security," *Bulletin of the Atomic Scientists* 41: 7, August, 1985.

27. Robert Jungk, *Brighter Than A Thousand Suns*, trans. James C. Cleugh (New York: Harcourt, Brace, World, 1958). Cf. President Truman's announcement of the bombing of Hiroshima: "The fire from which the sun draws its power has been loosed." (*New York Times*, August 7, 1945, p. 4).

28. Mircea Eliade, *Patterns in Comparative Religion*, trans. Rosemary Sheed (Cleveland: World Publishing Co., 1963), pp. 124, 150.

29. Private diary entry, cited by Gregg Herken, *The Winning Weapon: The Atomic Bomb in the Cold War, 1945–1950* (New York: Alfred A. Knopf, 1980), p. 17.

30. Eliade, *Patterns*, p. 136.

31. Ibid., p. 149.

31a. Mircea Eliade, *The Two and the One*, trans. J.M. Cohen (New York: Harper Torchbooks, 1967), p. 159.

32. Weart, *Nuclear Fear*, uses historically grounded arguments to come to the same conclusion about nuclear imagery as a whole.

33. Herken, *Winning Weapon*, provides a good summary.

Chapter 11. The Hell and Renaissance of Madness

1. James Hillman and Lauro Pozzo, *Inter Views* (New York: Harper & Row, 1983), p. 126.

2. James Hillman, "Anima Mundi: The Return of Soul to the World," *Spring*, 1982, p. 83.

3. Robert Jay Lifton and Kai Erikson, "Nuclear War's Effect on the Mind," in Robert Jay Lifton and Richard Falk, *Indefensible Weapons* (New York: Basic Books, 1982), p. 278.

4. James Hillman, *The Dream and the Underworld* (New York: Harper & Row, 1979), p. 58.

5. Ibid., p. 49.

6. James Hillman, "Mars, Arms, Rams, Wars: On the Love of War," in Richard Grossinger and Lindy Hough, eds., *Nuclear Strategy and the Code of the Warrior* (Berkeley, Cal.: North Atlantic Books, 1984); reprinted in V. Andrews, R. Bosnak, and K. Goodwin, eds., *Facing Apocalypse* (Dallas: Spring Publications, 1987). For other interpretations of the nuclear age by archetypal psychologists, see Andrews, Bosnak, and Goodwin, eds., *Facing Apocalypse*; Evelyn McConeghey and James McConnell, eds., *Nuclear Reactions* (Albuquerque: Image Seminars, Inc., 1984); Michael Perlman, *Imaginal Memory and the Place of Hiroshima* (Albany: SUNY Press, 1988); Wolfgang Giegerich, "The Nuclear Bomb and the Fate of God: On the First Nuclear Fission," *Spring*, 1985; Daniel C. Noel, "The Nuclear Horror and the Hounding of Nature," in Ira Chernus and Edward T. Linenthal, eds., *A Shuddering Dawn: Religious Studies and the Nuclear Age* (Albany: SUNY Press, 1989).

7. Hillman, "Mars, Arms, Rams, Wars," pp. 259-260.

8. Edward T. Linenthal, *Changing Images of the Warrior Hero in America* (New York and Toronto: Edwin Mellen Press, 1982).

9. Hillman, *Dream and Underworld*, p. 111.

10. Hillman, "Mars, Arms, Rams, Wars," p. 260.

11. Hillman, "Anima Mundi," pp. 90, 91.

12. James Hillman, *Re-Visioning Psychology* (New York: Harper & Row, 1975), p. 207.

13. Ibid., p. 109.

14. Ibid., p. 148.

15. Ibid., p. 224.

16. Hillman, *Dream and Underworld*, p. 84; see Hillman, *Inter Views*, pp. 120–122 on contemporary political dualism.

17. Hillman, *Re-Visioning Psychology*, p. ix.

18. James Hillman, "Psychology: Monotheistic or Polytheistic?", in David Leroy Miller, *The New Polytheism*, 2d ed. (Dallas: Spring Publications, 1981), p. 131.

19. Hillman, *Re-Visioning Psychology*, p. 221.

20. Hillman, *Dream and Underworld*, p. 84.

21. James Hillman, "On the Necessity of Abnormal Psychology," *Eranos Yearbook* 43 (Leiden: E.J. Brill, 1977), p. 96. See Giegerich, "The Nuclear Bomb and the Fate of God," for a rich discussion of this issue, specifically in the context of nuclear weapons.

22. Hillman, *Re-Visioning Psychology*, pp. 171, 246 (n. 6), 248 (n. 24). See the brief discussion in Hillman, "Psychology: Monotheistic or Polytheistic?", p. 131 (reprinted in James Hillman, *A Blue Fire*, ed. Thomas Moore [New York: Harper & Row, 1989], p. 42), where he endorses the cryptic formula, "The many contains the unity of the one without losing the possibilities of the many," and comments, "Unity too can be imagined polytheistically." See also the analogous argument on the "marriage" of monotheistic spirit and polytheistic soul in *a Blue Fire*, pp. 118–120 (originally published in James Hillman, "Peaks and Vales," *Puer Papers* [Dallas: Spring Publications, 1979]).

23. Hillman, *Re-visioning Psychology*, pp. 206, 221.

24. Ibid., p. 210.

25. James Hillman, *Suicide and the Soul* (New York: Harper & Row, 1973), p. 63.

26. Ibid., pp. 68, 67, 73.

27. Ibid., p. 86.

28. Ibid., pp. 69, 70.

29. Ibid., p. 70.

30. Ibid., pp. 89, 93.

31. Ibid.

32. Hillman, *Inter Views*, p. 78.

33. Hillman, *Dream and Underworld*, p. 44.

34. Hillman, *Re-Visioning Psychology*, p. 219: "The overhanging menace of breakdown, individual and societal, fills the air with questions of survival similar to those of the Renaissance."

35. Michel Foucault, *Madness and Civilization*, trans. Richard Howard (New York: Vintage Books, 1965), p. 17.

36. Hillman, *Re-Visioning Psychology*, p. 207.

37. Hillman, *A Blue Fire*, pp. 215, 216 (originally published in James Hillman, "The 'Negative' Senex and a Renaissance Solution," *Spring*, 1975).

38. James Hillman, "*Senex* and *Puer*: An Aspect of the Historical and Psychological Present," *Eranos Yearbook* 36 (Zurich: Rhein-Verlag, 1968), p. 354.

39. Hillman, *A Blue Fire*, p. 215.

40. On the monotheism of puer and senex in contemporary politics, see Hillman, *Inter Views*, pp. 117–123.

41. Hillman, *A Blue Fire*, p. 119. Since spirit is always a monotheistic phenomenon in Hillman's view, his claim "that there is madness in one's spirit, and there is spirit in one's madness" (ibid.) is one more indication that madness must make room for monotheism.

42. Hillman, *Re-Visioning Psychology*, p. 218.

Chapter 12. Madness and Peace

1. For examples in the history of Western culture, see James Turner Johnson, *The Quest for Peace* (Princeton: Princeton University Press, 1987).

2. Those who hold this view often argue that the term *nuclear war* is an oxymoron, since war necessarily implies the possibility of a winner as well as a loser.

3. Paul Tillich, *Dynamics of Faith* (New York: Harper Torchbooks, 1957), p. 43.

4. On the concept of war as work and play see James A. Aho, *Religious Mythology and the Art of War* (Westport, Conn.: Greenwood

Press, 1981) and Ira Chernus, "War and Myth: 'The Show Must Go On,'" *Journal of the American Academy of Religion* 52, no. 3 (September, 1985).

5. C. Wright Mills, *The Causes of World War III* (New York: Ballantine Books, 1958), pp. 133-134.

6. See Chernus, "War and Myth," pp. 461-462, and the brief reference to William Blake below.

7. Roger Caillois noted long ago that the threat of nuclear war now fills the role once played by religious festivals in human culture. For Caillois the essence of the festival was imagination, dance, and play that "pantomimed the destruction of the universe, in order to assure its periodic restoration." So he warned that an "excess of seriousness in the festival would make it fatal." (*Man and the Sacred*, trans. Meyer Barash [Glencoe, Ill.: The Free Press, 1959], p. 180).

8. Some initial efforts in this direction have been made, especially by archetypal psychologists; see the sources cited in chapter 11, note 6, above. Other useful approaches include Richard Grossinger and Lindy Hough, eds., *Nuclear Strategy and the Code of the Warrior* (Berkeley, Cal.: North Atlantic Books, 1984), Spencer Weart, *Nuclear Fear: A History of Images* (Cambridge, Mass.: Harvard University Press, 1988), and Paul Boyer, *By the Bomb's Early Light: American Thought and Culture at the Dawn of the Atomic Age* (New York: Pantheon Books, 1985). Unfortunately academic religious studies has just begun to respond to the task. Some initial efforts are presented in Ira Chernus and Edward T. Linenthal, eds., *A Shuddering Dawn: Religious Studies and the Nuclear Age* (Albany: SUNY Press, 1989) and Ira Chernus, *Dr. Strangegod: On the Symbolic Meaning of Nuclear Weapons* (Columbia, S.C.: University of South Carolina Press, 1986).

9. See Chernus, *Dr. Strangegod*, pp. 149-168. One approach is suggested by Robert Jay Lifton and Nicholas Humphrey, eds., *In a Dark Time* (Cambridge, Mass.: Harvard University Press, 1984).

10. William Blake, "Laocoon"; *Milton*, Preface; *Milton*, 30:19 (*Complete Writings*, ed. Geoffrey Keynes [Oxford: Oxford University Press, 1979], pp. 775, 480, 519).

11. Mircea Eliade, *The Forbidden Forest*, trans. Mac Linscott Ricketts and Mary Park Stevenson (Notre Dame, Ind.: University of Notre Dame Press, 1978), p. 304.

12. Robert Jay Lifton and Richard Falk, *Indefensible Weapons* (New York: Basic Books, 1982), p. 111.

Bibliography

Abas, Bryan. "Rocky Flats is Back." *Westword*, March 21–27, 1990.

Aho, James A. *Religious Mythology and the Art of War*. Westport, Conn.: Greenwood Press, 1981.

Aldridge, Robert C. *Nuclear Empire*. Vancouver: New Star Books, 1988.

———. *First Strike! The Pentagon's Strategy for Nuclear War*. Boston: South End Press, 1983.

Anders, Gunther. "Reflections on the H Bomb." Translated by Norbert Guterman. *Dissent*, Spring 1956.

Andrews, V.; Bosnak, R.; and Goodwin, K., eds. *Facing Apocalypse*. Dallas: Spring Publications, 1987.

Arnold, H.H. "The 36-Hour War." *Life*, Nov. 19, 1945.

Barnet, Richard. *Real Security: Restoring American Power in a Dangerous Decade*. New York: Simon & Schuster, 1981.

Barron, John. "The KGB's Magical War for Peace." *Reader's Digest*, October 1982.

Baruch, Bernard. "Spiritual Armageddon Is Here—Now." *Reader's Digest*, March 1951.

Benford, Robert D. "The Nuclear Disarmament Movement." In *The Nuclear Cage: A Sociology of the Arms Race*, by Lester R. Kurtz. Englewood Cliffs, N.J.: Prentice Hall, 1988.

Benford, Robert D. and Kurtz, Lester R. "Performing the Nuclear Ceremony: The Arms Race as Ritual." In *A Shuddering Dawn: Religious Studies and the Nuclear Age*, edited by Ira Chernus and Edward T. Linenthal. Albany: SUNY Press, 1989.

Betts, Richard. *Nuclear Blackmail and Nuclear Balance*. Washington, D.C.: The Brookings Institution, 1987.

Blake, William. *Complete Writings*. Edited by Geoffrey Keynes. Oxford: Oxford University Press, 1979.

Blight, James G. "Toward a Policy-Relevant Psychology of Avoiding Nuclear War." *American Psychologist* 42, no. 1 (January 1987).

Bottome, Edgar M. *The Missile Gap: A Study of the Formulation of Military and Political Policy*. Rutherford, N.J.: Fairleigh Dickinson University Press, 1971.

Boyer, Paul. *By the Bomb's Early Light: American Thought and Culture at the Dawn of the Atomic Age*. New York: Pantheon Books, 1985.

———. "From Activism to Apathy: The American People and Nuclear Weapons, 1963-1980." *Journal of American History* 70 (March 1984).

———. "Arms Race as Sitcom Plot." *Bulletin of the Atomic Scientists* 45, no. 5 (June, 1989).

Broad, William. "From Cold War to Nuclear Nostalgia." *New York Times*, Dec. 12, 1989.

Buber, Martin. *The Knowledge of Man*. Edited by Maurice Friedman. New York: Harper Torchbooks, 1966.

Caillois, Roger. *Man and the Sacred*. Translated by Meyer Barash. Glencoe, Ill.: The Free Press, 1959.

Chernus, Ira. *Dr. Strangegod: On the Symbolic Meaning of Nuclear Weapons*. Columbia, S.C.: University of South Carolina Press, 1986.

———. "War and Myth: 'The Show Must Go On'." *Journal of the American Academy of Religion* 52, no. 3 (September 1985).

Chernus, Ira, and Linenthal, Edward T., eds. *A Shuddering Dawn: Religious Studies and the Nuclear Age*. Albany: SUNY Press, 1989.

Cohn, Carol. "Sex and Death in the Rational World of Defense Intellectuals." *Signs* 12, no. 4 (Summer 1987).

Dorman, William. "The Media: Playing the Government's Game." *Bulletin of the Atomic Scientists* 41, no. 7 (August 1985).

Dowd, Maureen. "No. 1 Concerns: The New Dawn is Casting Some Things in a Bad Light." *New York Times*, March 4, 1990.

Dower, John. *War Without Mercy: Race and Power in the Pacific War*. New York: Pantheon Books, 1986.

Dumas, Lloyd, ed. *The Political Economy of Arms Reduction: Reversing Economic Decay*. Boulder, Colo.: Westview Press, 1982.

Eliade, Mircea. *Cosmos and History: The Myth of the Eternal Return.* Translated by Willard R. Trask. New York: Harper Torchbooks, 1959.

———. *The Forbidden Forest.* Translated by Mac Linscott Ricketts and Mary Park Stevenson. Notre Dame, Ind.: University of Notre Dame Press, 1978.

———. *The Forge and the Crucible.* Translated by Stephen Corrin. New York: Harper Torchbooks, 1971.

———. *A History of Religious Ideas,* Vol. I. Translated by Willard R. Trask. Chicago: University of Chicago Press, 1978.

———. *A History of Religious Ideas,* Vol. II. Translated by Willard R. Trask. Chicago: University of Chicago Press, 1982.

———. *A History of Religious Ideas,* Vol. III. Translated by Alf Hiltebeitel and Diana Apostolos-Cappadona. Chicago: University of Chicago Press, 1985.

———. "Homo Faber and Homo Religiosus." In *The History of Religions: Retrospect and Prospect,* edited by Joseph Kitagawa and Gregory Alles. Chicago: University of Chicago Press, 1986.

———. *Images and Symbols.* Translated by Phillip Mairet. New York: Sheed and Ward, 1961.

———. *Myth and Reality.* Translated by Willard R. Trask. New York: Harper Torchbooks, 1968.

———. *Myths, Dreams, and Mysteries.* Translated by Phillip Mairet. New York: Harper Torchbooks, 1967.

———. *No Souvenirs: Journal, 1957–1969.* Translated by Fred H. Johnson, Jr. New York: Harper & Row, 1977.

———. *Occultism, Witchcraft and Cultural Fashions.* Chicago: University of Chicago Press, 1976.

———. *Ordeal by Labyrinth: Conversations with Claude-Henri Rocquet.* Translated by Derek Coltman. Chicago: University of Chicago Press, 1982.

———. *Patterns in Comparative Religion.* Translated by Rosemary Sheed. Cleveland: World Publishing Company, 1963.

———. *The Quest.* Chicago: University of Chicago Press, 1969.

———. *Rites and Symbols of Initiation.* Translated by Willard R. Trask. New York: Harper Torchbooks, 1965.

———. *Shamanism: Archaic Techniques of Ecstasy.* Translated by Willard R. Trask. Princeton: Princeton University Press, 1964.

———. *The Sacred and the Profane.* Translated by Willard R. Trask. Princeton: Princeton University Press, 1964.

———. *Symbolism, the Sacred, and the Arts.* Edited by Diana Apostolos-Cappadona. New York: Crossroad Publishing Co., 1985.

———. *Tales of the Sacred and the Supernatural.* Philadelphia: Westminster Press, 1981.

———. *The Two and the One.* Translated by J. M. Cohen. New York: Harper Torchbooks, 1969.

———. "Waiting for the Dawn." In *Waiting for the Dawn: Mircea Eliade in Perspective,* edited by David Carrasco and Jane Marie Swanberg. Boulder, Colo.: Westview Press, 1985.

Ellsberg, Daniel. "How We Use Our Nuclear Arsenal." In *Protest and Survive,* edited by E. P. Thompson and Dan Smith. New York: Monthly Review Press, 1981.

Evans, Richard I. *R. D. Laing: The Man and His Ideas.* New York: Dutton & Co., 1976.

Foucault, Michel. *Madness and Civilization.* Translated by Richard Howard. New York: Vintage Books, 1965.

Frank, Jerome D. *Sanity and Survival.* New York: Random House, 1967.

Giegerich, Wolfgang. "The Nuclear Bomb and the Fate of God: The First Nuclear Fission." *Spring* 1985.

Glover, Edward. *War, Sadism, and Pacifism.* London: Allen & Unwin, 1946.

Gray, Colin, and Payne, Keith. "Victory Is Possible." *Foreign Policy* 39 (Summer 1980).

Gray, J. Glenn. *The Warriors.* New York: Harper Torchbooks, 1970.

Haldeman, H.R., and Dimona, Joseph. *The Ends of Power.* New York: New York Times Books, 1978.

Halperin, Morton H. "Secrecy and National Security." *Bulletin of the Atomic Scientists* 41, no. 7 (August 1985).

Herken, Gregg. *Counsels of War.* New York: Alfred A. Knopf, 1985.

———. *The Winning Weapon: The Atomic Bomb in the Cold War, 1945–1950.* New York: Alfred A. Knopf, 1980.

Hillman, James. "Anima Mundi: The Return of Soul to the World." *Spring* 1982.

———. *A Blue Fire*. Edited by Thomas Moore. New York: Harper & Row, 1989.

———. *The Dream and the Underworld*. New York: Harper & Row, 1979.

———. "Mars, Arms, Rams, Wars: On the Love of War." In *Nuclear Strategy and the Code of the Warrior*, edited by Richard Grossinger and Lindy Hough. Berkeley, Calif.: North Atlantic Books, 1984.

———. *The Myth of Analysis*. Evanston, Ill.: Northwestern University Press, 1972.

———. "On the Necessity of Abnormal Psychology." *Eranos Yearbook*, vol. 43. Leiden: E. J. Brill, 1977.

———. "Psychology: Monotheistic or Polytheistic?" In *The New Polytheism*, by David Leroy Miller. 2d ed. Dallas: Spring Publications, 1981.

———. *Puer Papers*. Dallas: Spring Publications, 1979.

———. *Re-Visioning Psychology*. New York: Harper & Row, 1975.

———. "*Senex* and *Puer*: An Aspect of the Historical and Psychological Present." *Eranos Jahrbuch*, vol. 36. Zurich: Rhein-Verlag, 1968.

———. *Suicide and the Soul*. New York: Harper & Row, 1973.

Hillman, James, and Pozzo, Laura. *Inter Views*. New York: Harper & Row, 1983.

Hirschbein, Ron. *Newest Weapons / Oldest Psychology: The Dialectics of American Nuclear Strategy*. New York: Peter Lang, 1989.

Johnson, James Turner. *The Quest for Peace: Three Moral Traditions in Western Cultural History*. Princeton: Princeton University Press, 1987.

Jungk, Robert. *Brighter Than a Thousand Suns*. Translated by James C. Cleugh. New York: Harcourt, Brace, World, 1958.

Kaku, Michio, and Axelrod, Daniel. *To Win a Nuclear War: The Pentagon's War-Fighting Plan*. Boston: South End Press, 1987.

Kaplan, Fred. *The Wizards of Armageddon*. New York: Simon & Schuster, 1983.

Kovel, Joel. *Against the State of Nuclear Terror*. Boston: South End Press, 1983.

Kull, Stephen. *Minds At War: Nuclear Reality and the Inner Conflicts of Defense Policymakers.* New York: Basic Books, 1988.

Kurtz, Lester R. *The Nuclear Cage.* Englewood Cliffs, N.J.: Prentice-Hall, 1988.

Laing, R. D. *The Divided Self.* 2d ed. Baltimore: Penguin Books, 1965.

———. *The Politics of Experience.* New York: Ballantine Books, 1967.

———. *The Politics of the Family.* New York: Vintage Books, 1972.

———. *The Self and Others.* 2d ed. New York: Pantheon Books, 1969.

———. *The Voice of Experience.* New York: Pantheon Books, 1982.

Laing, R. D., and Esterson, Aaron. *Sanity, Madness, and the Family.* New York: Basic Books, 1965.

Laing, R. D.; Phillipson, H.; and Lee, A. R. *Interpersonal Perception: A Theory and Method of Research.* London: Tavistock Publications, 1966.

La Rocque, Gene R. "Prospects for Change in the U.S. and Soviet Military." *The Defense Monitor* 18, no. 8 (1989).

Lifton, Robert Jay. *Boundaries: Psychological Man in Revolution.* New York: Random House, 1970.

———. *The Broken Connection.* New York: Simon & Schuster, 1979.

———. *Death in Life: Survivors of Hiroshima.* New York: Random House, 1967.

———. *The Future of Immortality and Other Essays for a Nuclear Age.* New York: Basic Books, 1987.

———. *History and Human Survival.* New York: Random House, 1970.

———. "The Image of the 'End of the World': A Psychological View." *Michigan Quarterly Review* 24, no. 1 (Winter 1985).

———. *The Life of the Self: Toward a New Psychology.* New York: Simon & Schuster, 1976.

———. *Nazi Doctors: Medical Killing and the Psychology of Genocide.* New York: Basic Books, 1986.

Lifton, Robert Jay, and Erikson, Kai. "Nuclear War's Effect on Mind." *Indefensible Weapons.* By Robert Jay Lifton and Richard Falk. New York: Basic Books, 1982.

Lifton, Robert Jay, and Falk, Richard. *Indefensible Weapons.* New York: Basic Books, 1982.

Lifton, Robert Jay, and Humphrey, Nicholas. *In A Dark Time.* Cambridge, Mass.: Harvard University Press, 1984.

Lifton, Robert Jay, and Olson, Eric. *Living and Dying.* New York: Praeger, 1974.

"Let's Prepare Shelters." *Life,* Oct. 13, 1961.

Linenthal, Edward T. "Restoring America: Political Revivalism in the Nuclear Age." In *Religion in the Life of the Nation: American Recoveries,* edited by Roland A. Sherrill. Urbana, Ill.: University of Illinois Press, 1989.

———. *Symbolic Defense: The Cultural Significance of the Strategic Defense Initiative.* Urbana, Ill.: University of Illinois Press, 1989.

———. *Changing Images of the Warrior Hero in America.* New York and Toronto: Edwin Mellen Press, 1982.

McConeghey, Evelyn, and McConnell, James, eds. *Nuclear Reactions.* Albuquerque: Image Seminars, Inc., 1984.

Mills, C. Wright. *The Causes of World War III.* New York: Ballantine Books, 1958.

Molander, Roger. "How I Learned to Start Worrying and Hate the Bomb." *Washington Post,* March 21, 1982.

Moss, Norman. *Men Who Play God.* New York: Harper & Row, 1968.

Noel, Daniel C. "The Nuclear Horror and the Hounding of Nature: Listening to Images." In *A Shuddering Dawn: Religious Studies and the Nuclear Age,* edited by Ira Chernus and Edward T. Linenthal. Albany: SUNY Press, 1989.

Perlman, Michael. *Imaginal Memory and the Place of Hiroshima.* Albany: SUNY Press, 1988.

Pipes, Richard. *Survival is Not Enough: Soviet Realities and America's Future.* New York: Simon & Schuster, 1984.

Powaski, Ronald E. *March to Armageddon.* New York: Oxford University Press, 1987.

Pringle, Peter, and Arkin, William. *SIOP: The Secret U.S. Plan for Nuclear War.* New York: W. W. Norton & Co., 1983.

The Public Agenda Foundation. *Voter Options on Nuclear Arms Policy.* New York: The Public Agenda Foundation, 1984.

Rhodes, Richard. *The Making of the Atomic Bomb.* New York: Simon & Schuster, 1986.

Ricketts, Mac Linscott. *Mircea Eliade: The Romanian Roots, 1907–1945.* 2 vols. Boulder, Colo.: East European Monographs, 1988.

Rowny, Edward V. "How Not to Negotiate With the Russians." *Reader's Digest*, June 1981.

Scheer, Robert. *With Enough Shovels.* New York: Random House, 1982.

Schell, Jonathan. *The Fate of the Earth.* New York: Avon Books, 1982.

Schwartz, William, and Derber, Charles, et al. *The Nuclear Seduction.* Berkeley, Cal.: University of California Press, 1990.

Shattuck, John, and Spence, Muriel Morisey. "Government Information Controls: Implications for Scholarship, Science, and Technology." Report to the Association of American Universities, 1988.

Sherwin, Martin J. *A World Destroyed: Hiroshima and the Origins of the Arms Race.* 2d ed. New York: Vintage Books, 1987.

"The Soul-Searchers Find No Answer." *Life*, Feb. 27, 1950.

Stone, Ronald H. *Paul Tillich's Radical Social Thought.* Atlanta: John Knox Press, 1980.

Talbott, Strobe. *The Russians and Reagan.* New York: Vintage Books, 1984.

———. "Rethinking the Red Menace." *Time*, Jan. 1, 1990.

Talmon, Jacob. *The Origins of Totalitarian Democracy.* London: Mercury, 1961.

Thomas, Evan. "From Abyss to Brink: Will United States be More Interventionist in a Post-Cold-War World?" *Newsweek*, Jan. 8, 1990.

Thompson, E. P., and Smith, Dan, eds. *Protest and Survive.* New York: Monthly Press Review, 1981.

Tillich, Paul. *The Courage to Be.* New Haven: Yale University Press, 1952.

———. *Dynamics of Faith.* New York: Harper Torchbooks, 1957.

———. *Love, Power, and Justice.* New York: Oxford University Press, 1954.

———. *My Search for Absolutes.* New York: Simon & Schuster, 1967.

———. *Political Expectation.* New York: Harper & Row, 1971.

———. *The Protestant Era.* Translated by J. L. Adams. Chicago: University of Chicago Press, 1957.

———. *The Religious Situation.* Translated by H. R. Niebuhr. New York: Henry Holt & Co., 1932.

———. *Systematic Theology.* 3 vols. Chicago: University of Chicago Press, 1951–1963.

———. *The Socialist Revolution.* Translated by Franklin Sherman. New York: Harper & Row, 1977.

———. *Theology of Culture.* Edited by R. C. Kimball. New York: Oxford University Press, 1959.

———. *What is Religion?* Edited by J. L. Adams. New York: Harper & Row, 1969.

Toth, Robert. "U.S. Shifts Nuclear Response Strategy." *Los Angeles Times,* July 23, 1989.

———. "Planners Split on How to Meet Nuclear Threat." *Los Angeles Times,* July 24, 1989.

Tyroler, Charles, II, ed. *Alerting America: The Papers of the Committee on the Present Danger,* Washington, D.C.: Pergamon-Brassey's, 1984.

Weart, Spencer. *Nuclear Fear: A History of Images.* Cambridge, Mass.: Harvard University Press, 1988.

Weida, William J. and Gertcher, Frank L. *The Political Economy of National Defense.* Boulder, Colo.: Westview Press, 1987.

Index

Alchemists, nuclear scientists as, 240
Alchemy, 240, 310n.19
Annihilation, fantasies of, 23-24, 299n.16; and dual track fantasy, 169, 171, 173; and nuclear deterrence, 163, 165-66; and nuclear disarmament, 81, 188; and nuclear madness, 135, 138-41, 143-44, 148-49, 210, 247; and nuclear superpower, 28; and safe bomb fantasy, 92; and schizophrenia, 124-31, 164; as resurrection fantasy, 267; in Cold War era, 149-56, 157-58, 160-61; in nuclear imagery, 65; in nuclear superpower relations, 12-14; in schizoid strategy, 117. See also Laing, R.D.
Antinuclear movement, 1-2, 3, 4-5,11; and dual track fantasy, 184-89; and family systems, 42; and invalidation, 42; and psychic numbing, 174; and social renaissance, 285; antinuclear protest, 4-5, 42-4, 295n.21; as schizophrenic fantasy, 159
Apocalypse, fantasies of: and Bomb as image of pollution, 183; and dual track fantasy, 170, 173-74, 175, 178, 180-82, 186; and nuclear cataclysm, fantasies of, 64, 257; and nuclear disarmament, 177, 185, 280, 283; and United States nuclear policy, 301n.13, 306n.24; in Cold War era, 157, 160-61, 180, 247
Arnold, H.H. ("Hap"), 150

Baruch, Bernard, 154
Bateson, Gregory, 129
Being, Paul Tillich's concept of, 48-49, 68
Blake, William, 287
Boehme, Jakob, 287
Bomb: and anxiety of meaninglessness, 58; and desire for infinitude, 68-69, 118; and ontological insecurity, 36, 66, 148; and social neurosis, 66-67; as enforcer of nuclear madness, 135, 141; as guarantor of world peace, 18, 77, 226-27, 237, 292n.13; as image of chaos, 250; as image of family violence, 39; as image of God, 151; as image of Hades, 257, 259; as image of suicidal transformation, 265; as magical weapon, 235, 236, 243; as religious image, 118, 154, 155, 156, 184, 189, 216, 228, 232, 242, 250-51, 268; as image of pollution, 182-83, 288; as schizophrenic image, 135, 137, 148-49, 155-56; as solar symbol, 239-40; as symbol of ultimate concern, 69
Bomb shelter: as religious image, 158; craze, 158-59
Broad, William, 78

Brown, Harold, 299n.24
Buber, Martin, 187
Bush, George, 172
Bush administration, 79, 179–80, 297n.7, 298nn.9, 10, 12, 298–99n.14a, 306n.21

CPD. *See* Committee on the Present Danger
Canticle for Leibowitz, A, 157
Causes of World War III, The, 282
Carter administration, 168
Cheney, Richard, 298n.9
Churchill, Winston, 164, 179
Cold War: and annihilation fantasies, 20, 139, 149; and apocalypse fantasies, 157, 160–61, 170, 180; and monotheistic consciousness, 84; and nuclear madness, 142–43, 146–61; and omnipotence fantasies, 20, 150–56, 157, 160–61, 172, 173; and schizoid strategy, 20, 29; and schizophrenia, 149–61, 170; as religious war, 225–27
Collusion, 43–4. *See also* Laing, R.D.
Committee on the Present Danger (CPD), 172, 173
Conrad, Joseph, 269
Cosmos and chaos: and *homo religiosus,* 199–201, 208–11, 249–51; and nuclear state, 240–41; and ontological security, 208–09; and nuclear expert, 236; and shamanism, 212; and temporality, 195–97; and world renewal, 202–04; chaos as madness, 216; defined, 194–95; in nuclear madness, 244–45; problem of in nuclear age, 204, 249–51; war as struggle between, 222, 224, 226; war between, in myth of nuclear origins, 242, 246–51

Cuban missile crisis, 158–59, 166

Day After, The, 175–78, 188, 305n.16
Death in life, 10, 11; and literalism, 118, 250; and safe bomb fantasy, 82; defined, 10; in schizophrenia, 129; in superpower policies, 27–28. *See also* Psychic numbing
Divided Self, The, 15, 20, 29, 45
Dr. Strangelove, 157, 296n.16
Dual track: and monotheistic consciousness, 270; and myth of nuclear origins, 247; and safe bomb fantasy, 179–81, 184, 187, 257, 258; and war as ritual play, 280; and world peace, 274, 275, 288; as heroic ego fantasy, 254; as religious image and ritual, 169–70; as schizoid fantasy, 168–75, 178–82, 184; defined, 168

Ego: and antinuclear activism, 186; and literalism, 88–89; and nuclear deterrence, 164; and nuclear disarmament, 73–74, 77–78, 81–82, 166, 177; and nuclear madness, 133, 142, 149; and science and technology, images of, 73; and world peace, 277, 281; in Cold War era, 173. *See also* Laing, R.D.
Eisenhower, Dwight, 224
Eliade, Mircea 4, 241, 250, 251, 253, 256, 259, 260, 261, 267, 290; cosmos and chaos, 194–204, 213; death in life, 198; end of the world, meaning of, 201–17; *Forbidden Forest, The,* 197, 203, 205–08; historical time, problem of,

196-97, 200-01, 205, 209-10, 215; *homo religiosus*, 193-94, 199-204; 206-17; initiation, 230; literalism, 198-99, 208, 209; metallurgy, 229-30; modern man, 193-94, 196-99, 204-05; modernity, 193, 196-99, 204, 209, 211, 213, 214; nuclear madness, 205-06; origin myths, 219, 221; religion, defined, 200; sacred, defined, 200; secular symbols as religious symbols, 214-16; shamanism, 211-14, 235-37; solar symbolism, 239; transcendence of time, 201-03, 206, 231, 232; war as ritual hunting, 221-22; weapons as religious objects, 229-31; world creation, 229, 236-37; world destruction, 205-08, 211, 213; world renewal, 201-04, 213, 222
Engulfment, fantasies of: defined, 16; in international relations, 23; in nuclear imagery, 17; in nuclear madness, 142-43, 209, 210, 247; in schizophrenia, 118; in superpower policies, 28, 82. *See also* Laing, R.D.
Environmental concerns, 79-80, 179
Erikson, Kai, 148, 254

Fail-safe, 157
False self, 45; and dual track fantasy, 169, 172, 183, 184; and nuclear madness, 133, 135-37, 139, 142, 144, 184; and psychic numbing, 17, 33, 45, 75, 115, 116-17; and need for religious imagery, 214; and United States nuclear policy, 19, 75-76, 172; and world peace, 276, 277; defined, 17; in American attitudes toward Soviet Union, 36, 74-75, 167; in Cold War era fantasies, 151, 154-56, 161; in family systems, 38-40, 45; in schizophrenia, 130, 209. *See also* Laing, R.D.; Schizoid strategy
"Family of nations": defined, 37; in international relations, 37-40, 45, 75
Family systems, 42-44. *See also* Laing, R.D.
Fate of the Earth, The, 175-78, 188, 305n.16
Finitude: and freedom, 60-61; and psychic numbing, 112-13, 116-17; and schizophrenia, 130-31, 148; desire for, and infinitude, 118, 303-04n.25; in Cold War era fantasies, 151, 155. *See also* Tillich, Paul; Lifton, Robert Jay
Forbidden Forest, The, 197, 203, 205-08
Forrestal, James, 301n.11
Foucault, Michel, 262
Freud, Sigmund, 195

Gergen, David R., 301n.14
Glover, Edward, 155-56
Gorbachev, Mikhail, 174
Gray, Colin, 18
Groves, Leslie, 303n.18

Hades (hell), 253-60; as image of nuclear holocaust, 254; as image of postholocaust world, 254; as image of psychic numbing, 254-55; as nuclear hell, 254-60; as psychological archetype of self-destruction, 254; as reinforcer of psychic numbing, 258-59
Hallucinogenic use as shamanic initiation, 211-13

Index

Hanford, Washington, 237
Heller, Eric, 204, 206
Heroic ego, fantasy of: and dual track, 169, 180, 181, 184, 254; and literalism 116-17; and nuclear arms race, 84-85; and nuclear deterrence, 165, 254; and nuclear madness, 134-37, 141-42, 184; and social renaissance, 267; and safe bomb fantasy, 91, 183; and schizoid strategy, 93, 135; and war as work, 280; and world peace, 276; in Cold War era, 150-151, 155. *See also* Hillman, James
Hibakusha, 9, 10
Hillman, James, 4, 90, 114, 116, 118, 124, 208, 251, 278, 289; Bomb, imagery of, 255-56; Hades 253-63, 267; heroic ego, 83-84, 86, 93, 254-57, 262, 266; literalism, 85-88, 91-92, 257, 258, 261, 262; monotheistic consciousness, 83-84, 86-87, 186, 256, 257, 260-68, 270, 313n.22, 314n.41; nominalism, 87-88; polytheistic consciousness, 86, 260-68, 313n.22; psychosis, defined, 260; *puer* and disarmament movement, 270; Renaissance, 263-64, 266-71; *Re-visioning Psychology*, 261, 263; schizophrenia, 254; social madness, defined, 254; *Suicide and the Soul*, 264, 266; suicide, 264-67; war as religious sacrifice, 256
Hiroshima, atomic bombing of, 9, 10, 12, 18, 145, 220, 223, 242, 310n.18, 311n.27
Hitler, Adolf, 219
Homo religiosus: and cosmos and chaos, 199-201, 208-11, 249-51; and freedom, 202; and metallurgy 229, 232; and origin myths, 219; and historical time, 200-01; and transcendence of time, 201-03, 206; and world destruction 206-08; and world renewal, 201-04, 216-17, 241, 245-49; as shamanic initiate, 211-14; compared with schizophrenic, 209-11; defined, 193-94

Implosion, fantasies of, 26; and schizophrenia, 129-31, 148; defined, 16; in Cold War era, 154; in international relations, 23; in nuclear imagery, 17; in nuclear madness, 142-43, 209, 247; in superpower policies, 28, 82. *See also* Laing, R.D.
Infinitude: and finitude, desire for, 68, 112-13, 303-04n.25; and nuclear disarmament, 177, 187; and world peace, 278, 282, 283; desire to escape, in nuclear age, 297n.20; fear of, in schizophrenia 127-31, 148, 209; in Cold War era fantasies 154, need for grounding of, in religious imagery, 210-11. *See also* Tillich, Paul
Initiation: and nuclear technology, 236-38; as process of social transformation, 244-45, 248; shamanic, 211-13; world destruction as form of, 244-45, 248
Intermediate Nuclear Forces (INF) Treaty, 79, 175
Invalidation, 41-44. *See also* Laing, R.D.

Johnson administration, 168
Jung, C.G., 83

Kahn, Herman, 157-58, 165
Kaltenborn, H.V., 145, 146
Kennedy administration, 168
Kierkegaard, Soren, 16
Kissinger, Henry, 165
Kubrick Stanley, 157, 296n.16

La Rocque, Gene, 79
Laing, R.D. 3, 15-18, 20-23, 24-25, 29, 33, 39, 46, 48, 69, 77, 92, 118, 119, 189, 194, 208, 211; and Jung, C.G., 83; and Lifton, Robert Jay, 11, 17, 47, 125; and Tillich, Paul, 16, 47, 69; annihilation, fantasies of, 20, 24; Bomb, 135; collusion, 40; *Divided Self, The*, 15, 20, 29, 45, 119; engulfment, fantasies of, 16, 17, 25-26, 114-15; false self 11, 17, 21, 29-31, 45, 72-74; family systems, defined, 34, 36, 37, 45, 75; implosion, fantasies of, 16, 17, 114-15; invalidation, 40; mapping, 30-32, 34, 40; mystification, 40; omnipotence, fantasies of, 18, 20-21; ontological insecurity 15-17, 21, 29, 32, 34, 45, 70, 105, 114; petrification, fantasies of, 16, 17, 25-26, 114-15; *Politics of Experience, The*, 83; rational ego, 71-73; schizoid strategy 17-18, 20-21, 25-27, 28, 29-31, 45, 69, 72-73, 84, 93, 114, 116; schizophrenia 124, 125, 126, 128, 129, 132, 147
Laurence, William L., 147
Lawrence Laboratories, 237
Lifton, Robert Jay, 2, 3, 9-15 17, 46, 118, 138-39, 177, 208, 210, 211, 290; and Laing, R.D. 3, 11, 17, 125; and Tillich, Paul, 3, 11, 52, 102; Bomb, 135; death in life, 10, 11, 100, 115, 148, 254; experiential transcendence, 101-105, 129; finitude. 103-113; Hiroshima study, 9; infinitude, 105-113; psychic numbing, 2, 9-15, 46, 52, 69-70, 93, 95, 100-102, 105-106, 110-11, 113-15, 116, 144; psychological health, theory of, 95-98; schizophrenia 123, 124-29, 132, 187-88; symbolic immortality and, 10, 11, 12-13, 98-105; totalism 13-14, 112, 124
Limited Test Ban Treaty, 166
Literalism: and antinuclear activism, 185, 188; and Bomb as image of pollution, 183; and dual track fantasy, 169, 171; and nuclear imagery, 86-87, 148; and nuclear madness, 133, 136, 140-44, 149, 247; and psychic numbing, 88-90, 116-117, 165; and religious imagery, 117, 249, and safe bomb fantasy, 90, 91; and schizoid strategy, 93, 116-18; and schizophrenia, 127-131, 187-88; and world peace, 282, 283, 284, 286, 287; in Cold War era fantasies, 151-56, 157, 158-61. *See also* Eliade, Mircea; Hillman, James
Livermore, California, 237
Los Alamos, 237

MAD (Mutually Assured Destruction), 163, 164-165, 166, 172, 225, 228
"Madman Theory", 165
Madness and Civilization, 269
Manhattan Project, 233, 237, 303n.18
Mapping, 44. *See also* Laing, R.D.
Men Who Play God, 234

Metallurgists, nuclear scientists as, 233–34
Metallurgy, 229–31, 233, 234
Meyer, Nicholas, 175–78
Miller, Walter, Jr., 157
Mills, C. Wright, 282
Modern man, Mircea Eliade's concept of: and death in life, 198; and historical time, 196–97, 246–47; and transcendence of time, 203–04, 232, 246–47; as schizoid, 209; defined, 193–94; nuclear scientist as, 204–05
Modernity: and meaninglessness of chaos, 247, 249–50; and ontological insecurity, 132; and religious imagery, 118–19, 213–14, 248–49, 271–72; and suicide, 267; as age of neurosis, 56; as schizoid strategy, 116–19, 135; madness of, in Cold War fantasies, 150–56; self-annihilation as goal of, 146–47; use of, in text, 291n.3. *See also* Eliade, Mircea; Tillich, Paul
Monotheistic consciousness 313n.22, 314n.41; and antinuclear activism, 186, 262; and deicide, 262, 267; and nuclear arms race, 84–85; and nuclear disarmament, 84–85, 270; and nuclear madness, 134, 135; and desire for self-destruction, 260, 268; in Cold War era, 84, 151. *See also* Hillman, James
Moss, Norman, 234
Murrow, Edward R., 145–46
Mutually Assured Destruction. *See* MAD
Mystification, 40–41, 43–44, 77–78. *See also* Laing, R.D.
Myth of nuclear origins: as embodiment of war experience and values, 228–29; historical origins, 219–20; indicative of nuclear age attitudes, 221; themes, 220; war between cosmos and chaos in, 242, 246–51; weapons as religious objects in, 241; world renewal as theme of, 242, 244–45
Myth of world destruction, 243, 244, 245–49

Nagasaki, atomic bombing of, 12, 145, 220, 224, 242
Neurosis: and Bomb, 66–67; and modernity, 56; and nuclear politics, 66; and psychic numbing, 57; and radical finitude, 57; and religious imagery, 210–11; characteristics of, 56–57; defined, 11; in nuclear images, 63–64; in U.S.-U.S.S.R. relations, 63; nuclear age as age of, 56. *See also* Tillich, Paul
Nixon, Richard, 165
Nixon administration, 75
Nuclear armament, origins of, 4
Nuclear arms race: and family system, 37; and heroic ego, 84–85; and monotheistic consciousness, 84–85; and psychic numbing, 93; as schizoid strategy, 20, 77, 78, 124; as nuclear madness, 124
Nuclear deterrence, 21; and heroic ego, 165; and omnipotence fantasies, 19–20; as nuclear madness, 163–89; as part of dual track fantasy, 168–75, 184, 185, 254, 288; as schizoid strategy, 19, 22, 25–26, 36, 76; in nuclear imagery, 66; theory of, 164–165, 166
Nuclear disarmament, 3, 4–5, 71,

78-81, 288, 298n.11; and ego, 74; and false self, 73-76, 78; and literalism, 90; and monotheistic consciousness, 84-85, 270; and myth of nuclear origins, 247; and nuclear expert as shaman, 236-39; and radical finitude, 175-78; and safe bomb fantasy, 76-81, 137; and weapons as religious objects, 234-35; as nuclear madness, 166-89; as part of dual track fantasy, 168-75, 178-82, 184, 254; as play, 285; as schizoid strategy, 136, 138, 167-68; defined, 166; discourse and psychic numbing, 11; fantasy of, and media, 167

Nuclear images: and literalism, 86-87; and mapping, 31; and nuclear deterrence, 66; as mode of symbolic immortality, 12; as reinforcers of psychic numbing, 30, 31, 46, 69, 82, 93, 161; as religious images of infinitude, 67; examples of 12, 23, 25, 26, 28, 62-66, 306n.36

Nuclear madness: and nuclear arms race, 124; as defense against ontological insecurity, 250; as initiatory journey, 104, 269; as model of schizophrenic social process, 123, 131-161, 250; as religious experience of chaos 216-17, 249-50; defined, 3; historical origins, 134-35, 286

Nuclear policy, United States, 146; and nuclear madness, 137-138; in 1950s, 18, 145-51 (*see also* Cold War); in 1960s, 163-68; in 1970s, 75, 168, 172-73; in 1980s, 71, 75, 173-175, 178-80, 306n.21; in 1990s, 184

Nuclear waste disposal, 79-80
Nuclear weapons. *See* bomb
Nuclearism, 13

Oak Ridge, Tennessee, 237
Omnipotence, fantasies of: and dual track, 169, 171, 173, 175, 179-82, 184; and heroic ego, 93; and nuclear deterrence, 19-20, 163, 165-66; and nuclear disarmament, 166-68, 188; and safe bomb fantasy, 76, 81, 92; and United States as nuclear superpower, 18-28, 76-77, 146; and world peace, 275; in Cold War era, 150-56, 157, 160-61, 172, 173; in international relations, 23; in nuclear madness, 135, 136, 137, 140, 141, 144, 184; in schizophrenia, 130. *See also* Laing, R.D.

On the Beach, 157
Ontological insecurity: and dual track fantasy 170, 171, 182, 184; and false self, 116; and heroic ego, 93; and literalism, 90; and nuclear disarmament, 78, 82, 168, 188; and radical finitude, 62, 142, 176; and religious imagery, 114, 141, 210; and schizophrenia, 131, 144; and world peace, 276-77; as primary obstacle to peace, 276; as social and political phenomenon, 29, 45; defined, 15-16; historical sources of, 46, 48; in Cold War era, 153, 160, 173; in modern age, 132, 249. *See also* Laing, R.D.; Tillich, Paul

Oppenheimer, Robert, 84, 303n.21
Orwell, George, 88

Pantex plant, 237
Peace: and psychic numbing, 280; as form of social madness, 275-78, 287; as imaginative act, 286-287; as play, 281, 282-86, 288, 290; as theater, 284; as ultimate concern, 281, 287; as work, 281, 283; concept of, defined, 273-74, 275; movement 283-86, 290; nuclear weapons as guarantor of, 18, 77, 226-27, 237, 292n.13; world, as religious image, 274, 278, 281, 282-83, 286, 290
Petrification, fantasies of: and dual track, 170, 171, 182; and nuclear madness, 133, 142, 209, 210; and world peace, 275; defined, 16; in international relations, 23, 25-26; in nuclear imagery, 17; in superpower policies, 25, 28, 75, 82. *See also* Laing, R.D.
Pipes, Richard, 172
Politics of Experience, The, 83
Polytheistic consciousness, 260, 267, 268, 313n.22. *See also* Hillman, James
Postmodernism, 286, 291n.3
Psychic numbing, 2, 9-15, 26; and false self, 17, 33, 45, 116; and desire for infinitude, 112-13; and fantasy of nuclear hell, 258-59; and literalism, 116-19, 188; and neurosis, 57; and nuclear arms race, 93; and nuclear madness, 133, 134, 138, 139, 140, 144; and peace, 276; and radical finitude, 111, 118, 132; and religious imagery, 111, 119, 132; and safe bomb fantasy, 81-82; and schizoid strategy, 114, 116; and schizophrenia, 124-31, 209; and world peace, 276, 280; as central fact of nuclear age, 10; as part of disarmament discourse, 11; as religious phenomenon, 62, 114; as social phenomenon, 13, 33-34; as ultimate concern, 117; counteracting of, 14, 270; defined, 10; historical origins, 13; in Cold War era, 151-54, 157, 161; origins of, in modernity's neurosis, 54, 118; reinforcement of, by antinuclear activism, 174-75; reinforcement of, by disarmament fantasy, 168; reinforcement of, by dual track fantasy, 170, 171, 178-82; reinforcement of, by news media, 137-40, 146; reinforcement of, by nuclear images, 30, 31, 46, 69, 82, 93. *See also* Death in life; Lifton, Robert Jay

Radical finitude: and antinuclear activism, 186-87, 188; and Bomb, 68, 81, 118; and dual track fantasy, 169; and neurosis, 57; and nuclear disarmament, 166, 175-78; and nuclear madness, 134, 140, 248; and ontological insecurity, 62, 141; and psychic numbing, 111, 118, 132; and schizoid strategy, 81, 115, 117, 209; and schizophrenia, 129, 148; and science and technology, 55; and world peace, 276, 277, 281, 282, 285; as modernity's ultimate concern, 76; in Cold War era, 152, 154, 160. *See also* Tillich, Paul
Rationality. *See* Ego
Reagan, Ronald, 19, 172, 173, 174, 175, 295n.21

Reagan administration, 19, 71, 75, 81, 168, 174, 182, 301n.14
Religious image, defined, 109
Renaissance: and antinuclear activism, 285; and world peace, 278, 282, 284-7; as model for transformation, 263-64, 266-72; as play, 281; as universal madness, 268-72
Revisioning Psychology, 261, 263
Rocky Flats, 237, 298n.12

SDI. *See* Strategic Defense Initiative
Safe bomb, fantasy of, 76-83, 283; and dual track fantasy, 179-81, 184, 187, 257; and heroic ego, 91; and literalism, 90-92; and monotheistic consciousness, 270; and nuclear madness, 136-37, 143-44; and omnipotence fantasy, 92
Sartre, Jean Paul, 16
Schell, Jonathan, 175-78
Schelling, Thomas, 164-65
Schizoid strategy: and "family of nations", 38-40, 45, 75; and heroic ego, 93; and nuclear arms race, 20, 77; and nuclear deterrence, 22, 76; and nuclear superpowers, 18-29, 74-76; and radical finitude, 115; as metaphor for nuclear madness, 45, 135-37; compared with schizophrenia, 119, 125; defined, 17; in American attitudes toward Soviet Union, 35, 74-75; origins in modern West, 23, 116, 117-18. *See also* Laing, R.D.
Schizophrenia: and annihilation fantasies, 124, 164; and Cold War fantasies, 149-56; and *homo religiosus*, 209-11; and ontological insecurity, 124, 131, 144; and religious imagery, 130-31, 141, 213-14; and shamanism, 212-13; and world-destruction fantasies, 126-29; contrasted with schizoid neurosis, 119, 125. *See also* Hillman, James; Laing, R.D.; Nuclear madness
Scientific objectivity. *See* Ego
Shaman: nuclear expert as, 236-239, 243, 244; nuclear state as, 238-41, 243
Shamanism, 211-13
Single Integrated Operating Plan (SIOP), 19, 80, 293n.18
Soviet Union as nuclear threat, 149-50, 158, 166, 173, 178, 179
Star Wars. *See* Strategic Defense Initiative
State, role of, 134-38, 238-43
Stimson, Henry L., 292n.13
Strategic Defense Initiative (SDI), 9, 175, 288, 311n.24
Suicide and the Soul, 264, 266
Suicide, 264-67
Symbolic immortality: and psychic numbing, 11, 113; and psychological health, 10-13, 98-105, 111, 211; expressed in nuclear images, 12. *See also* Lifton, Robert Jay
Szilard, Leo, 292n.13

Talbott, Strobe, 79
Theophrastus of Hohenheim (Paracelsus), 287
Thinking About the Unthinkable, 158
Tillich, Paul, 3, 15, 46, 62, 82, 93, 118, 124, 194, 208, 211, 276, 295n.1, 295-96n.3; and Laing, R.D., 16, 47, 69; and Lifton, Robert Jay, 11, 47, 102; Being, 48-49, 68; finitude, 48, 49, 50, 52-53, 54, 102,

106–107; freedom, 59–62; immortality, 64, 102; infinitude, 48, 49, 50, 52–53, 55, 102–103, 105; meaninglessness, anxiety of, 58; modernity, 53, 58, 72; neurosis, 11, 52–53, 56, 65, 69, 114, 116; nonbeing, 115; ontological insecurity, 47, 53, 69–70, 105–106; radical finitude, 53–54, 58, 69; ultimate concern, religion as, 48, 50, 61, 102–103
Truman, Harry S. 18, 145, 223, 239–40, 303n.21, 310n.18, 311n.27

Ultimate concern: Bomb as symbol of, 76; peace process as, 281; psychic numbing as, 117, 140; religion as, 48, 51; social neurosis as, 60–61. *See also* Tillich, Paul
United Nations, 220, 225, 241

Vietnam War, 172

War: and heroic ego, 280; as initiation, 222; as religious festival, 315n.7; as religious sacrifice, 256; as ritual hunting, 222–29, 242; as ritual play, 279–80, 284; as theater, 284; as work, 280; as world renewal, 222, 224, 226–27; concept of, defined, 274, 275, 279
Watkins, James, 79
Weapons as religous objects, 229–31, 235, 242
Weart, Spencer, 147, 158
World Wars as religious wars: World War I, 227; World II, 222–25, 227, 228, 242; World War III, 227
World-destruction, fantasy of: and world renewal, 244–45, 248–49; as nuclear hell, 260; in Cold War era, 153; in nuclear madness, 134–35, 137, 141, 153, 288–89; in schizophrenia, 126–29

NUCLEAR MADNESS
Religion and the Psychology of the Nuclear Age
Ira Chernus

"Chernus has energetically and imaginatively answered the challenge to scholars of religion to make the nuclear age a central focus of their research and reflection. Chernus's work does that, and has the additional benefit of demonstrating the need to do that in a way that integrates social science approaches with more traditional phenomenology of religion approaches."

—H. John McDargh, Boston Co[llege]

This book builds on Robert Jay Lifton's theory of psychic numbing, and takes madness as a guiding metaphor. It shows that public perceptions of the Bomb are a kaleidoscope of ever-changing i[deas] and images. Recent changes in public awareness only signal new symptoms of this public madness, symptoms unwittingly fostered by the antinuclear movement. Since the newest nuclear images follow [the] same psychological pattern as their predecessors, they are likely to lead us deeper into nuclear madness.

Chernus offers new interpretations of four major theorists in the psychology of religion — Paul Tillich, R.D. Laing, Mircea Eliade, and James Hillman — to trace the roots of nuclear madness b[ack] to the onset of modernity, when the West gained technological mastery at the price of losing religious imagination and ontological security. The author develops an interpretation of Lifton's own thought a[s] ontological and religious psychology. Drawing on the work of Eliade and Hillman, he goes on to sugg[est] that madness reflects a repressed desire to transform life by opening up the floodgates of imagination. conscious cultivation of the play of imagination can lead the way through madness to sanity and peace. But, imagination can only respond to the nuclear threat if it is acted out in a new brand of peace activi[sm] that blends pragmatic politics with psychological and religious transformation.

Ira Chernus is Associate Professor of Religious Studies at the University of Colorado at Boulder. He is co-author of *A Shuddering Dawn: Religious Studies and the Nuclear Age* with Edward Tabor Linenthal, also published by SUNY Press.

STATE UNIVERSITY OF NEW YORK PRESS
ISBN 0-7914-0504-4

LIBRARY OF DAVIDSON COLLEGE

Books on regular loan may be checked out for four weeks. Books must be presented at the Circulation Desk in order to be renewed.

A fine is charged after date due.

Special books are subject to special regulations at the discretion of the library staff.

MAY 1 2 1993